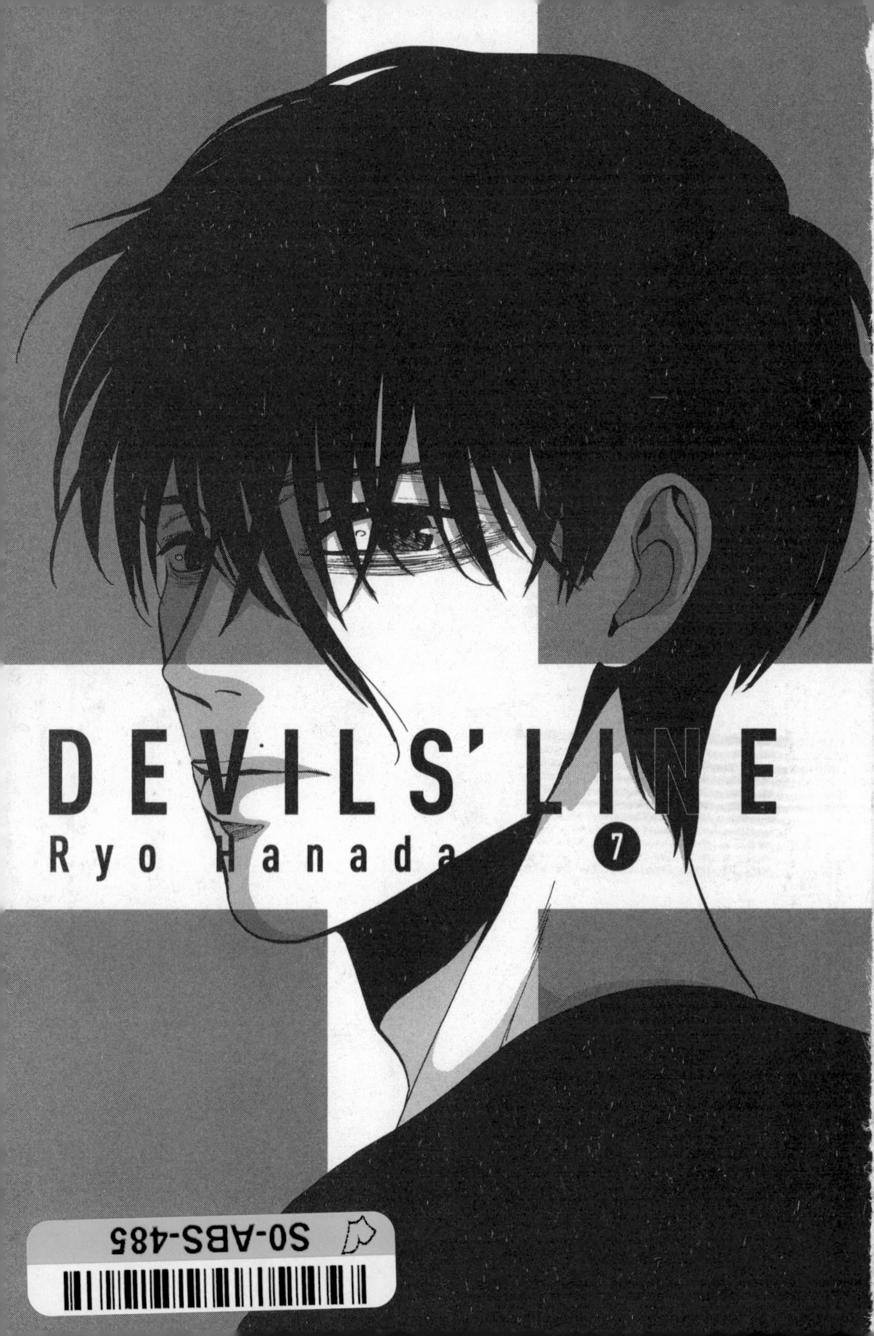
DEVILS' LINE
Ryo Hanada
7

Character and Relationship Diagram (based on relationships up to the last volume)

MPD PUBLIC SAFETY DIVISION 5

C SQUAD

NAOYA USHIO
(Zero Five)

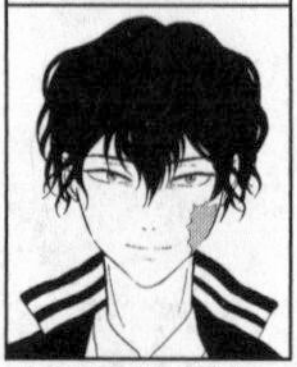

A member of the CCC along with Kikuhara and Makimura. He attacked Tsukasa in a hotel.

B SQUAD

TAKESHI MAKIMURA
(Zero Six)

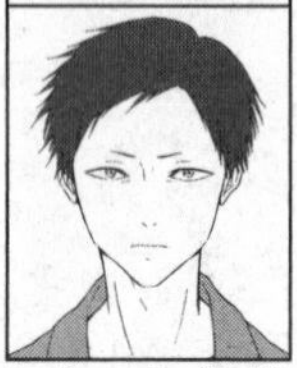

Secretly a member of the CCC. He previously instructed Zero Seven in sniping.

A SQUAD

KIRIO KIKUHARA
(Zero Two)

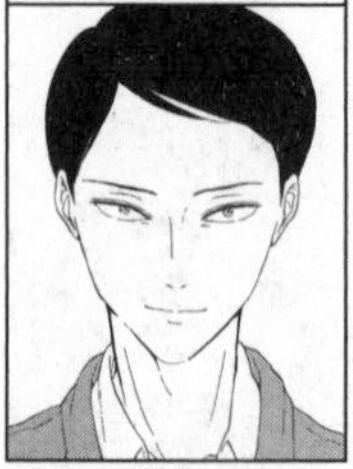

The leader of A Squad, he's also secretly the commander of the CCC, an organization dedicated to the extermination of devils.

F SQUAD

YUUKI ANZAI

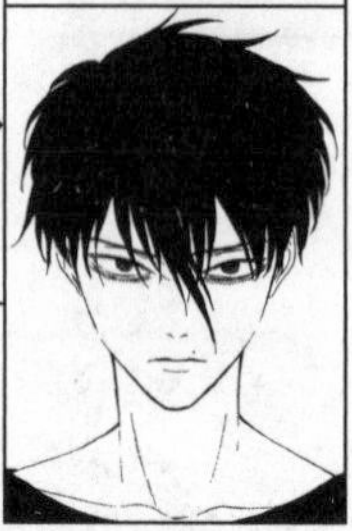

Half-devil, half-human police officer, he was pessimistic regarding the coexistence of devils and humans, but his thinking has been changing since he met Tsukasa.

MEGUMI ISHIMARU

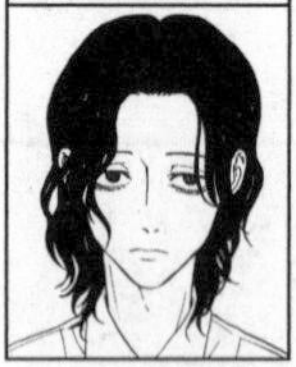

New F Squad leader. Came to F Squad at the recommendation of Kikuhara (Zero Two), who he secretly reports to.

TAKASHI SAWAZAKI

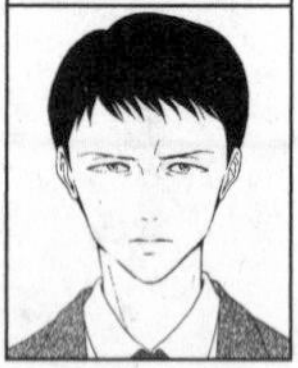

Former F Squad leader, his inability to control his devil subordinates was regarded as problematic, and he was demoted from his position as leader.

YOUSUKE ASAMI

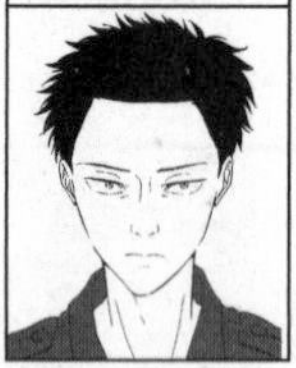

A member of Investigation Division 1, he was assigned temporarily to Public Safety Division 5, where he is part of the ongoing investigation.

JULIANA LLOYD

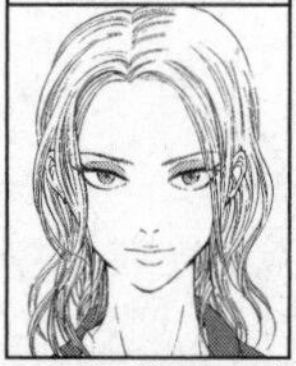

Devil police officer. Born and raised in Japan. She skillfully uses make-up to hide the bags under her eyes.

RYUUSEI YANAGI

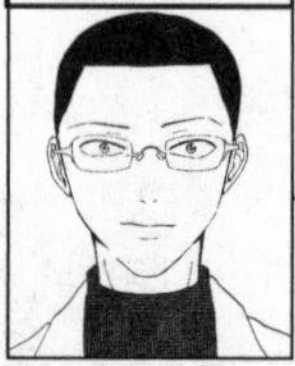

Doctor attached to F Squad specializing in the hematology of the redeye race (devils), he was apparently a punk in his youth.

Acquaintance

AKIO KANO

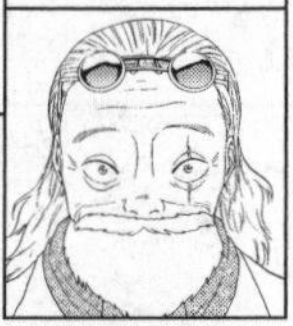

Psychosomatic doctor specializing in devil care, he is also a member of R2PC, a committee that works to protect devil rights.

*A more detailed *Devils' Line* Character and Relationship Diagram created by the author can be viewed online. (Japanese only.)
http://hanada.coln.biz/diagram/realpart/topmenu.html

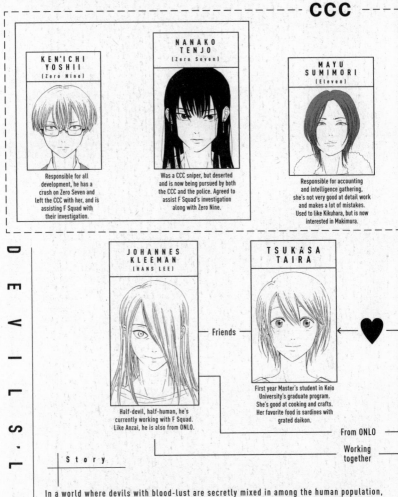

CCC

KEN'ICHI YOSHII
(Zero Nine)

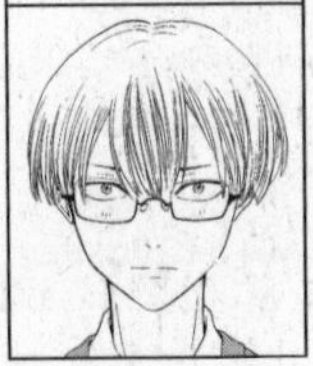

Responsible for all development, he has a crush on Zero Seven and left the CCC with her, and is assisting F Squad with their investigation.

NANAKO TENJO
(Zero Seven)

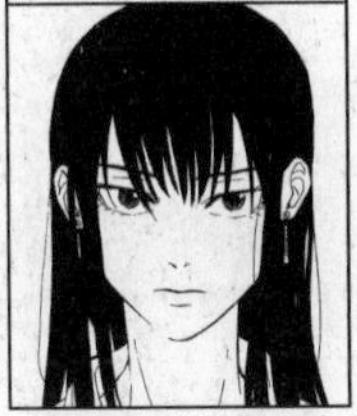

Was a CCC sniper, but deserted and is now being pursued by both the CCC and the police. Agreed to assist F Squad's investigation along with Zero Nine.

MAYU SUMIMORI
(Eleven)

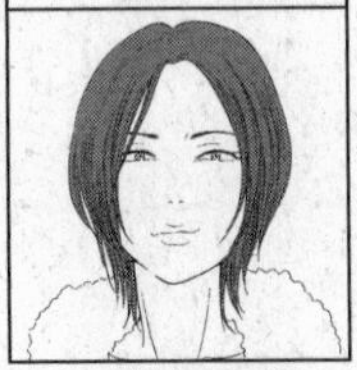

Responsible for accounting and intelligence gathering, she's not very good at detail work and makes a lot of mistakes. Used to like Kikuhara, but is now interested in Makimura.

DEVIL'S LINE

JOHANNES KLEEMAN
(HANS LEE)

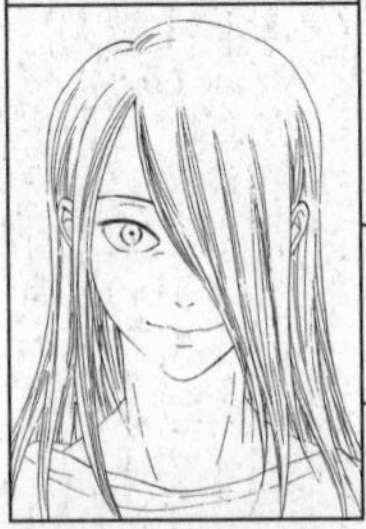

Half-devil, half-human, he's currently working with F Squad. Like Anzai, he is also from ONLO.

Friends

TSUKASA TAIRA

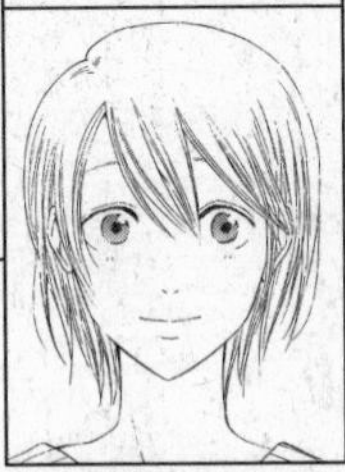

First year Master's student in Keio University's graduate program. She's good at cooking and crafts. Her favorite food is sardines with grated daikon.

From ONLO

Working together

Story

In a world where devils with blood-lust are secretly mixed in among the human population, graduate student Tsukasa Taira meets the half-devil half-human detective Yuuki Anzai, and they're immediately attracted to each other. But Anzai and Tsukasa's lives are in danger due to the secret maneuverings of the CCC, an organization intent on the annihilation of all devils. After many twists and turns, the two finally start dating. In the meantime, Ishimaru takes over the division Anzai belongs to, Public Safety Division 5's F Squad, which was previously led by Sawazaki. Ishimaru opens a thorough investigation into the CCC. The battle between the CCC and F Squad, full of half-truths and falsehoods, has begun.

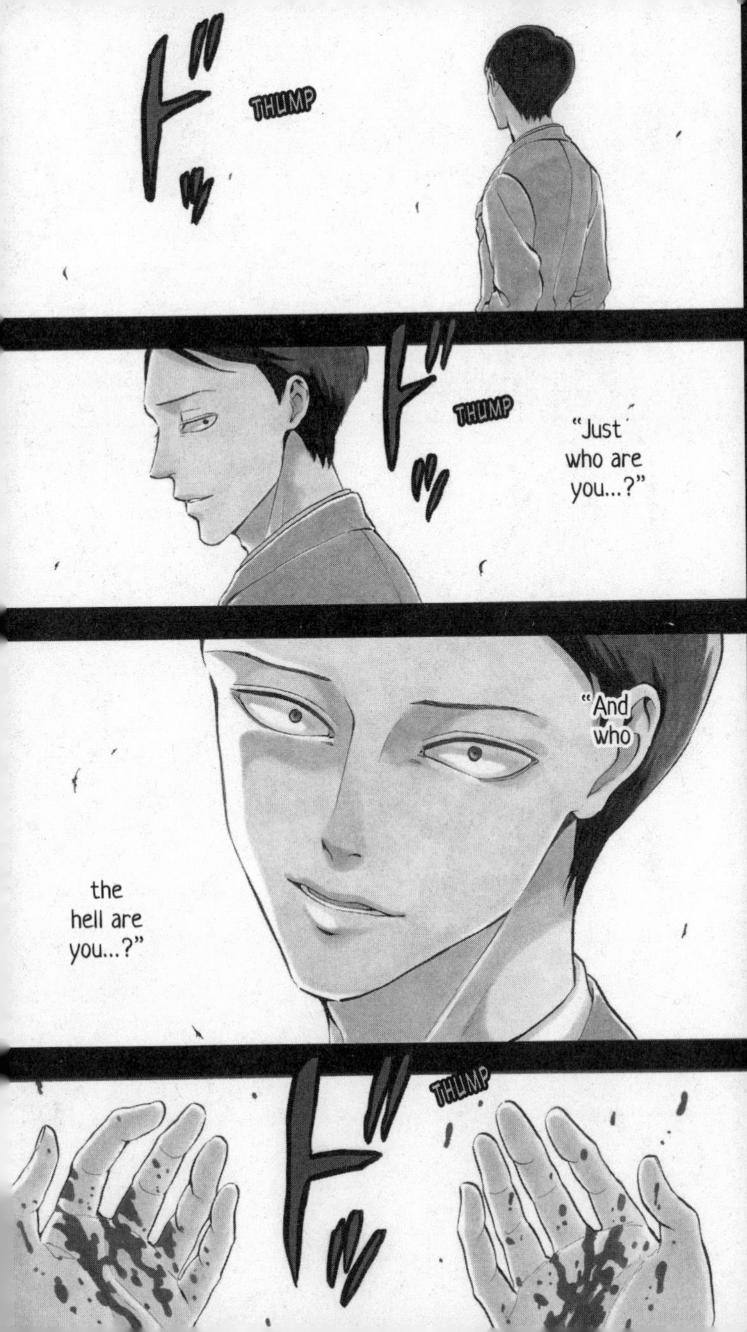
THUMP
THUMP
"Just who are you...?"
"And who
the hell are you...?"
THUMP

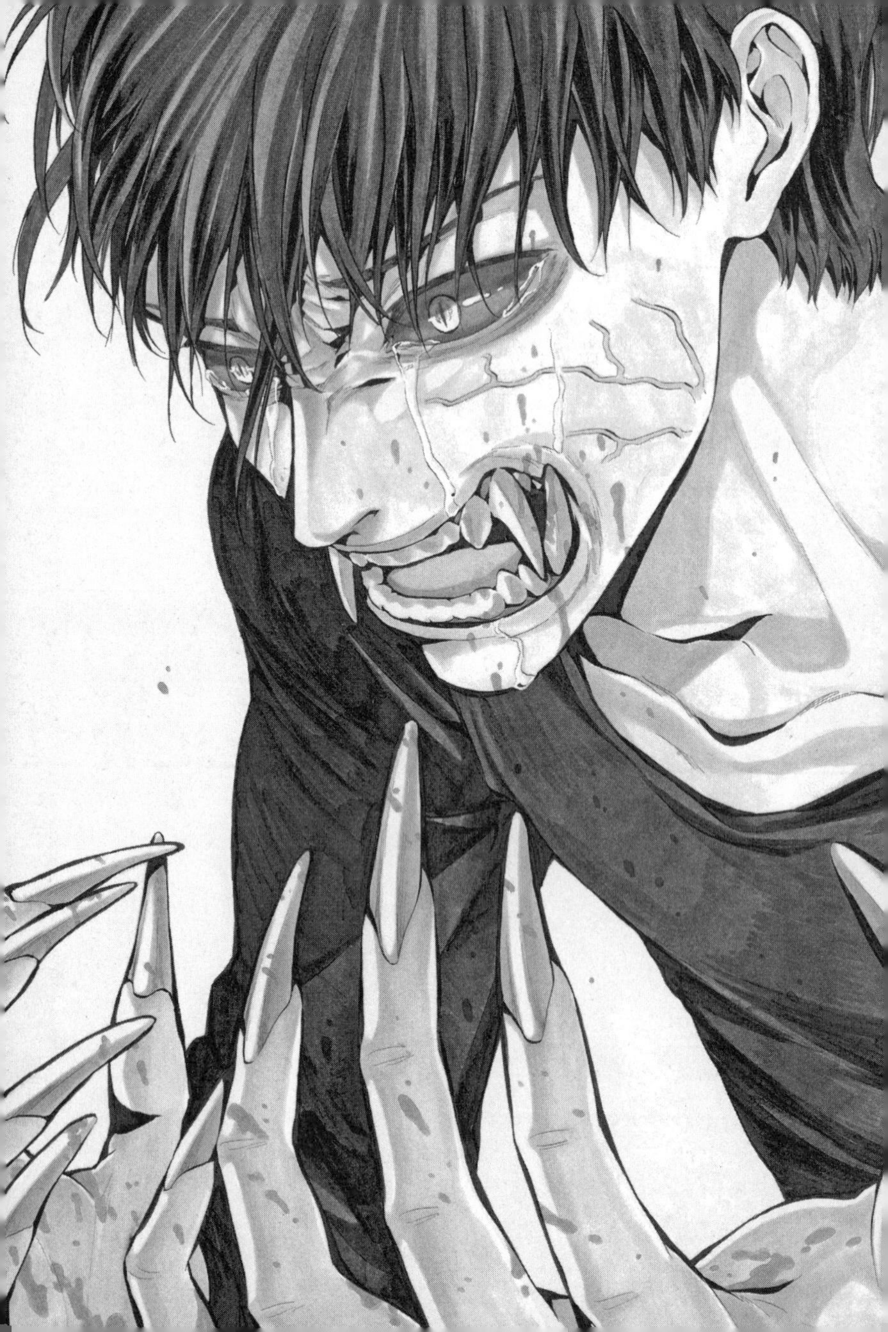

Line 33
Children

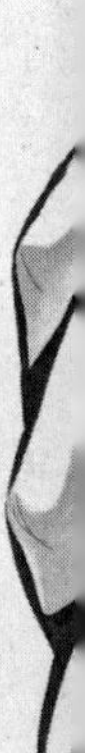

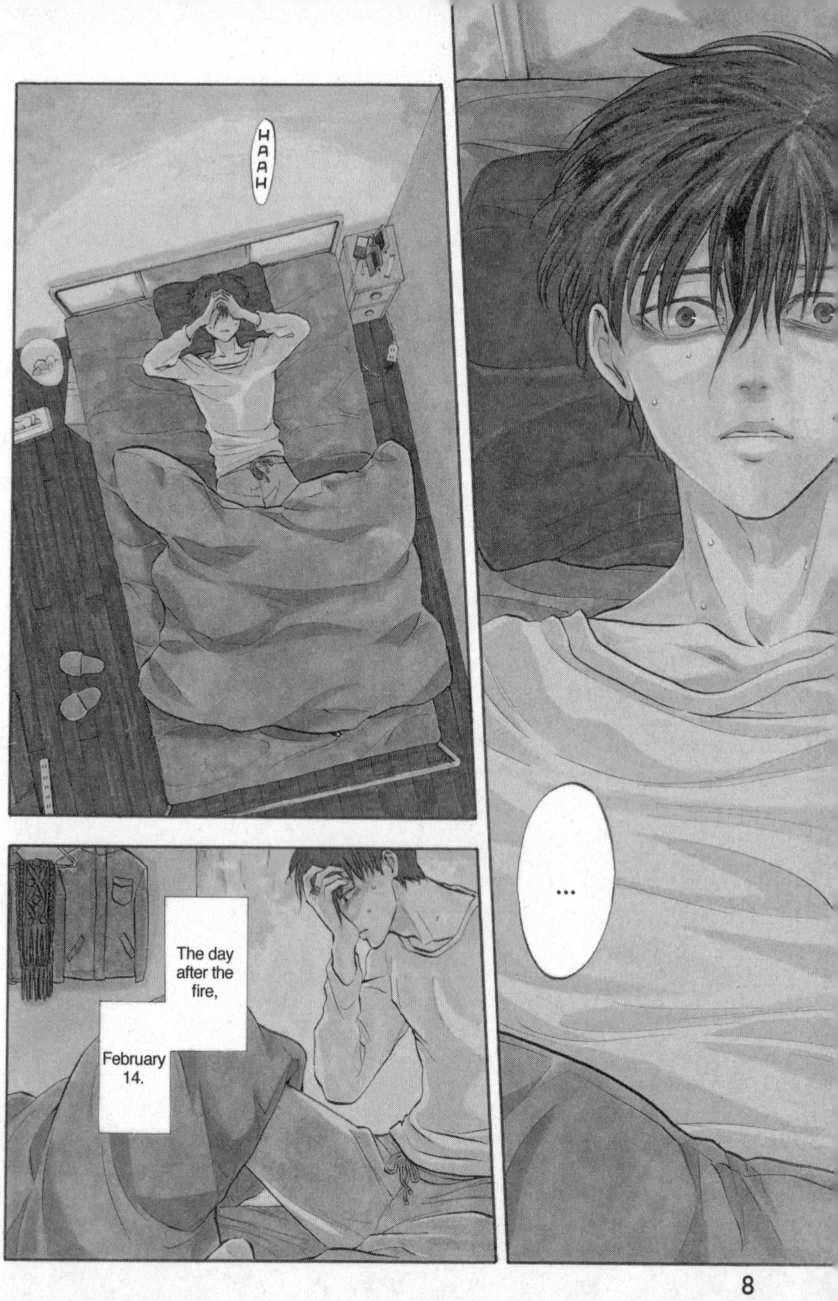
...
HAAH
The day after the fire,
February 14.

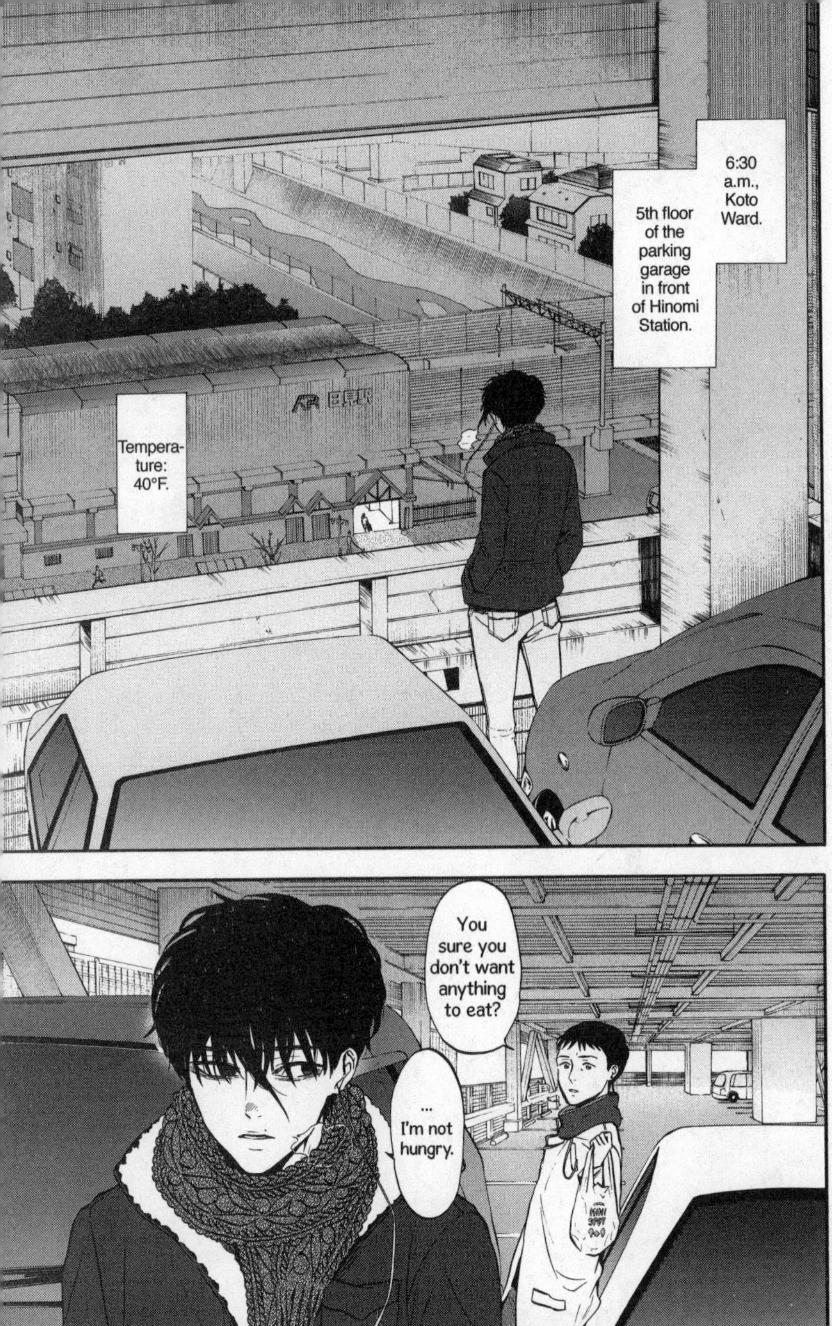
6:30 a.m., Koto Ward.
5th floor of the parking garage in front of Hinomi Station.
Tempera-ture: 40°F.
You sure you don't want anything to eat?
... I'm not hungry.

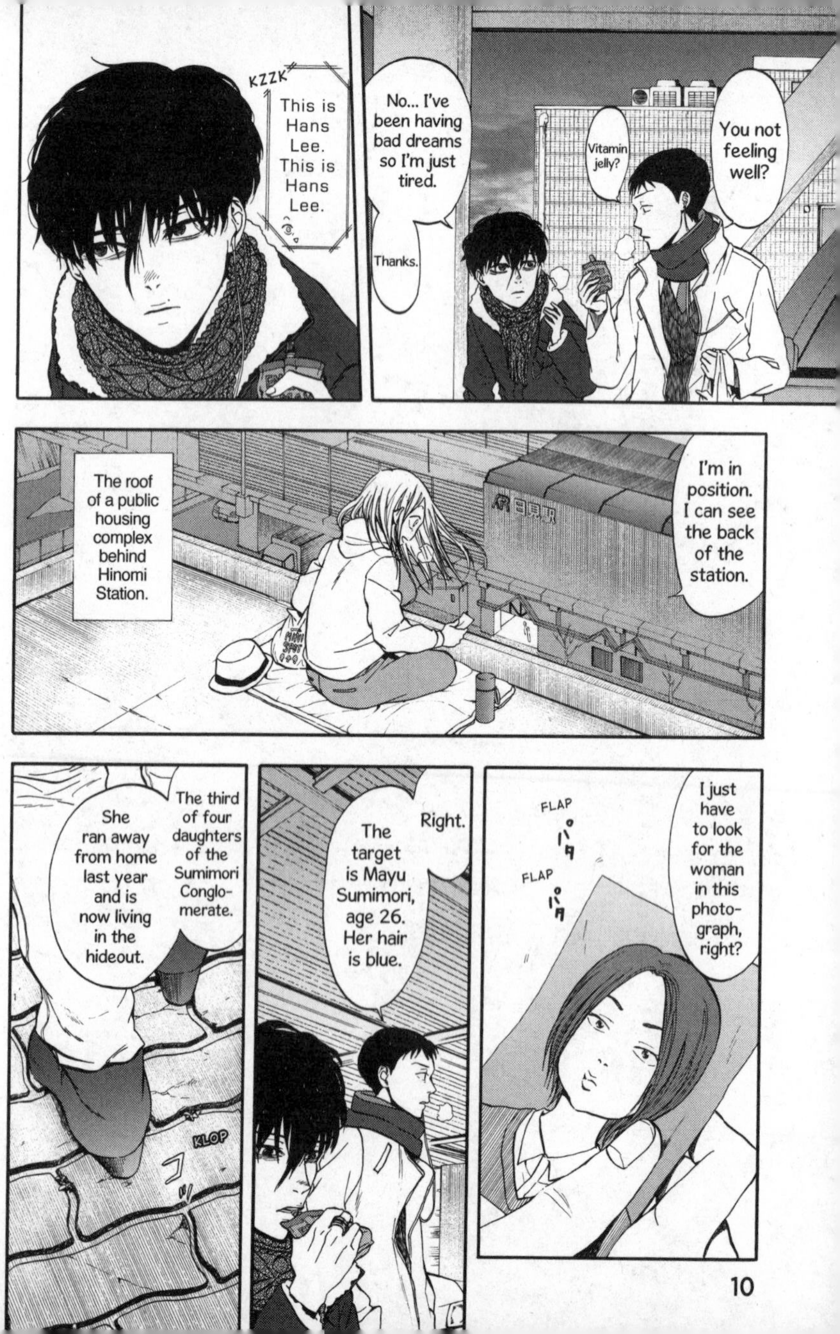
You not feeling well?
Vitamin jelly?
No... I've been having bad dreams so I'm just tired.
Thanks.
KZZK
This is Hans Lee. This is Hans Lee.
I'm in position. I can see the back of the station.
The roof of a public housing complex behind Hinomi Station.
I just have to look for the woman in this photograph, right?
FLAP
パタ
FLAP
パタ
Right.
The target is Mayu Sumimori, age 26. Her hair is blue.
The third of four daughters of the Sumimori Conglomerate.
She ran away from home last year and is now living in the hideout.
KLOP

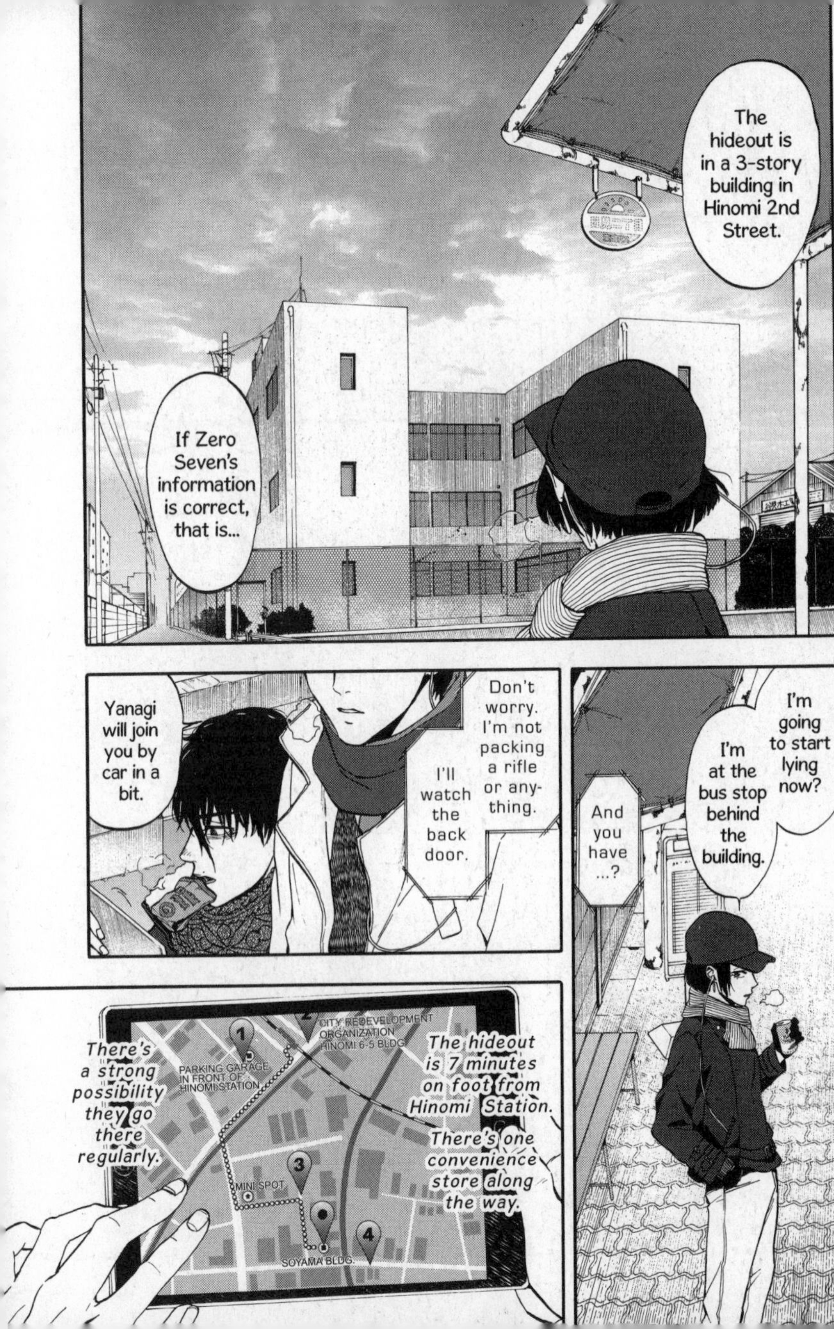

The hideout is in a 3-story building in Hinomi 2nd Street.
If Zero Seven's information is correct, that is...
I'm going to start lying now?
I'm at the bus stop behind the building.
And you have ...?
Don't worry. I'm not packing a rifle or anything.
I'll watch the back door.
Yanagi will join you by car in a bit.
The hideout is 7 minutes on foot from Hinomi Station.
There's one convenience store along the way.
There's a strong possibility they go there regularly.
CITY REDEVELOPMENT ORGANIZATION HINOMI 6-5 BLDG
PARKING GARAGE IN FRONT OF HINOMI STATION
MINI SPOT
SOYAMA BLDG.
1
2
3
4

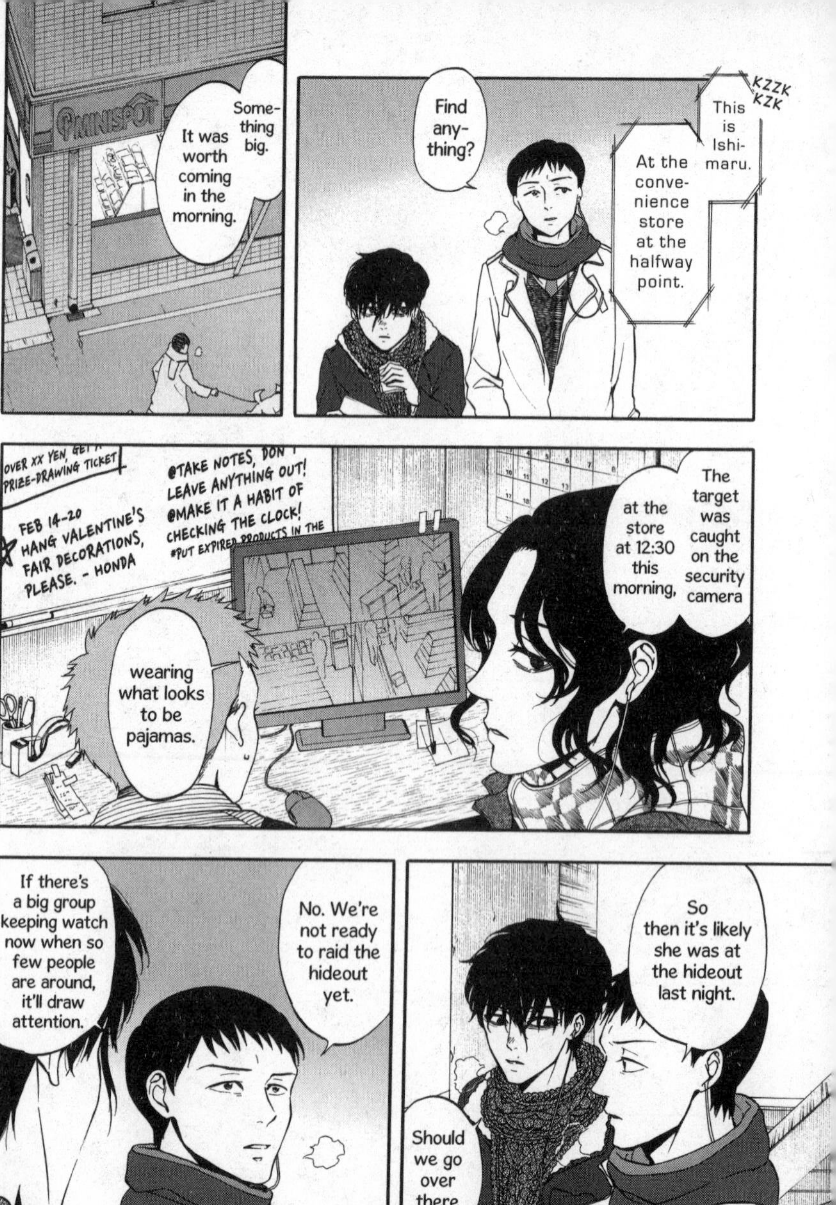
KZZK KZK
This is Ishimaru.
At the convenience store at the halfway point.
Find anything?
Something big.
It was worth coming in the morning.
The target was caught on the security camera
at the store at 12:30 this morning,
OVER XX YEN, GET A PRIZE-DRAWING TICKET
@TAKE NOTES, DON'T LEAVE ANYTHING OUT!
@MAKE IT A HABIT OF CHECKING THE CLOCK!
#PUT EXPIRED PRODUCTS IN THE
FEB 14-20 HANG VALENTINE'S FAIR DECORATIONS, PLEASE. - HONDA
wearing what looks to be pajamas.
So then it's likely she was at the hideout last night.
Should we go over there ...?
No. We're not ready to raid the hideout yet.
If there's a big group keeping watch now when so few people are around, it'll draw attention.

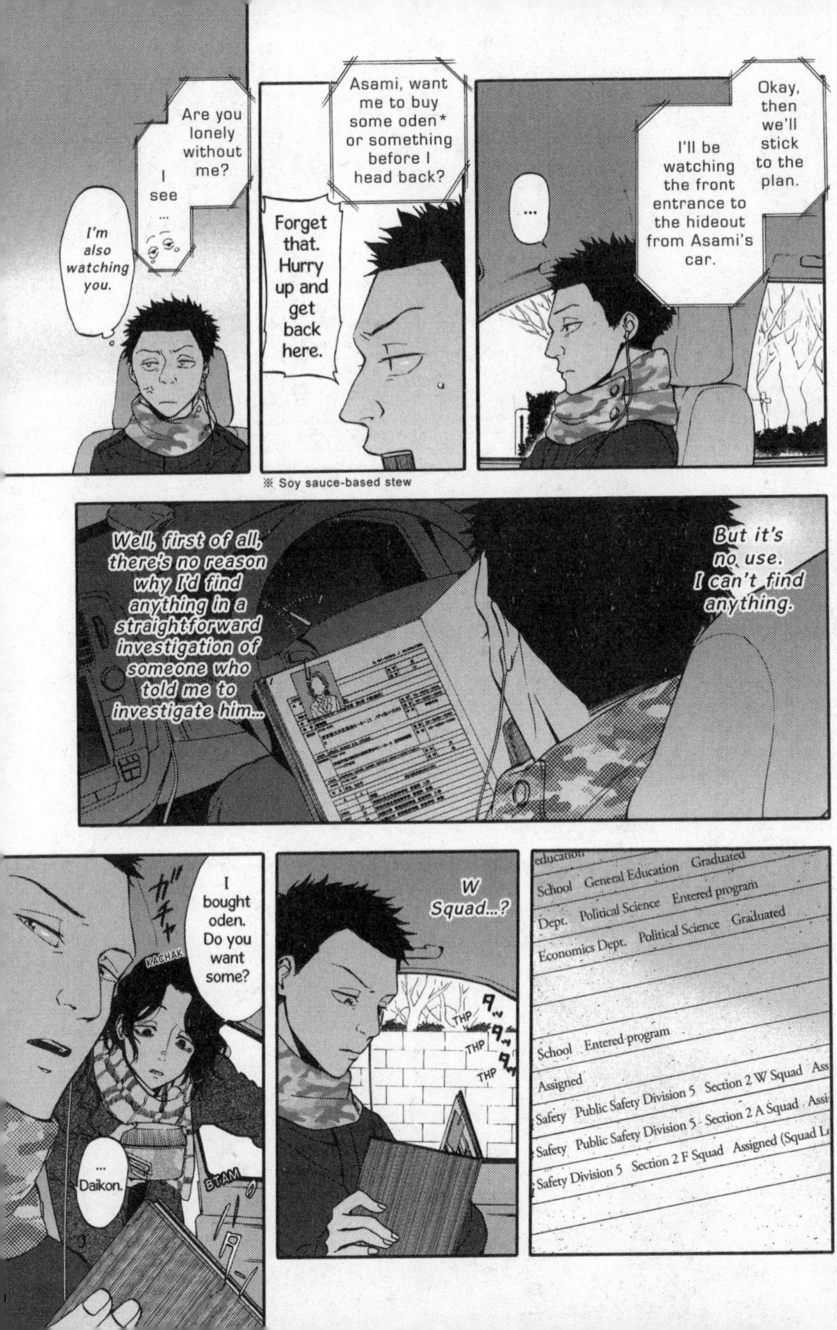
Okay, then we'll stick to the plan.
I'll be watching the front entrance to the hideout from Asami's car.
...
Asami, want me to buy some oden* or something before I head back?
Forget that. Hurry up and get back here.
Are you lonely without me?
I see ...
I'm also watching you.
But it's no use. I can't find anything.
Well, first of all, there's no reason why I'd find anything in a straightforward investigation of someone who told me to investigate him...
education
School General Education Graduated
Dept. Political Science Entered program
Economics Dept. Political Science Graduated
School Entered program
Assigned
Safety Public Safety Division 5 Section 2 W Squad Ass
Safety Public Safety Division 5 Section 2 A Squad Assi
Safety Division 5 Section 2 F Squad Assigned (Squad L
W Squad...?
THP
THP
THP
I bought oden. Do you want some?
KACHAK
BTAM
... Daikon.
※ Soy sauce-based stew

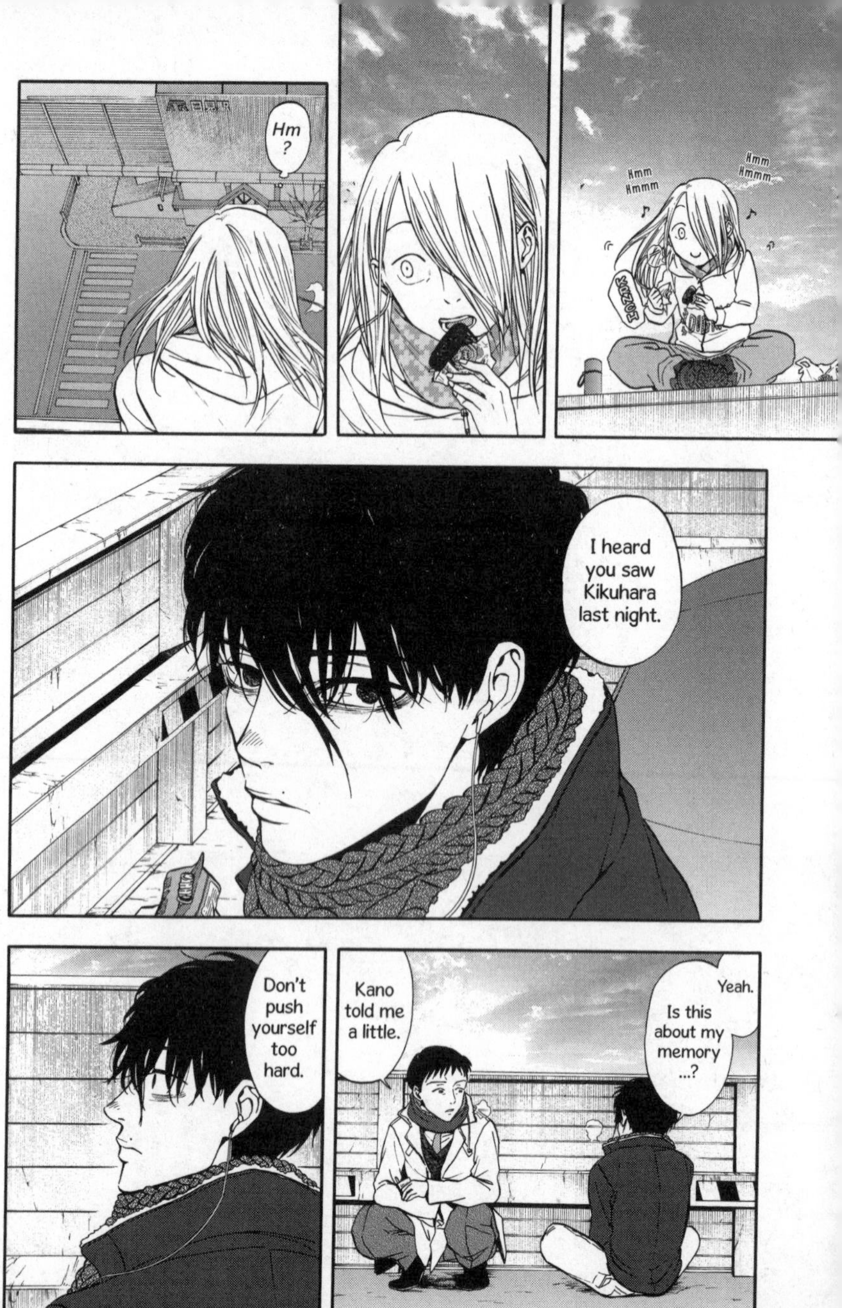
Hmm Hmmm
Hmm Hmmm
Hm?
I heard you saw Kikuhara last night.
Yeah.
Is this about my memory ...?
Kano told me a little.
Don't push yourself too hard.

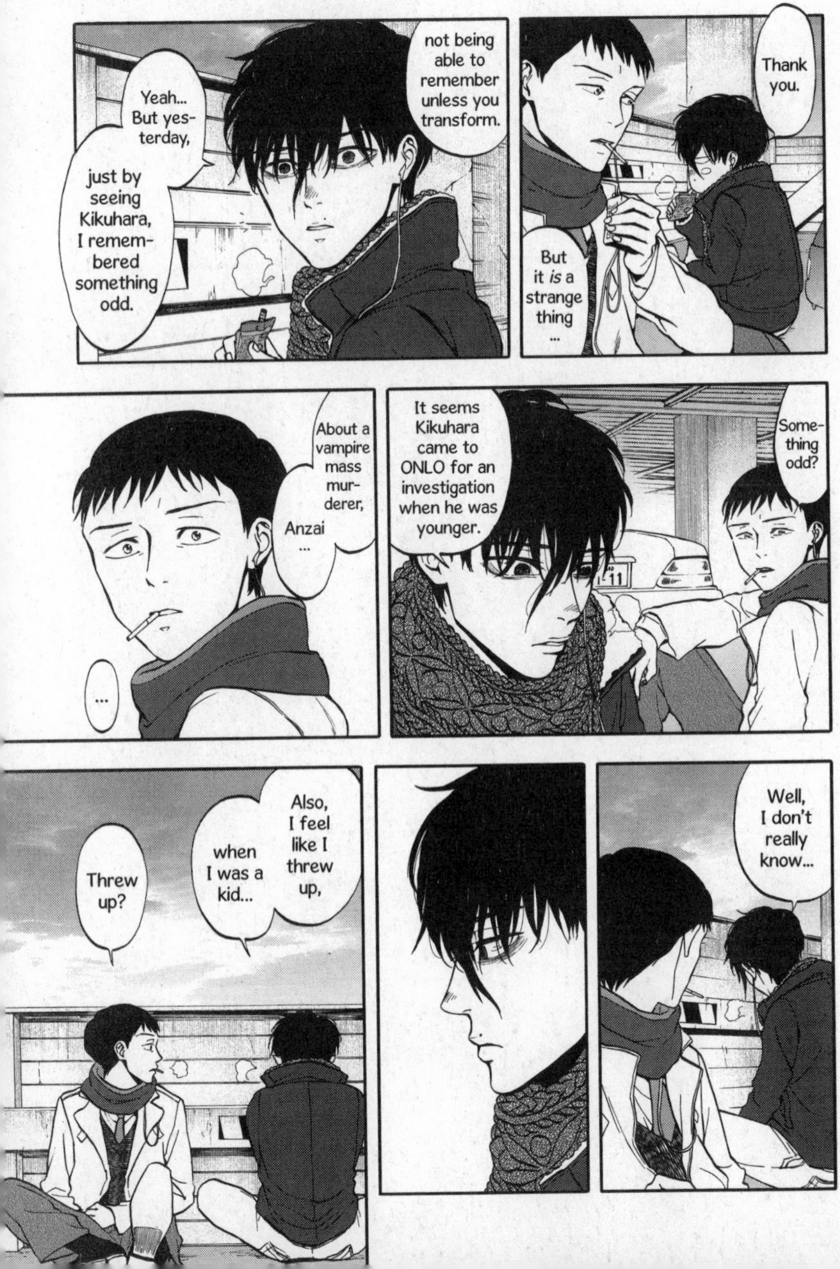

Thank you.
But it *is* a strange thing ...
not being able to remember unless you transform.
Yeah... But yesterday,
just by seeing Kikuhara, I remembered something odd.
Something odd?
It seems Kikuhara came to ONLO for an investigation when he was younger.
About a vampire mass murderer, Anzai ...
...
Well, I don't really know...
Also, I feel like I threw up,
when I was a kid...
Threw up?

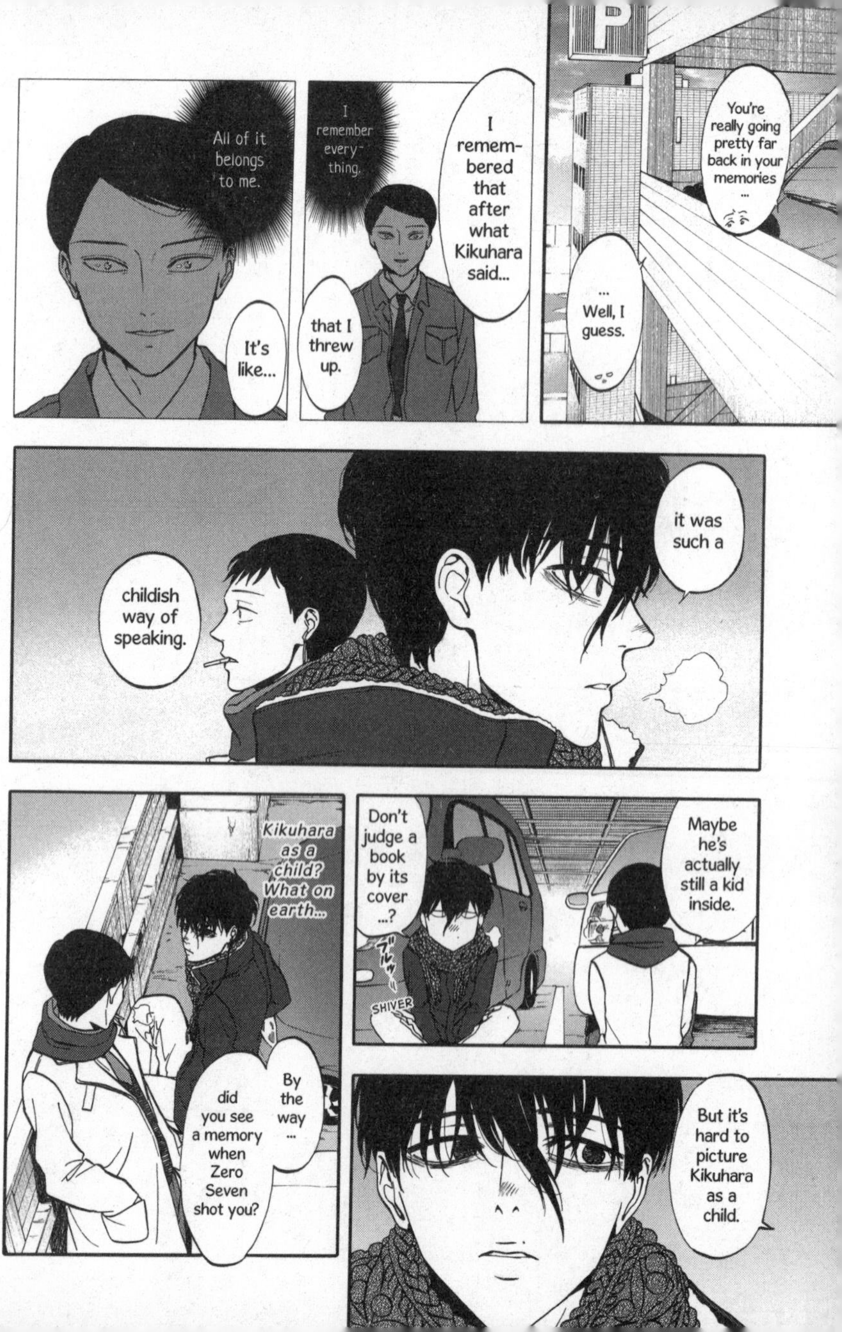

You're really going pretty far back in your memories ...
... Well, I guess.
I remembered that after what Kikuhara said...
I remember every-thing.
that I threw up.
All of it belongs to me.
It's like...
it was such a
childish way of speaking.
Maybe he's actually still a kid inside.
Don't judge a book by its cover ...?
SHIVER
But it's hard to picture Kikuhara as a child.
Kikuhara as a child? What on earth...
By the way ...
did you see a memory when Zero Seven shot you?

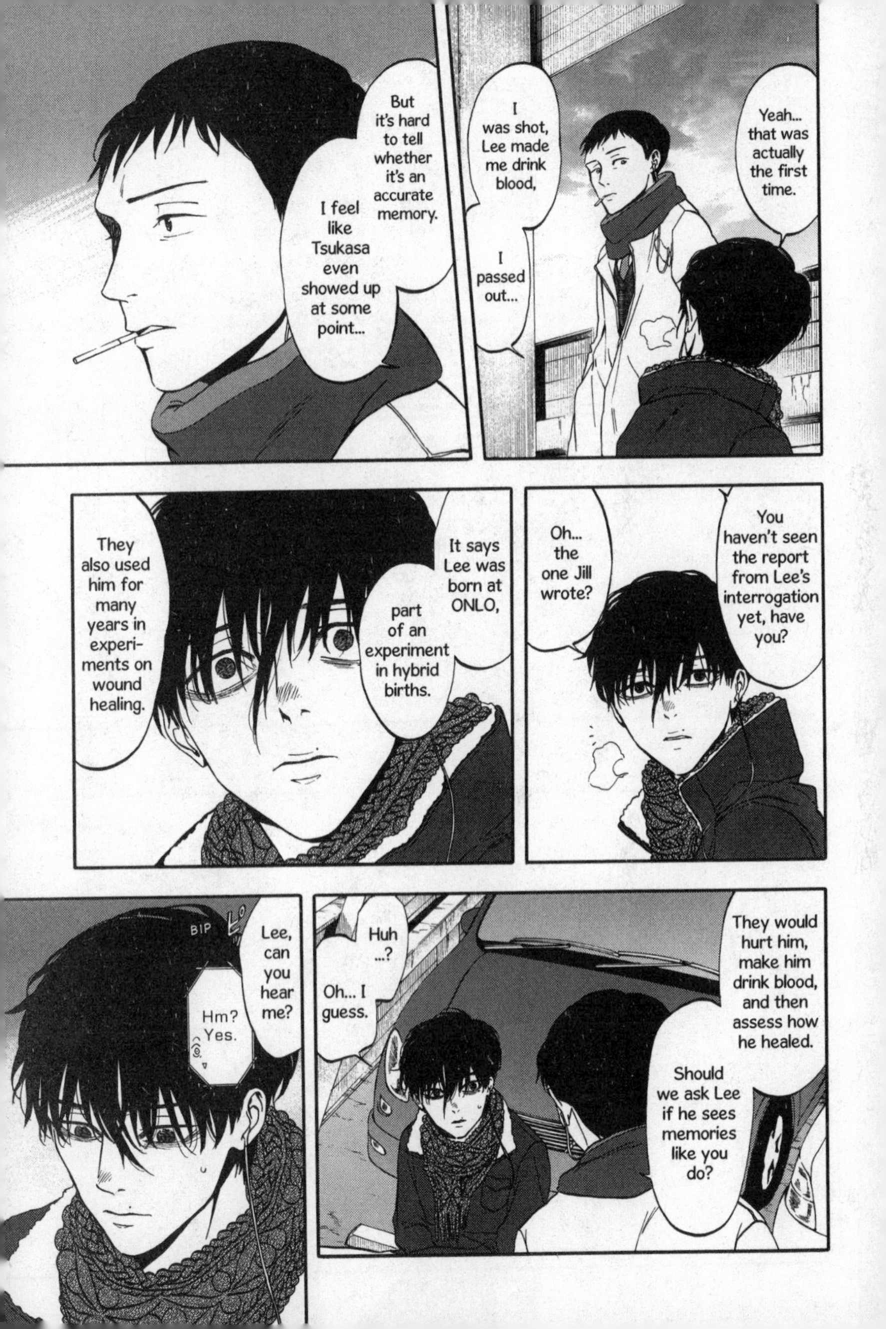
Yeah... that was actually the first time.
I was shot, Lee made me drink blood,
I passed out...
But it's hard to tell whether it's an accurate memory.
I feel like Tsukasa even showed up at some point...
You haven't seen the report from Lee's interrogation yet, have you?
Oh... the one Jill wrote?
It says Lee was born at ONLO,
part of an experiment in hybrid births.
They also used him for many years in experi-ments on wound healing.
They would hurt him, make him drink blood, and then assess how he healed.
Should we ask Lee if he sees memories like you do?
Huh ...?
Oh... I guess.
BIP
Lee, can you hear me?
Hm? Yes.

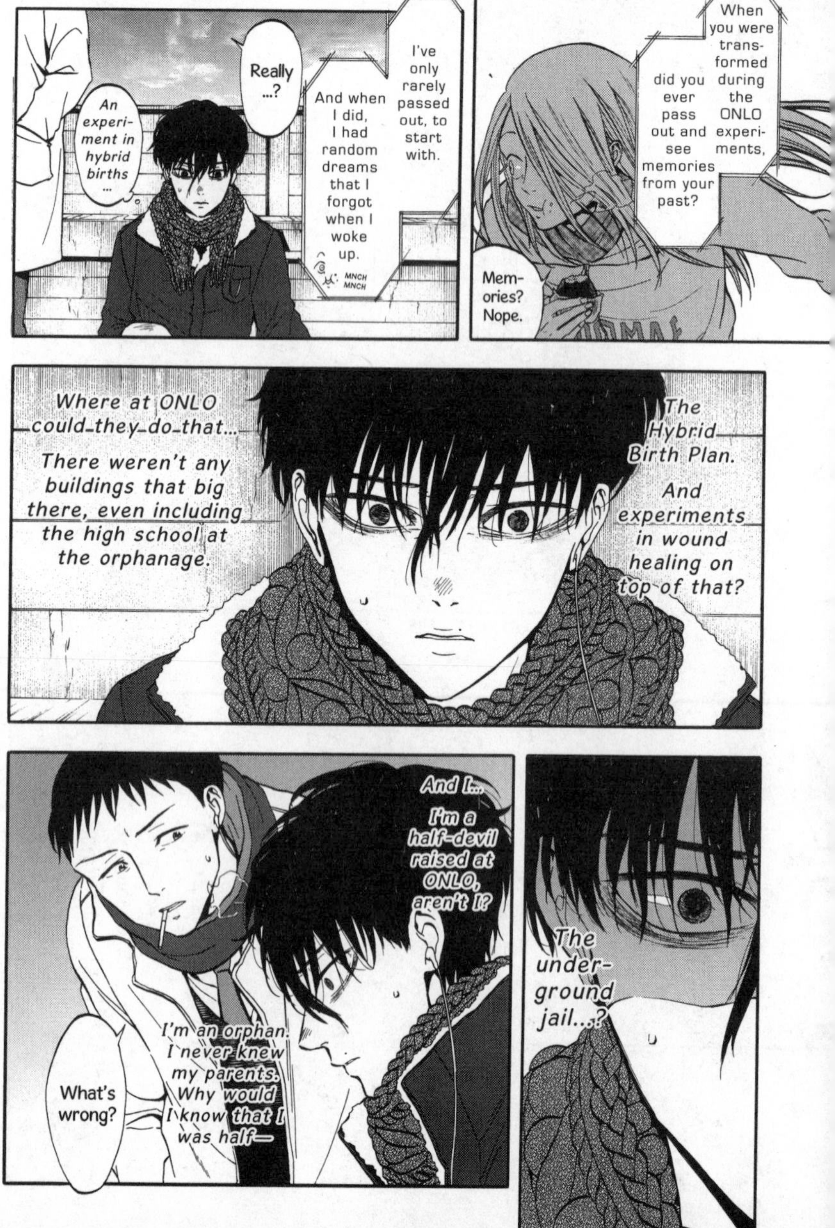
When you were trans-formed during the ONLO experi-ments, did you ever pass out and see memories from your past?
Memo-ries? Nope.
I've only rarely passed out, to start with.
And when I did, I had random dreams that I forgot when I woke up.
MNCH MNCH
Really ...?
An experi-ment in hybrid births ...
The Hybrid Birth Plan.
And experiments in wound healing on top of that?
Where at ONLO could they do that...
There weren't any buildings that big there, even including the high school at the orphanage.
The under-ground jail...?
And I...
I'm a half-devil raised at ONLO, aren't I?
I'm an orphan. I never knew my parents. Why would I know that I was half—
What's wrong?

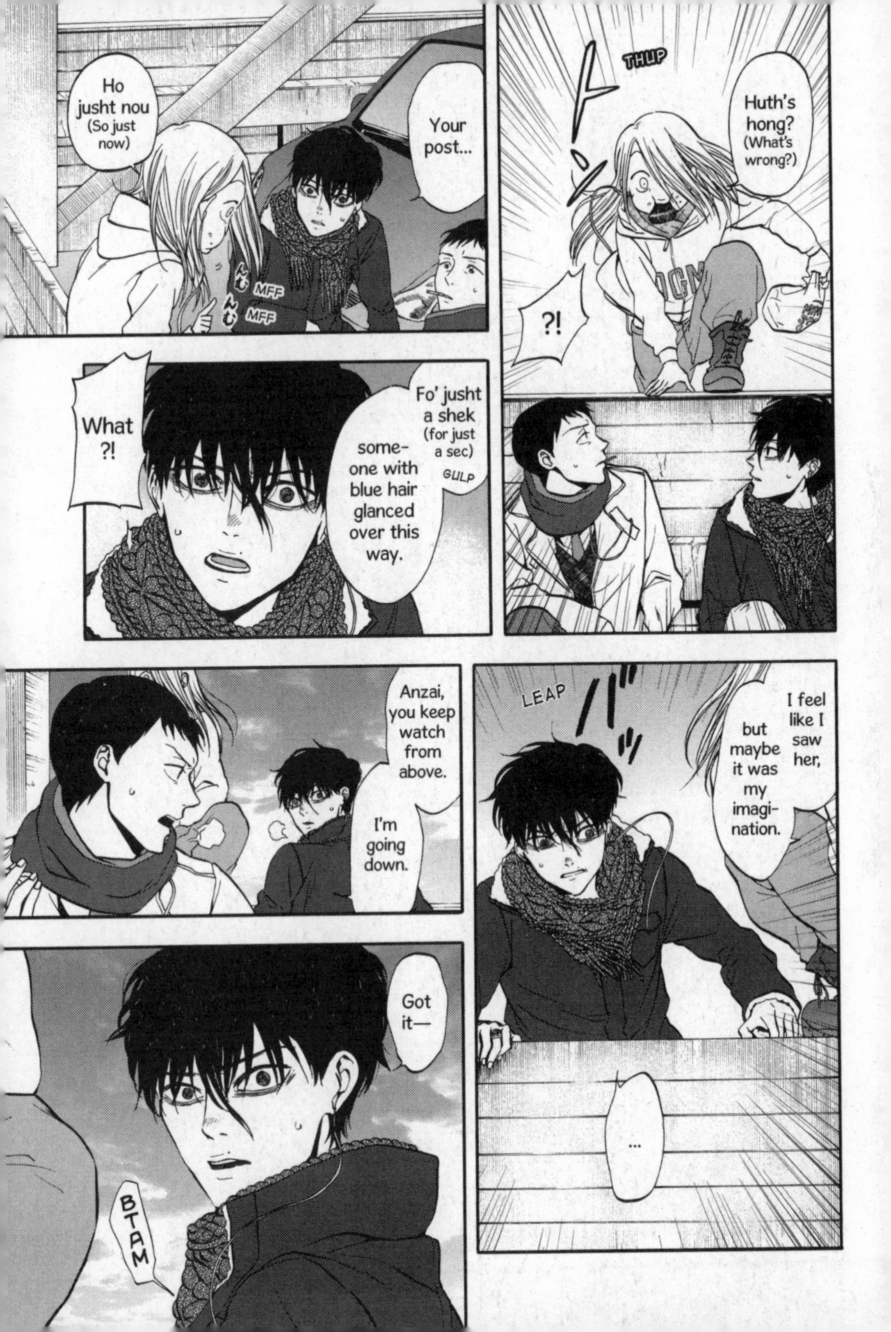
THUP
Huth's hong? (What's wrong?)
?!
Your post...
Ho jusht nou (So just now)
MFF
MFF
Fo' jusht a shek (for just a sec)
GULP
someone with blue hair glanced over this way.
What ?!
LEAP
I feel like I saw her,
but maybe it was my imagination.
...
Anzai, you keep watch from above.
I'm going down.
Got it—
BTAM

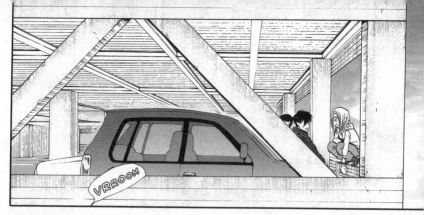

A car, right?

That sound just now...

BAM

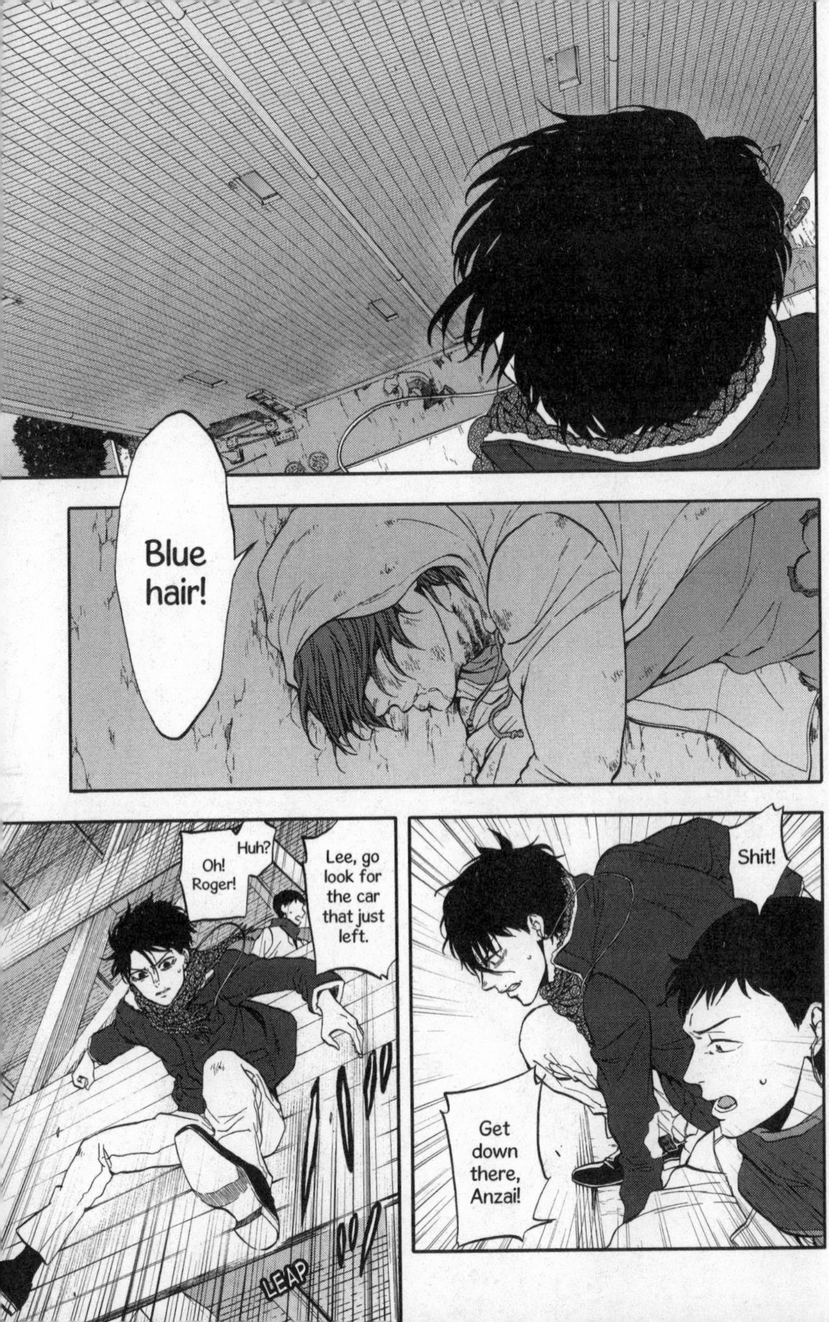
Blue hair!
Shit!
Get down there, Anzai!
Lee, go look for the car that just left.
Huh?
Oh! Roger!
LEAP

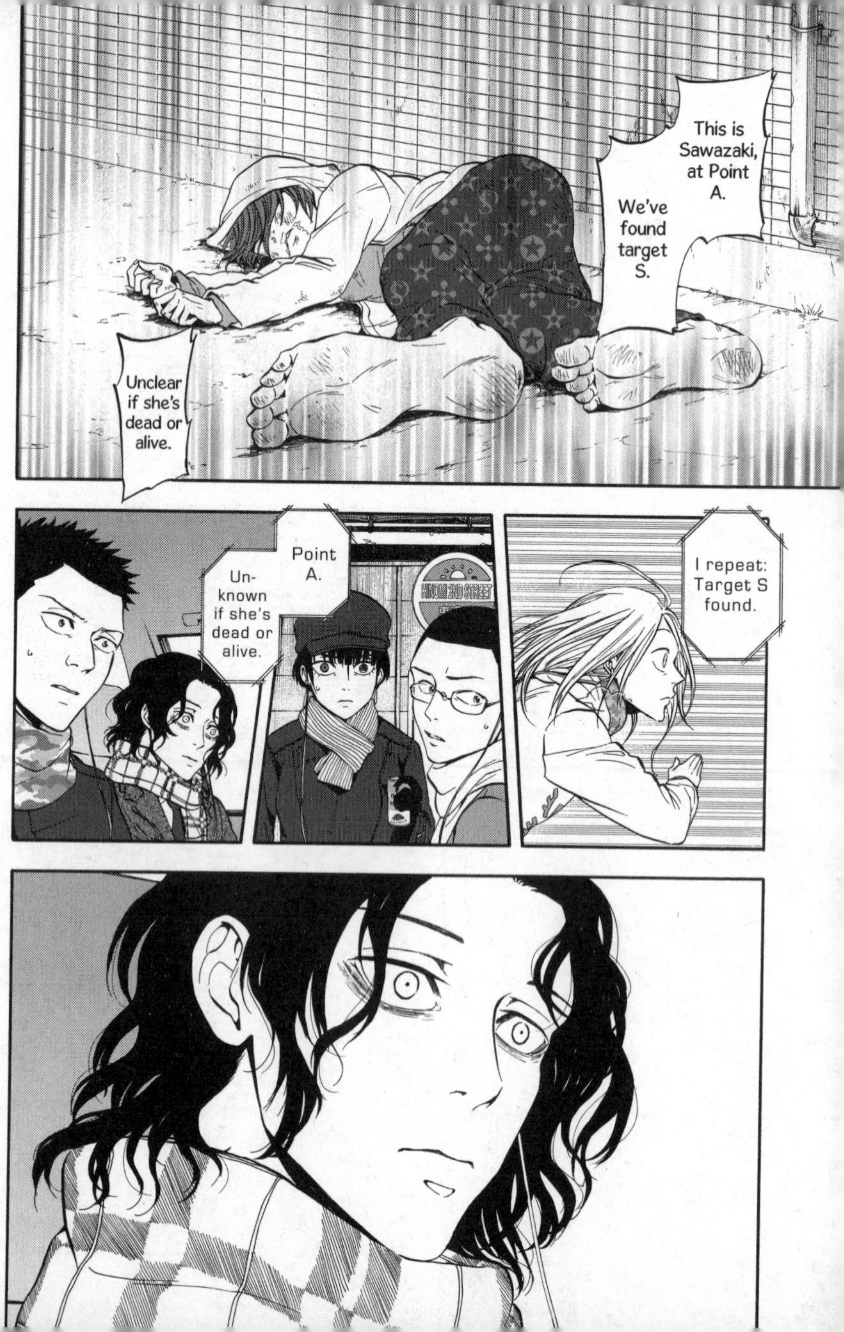
This is Sawazaki, at Point A.
We've found target S.
Unclear if she's dead or alive.
I repeat: Target S found.
Point A.
HINOMI 2ND STREET
Un-known if she's dead or alive.

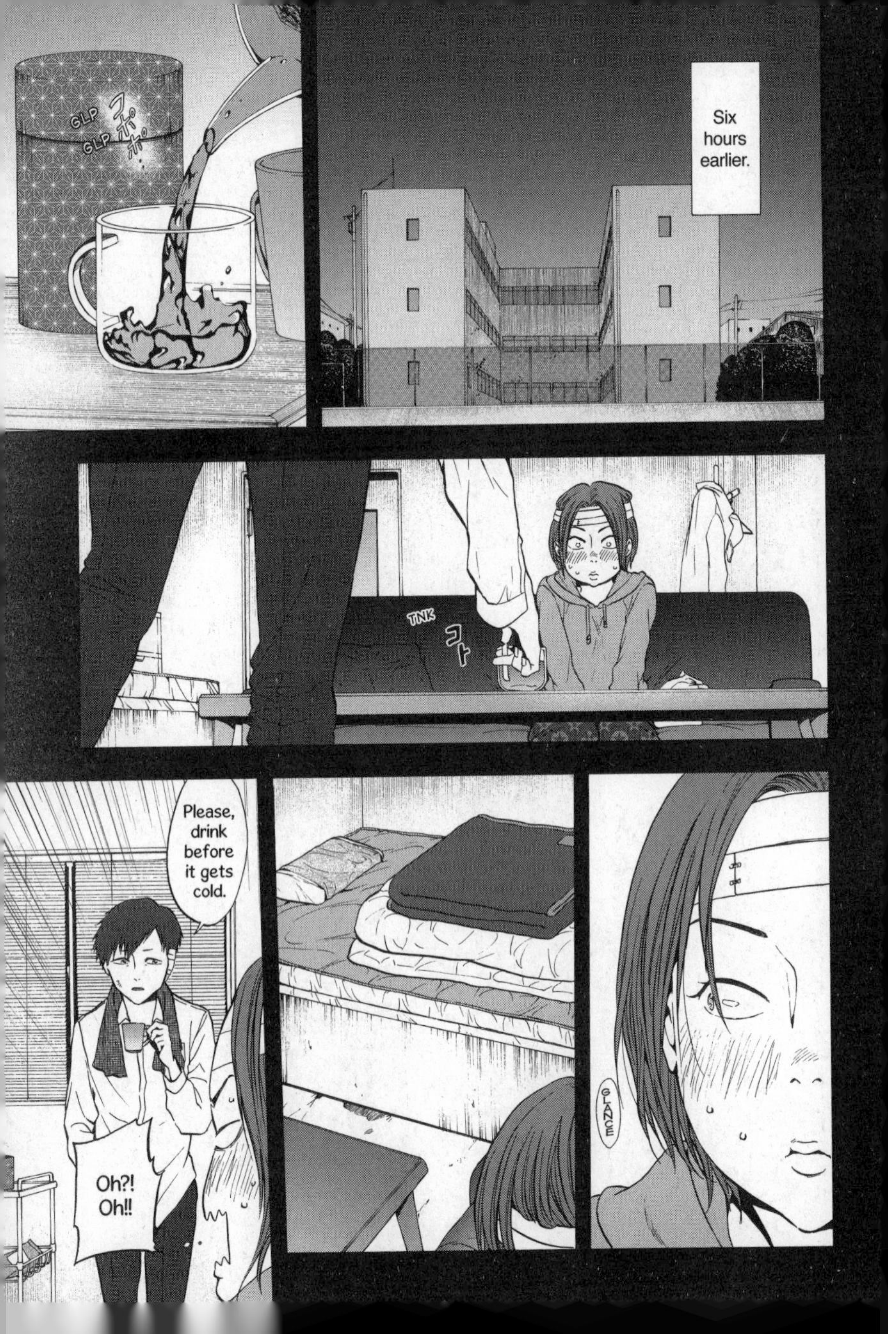
Six hours earlier.
GLP GLP
コポポ
TNK
コト
GLANCE
Please, drink before it gets cold.
Oh?! Oh!!

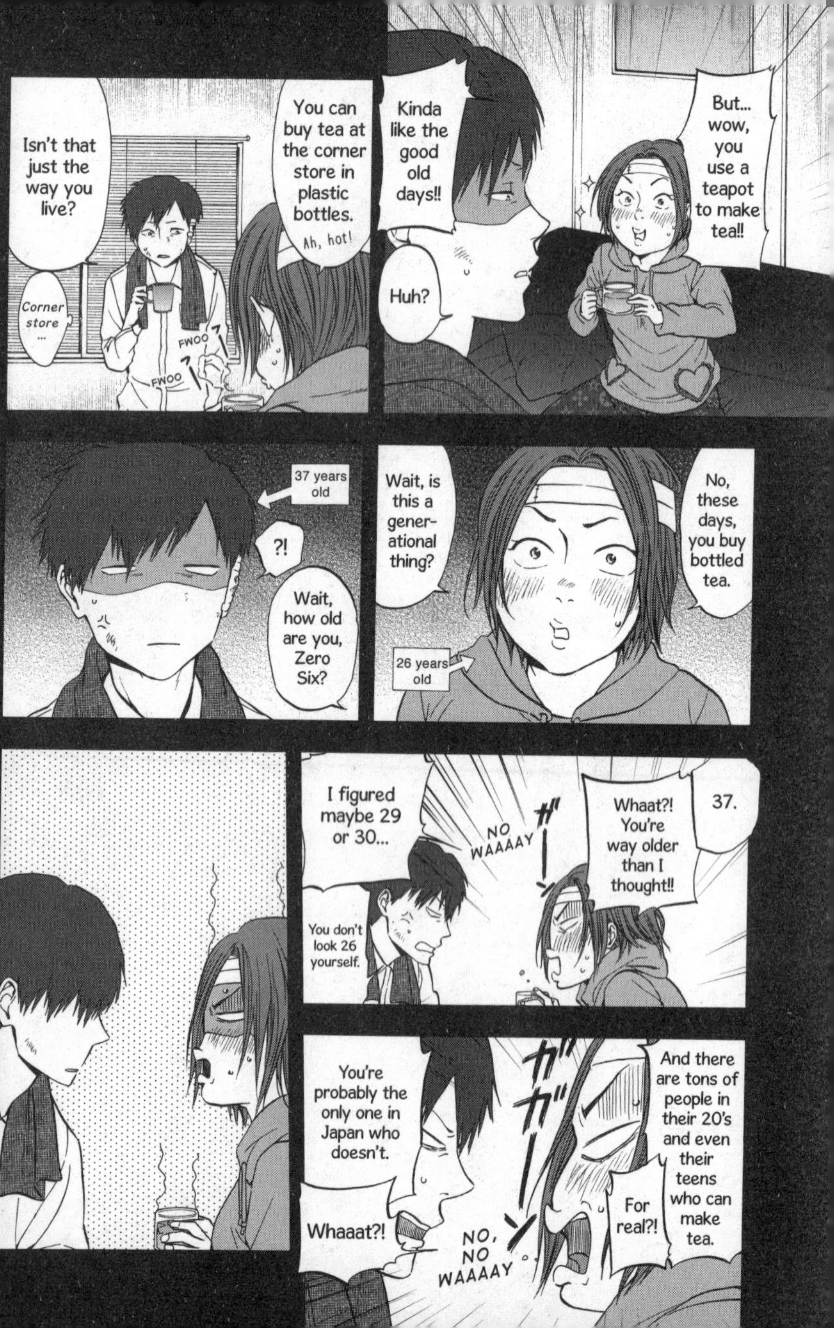

But... wow, you use a teapot to make tea!!
Kinda like the good old days!!
Huh?
You can buy tea at the corner store in plastic bottles.
Ah, hot!
Isn't that just the way you live?
Corner store ...
FWOO
FWOO
No, these days, you buy bottled tea.
Wait, is this a generational thing?
26 years old
37 years old
?!
Wait, how old are you, Zero Six?
37.
Whaat?! You're way older than I thought!!
NO WAAAAY
I figured maybe 29 or 30...
You don't look 26 yourself.
And there are tons of people in their 20's and even their teens who can make tea.
For real?!
NO, NO WAAAAY
You're probably the only one in Japan who doesn't.
Whaaat?!

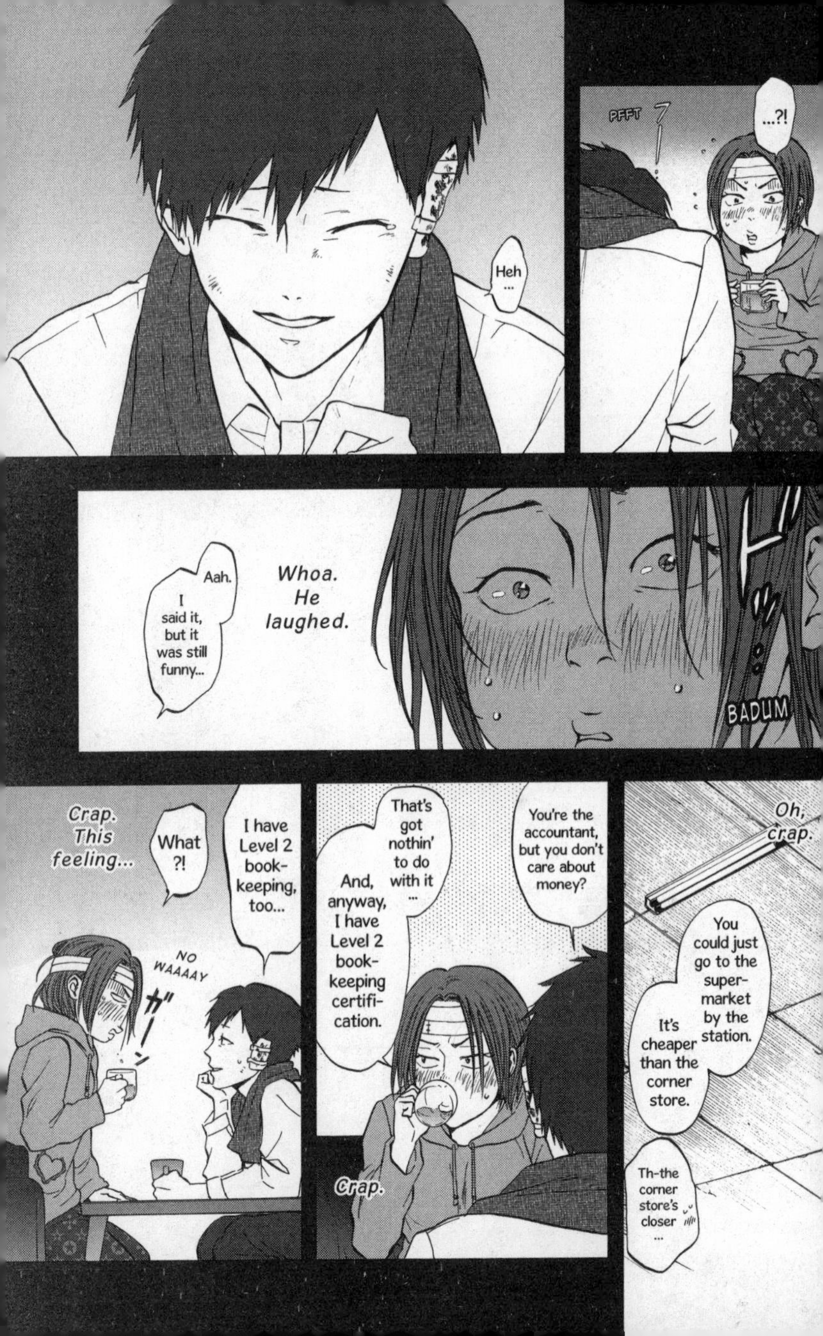
PFFT
...?!
Heh ...
BADUM
Whoa. He laughed.
Aah. I said it, but it was still funny...
Oh, crap.
You could just go to the super-market by the station.
It's cheaper than the corner store.
Th-the corner store's closer ...
You're the accountant, but you don't care about money?
That's got nothin' to do with it ...
And, anyway, I have Level 2 book-keeping certifi-cation.
Crap.
I have Level 2 book-keeping, too...
What ?!
Crap. This feeling...
NO WAAAAY

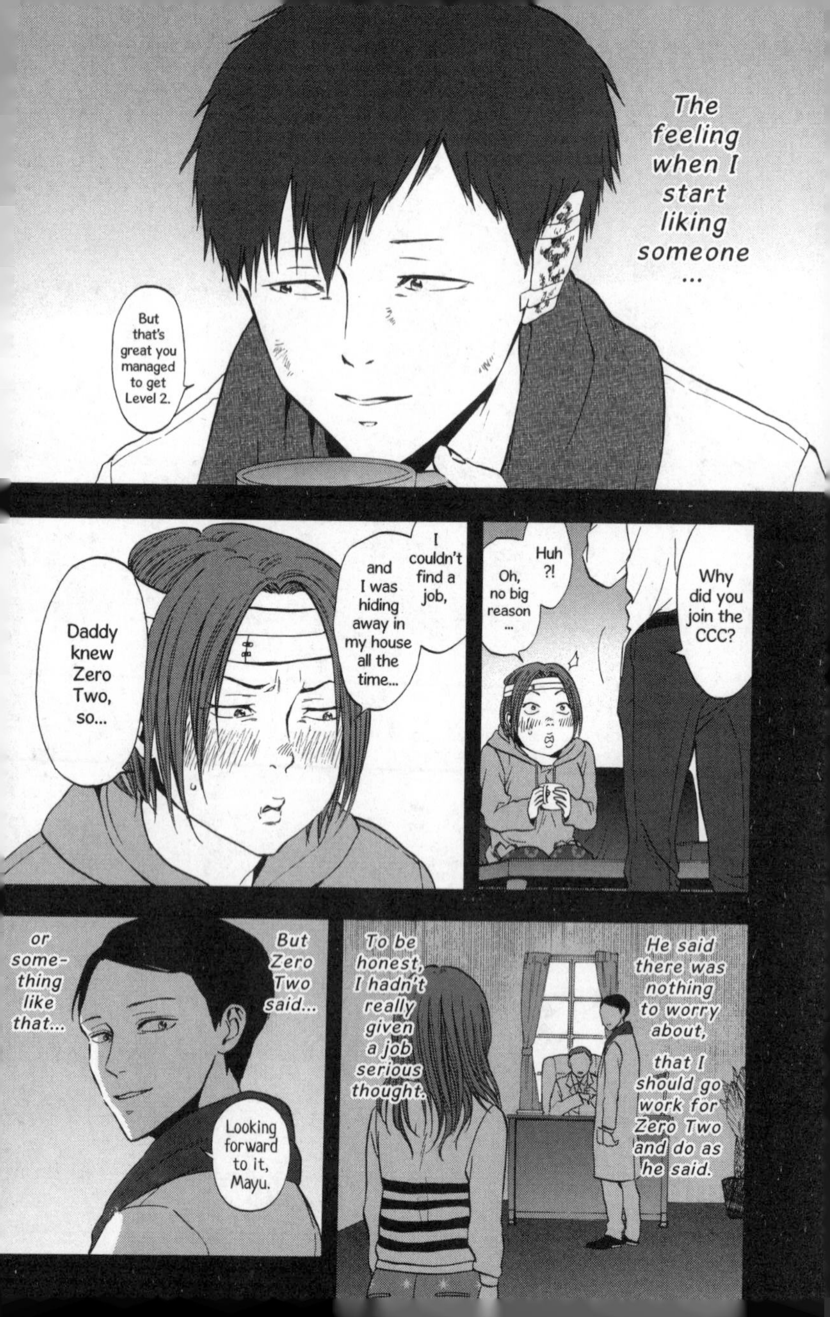
The feeling when I start liking someone ...
But that's great you managed to get Level 2.
Why did you join the CCC?
Huh ?!
Oh, no big reason ...
I couldn't find a job,
and I was hiding away in my house all the time...
Daddy knew Zero Two, so...
He said there was nothing to worry about,
that I should go work for Zero Two and do as he said.
To be honest, I hadn't really given a job serious thought.
But Zero Two said...
or some-thing like that...
Looking forward to it, Mayu.

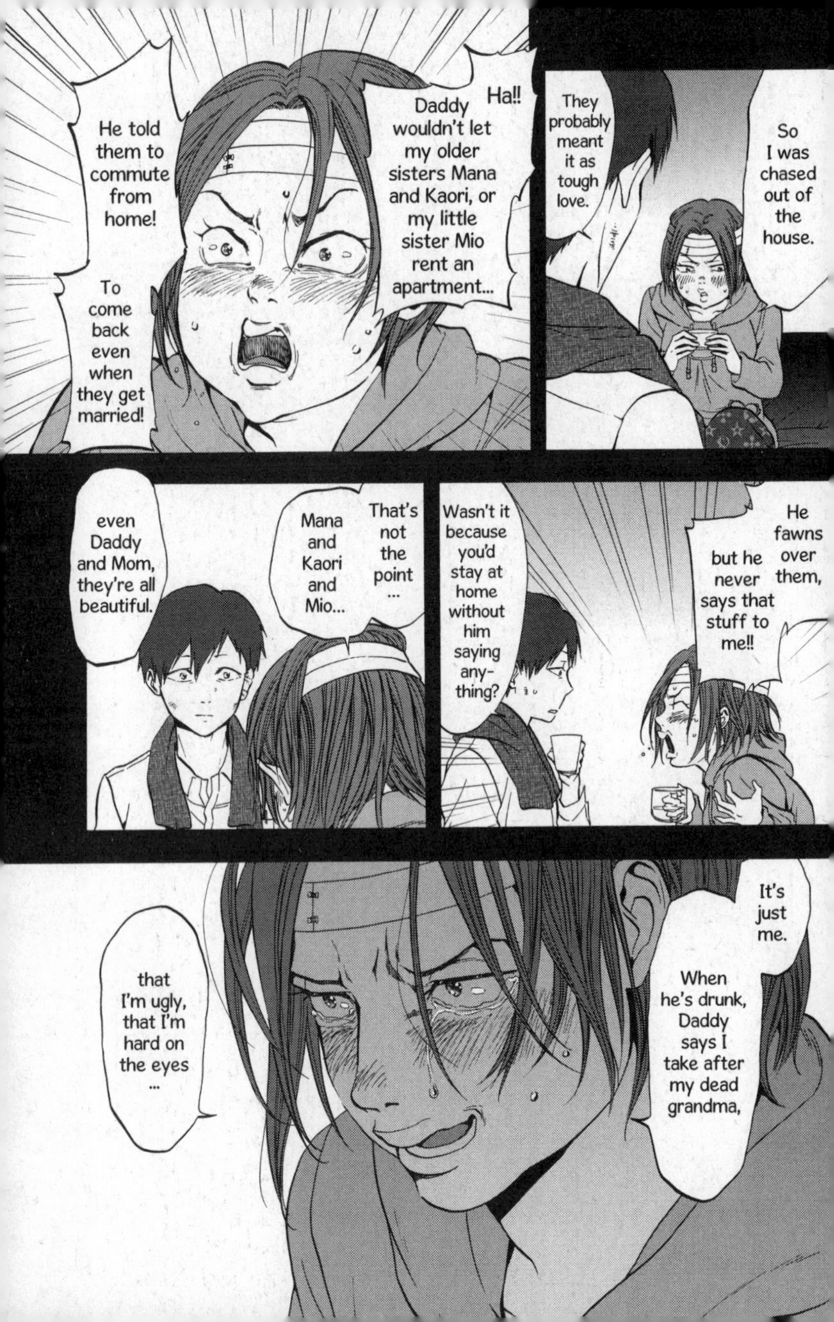

So I was chased out of the house.
They probably meant it as tough love.
Ha!!
Daddy wouldn't let my older sisters Mana and Kaori, or my little sister Mio rent an apartment...
He told them to commute from home!
To come back even when they get married!
He fawns over them,
but he never says that stuff to me!!
Wasn't it because you'd stay at home without him saying any-thing?
That's not the point ...
Mana and Kaori and Mio...
even Daddy and Mom, they're all beautiful.
It's just me.
When he's drunk, Daddy says I take after my dead grandma,
that I'm ugly, that I'm hard on the eyes ...

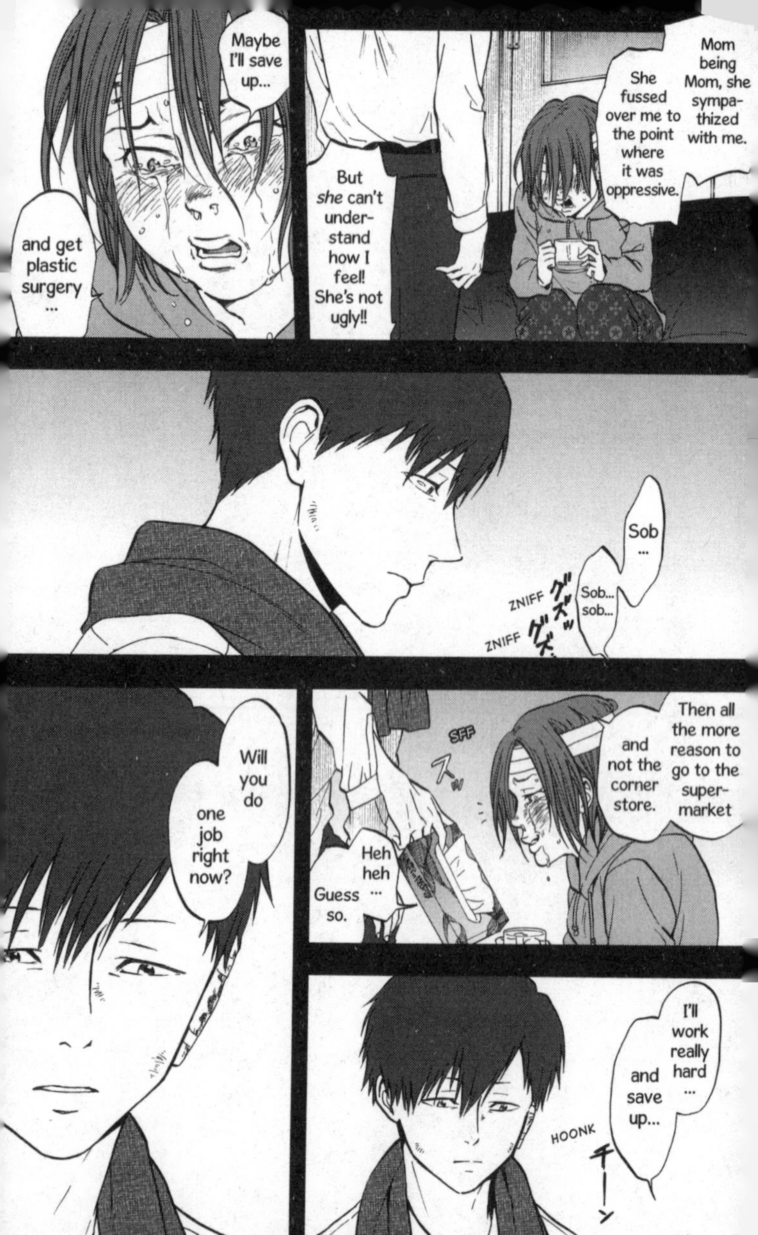
Mom being Mom, she sympathized with me.
She fussed over me to the point where it was oppressive.
But *she* can't understand how I feel! She's not ugly!!
Maybe I'll save up...
and get plastic surgery...
Sob...
Sob... sob...
ZNIFF
ZNIFF
Then all the more reason to go to the supermarket
and not the corner store.
SFF
Heh heh...
Guess so.
I'll work really hard...
and save up...
HOONK
Will you do one job right now?

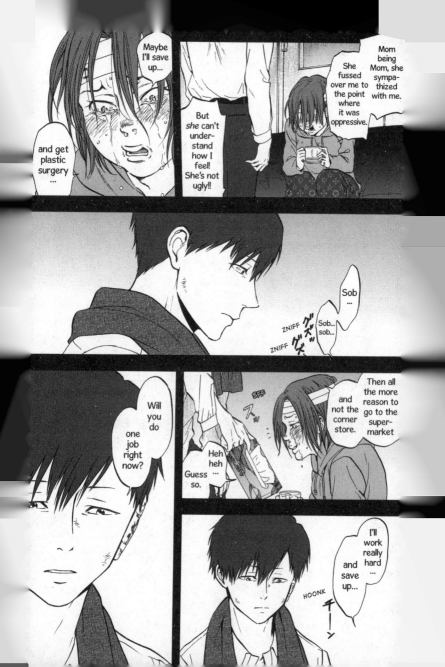

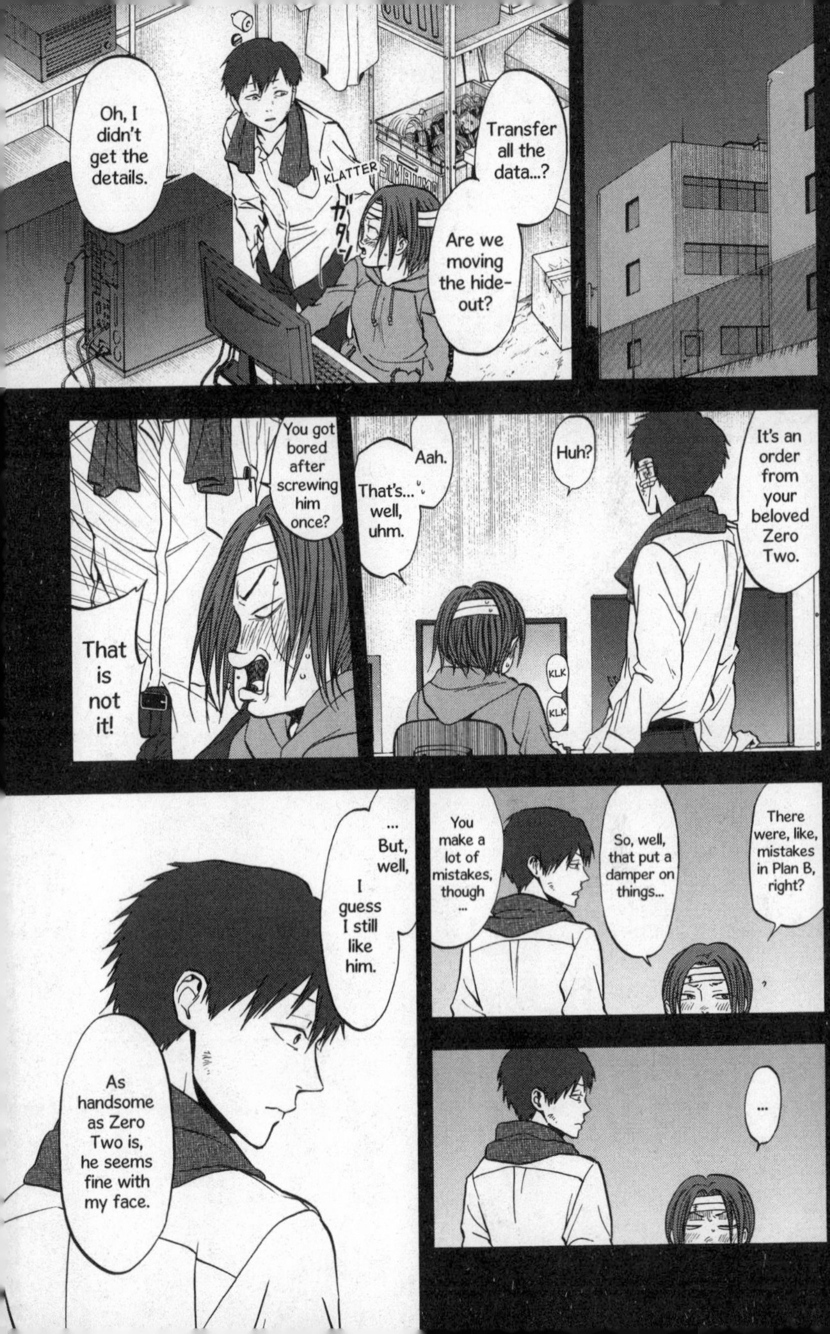
Transfer all the data...?
Are we moving the hide-out?
KLATTER
Oh, I didn't get the details.
It's an order from your beloved Zero Two.
Huh?
Aah.
That's... well, uhm.
KLK
KLK
You got bored after screwing him once?
That is not it!
There were, like, mistakes in Plan B, right?
So, well, that put a damper on things...
You make a lot of mistakes, though ...
...
... But, well, I guess I still like him.
As handsome as Zero Two is, he seems fine with my face.

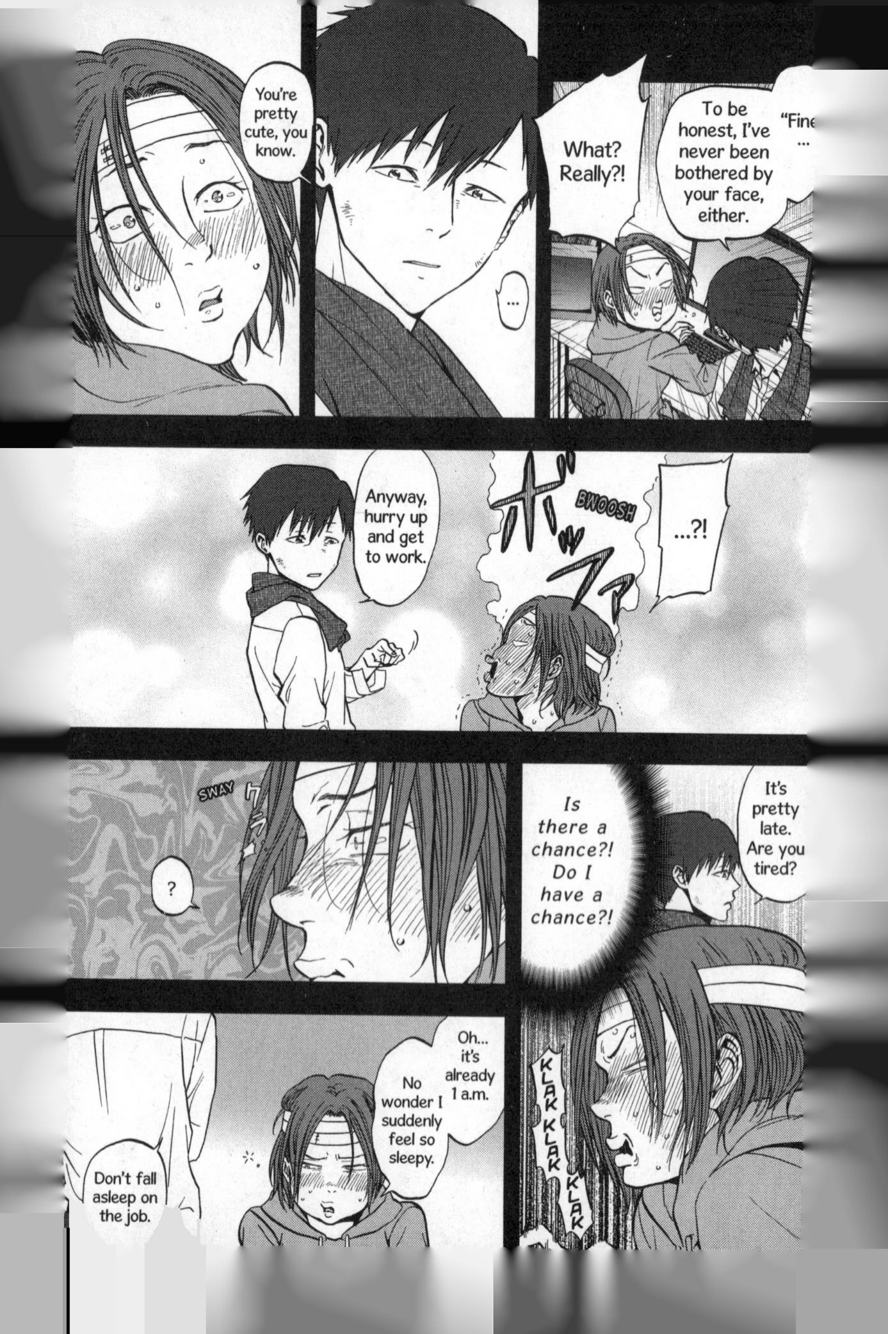
"Fine ...
To be honest, I've never been bothered by your face, either.
What? Really?!
...
You're pretty cute, you know.
...?!
BWOOSH
Anyway, hurry up and get to work.
It's pretty late. Are you tired?
Is there a chance?! Do I have a chance?!
SWAY
?
KLAK KLAK KLAK KLAK
Oh... it's already 1 a.m.
No wonder I suddenly feel so sleepy.
Don't fall asleep on the job.

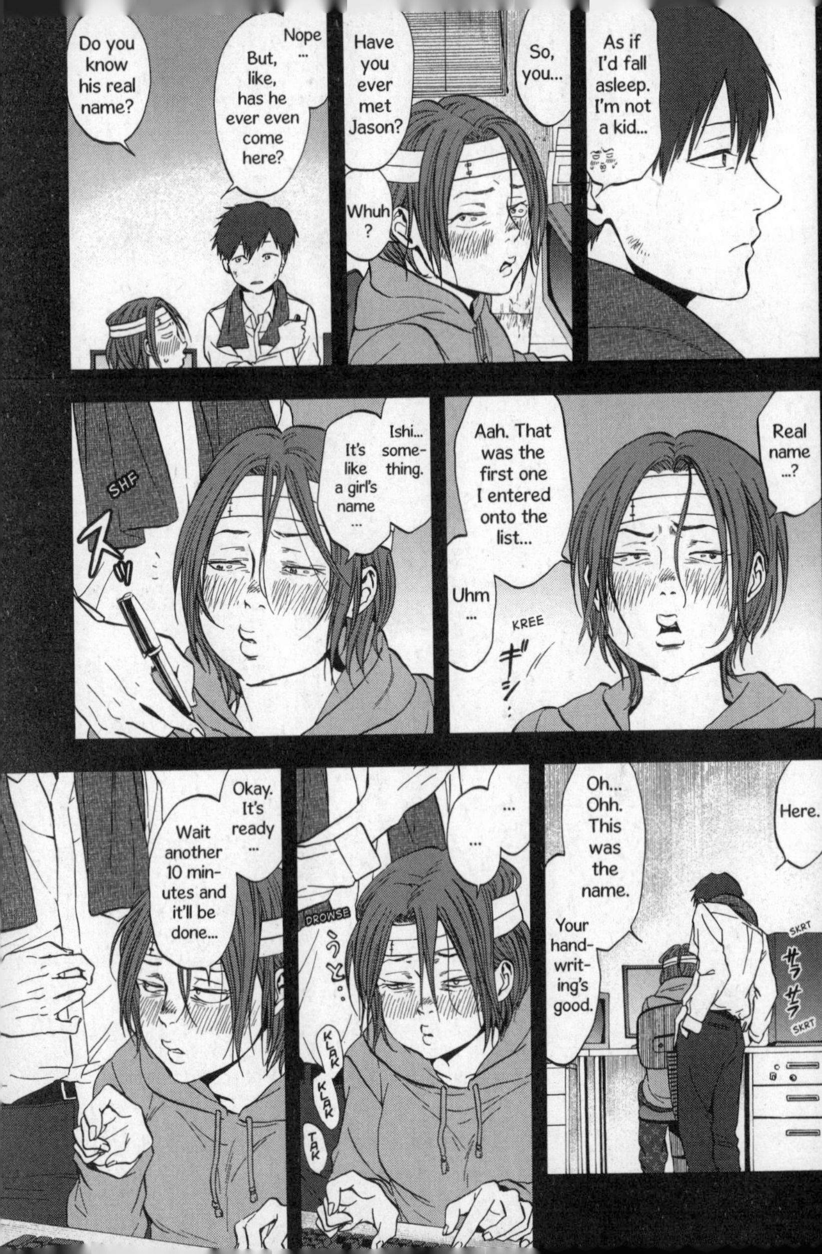
As if I'd fall asleep. I'm not a kid...
So, you...
Have you ever met Jason?
Whuh ?
Nope ...
But, like, has he ever even come here?
Do you know his real name?
Real name ...?
Aah. That was the first one I entered onto the list...
Uhm ...
KREE
Ishi... some-thing.
It's like a girl's name ...
SHF
Here.
Oh... Ohh. This was the name.
Your hand-writ-ing's good.
SKRT
SKRT
...
...
DROWSE
KLAK
KLAK
TAK
Okay. It's ready ...
Wait another 10 min-utes and it'll be done...

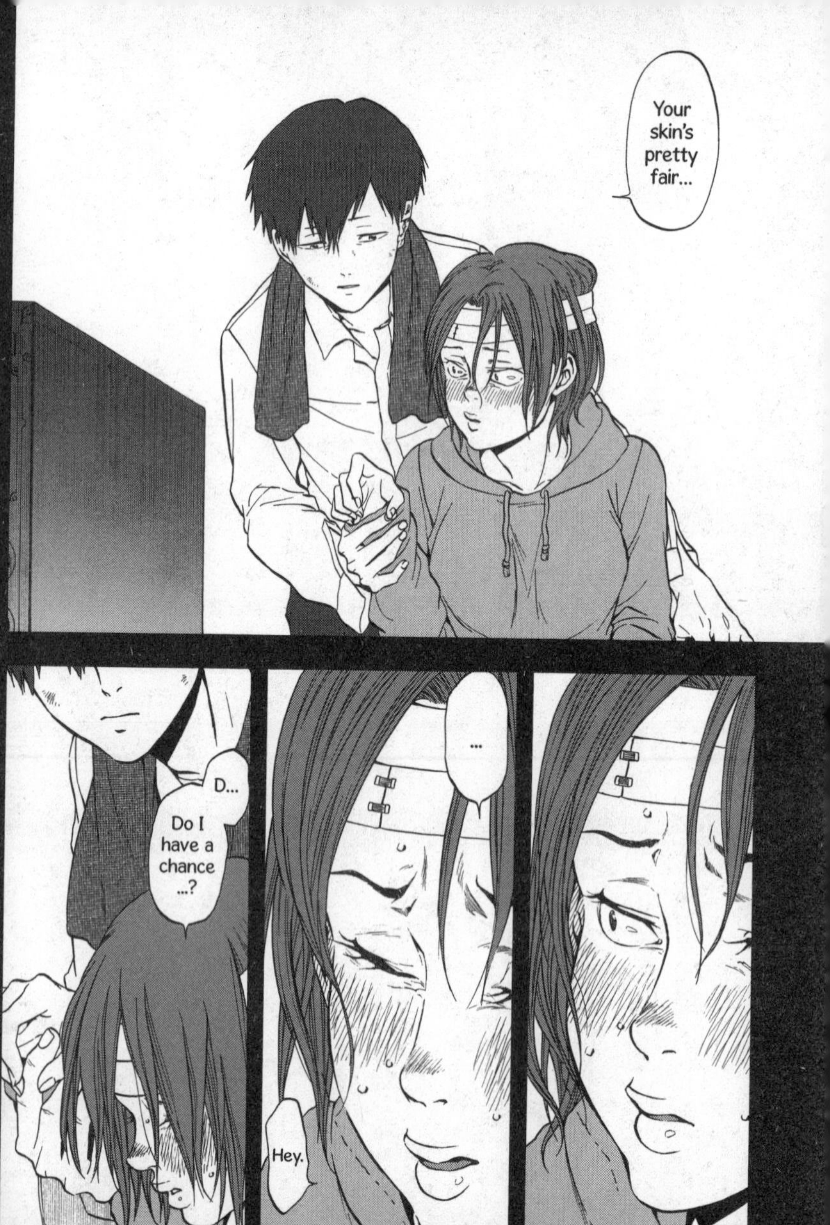
Your skin's pretty fair...
...
Hey.
D...
Do I have a chance ...?

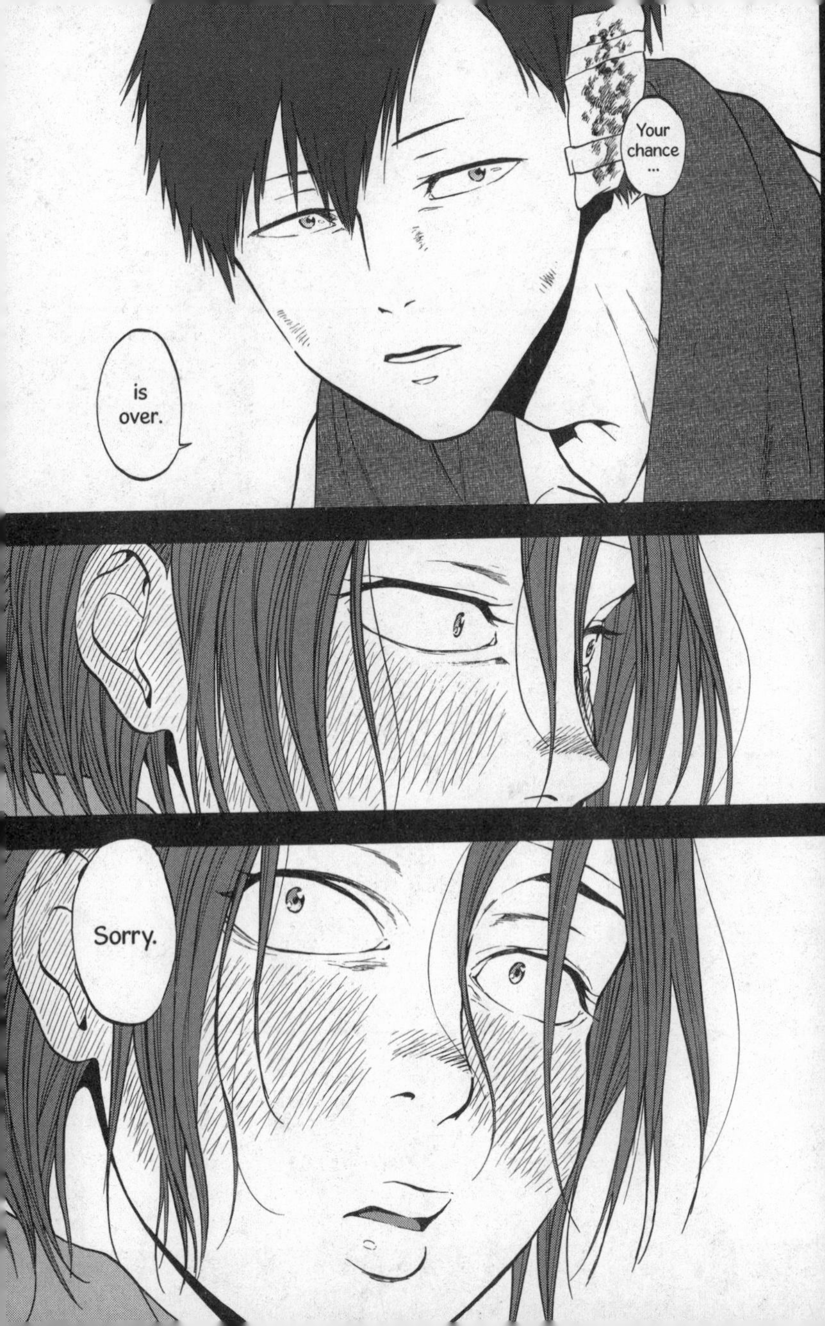
Your chance ...
is over.
Sorry.

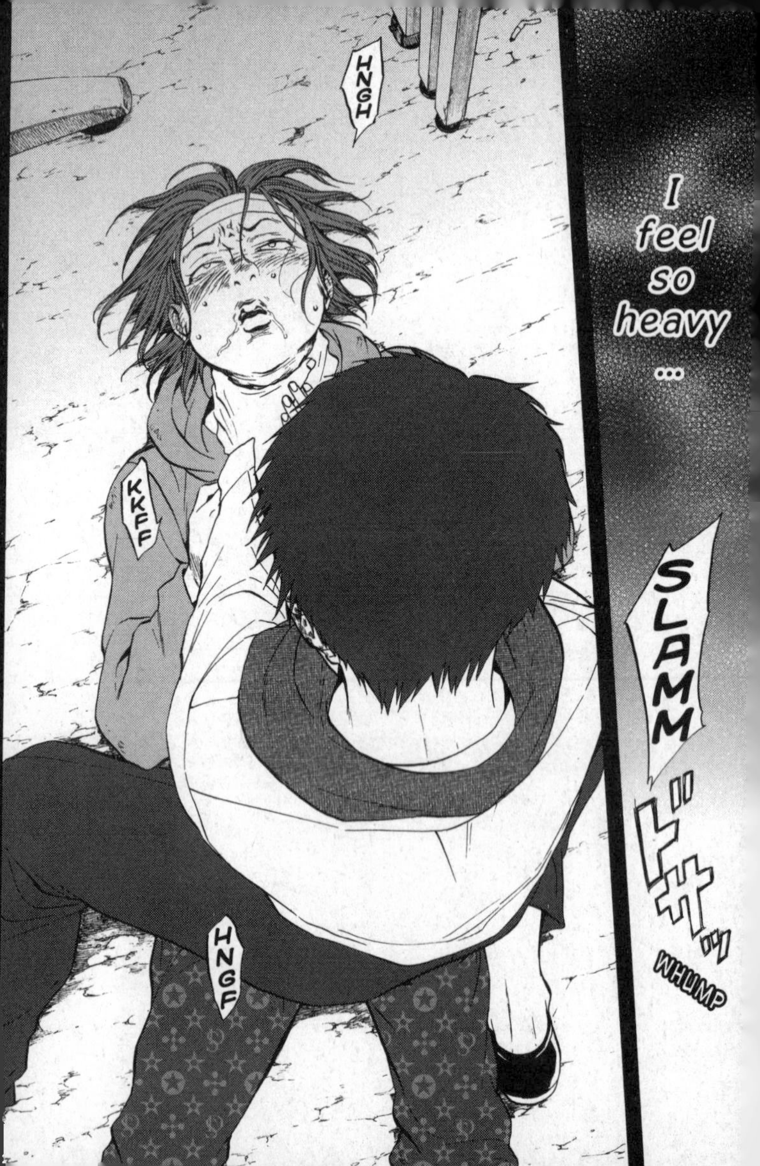
I feel so heavy ...
SLAMM
ドサッ
WHUMP
HNGH
KKFF
HNGF

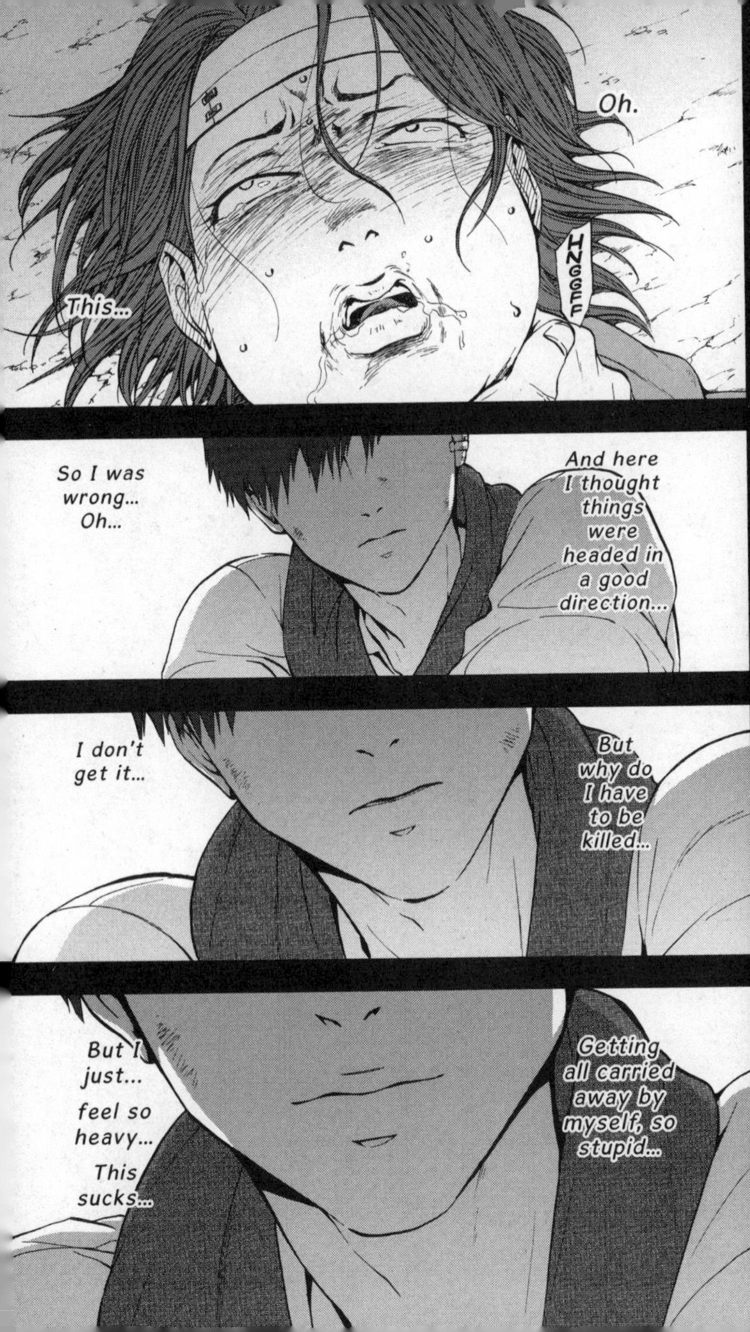
Oh.
HNGGFF
This...
And here I thought things were headed in a good direction...
So I was wrong... Oh...
But why do I have to be killed...
I don't get it...
Getting all carried away by myself, so stupid...
But I just...
feel so heavy...
This sucks...

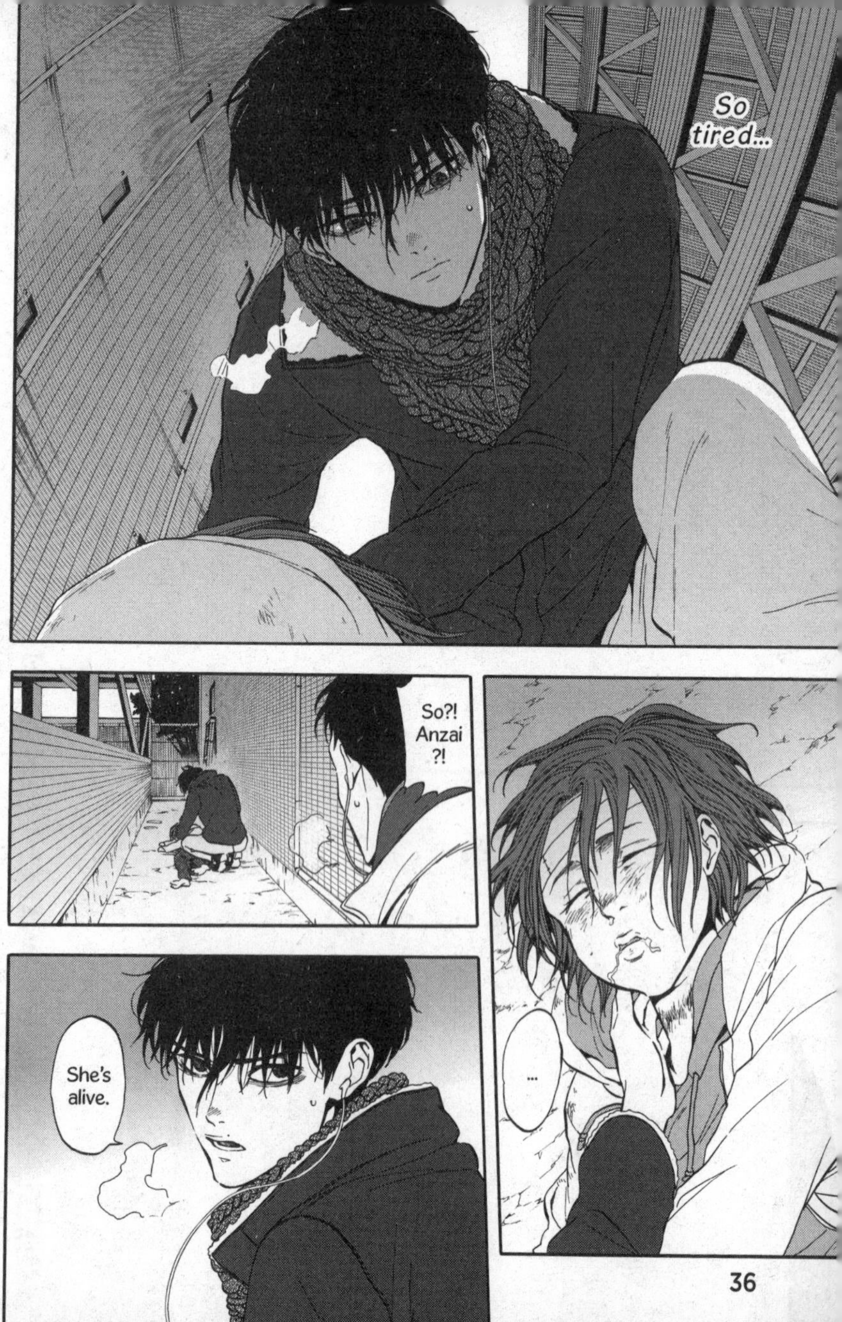
So tired...
...
So?! Anzai ?!
She's alive.

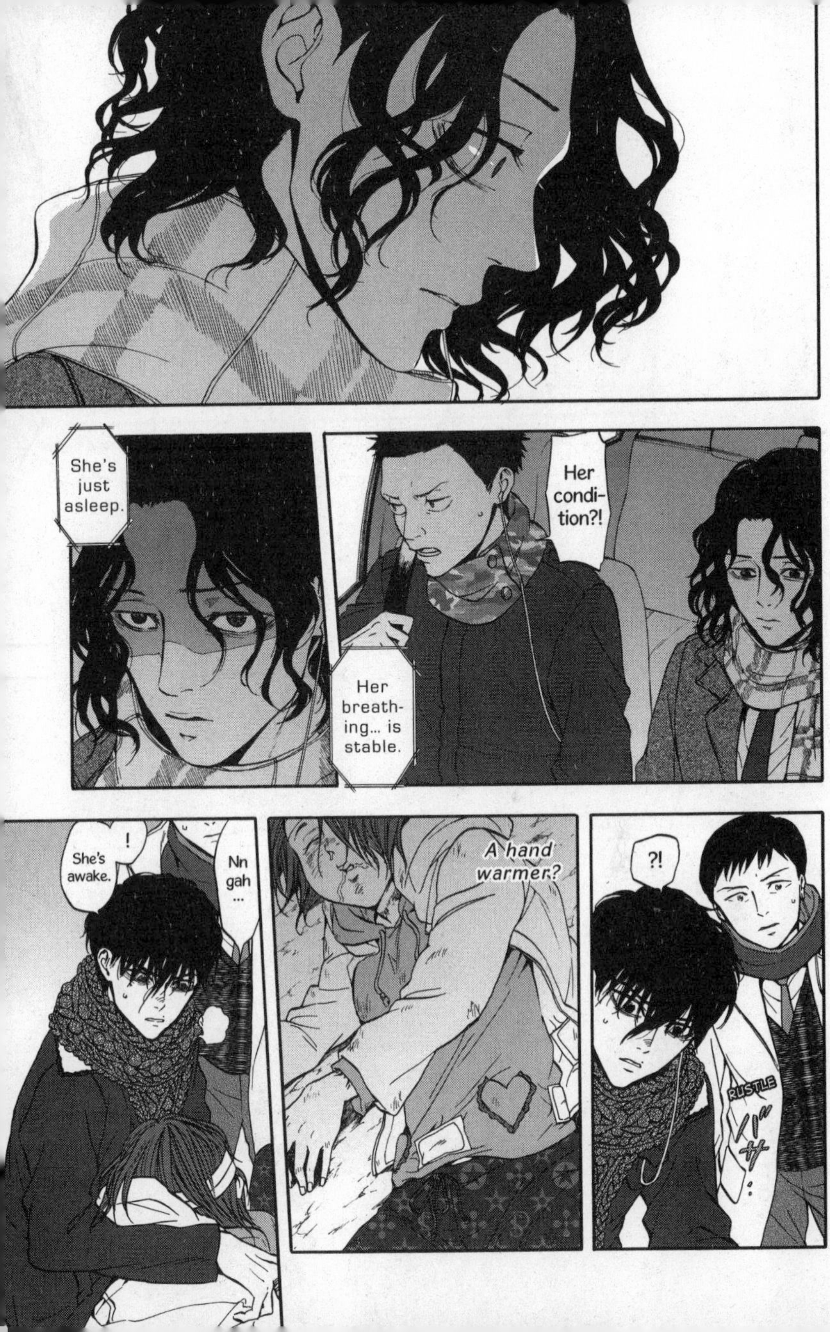
Her condition?!
Her breathing... is stable.
She's just asleep.
?!
RUSTLE
A hand warmer?
Nn gah ...
!
She's awake.

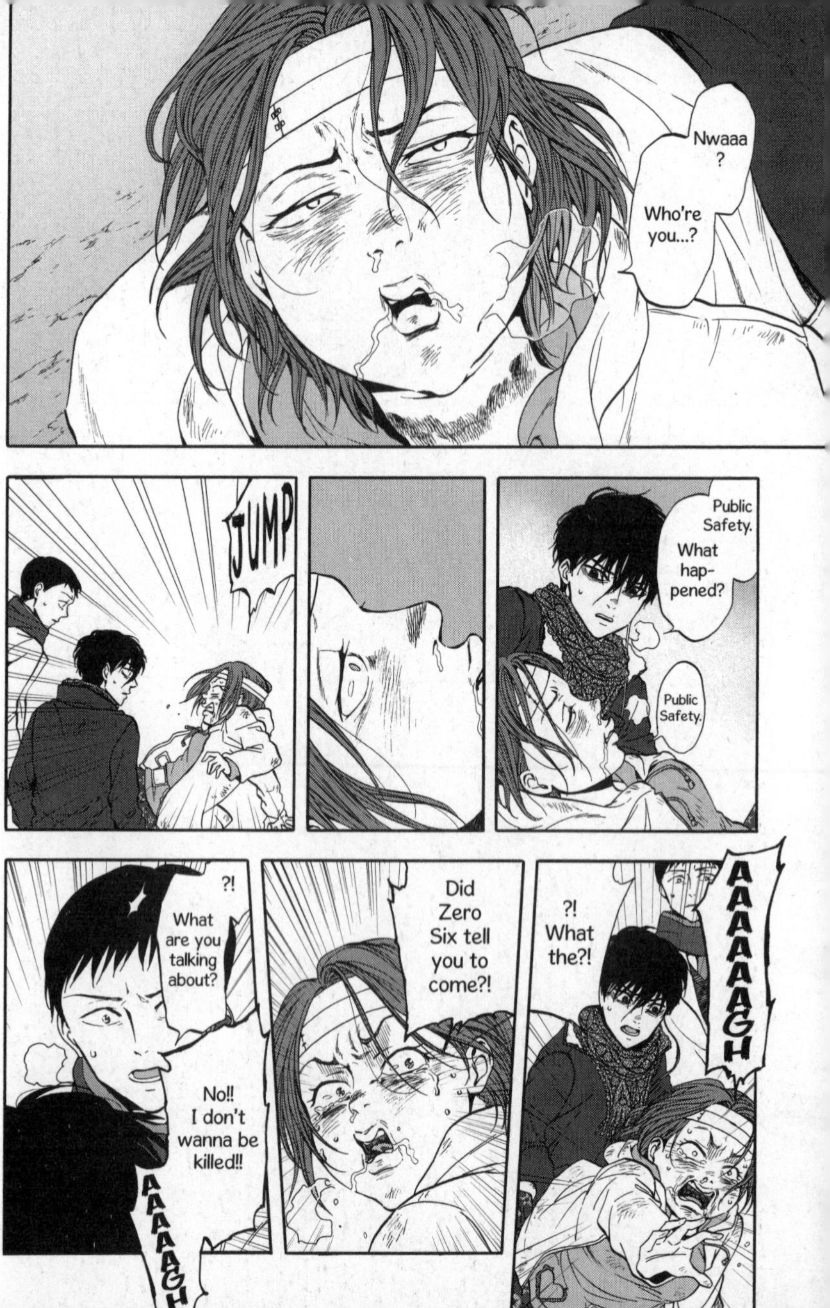

Nwaaa ?
Who're you...?
Public Safety.
What hap-pened?
Public Safety.
JUMP
AAAAAAAGH
?! What the?!
Did Zero Six tell you to come?!
No!! I don't wanna be killed!!
?!
What are you talking about?
AAAAAGH

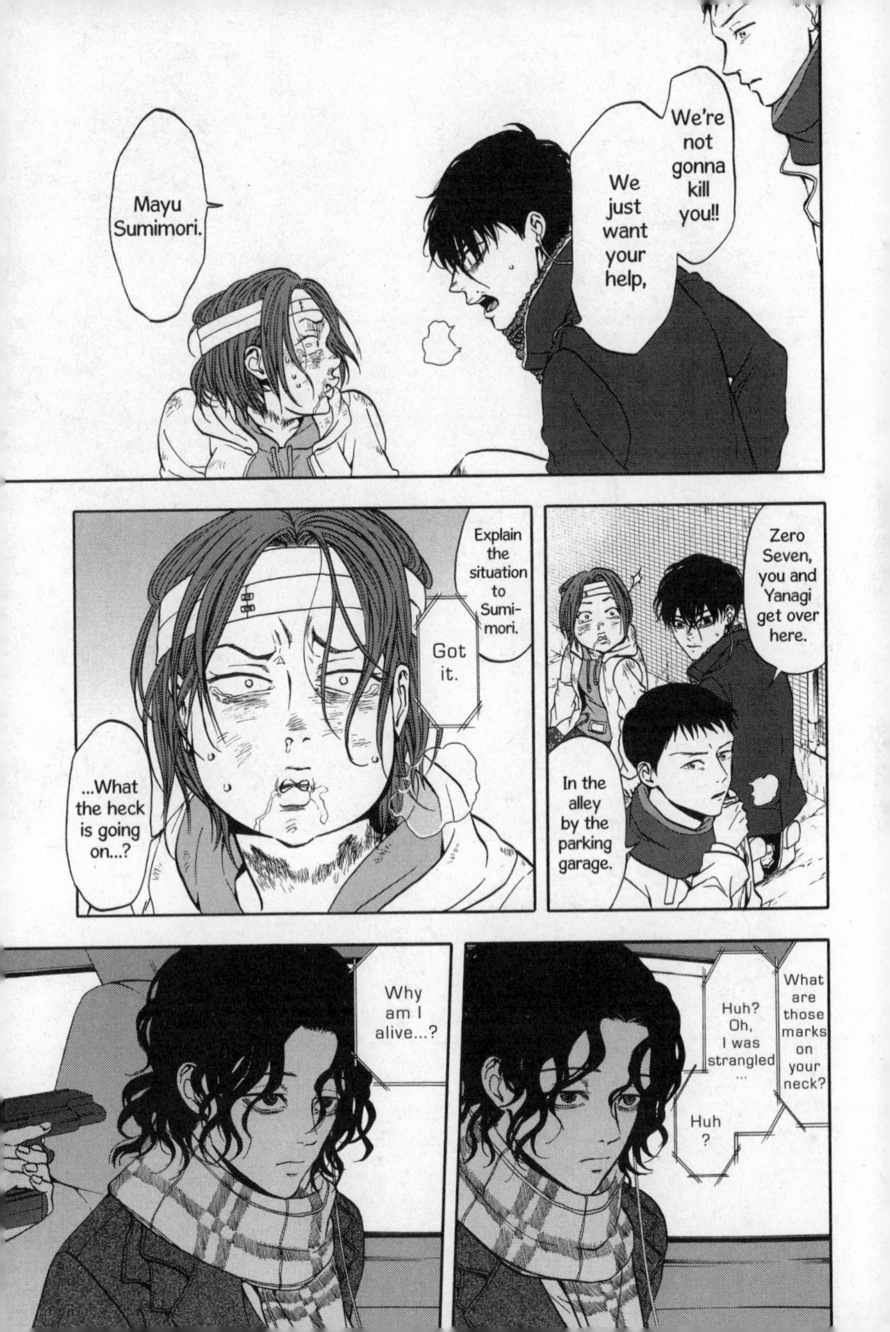
We're not gonna kill you!!
We just want your help,
Mayu Sumimori.
Zero Seven, you and Yanagi get over here.
In the alley by the parking garage.
Explain the situation to Sumi-mori.
Got it.
...What the heck is going on...?
What are those marks on your neck?
Huh? Oh, I was strangled ...
Huh ?
Why am I alive...?

Take your hand out of your pocket.

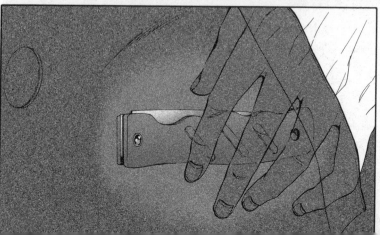

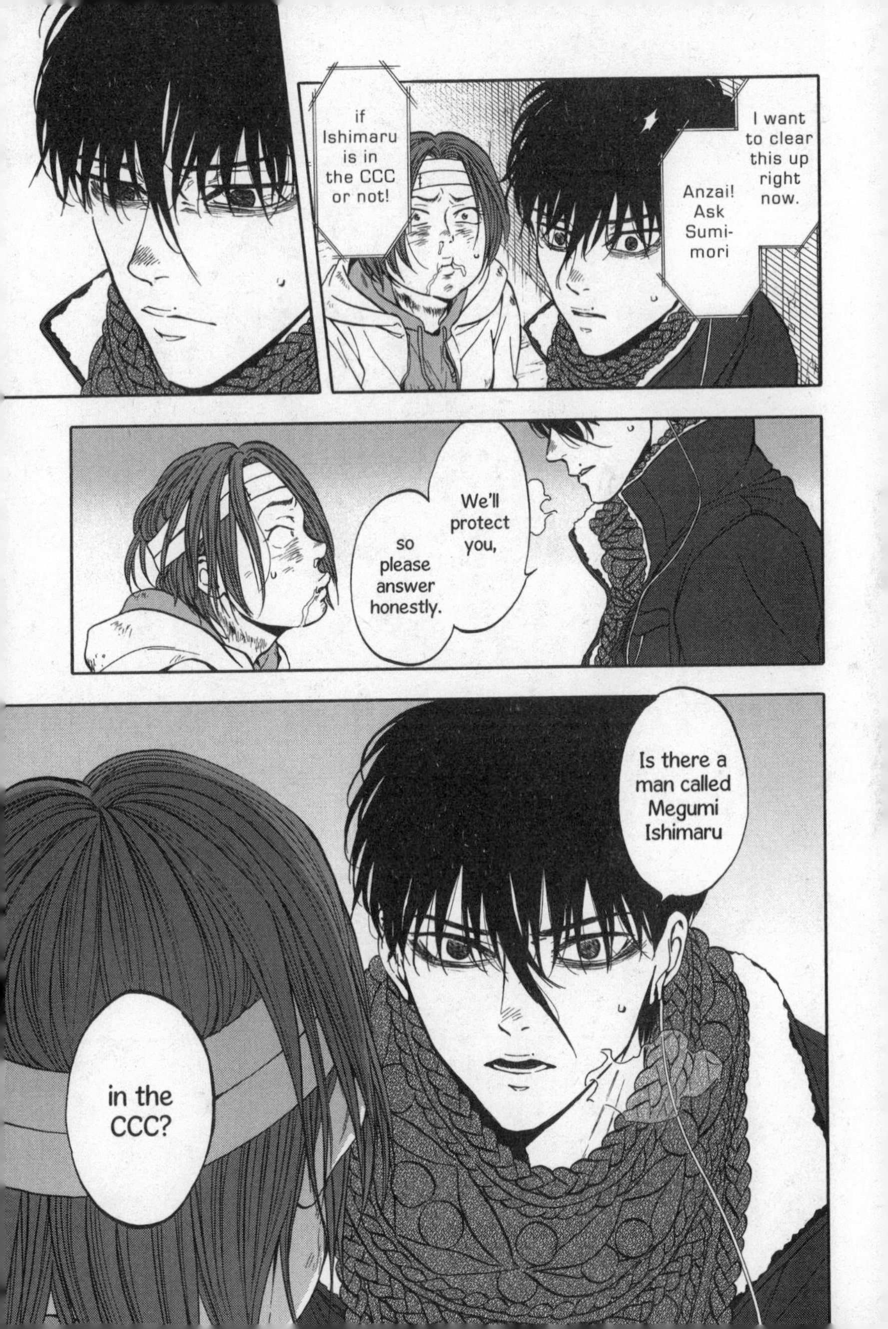
I want to clear this up right now.
Anzai! Ask Sumimori
if Ishimaru is in the CCC or not!
We'll protect you,
so please answer honestly.
Is there a man called Megumi Ishimaru
in the CCC?

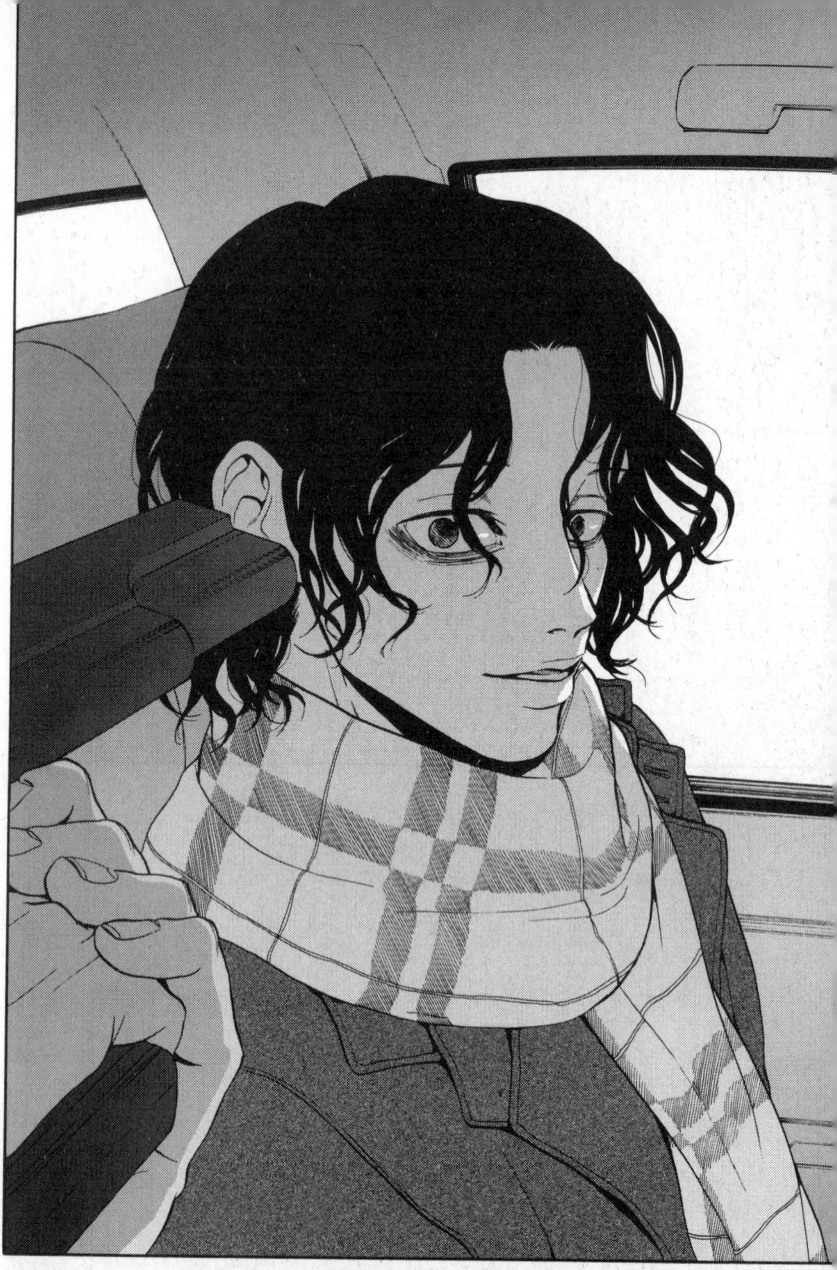

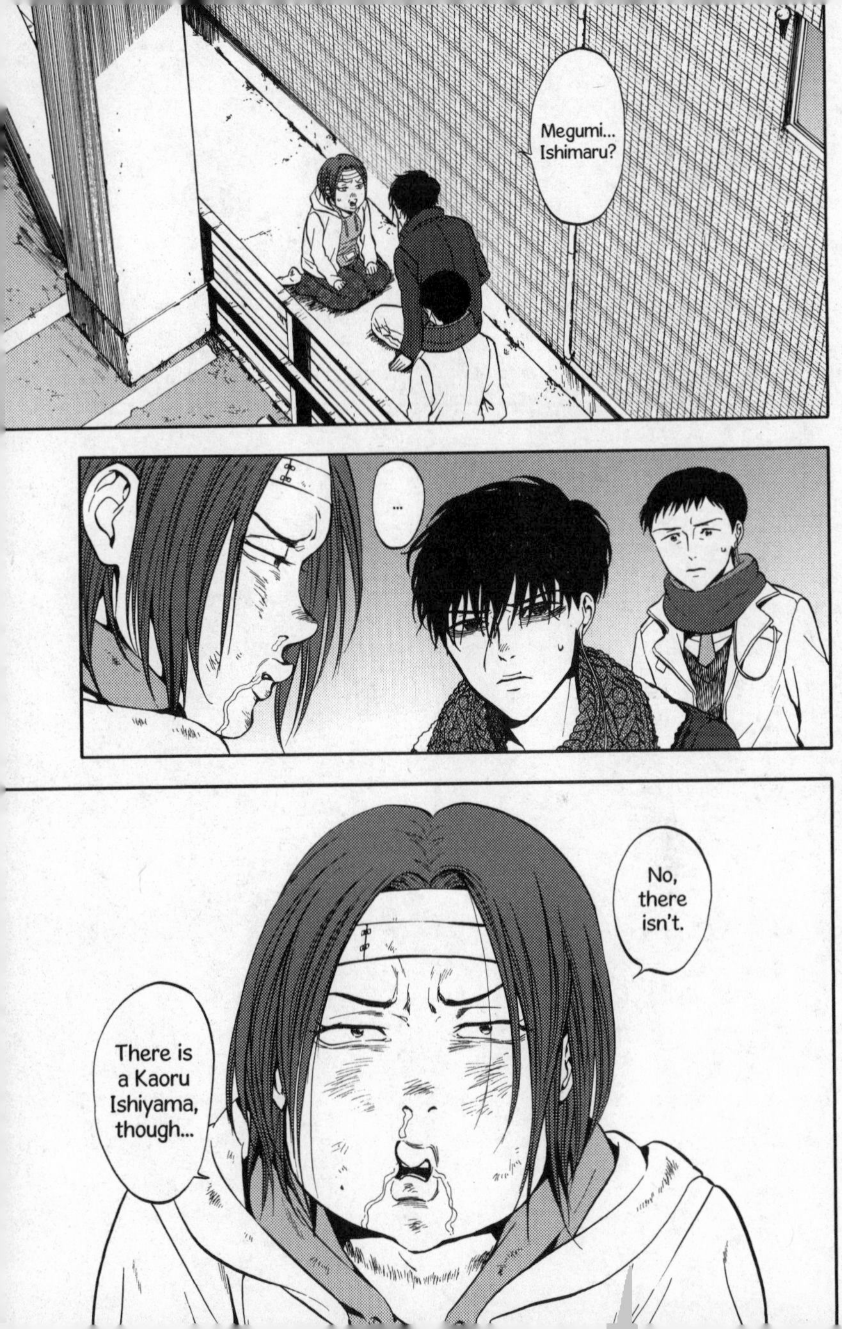
Megumi... Ishimaru?
...
No, there isn't.
There is a Kaoru Ishiyama, though...

Line 34
Outsider

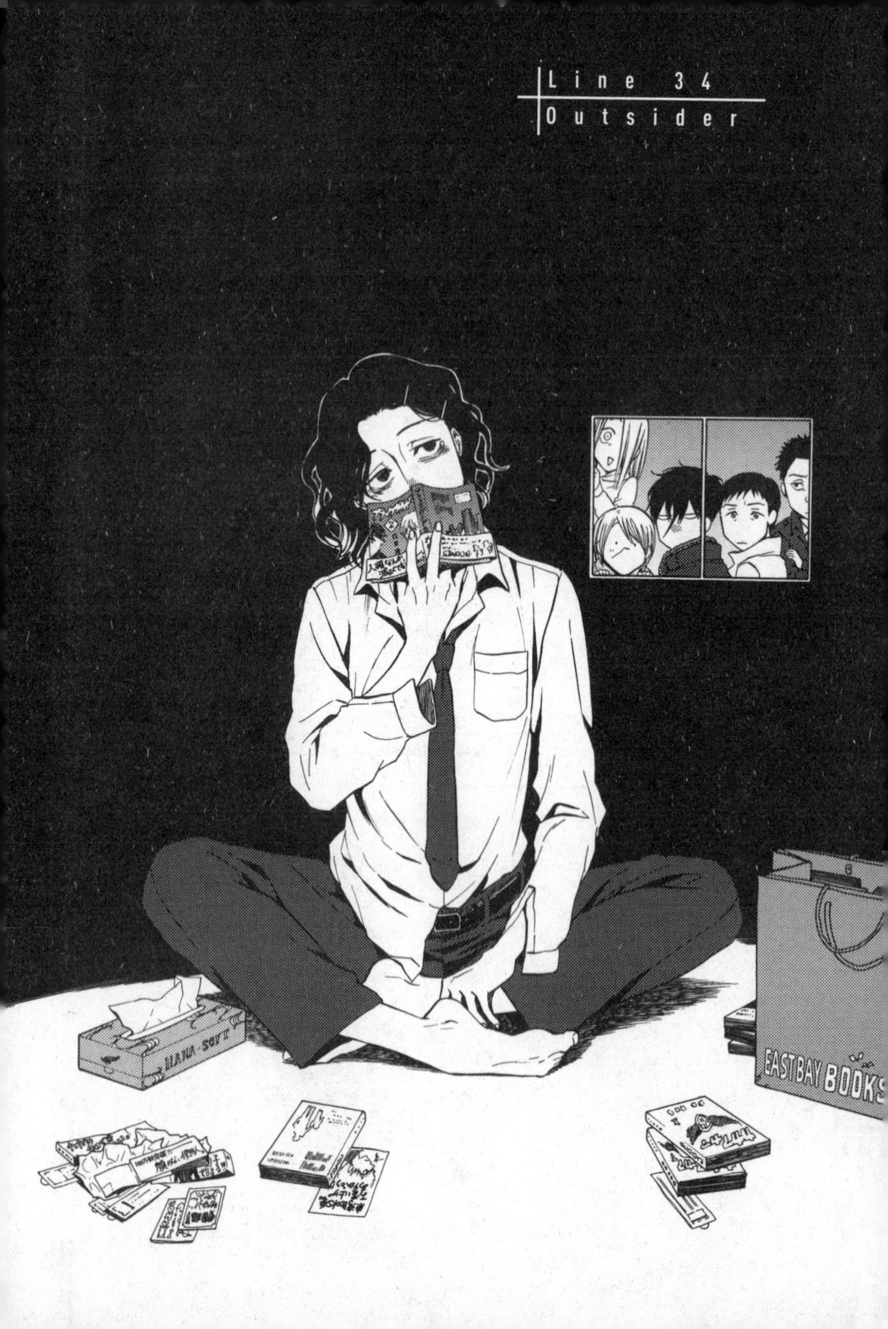

HANA SOFT
EASTBAY BOOKS

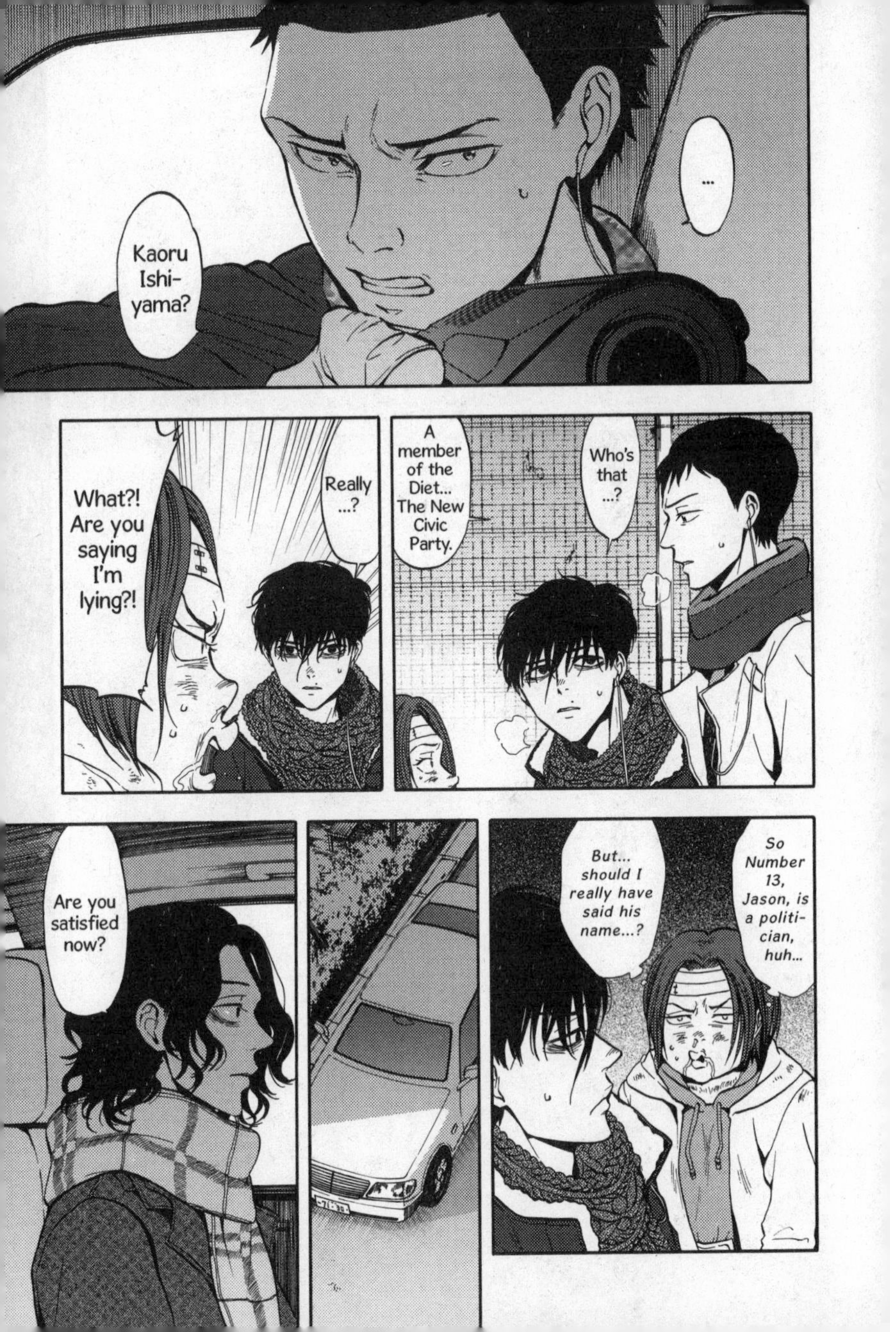
...
Kaoru Ishi-yama?
Who's that ...?
A member of the Diet... The New Civic Party.
Really ...?
What?! Are you saying I'm lying?!
So Number 13, Jason, is a politi-cian, huh...
But... should I really have said his name...?
Are you satisfied now?

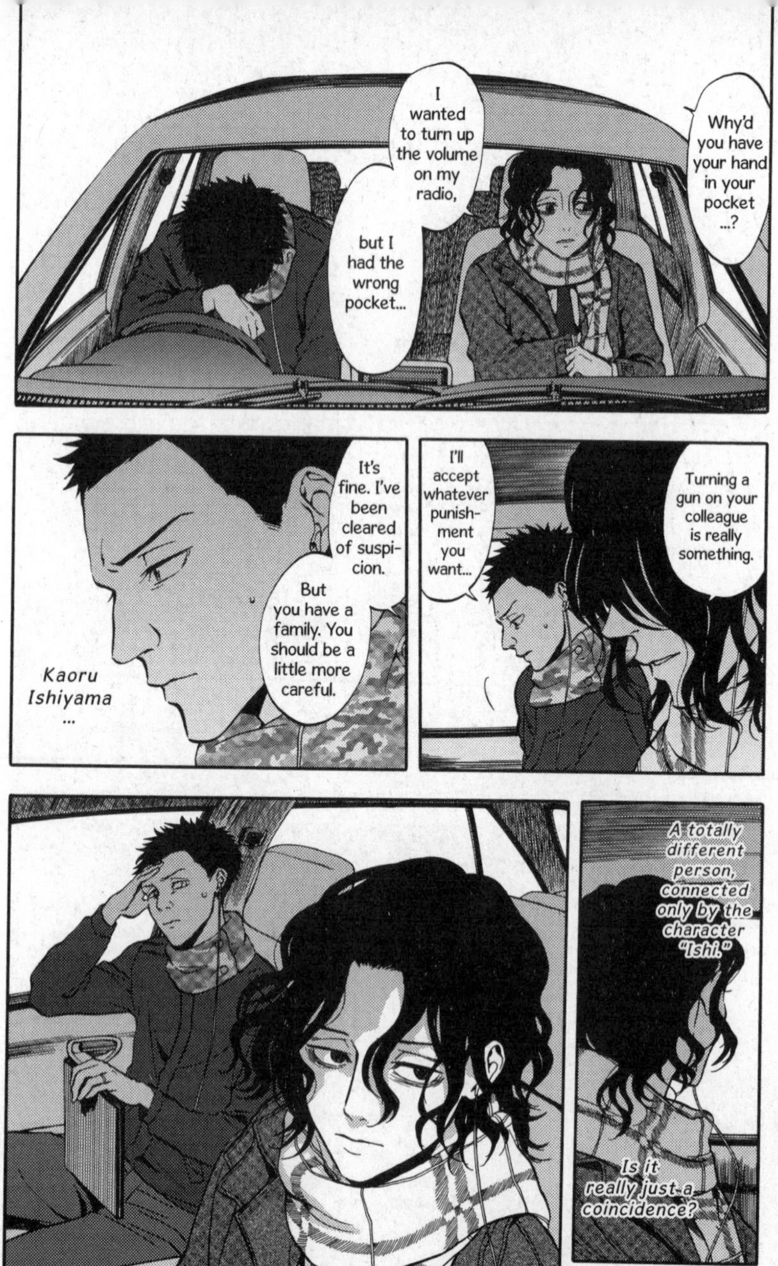
Why'd you have your hand in your pocket ...?
I wanted to turn up the volume on my radio,
but I had the wrong pocket...
Turning a gun on your colleague is really something.
I'll accept whatever punish-ment you want...
It's fine. I've been cleared of suspi-cion.
But you have a family. You should be a little more careful.
Kaoru Ishiyama ...
A totally different person, connected only by the character "Ishi."
Is it really just a coincidence?

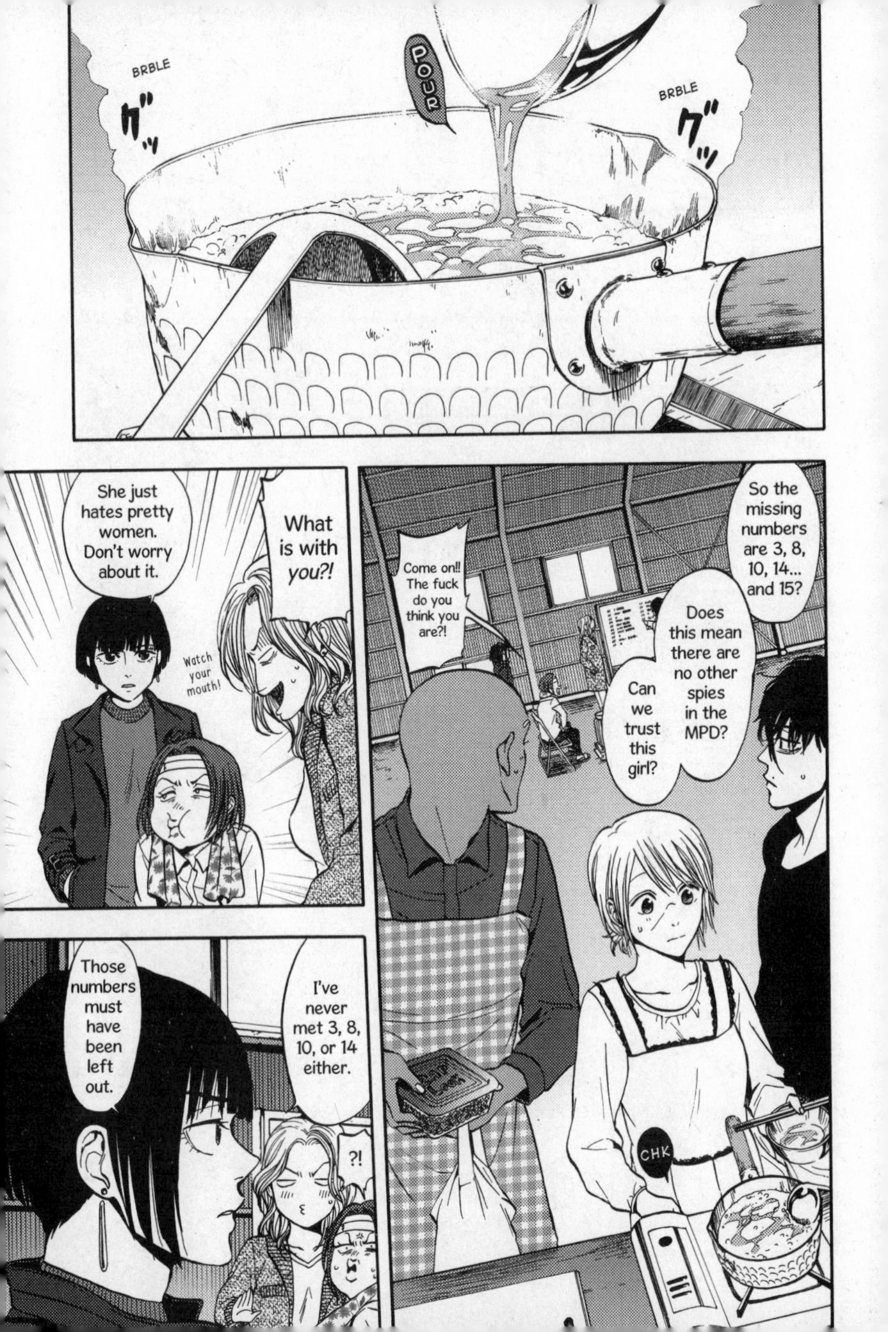
BRBLE
グツ
POUR
BRBLE
グツ
So the missing numbers are 3, 8, 10, 14... and 15?
Does this mean there are no other spies in the MPD?
Can we trust this girl?
Come on!! The fuck do you think you are?!
CHK
What is with *you?!*
She just hates pretty women. Don't worry about it.
Watch your mouth!
I've never met 3, 8, 10, or 14 either.
Those numbers must have been left out.
?!

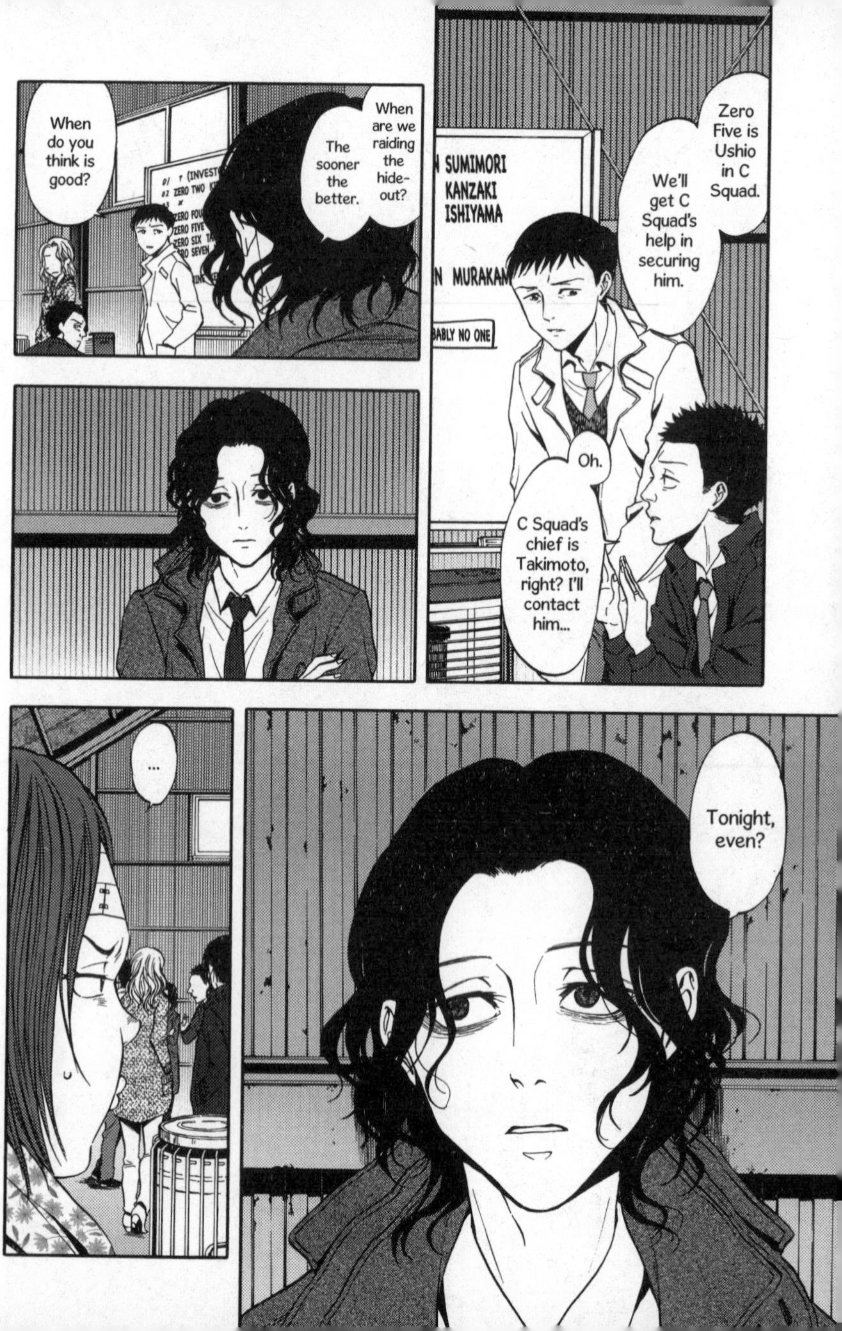
Zero Five is Ushio in C Squad.
We'll get C Squad's help in securing him.
SUMIMORI
KANZAKI
ISHIYAMA
Oh.
C Squad's chief is Takimoto, right? I'll contact him...
When are we raiding the hide-out?
The sooner the better.
When do you think is good?
Tonight, even?
...

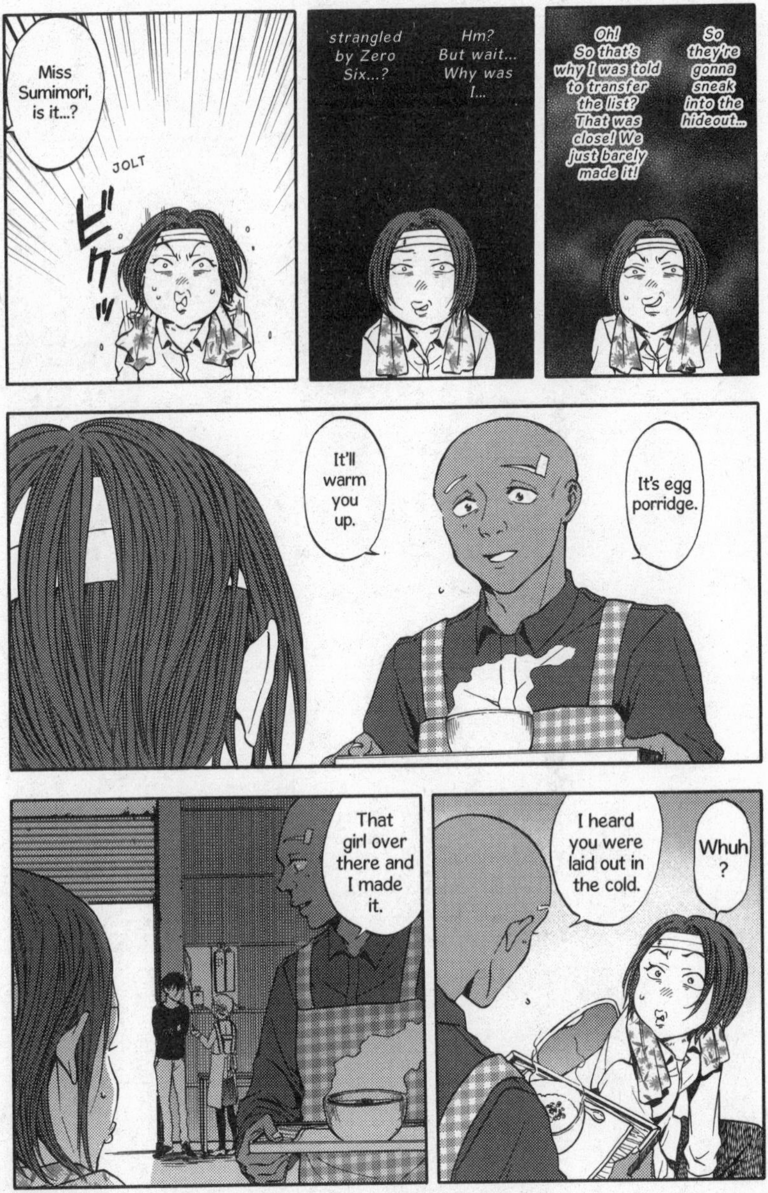

So they're gonna sneak into the hideout...
Oh! So that's why I was told to transfer the list? That was close! We just barely made it!
Hm? But wait... Why was I...
strangled by Zero Six...?
Miss Sumimori, is it...?
JOLT
ビクッ
It's egg porridge.
It'll warm you up.
Whuh?
I heard you were laid out in the cold.
That girl over there and I made it.

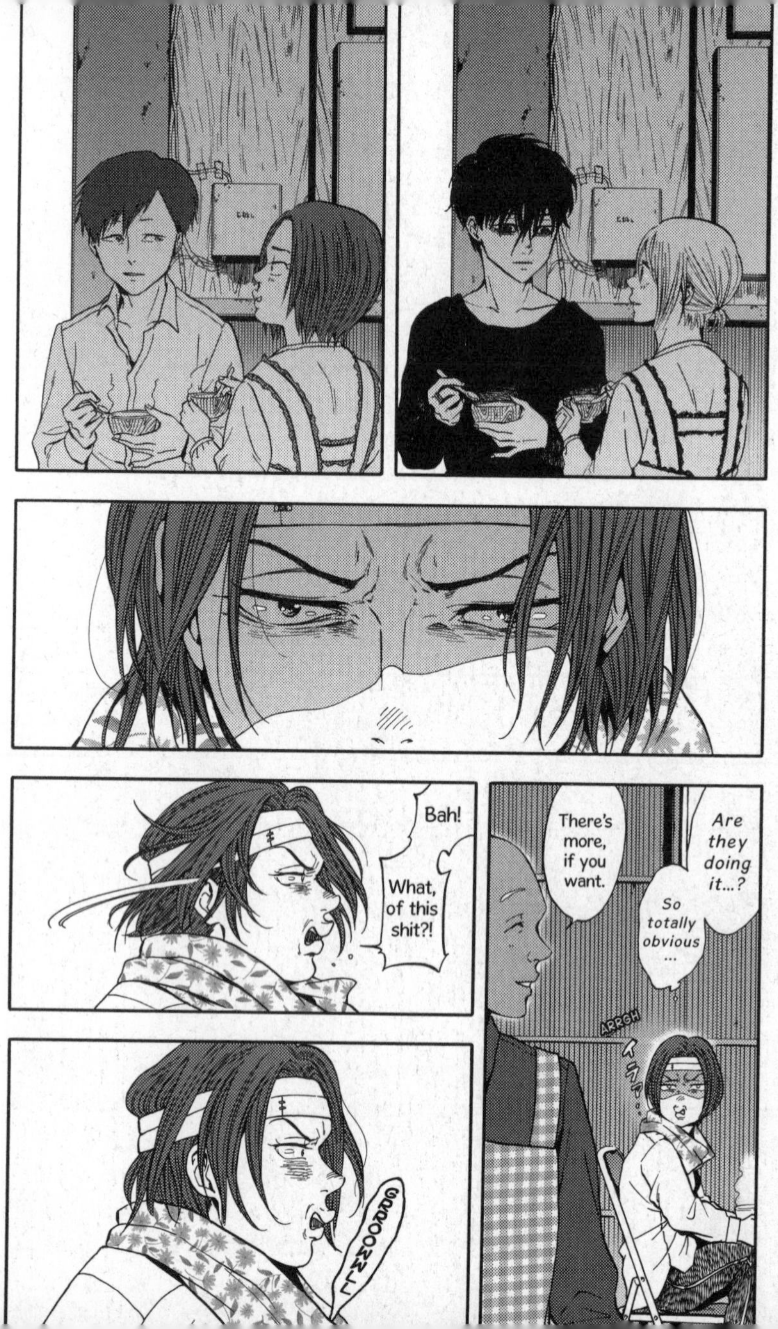
Are they doing it...?
There's more, if you want.
So totally obvious ...
ARRGH
Bah!
What, of this shit?!
GRROOWWLL

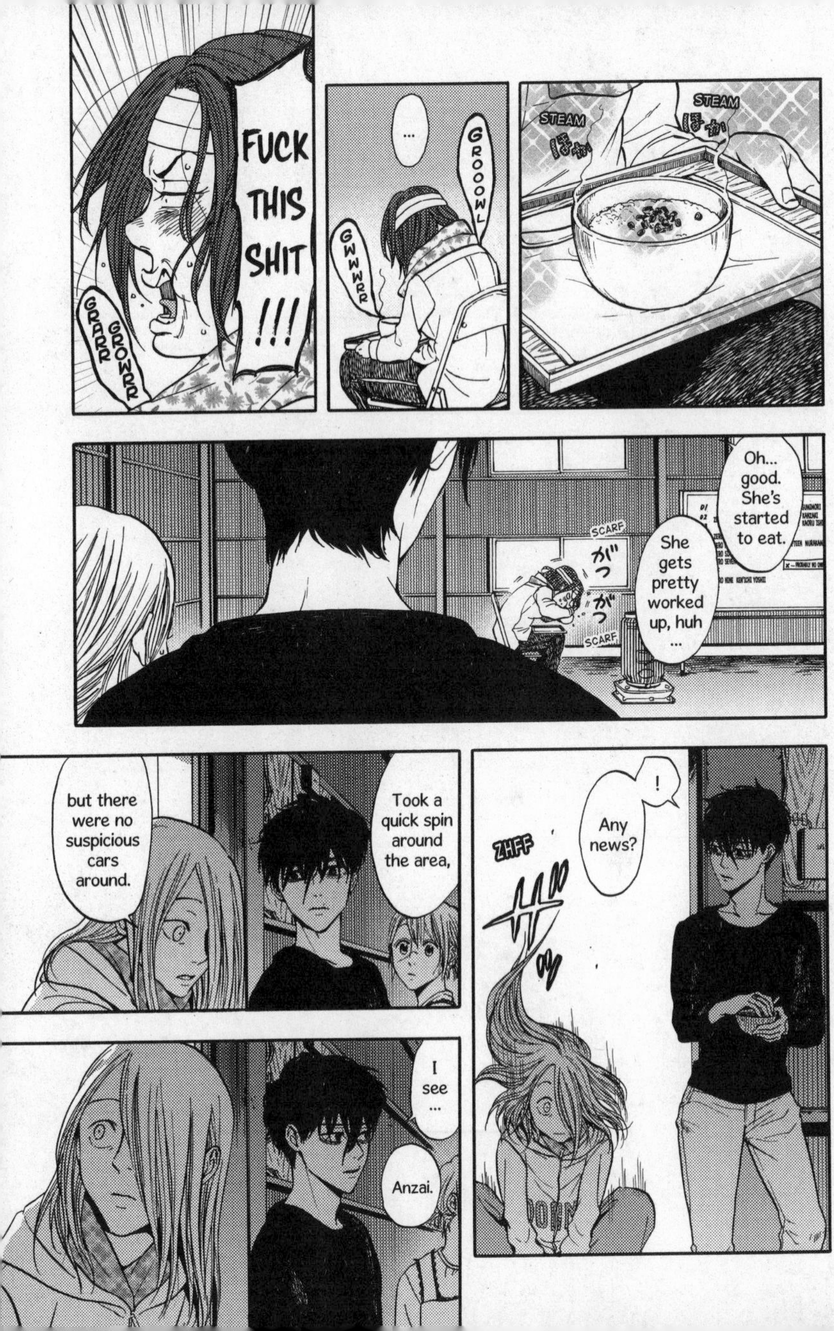
STEAM
STEAM
...
GROOOOWL
GWWWRR
FUCK THIS SHIT!!!
GRARR GROWRR
Oh... good. She's started to eat.
She gets pretty worked up, huh ...
SCARF
がつ
がつ
SCARF
!
Any news?
ZHFF
Took a quick spin around the area,
but there were no suspicious cars around.
I see ...
Anzai.

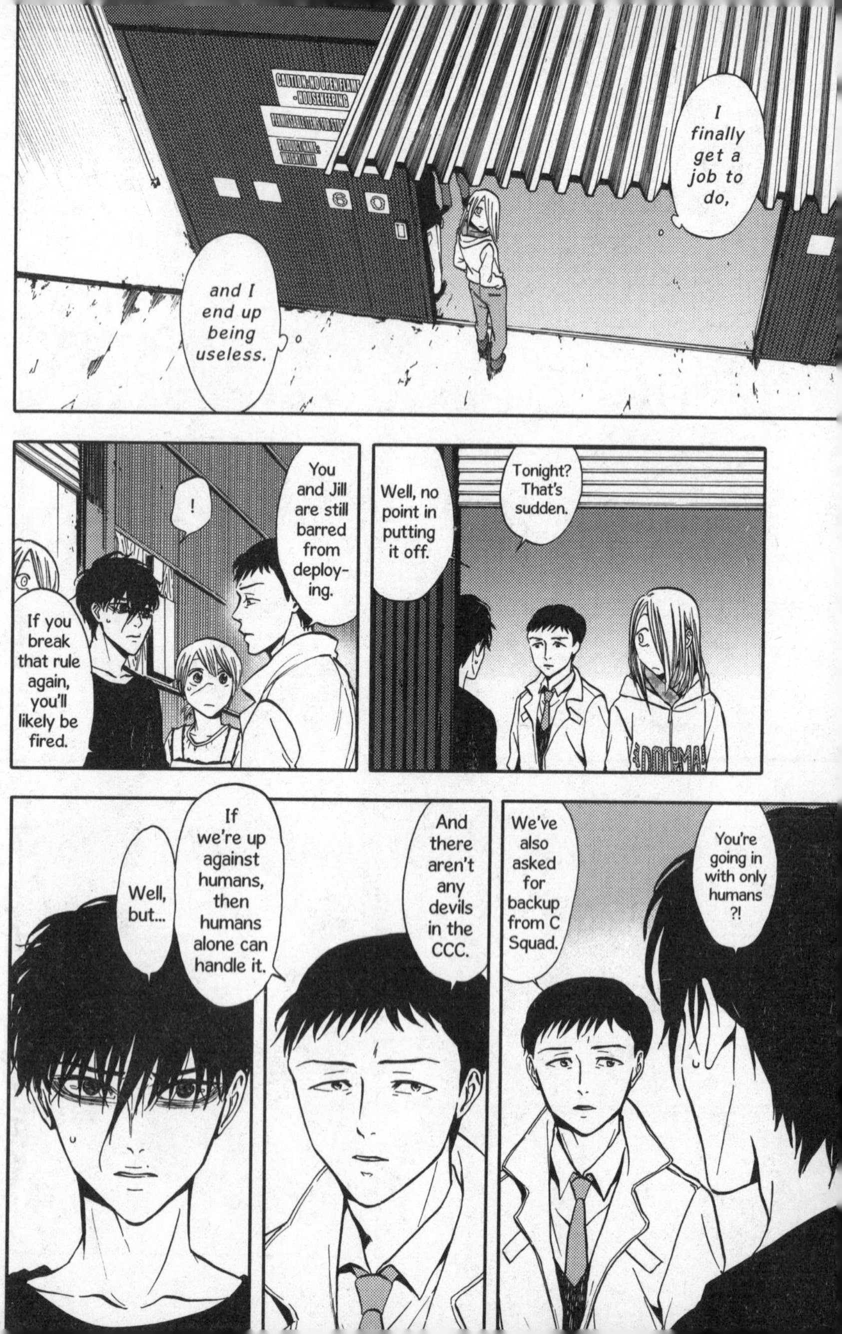
CAUTION: NO OPEN FLAME
- HOUSEKEEPING
I finally get a job to do,
and I end up being useless.
Tonight? That's sudden.
Well, no point in putting it off.
You and Jill are still barred from deploying.
!
If you break that rule again, you'll likely be fired.
You're going in with only humans?!
We've also asked for backup from C Squad.
And there aren't any devils in the CCC.
If we're up against humans, then humans alone can handle it.
Well, but...

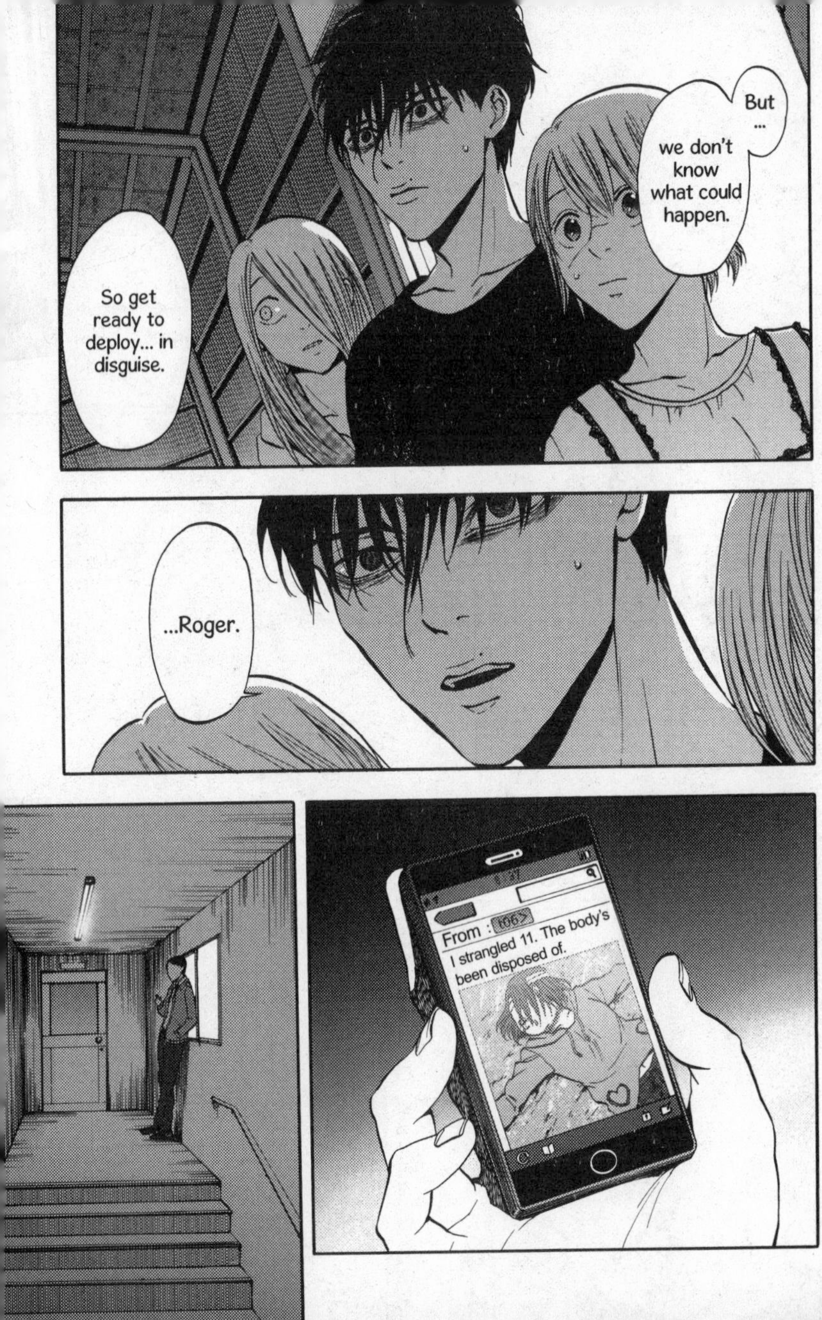
But ... we don't know what could happen.
So get ready to deploy... in disguise.
...Roger.
From : t06
I strangled 11. The body's been disposed of.

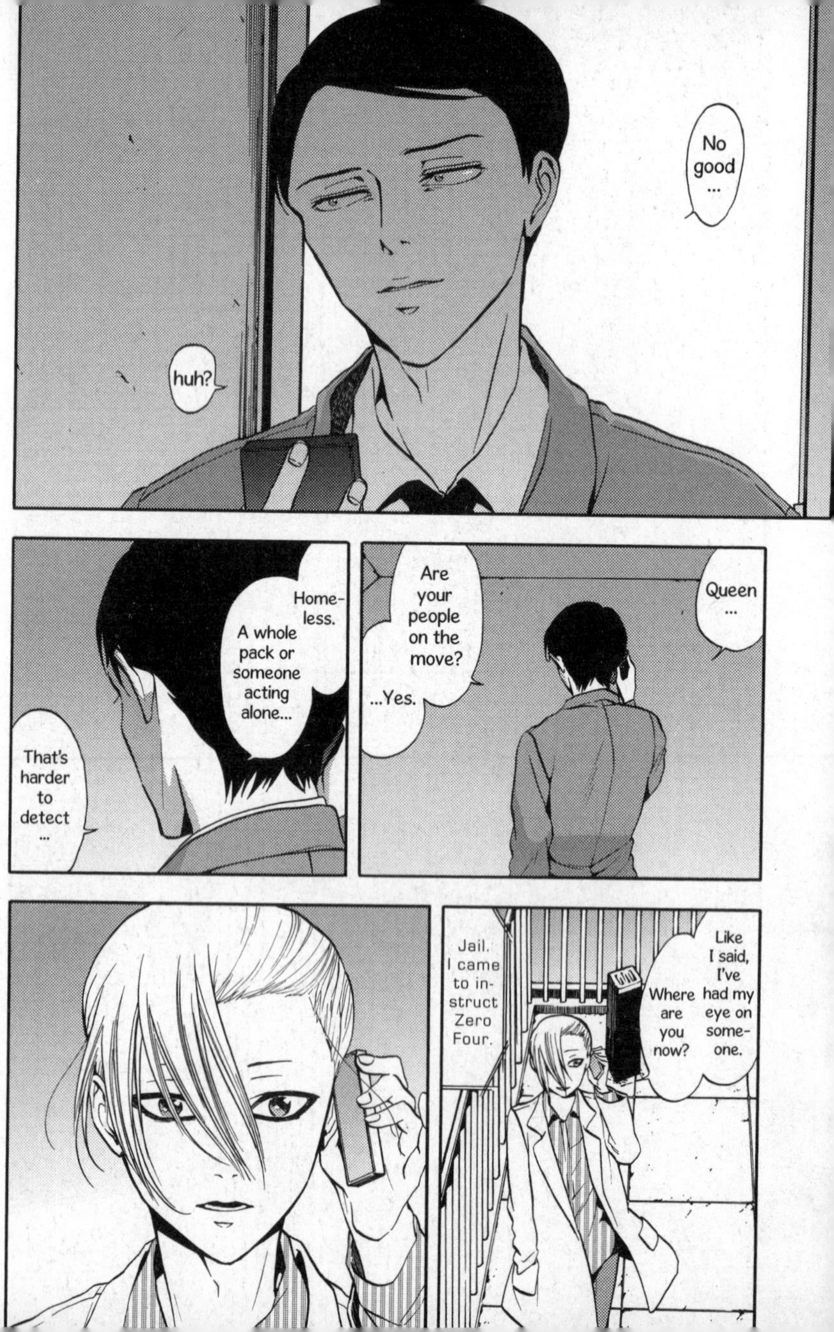
No good ...
huh?
Queen ...
Are your people on the move?
...Yes.
Home-less. A whole pack or someone acting alone...
That's harder to detect ...
Like I said, I've had my eye on some-one.
Where are you now?
Jail. I came to in-struct Zero Four.

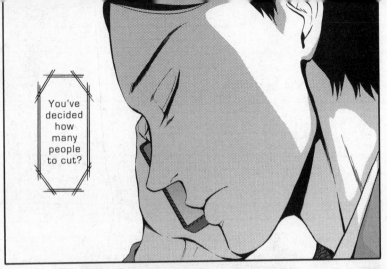

You've decided how many people to cut?

SEWING MACHINE CAFE
Sewing Lounge and Cafe
Weekdays 10 : 00 ~ 00
Weekends and holidays ~ 22 : 00

TAK
TAK
TAK
TAK
TAK
TAK
TAK
TAK

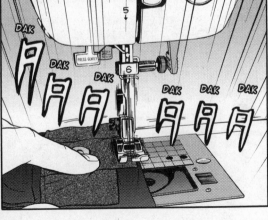

DAK
DAK
DAK
DAK
DAK
DAK

PRESS GENTLY

5
6

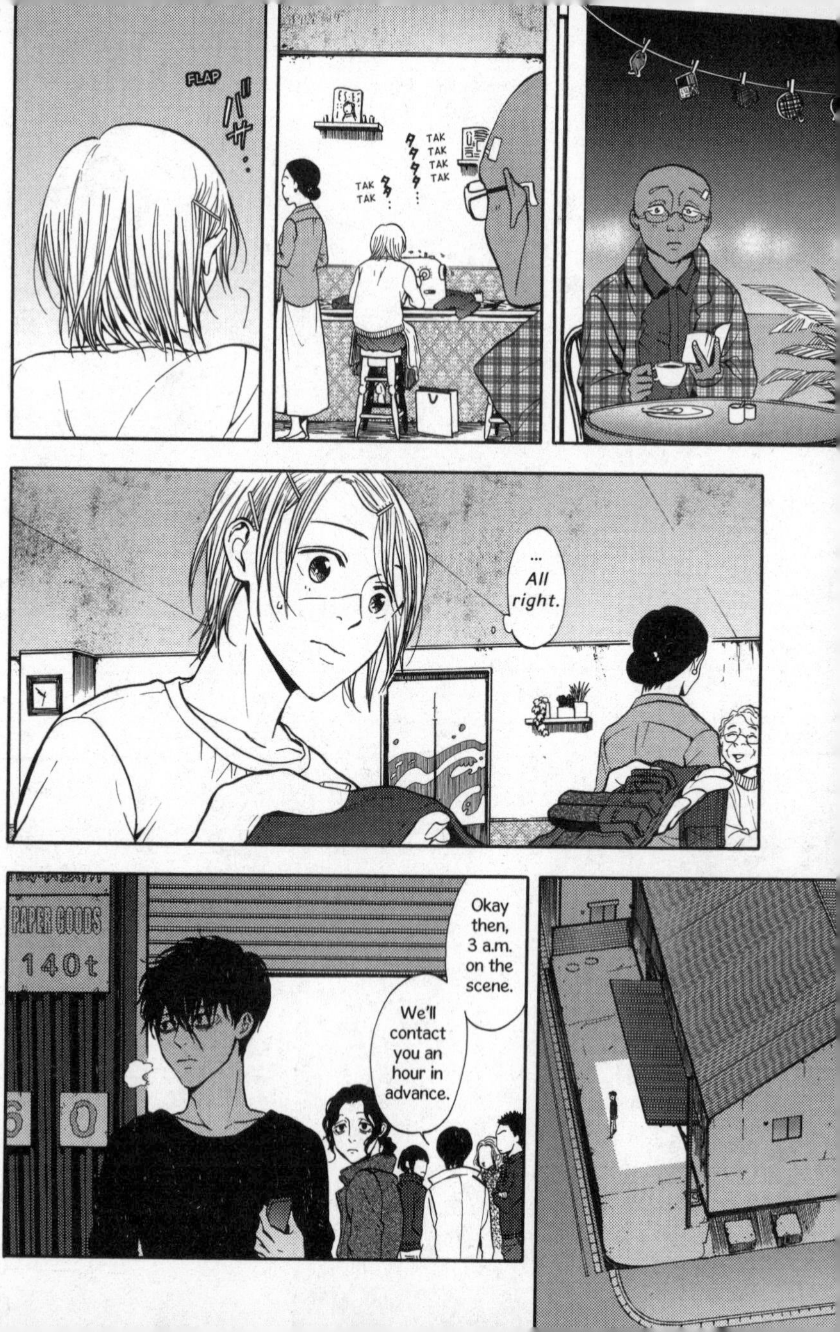

TAK TAK TAK TAK
TAK TAK
FLAP
バサ…
... All right.
Okay then, 3 a.m. on the scene.
We'll contact you an hour in advance.
PAPER GOODS
140t

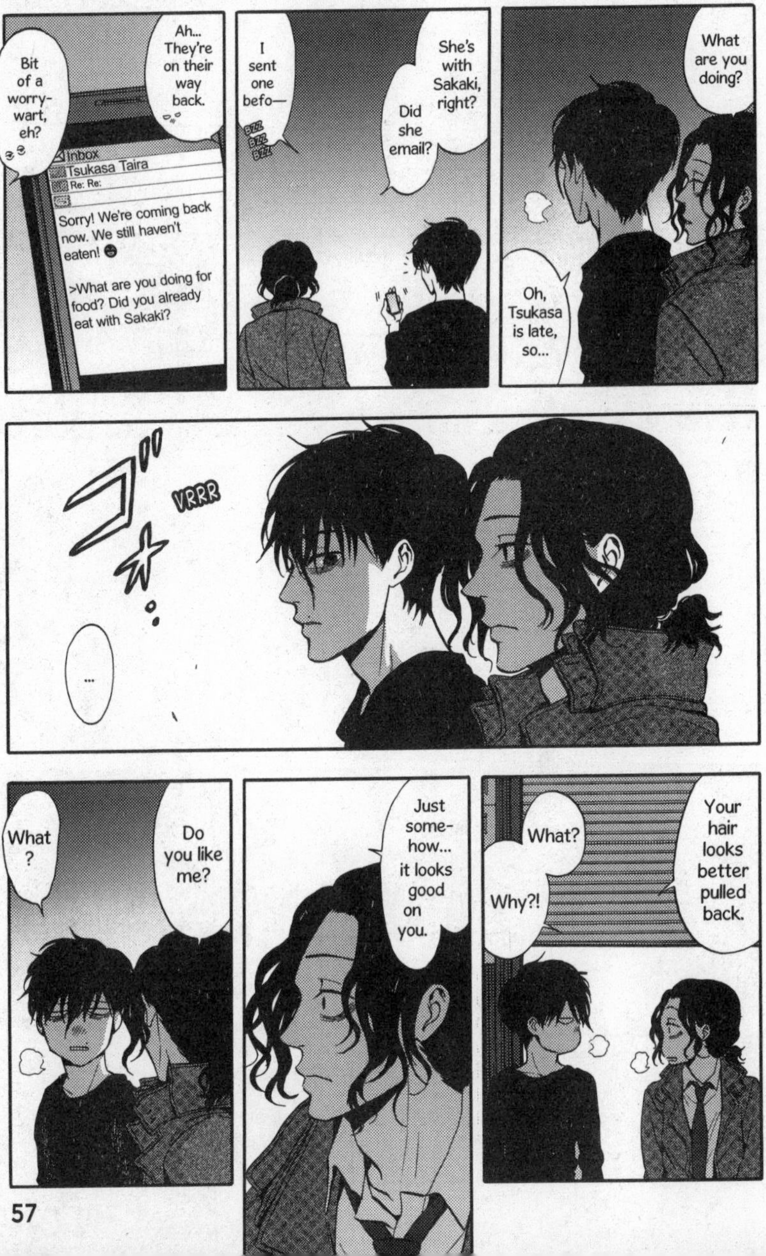
What are you doing?
Oh, Tsukasa is late, so...
She's with Sakaki, right?
Did she email?
I sent one befo—
BZZ BZZ BZZ
Ah... They're on their way back.
Bit of a worry-wart, eh?
Inbox
Tsukasa Taira
Re: Re:
Sorry! We're coming back now. We still haven't eaten!
>What are you doing for food? Did you already eat with Sakaki?
VRRR
...
Your hair looks better pulled back.
What?
Why?!
Just some-how... it looks good on you.
Do you like me?
What?

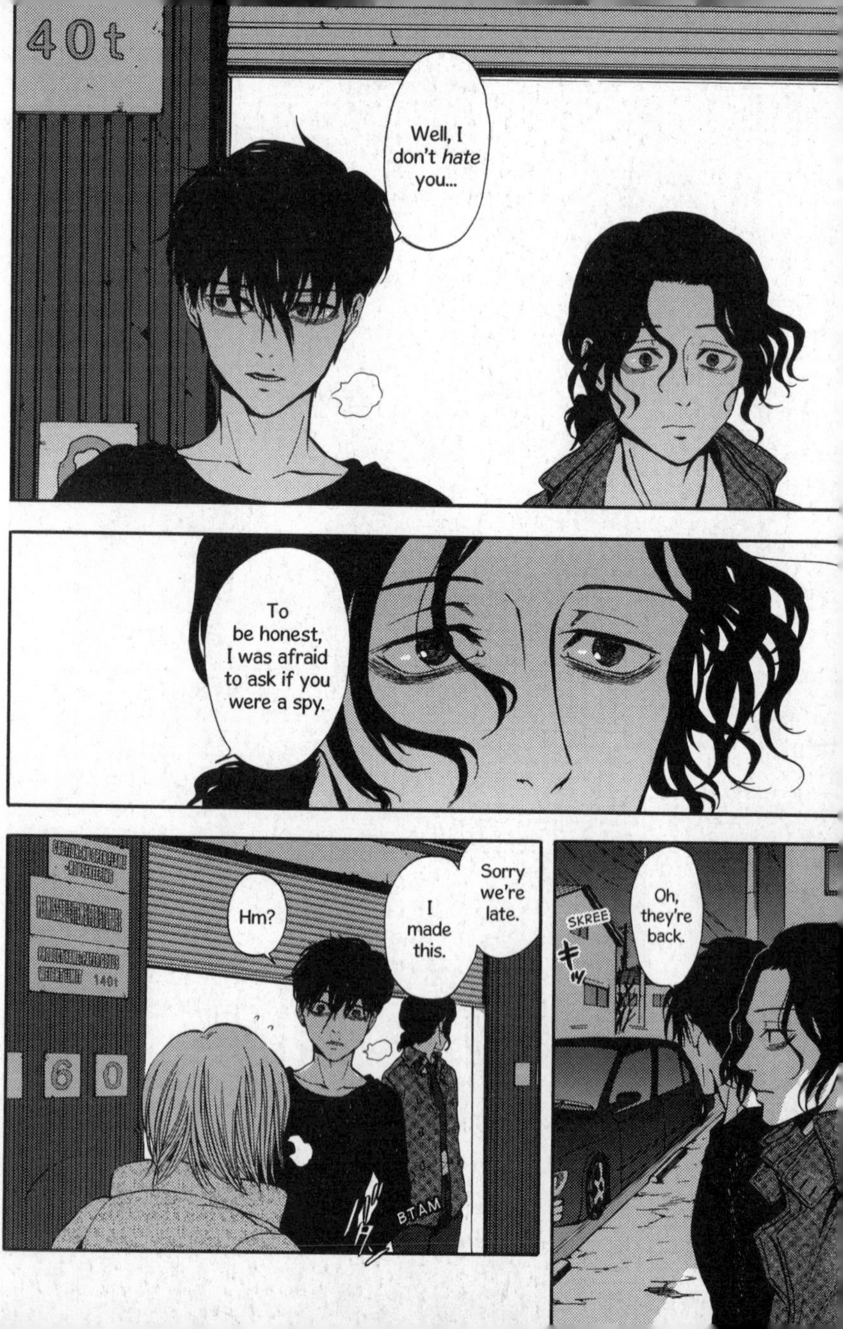
40t
Well, I don't *hate* you...
To be honest, I was afraid to ask if you were a spy.
SKREE
Oh, they're back.
Sorry we're late.
I made this.
Hm?
BTAM

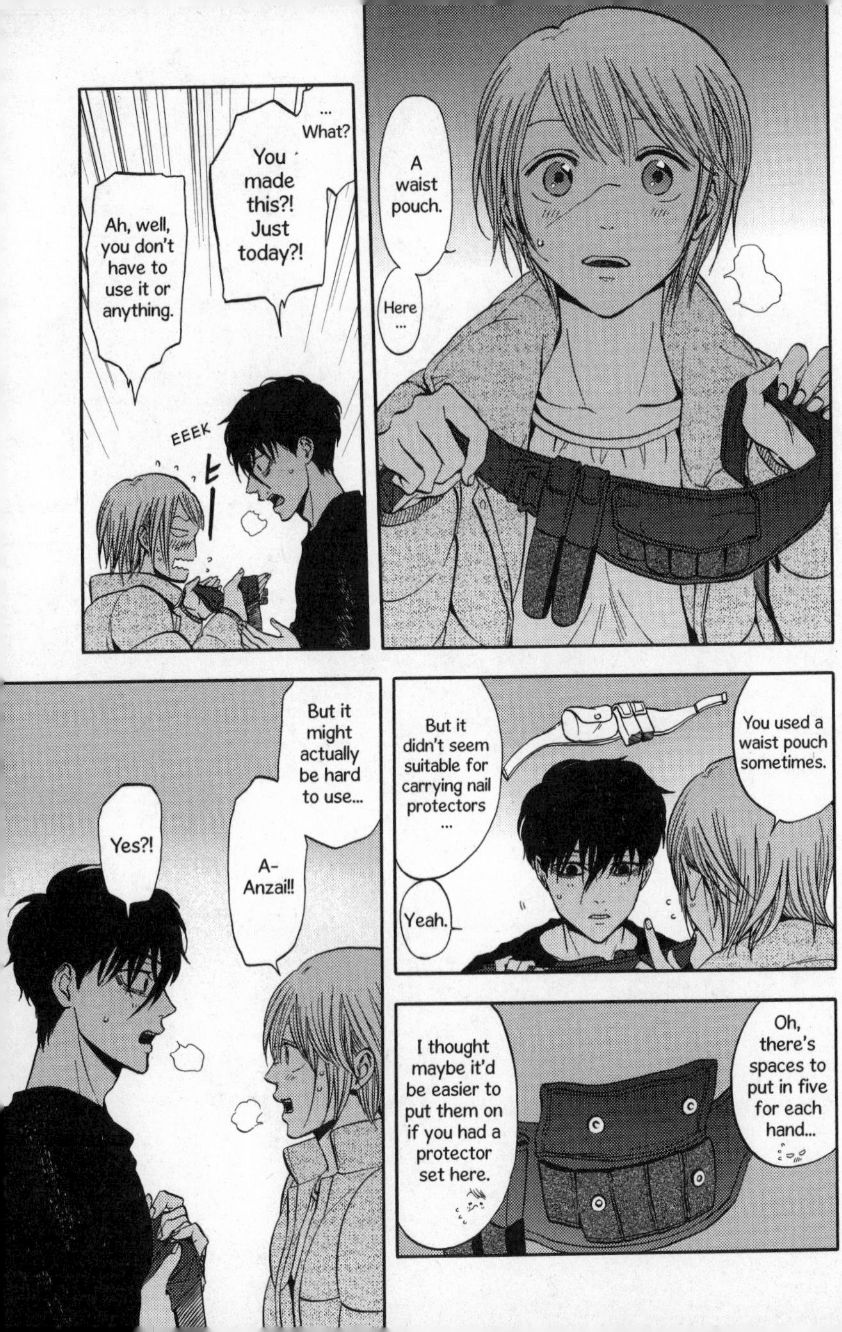
A waist pouch.
Here ...
... What?
You made this?! Just today?!
Ah, well, you don't have to use it or anything.
EEEK
You used a waist pouch sometimes.
But it didn't seem suitable for carrying nail protectors ...
Yeah.
Oh, there's spaces to put in five for each hand...
I thought maybe it'd be easier to put them on if you had a protector set here.
But it might actually be hard to use...
A- Anzai!!
Yes?!

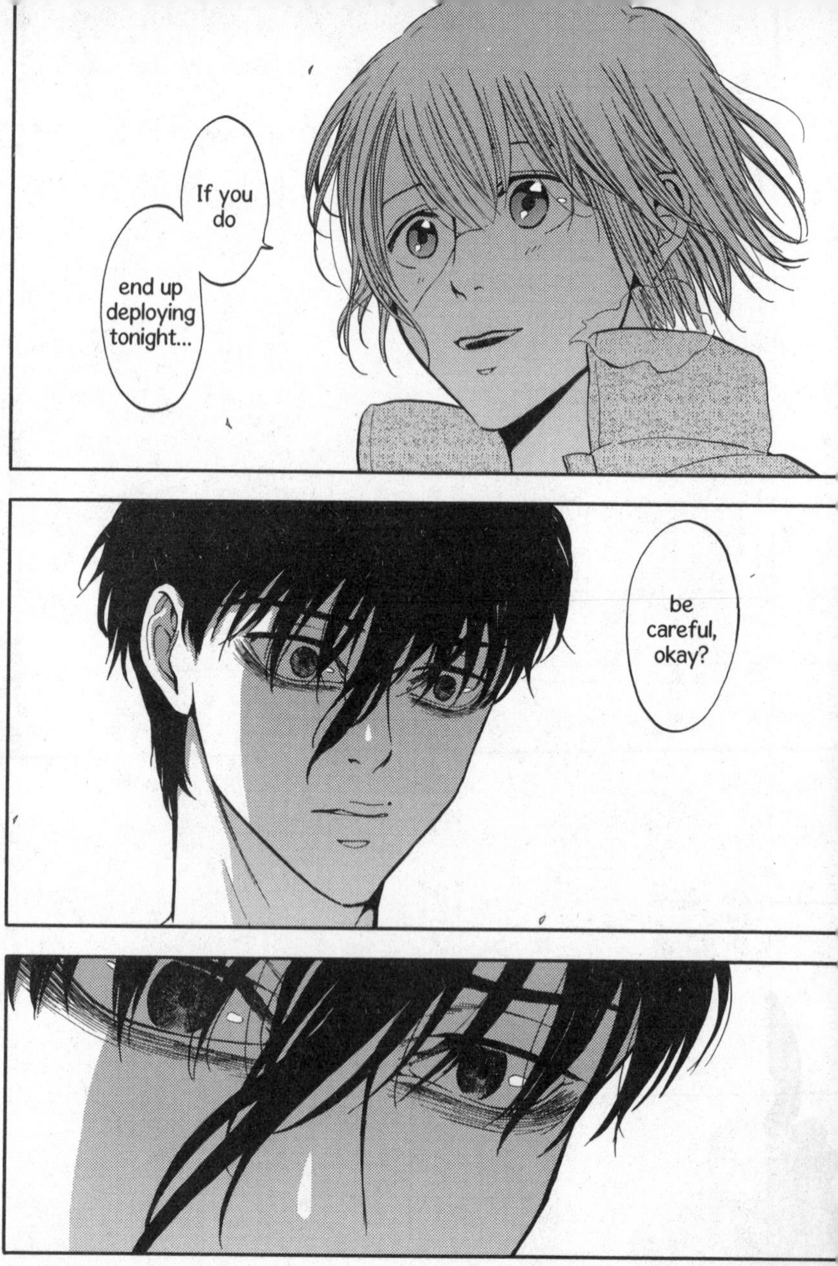
If you do
end up deploying tonight...
be careful, okay?

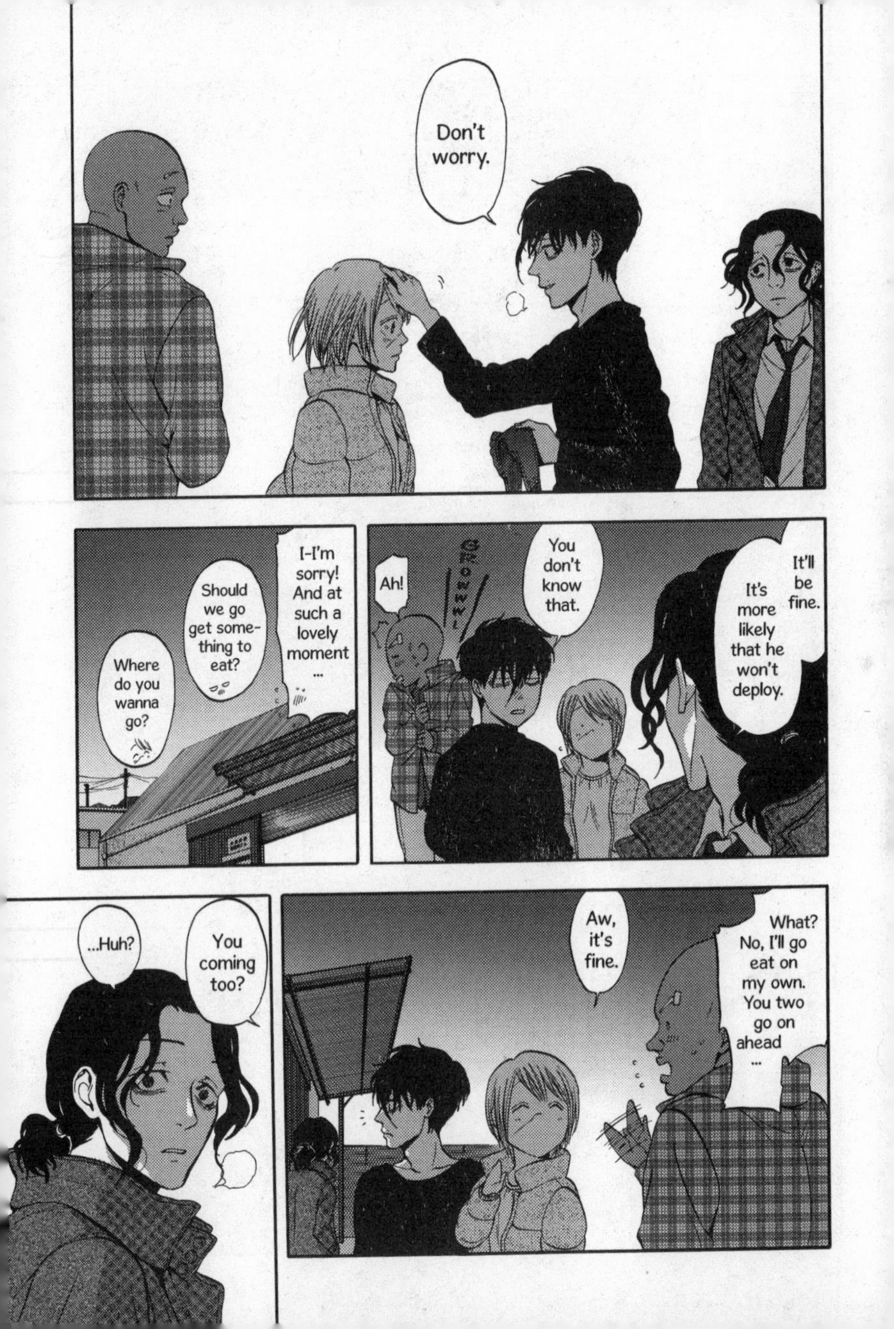
Don't worry.
It'll be fine.
It's more likely that he won't deploy.
You don't know that.
GROWWWL
Ah!
I-I'm sorry! And at such a lovely moment ...
Should we go get some-thing to eat?
Where do you wanna go?
What? No, I'll go eat on my own. You two go on ahead ...
Aw, it's fine.
You coming too?
...Huh?

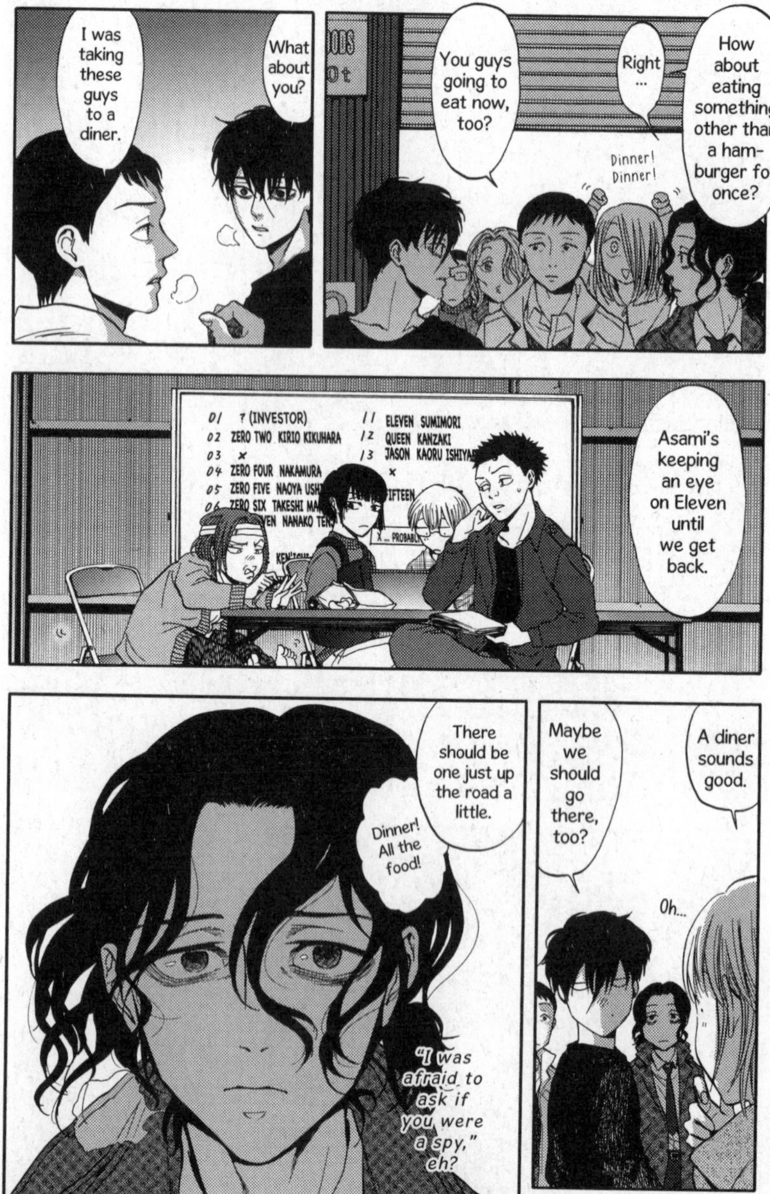
How about eating something other than a ham-burger for once?
Right ...
Dinner! Dinner!
You guys going to eat now, too?
What about you?
I was taking these guys to a diner.
Asami's keeping an eye on Eleven until we get back.
01 ? (INVESTOR)
02 ZERO TWO KIRIO KIKUHARA
03 ×
04 ZERO FOUR NAKAMURA
11 ELEVEN SUMIMORI
12 QUEEN KANZAKI
A diner sounds good.
Maybe we should go there, too?
Oh...
There should be one just up the road a little.
Dinner! All the food!
"I was afraid to ask if you were a spy," eh?

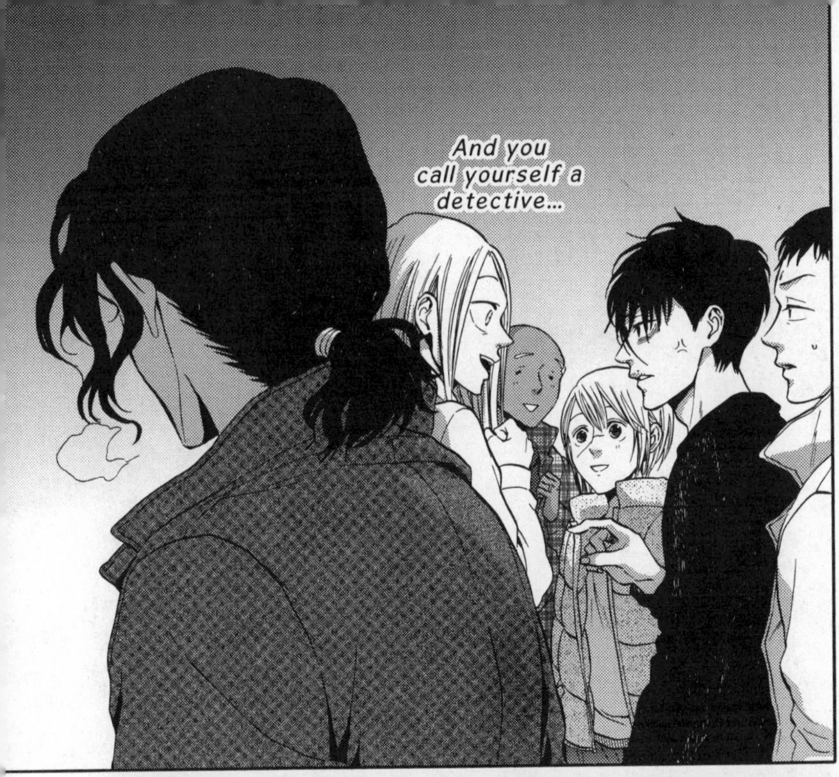
And you call yourself a detective...
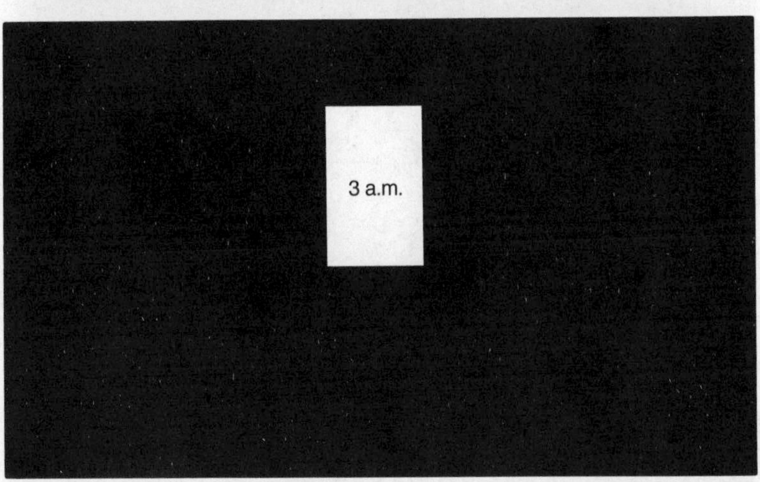
3 a.m.

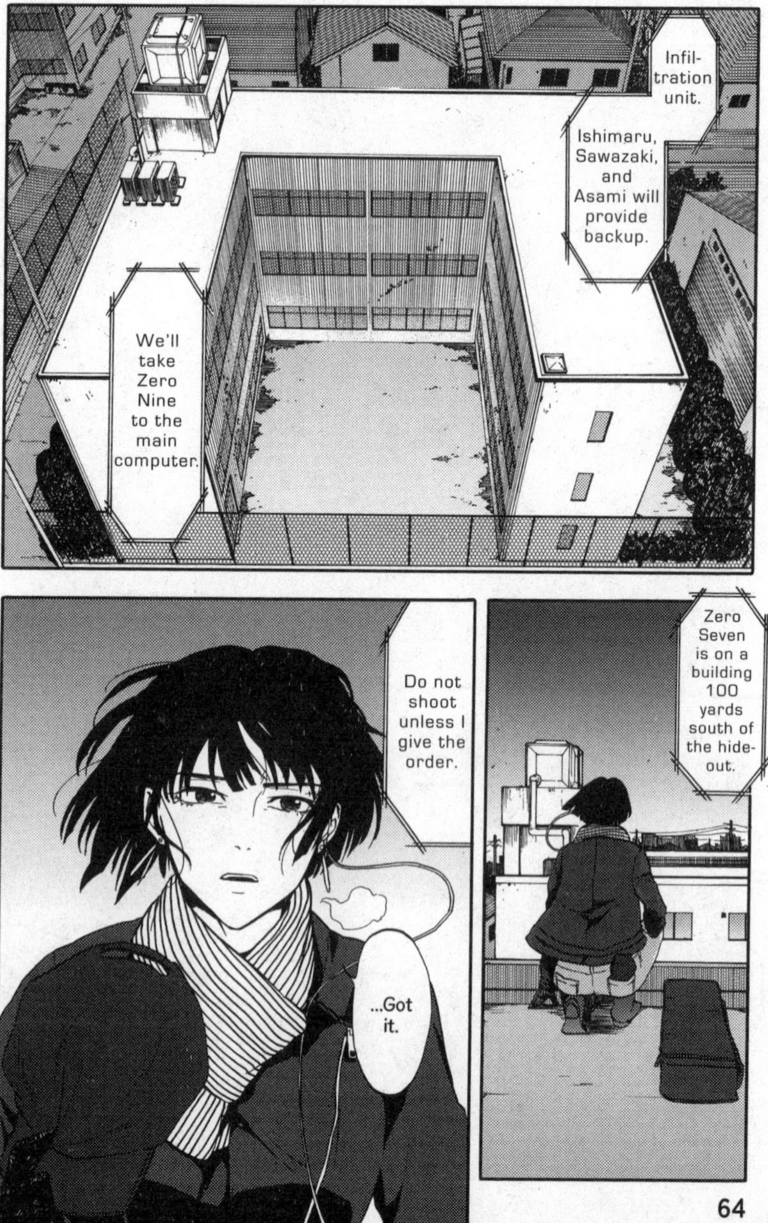
Infiltration unit.
Ishimaru, Sawazaki, and Asami will provide backup.
We'll take Zero Nine to the main computer.
Zero Seven is on a building 100 yards south of the hide-out.
Do not shoot unless I give the order.
...Got it.

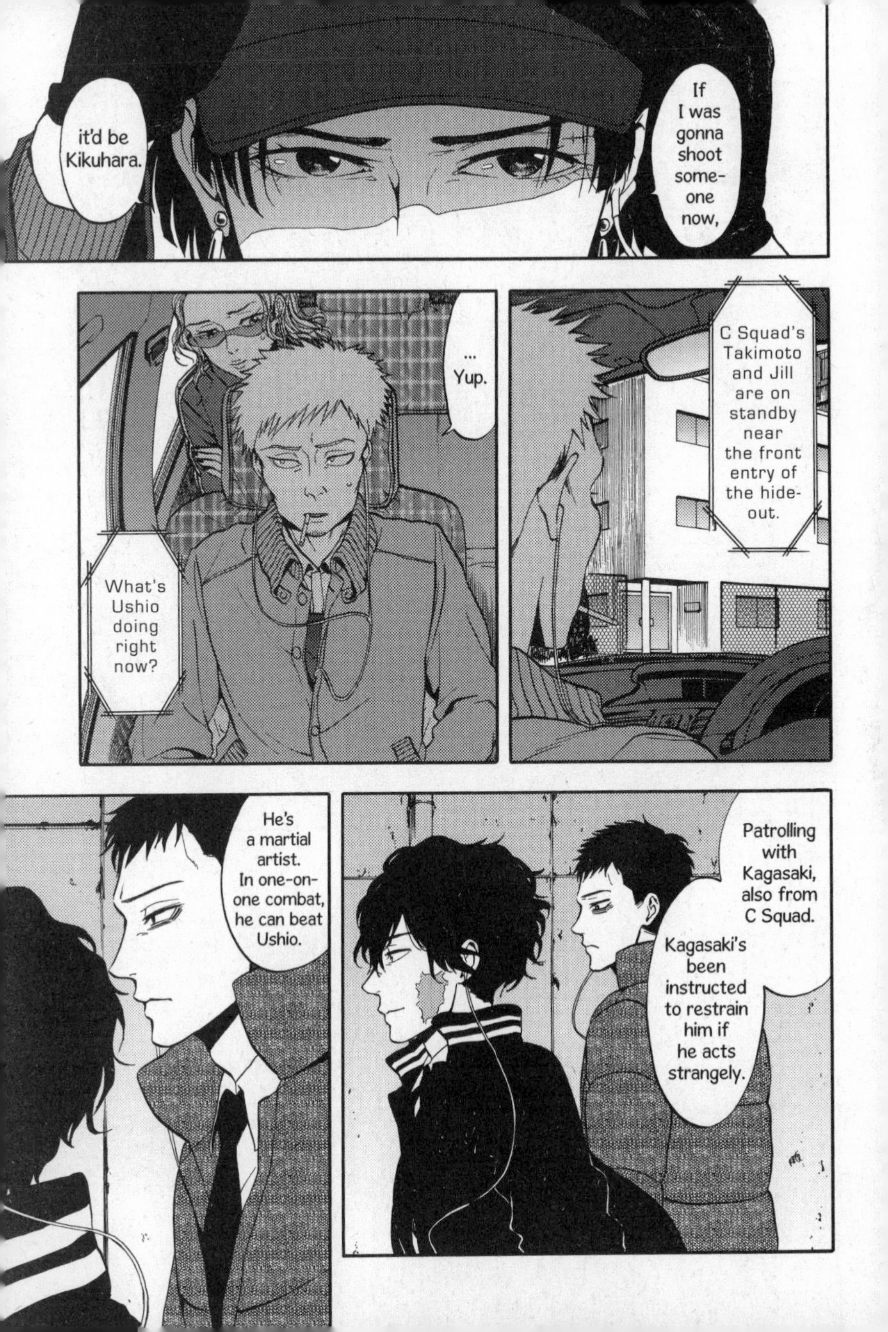

If I was gonna shoot some-one now,
it'd be Kikuhara.
C Squad's Takimoto and Jill are on standby near the front entry of the hide-out.
... Yup.
What's Ushio doing right now?
Patrolling with Kagasaki, also from C Squad.
Kagasaki's been instructed to restrain him if he acts strangely.
He's a martial artist. In one-on-one combat, he can beat Ushio.

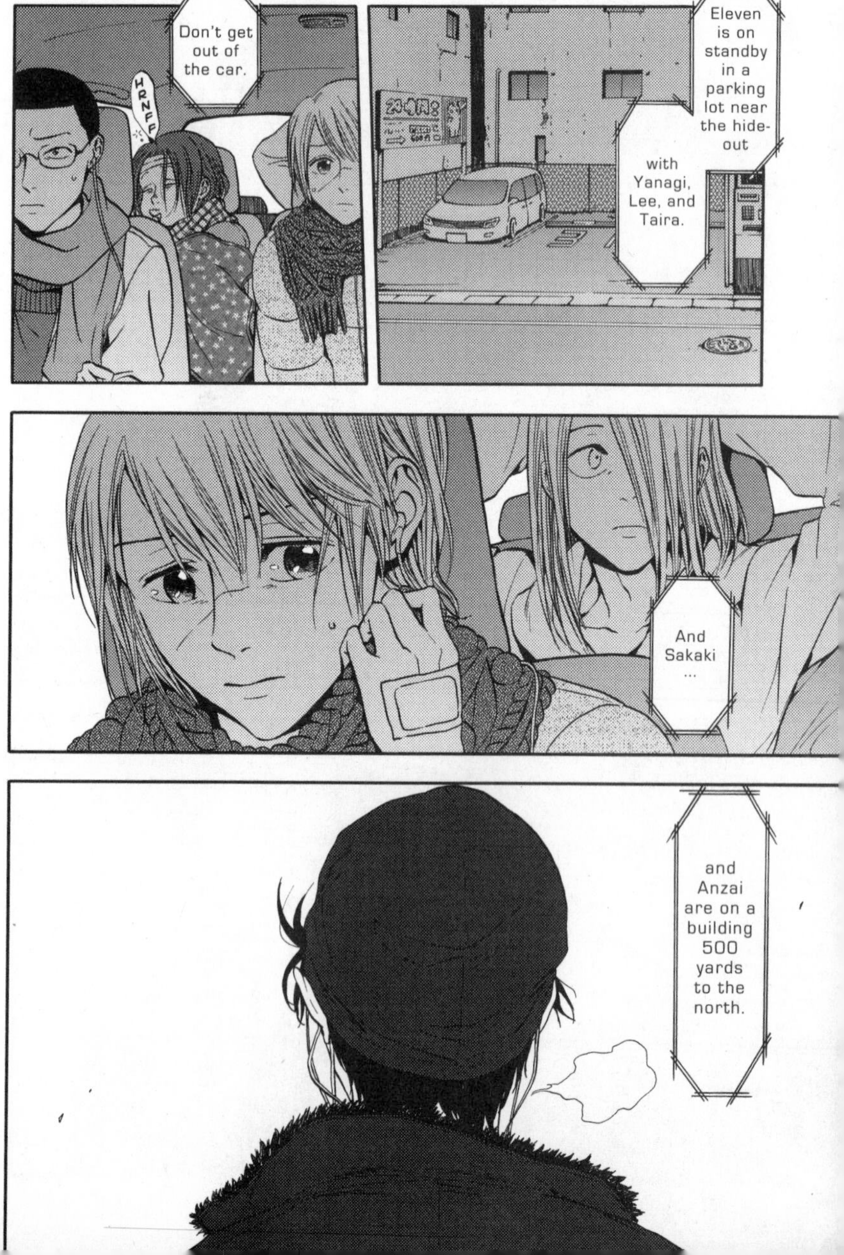
Eleven is on standby in a parking lot near the hide-out
with Yanagi, Lee, and Taira.
Don't get out of the car.
HRNFF
And Sakaki ...
and Anzai are on a building 500 yards to the north.

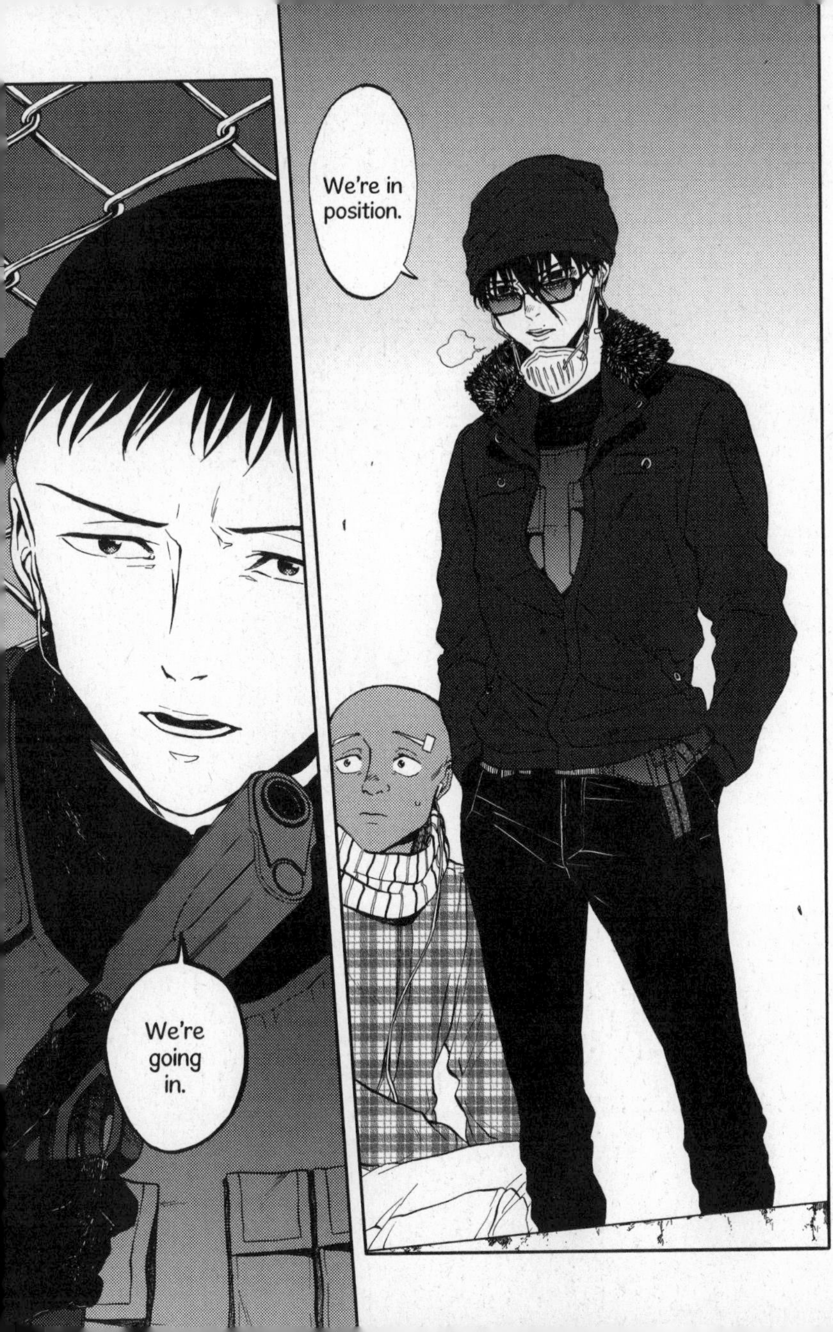
We're in position.
We're going in.

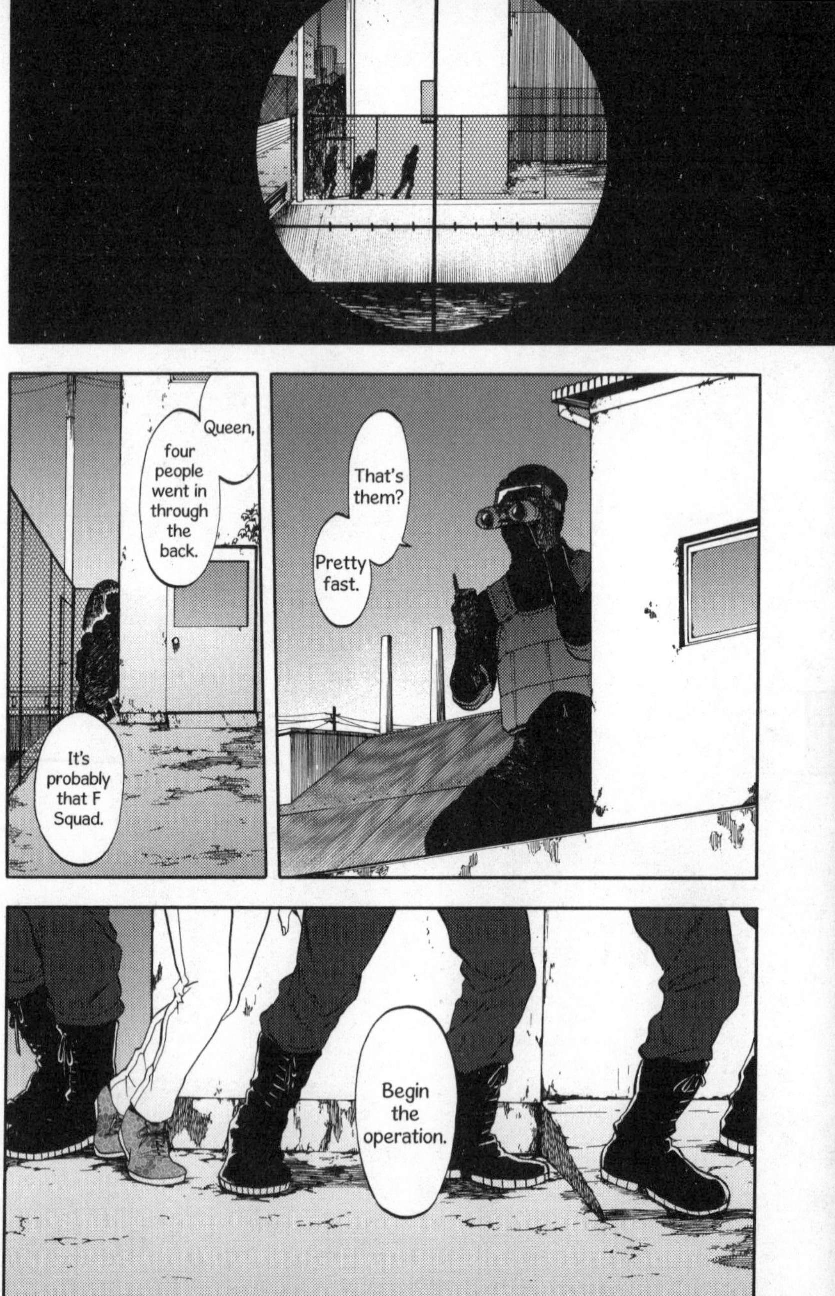
That's them?
Pretty fast.
Queen, four people went in through the back.
It's probably that F Squad.
Begin the operation.

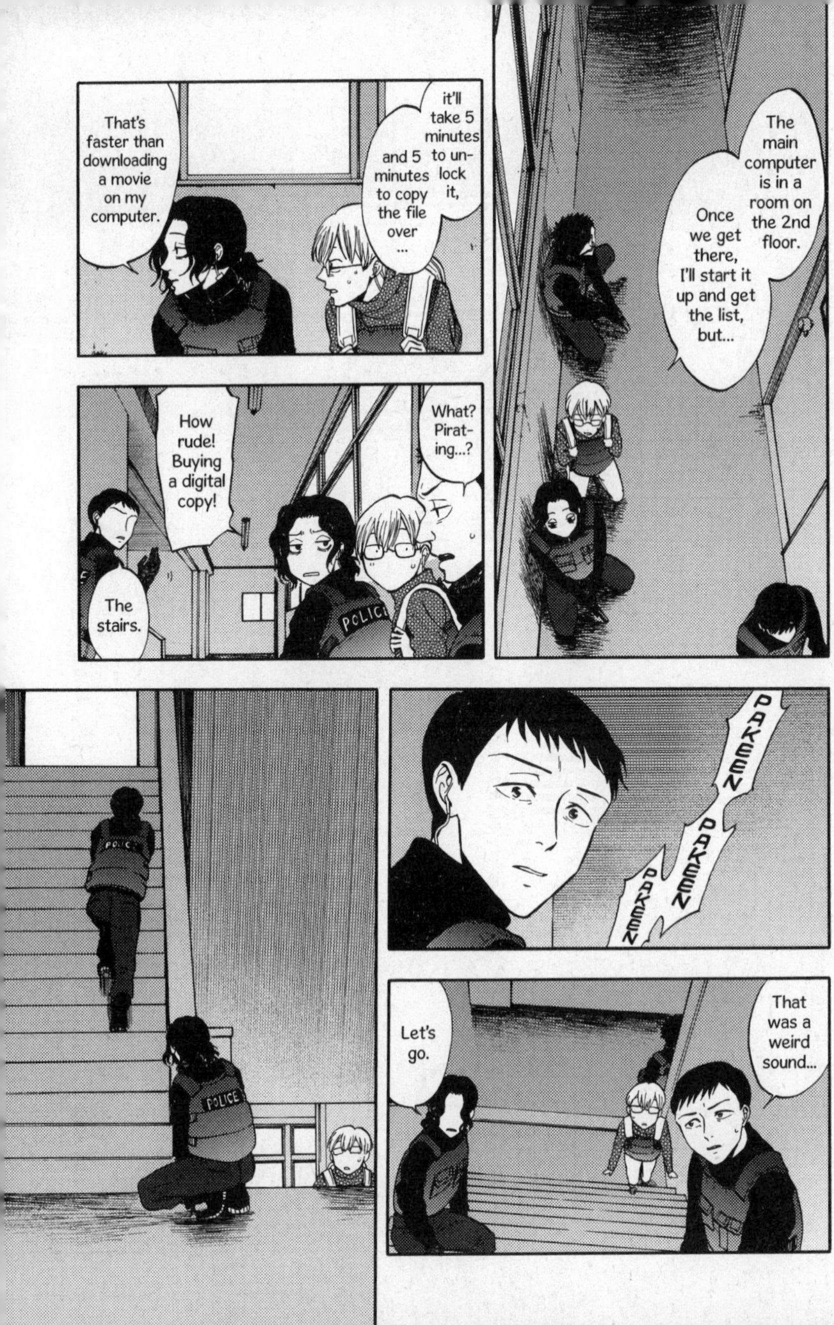
The main computer is in a room on the 2nd floor.
Once we get there, I'll start it up and get the list, but...
it'll take 5 minutes to un-lock it,
and 5 minutes to copy the file over ...
That's faster than downloading a movie on my computer.
What? Pirat-ing...?
How rude! Buying a digital copy!
The stairs.
PAKEEN
PAKEEN
PAKEEN
That was a weird sound...
Let's go.

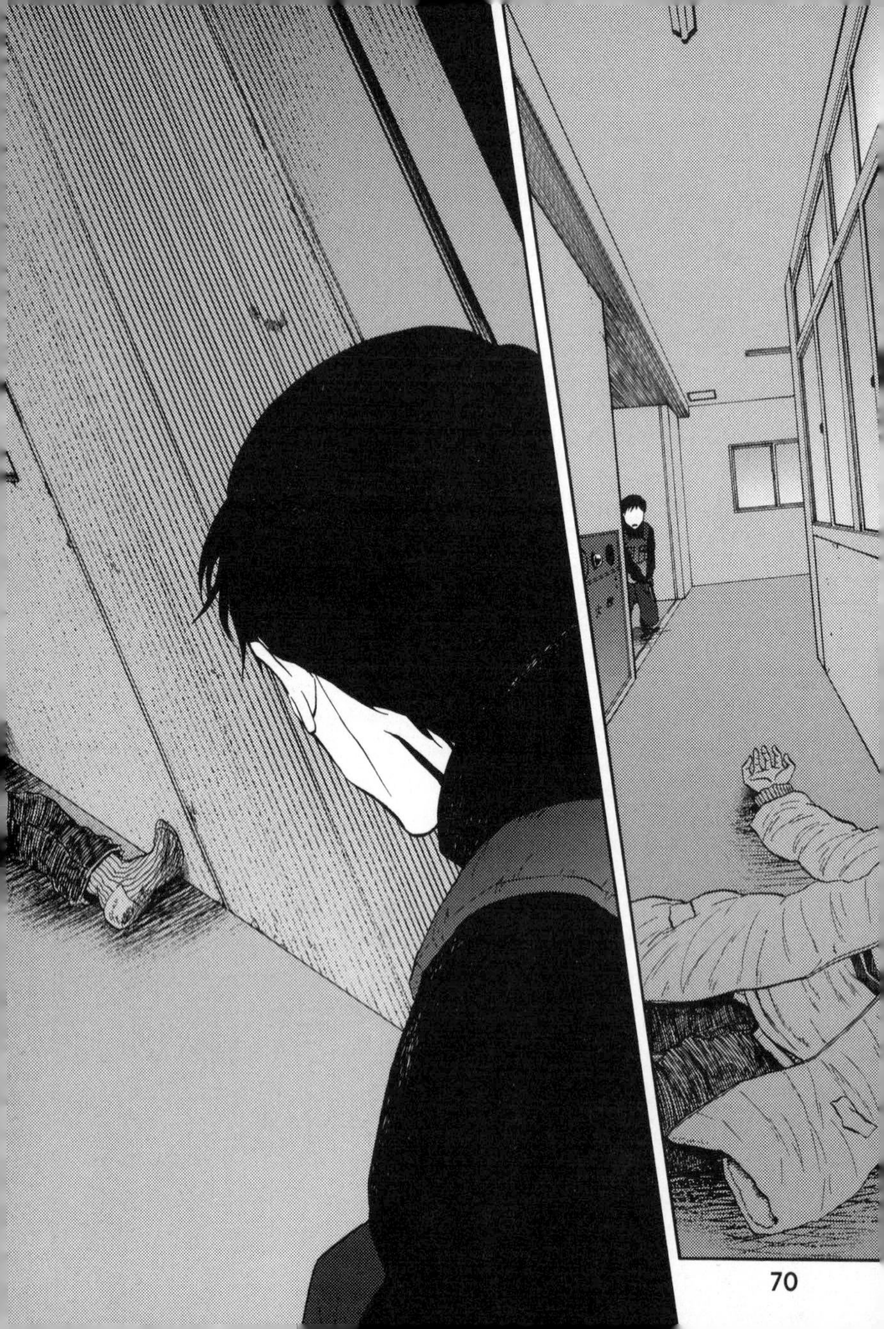

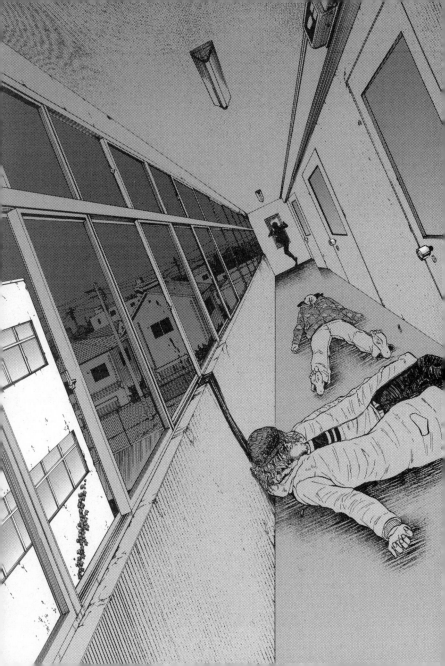

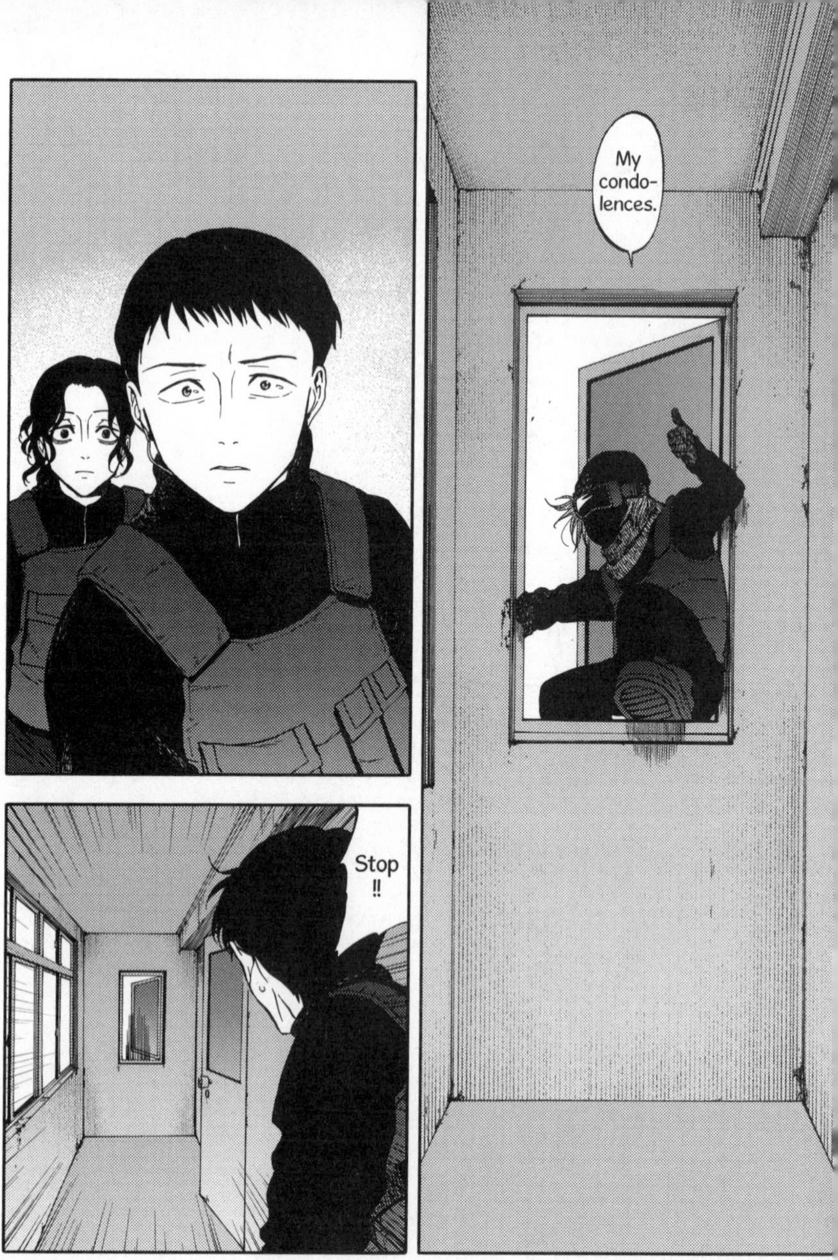
My condolences.
Stop !!

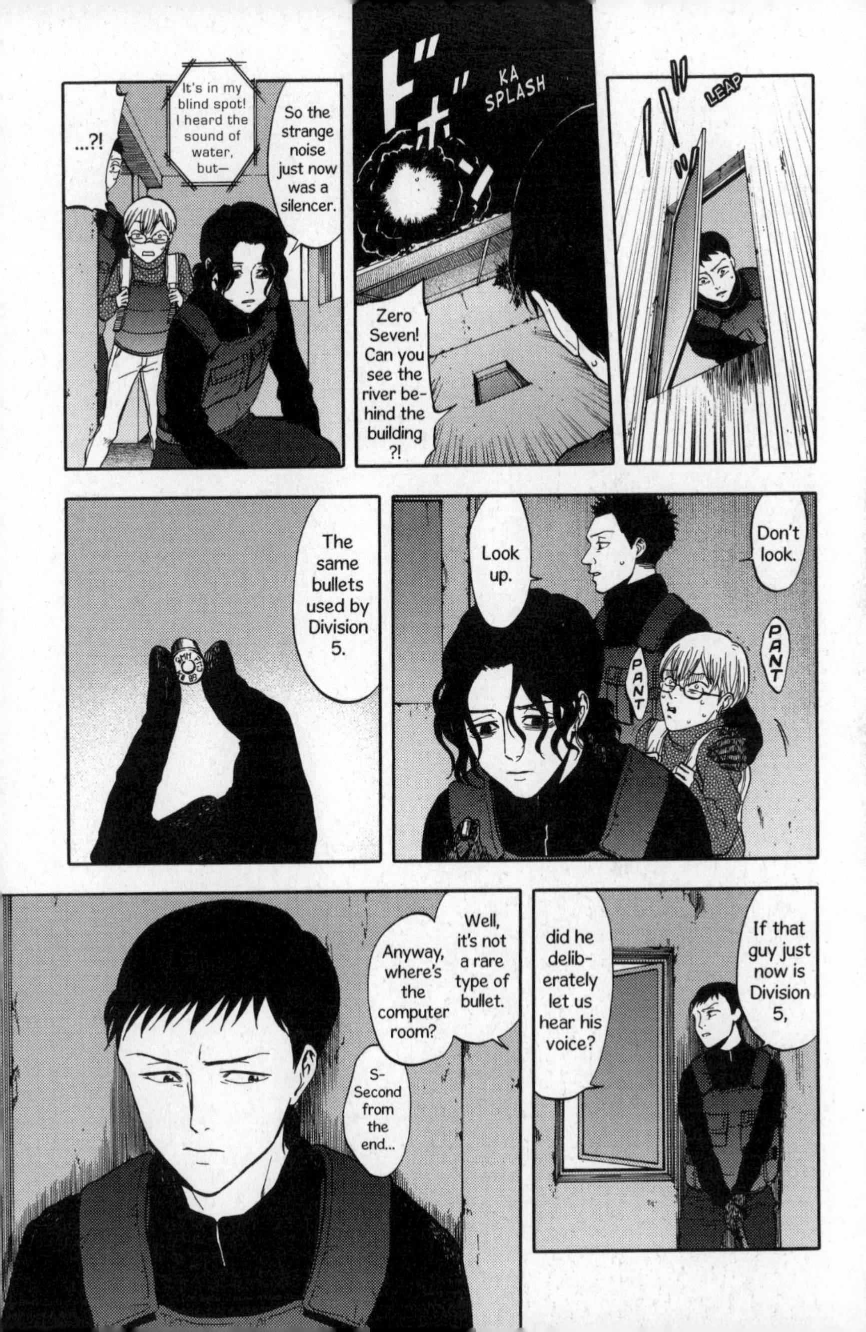
LEAP
KA SPLASH
Zero Seven! Can you see the river be-hind the building?!
So the strange noise just now was a silencer.
It's in my blind spot! I heard the sound of water, but—
...?!
Don't look.
Look up.
PANT
PANT
The same bullets used by Division 5.
If that guy just now is Division 5,
did he delib-erately let us hear his voice?
Well, it's not a rare type of bullet.
Anyway, where's the computer room?
S-Second from the end...

Who
is this
guy...?

Watch
your
step!

You're
gonna
...

SLIP

!!

PO

74

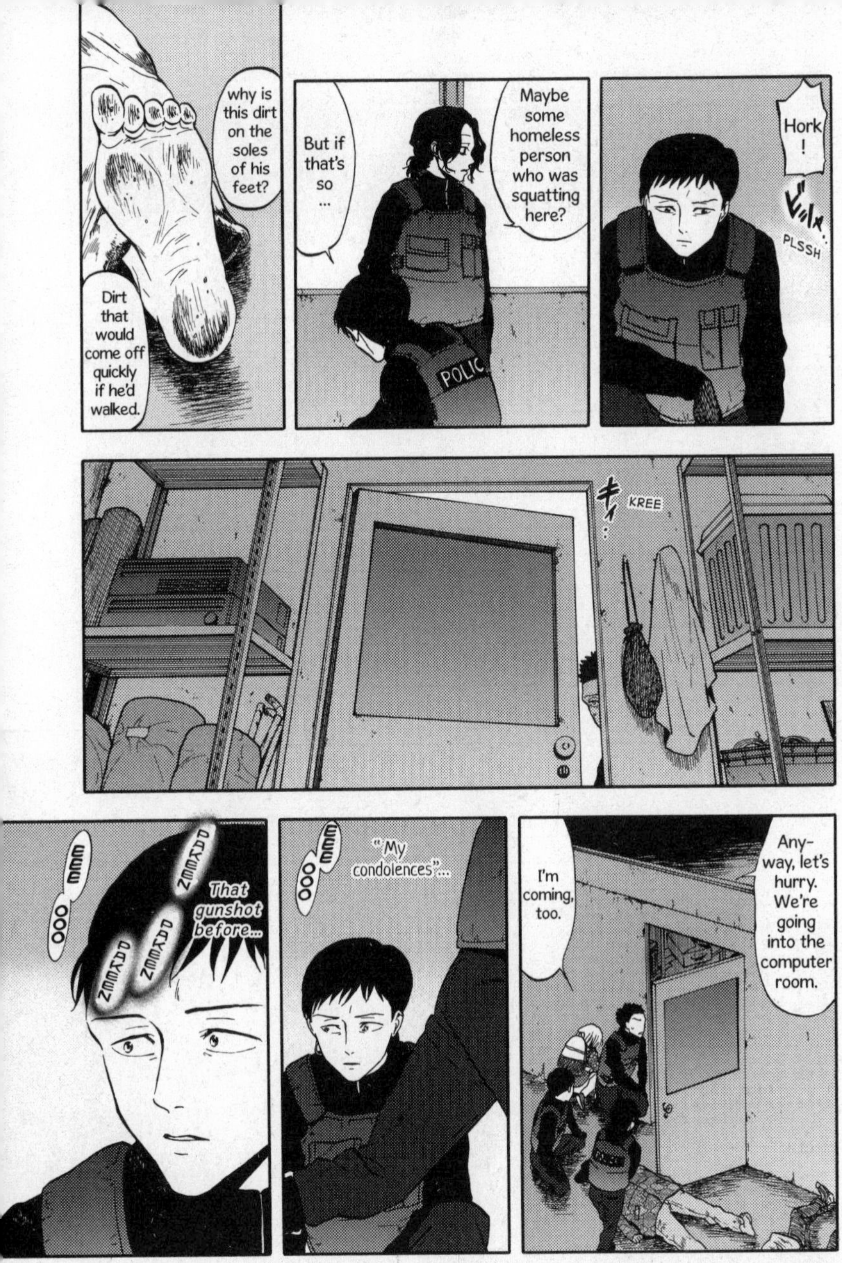
Hork!
PLSSH
Maybe some homeless person who was squatting here?
But if that's so ...
why is this dirt on the soles of his feet?
Dirt that would come off quickly if he'd walked.
POLIC
KREE
Any-way, let's hurry. We're going into the computer room.
I'm coming, too.
"My condolences"...
EEE OOO
That gunshot before...
DAKEEN DAKEEN DAKEEN
EEE OOO

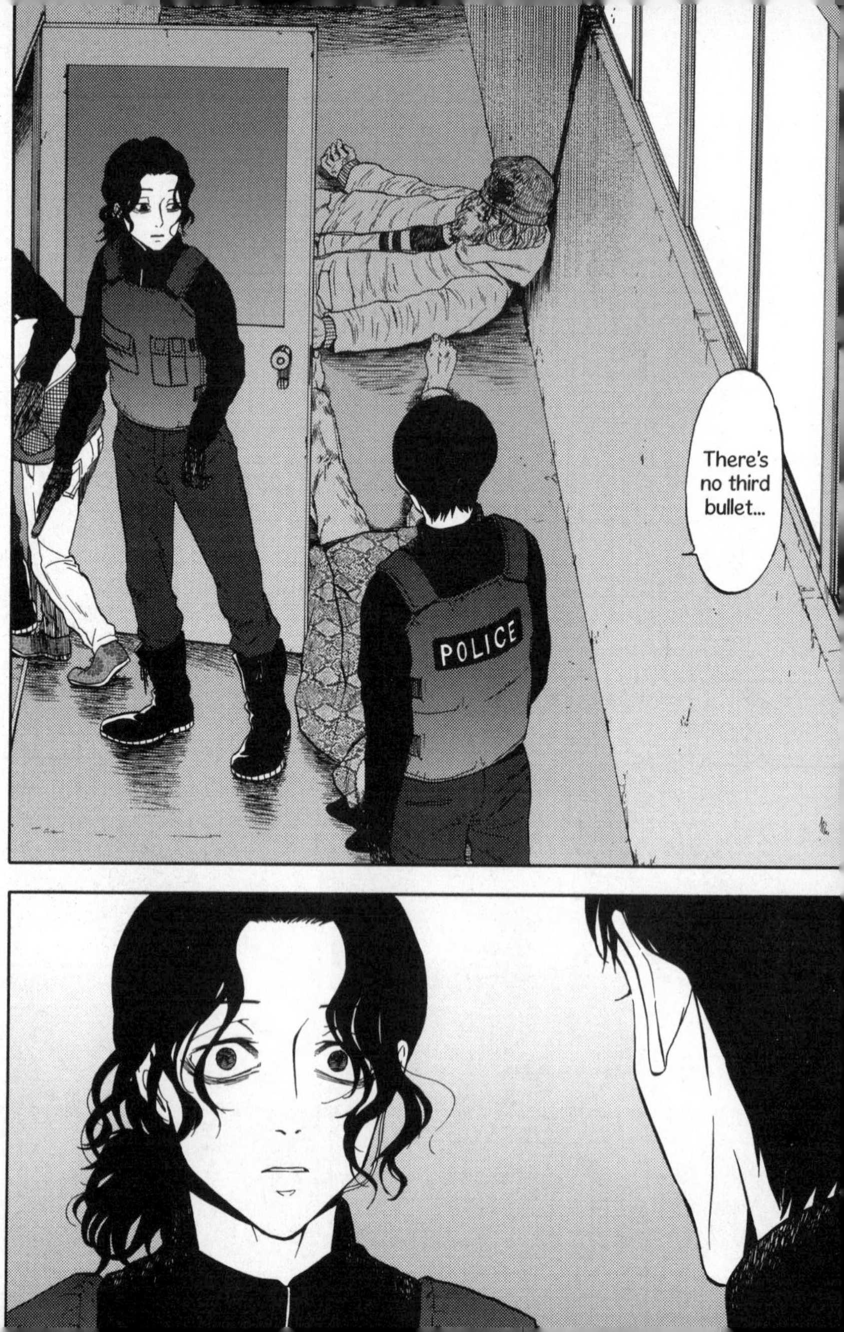
There's no third bullet...
POLICE

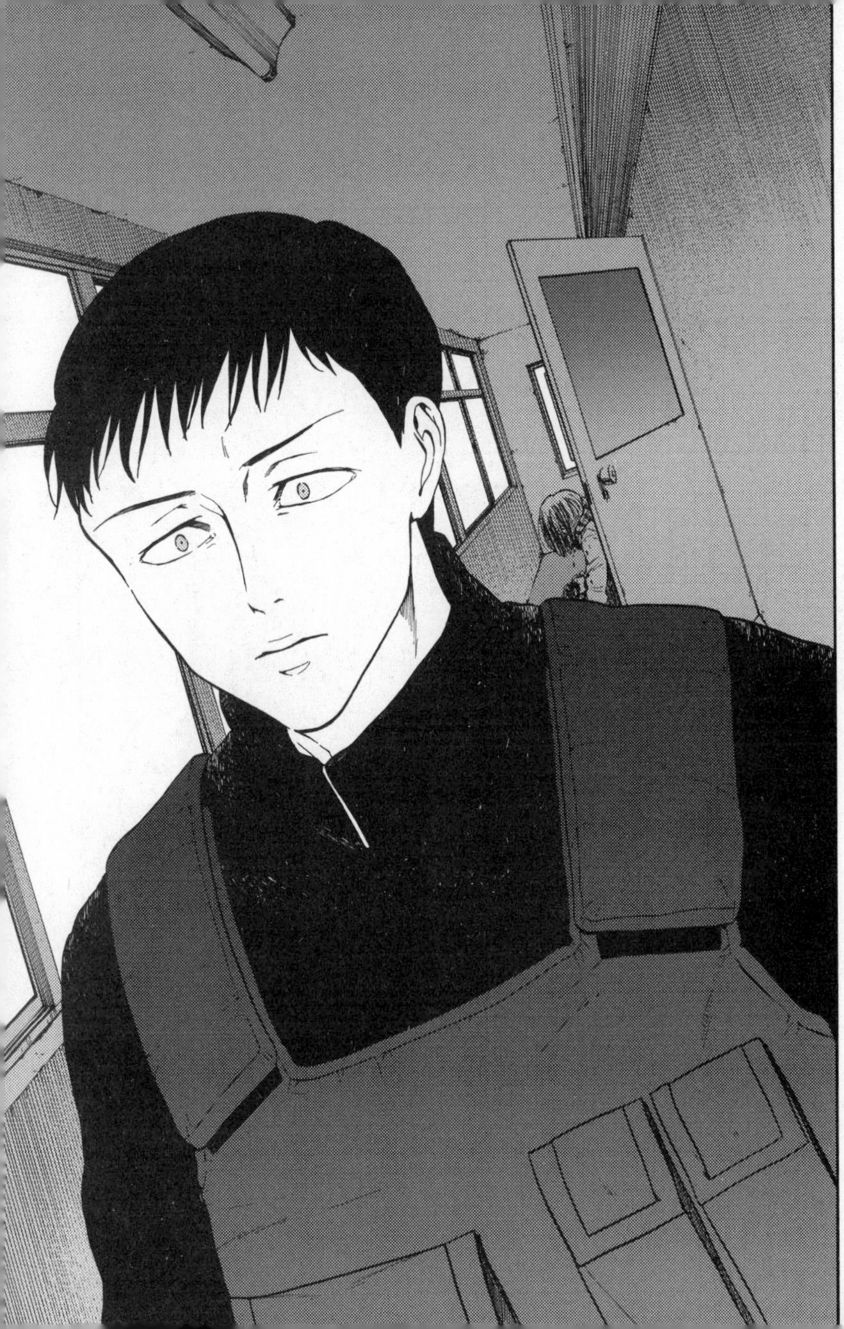

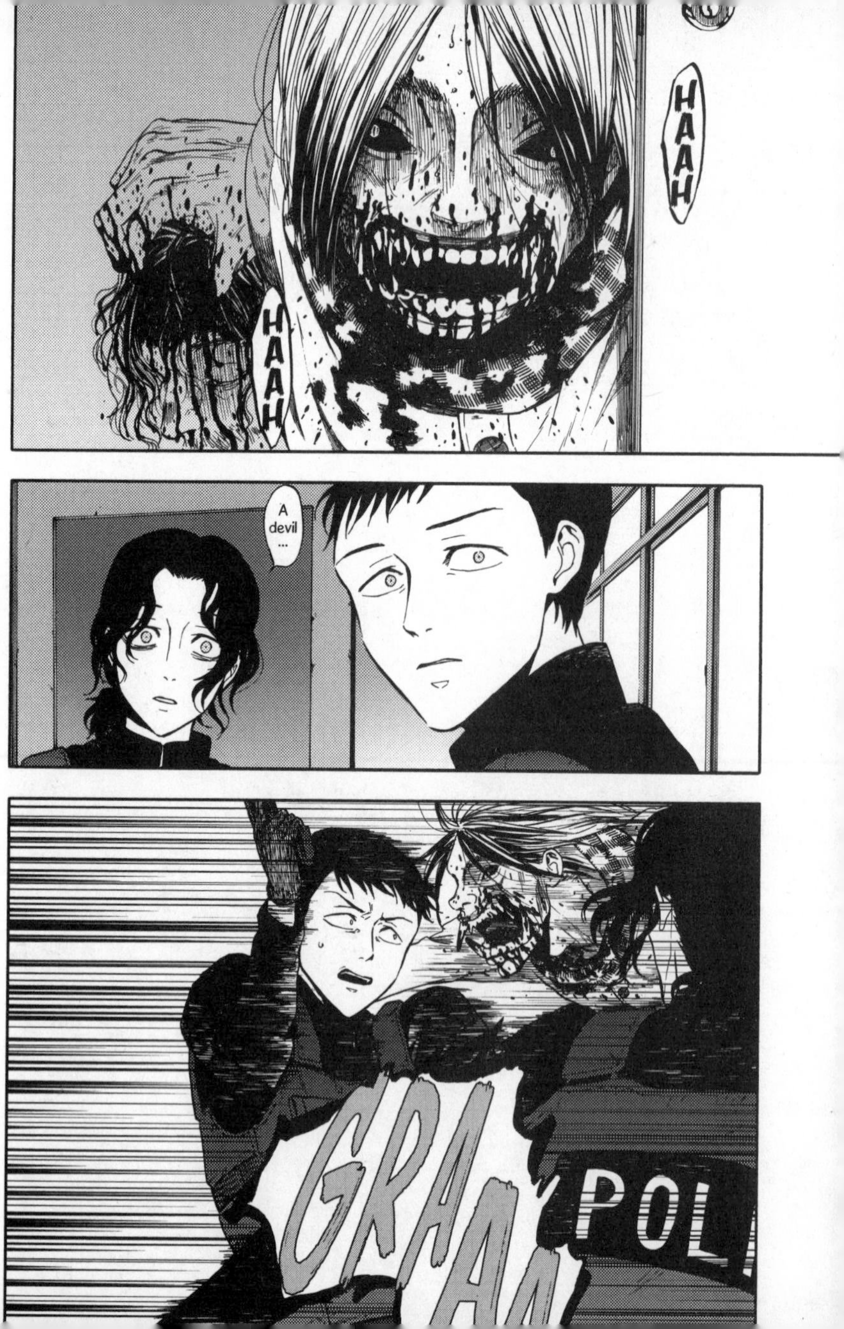
HAAH
HAAH
A devil ...
GRAAA
POL

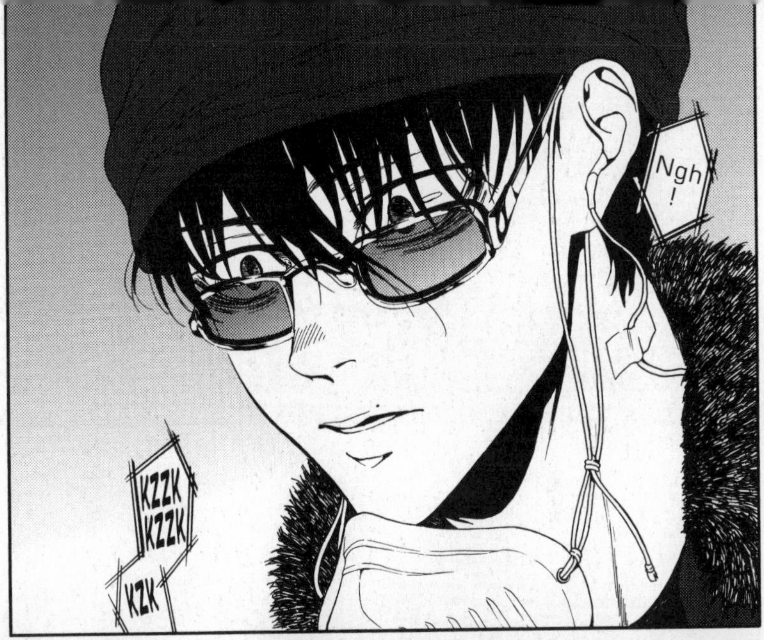
Ngh!
KZZK KZZK
KZK

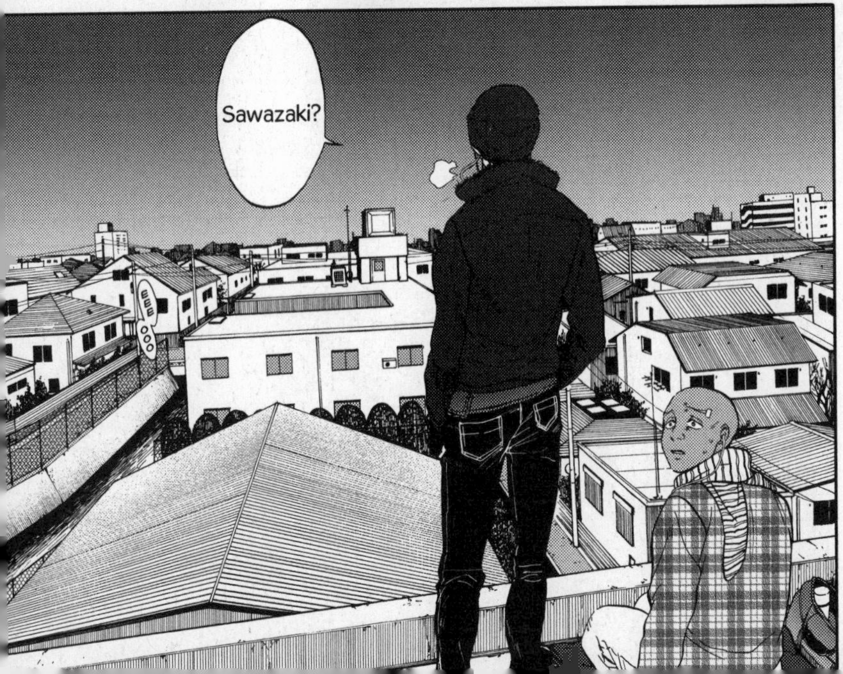
Sawazaki?
EEE
OOO

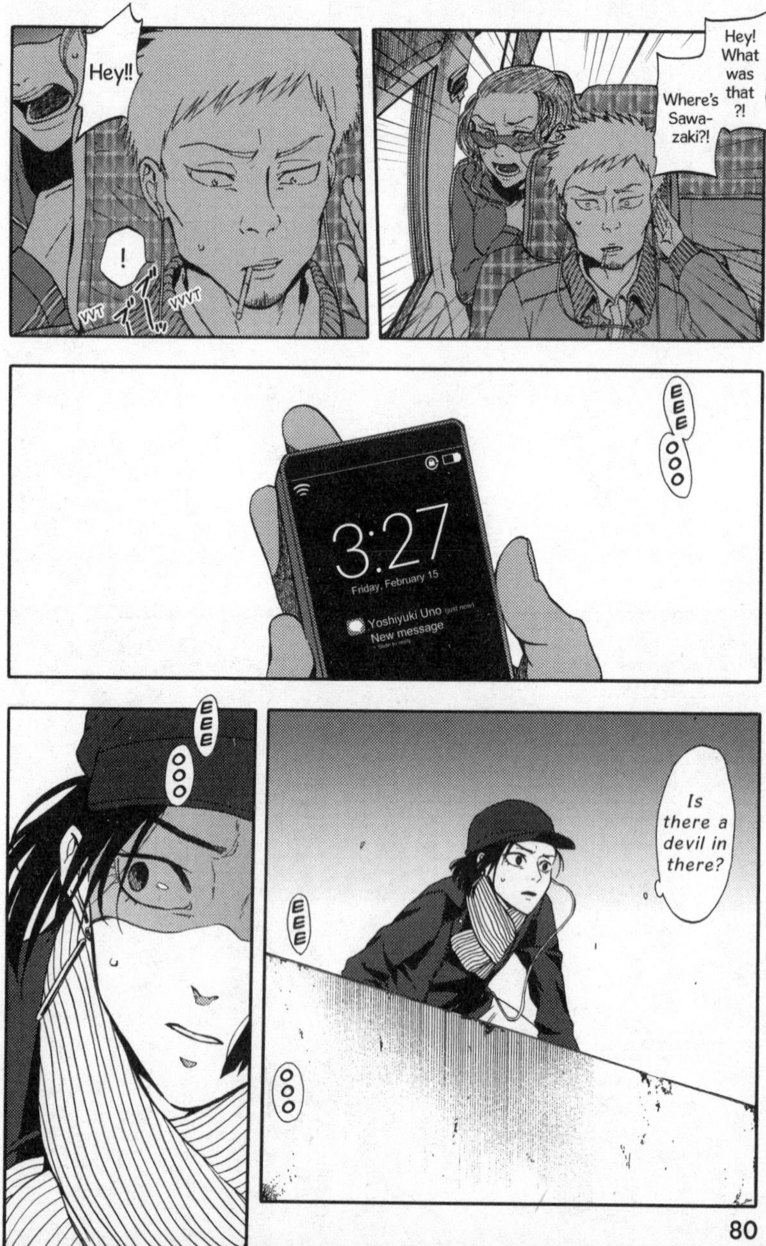
Hey! What was that ?!
Where's Sawa-zaki?!
Hey!!
!
VVT
VVVT
EEEOOO
3:27
Friday, February 15
Yoshiyuki Uno (just now)
New message
Is there a devil in there?
EEE
OOO
EEE
OOO

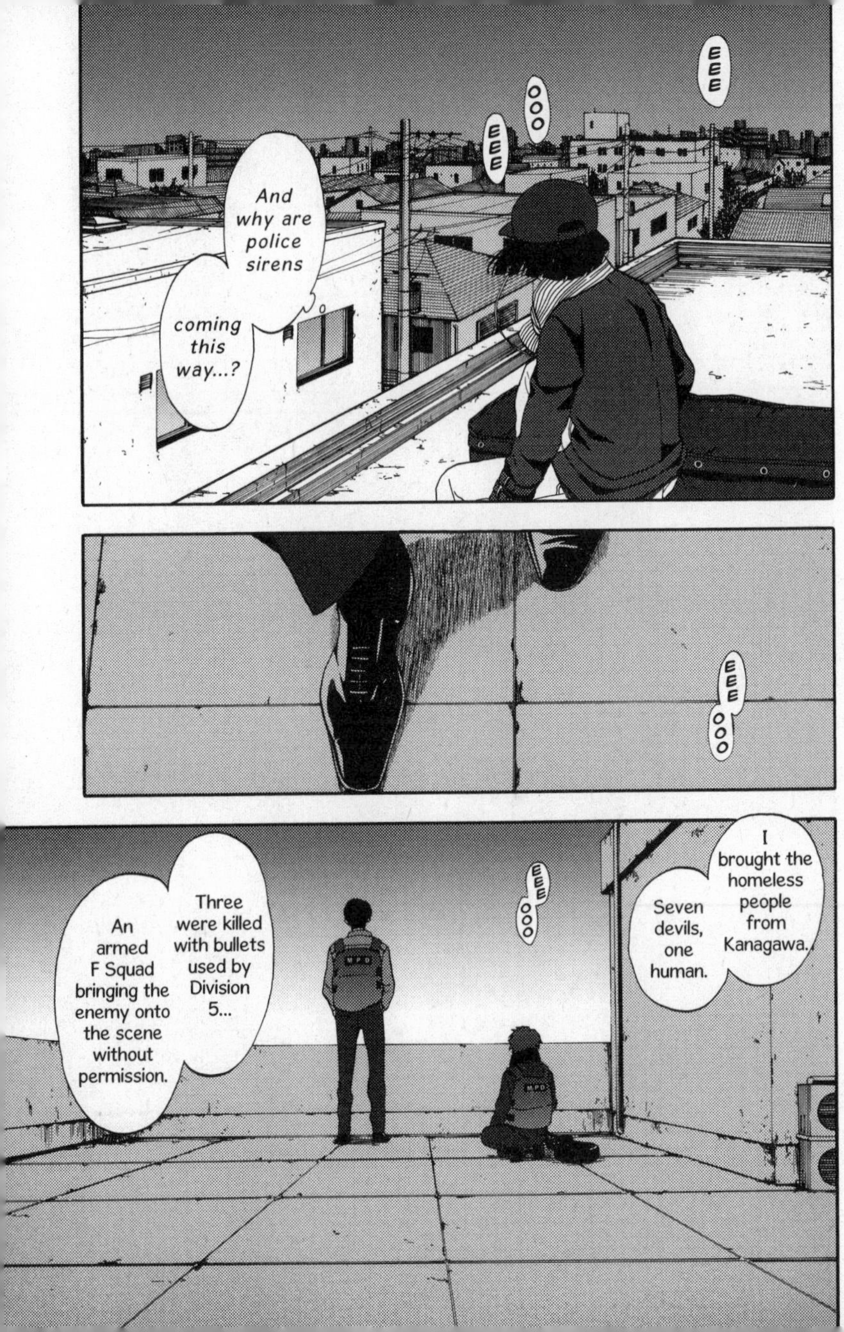
EEE
OOO
EEE
And why are police sirens coming this way...?
EEE
OOO
I brought the homeless people from Kanagawa...
Seven devils, one human.
EEE
OOO
Three were killed with bullets used by Division 5...
An armed F Squad bringing the enemy onto the scene without permission.

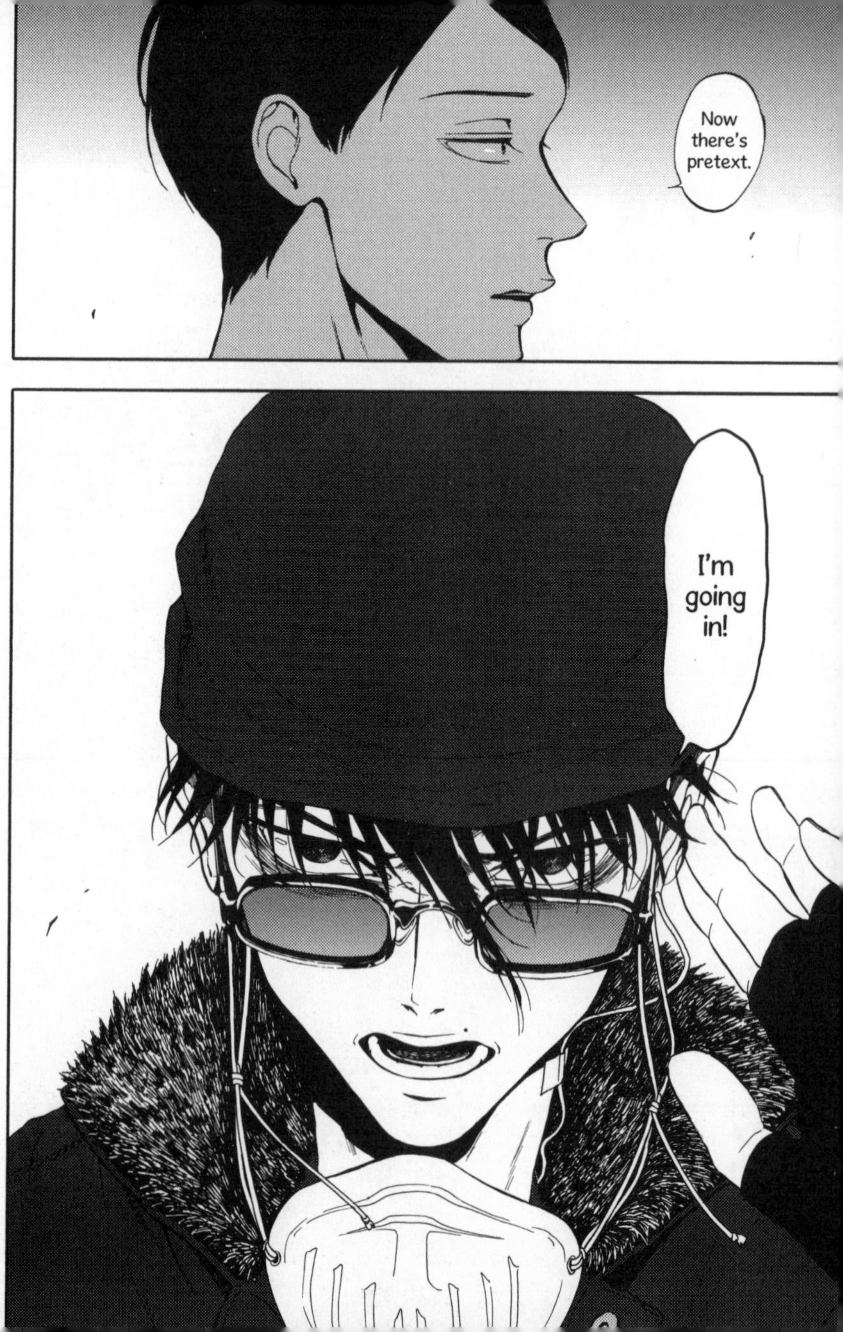
Now there's pretext.
I'm going in!

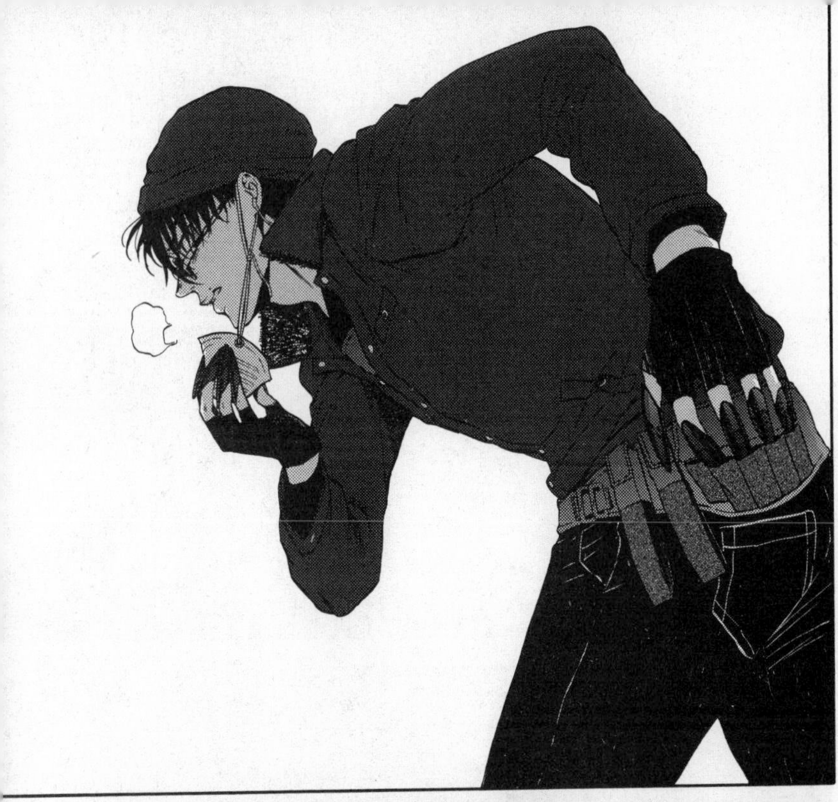

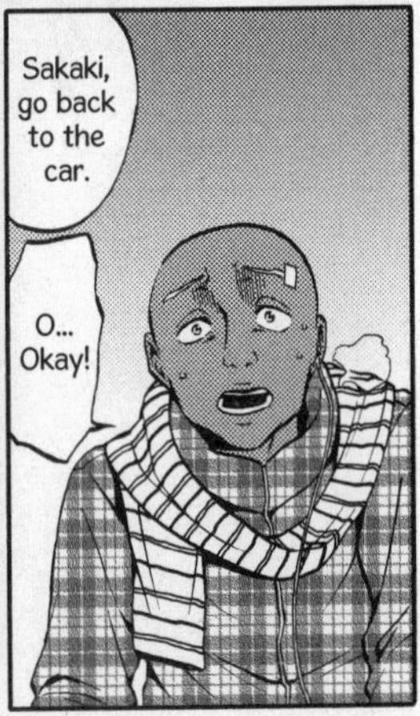
Sakaki, go back to the car.
O... Okay!

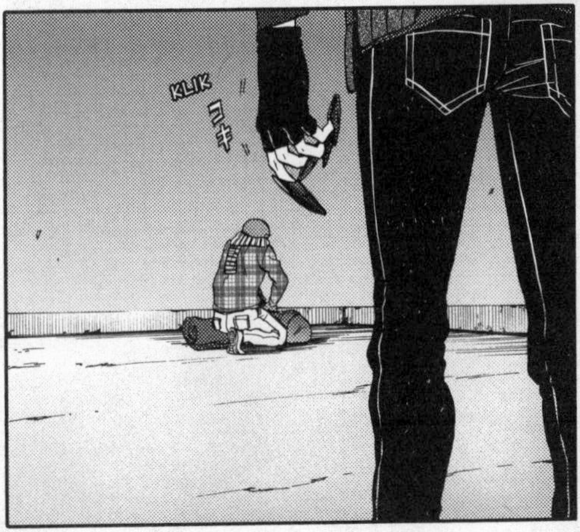
KLIK

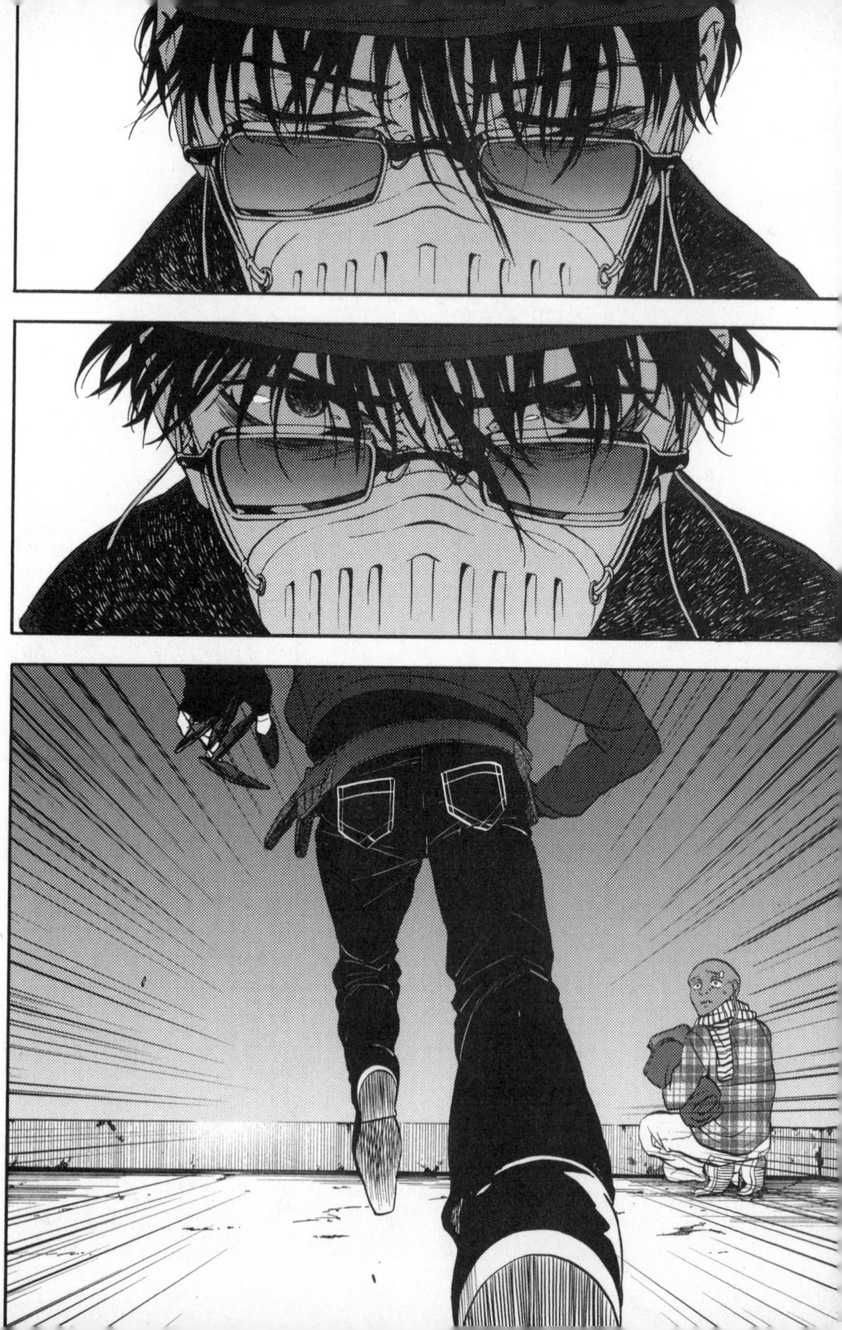

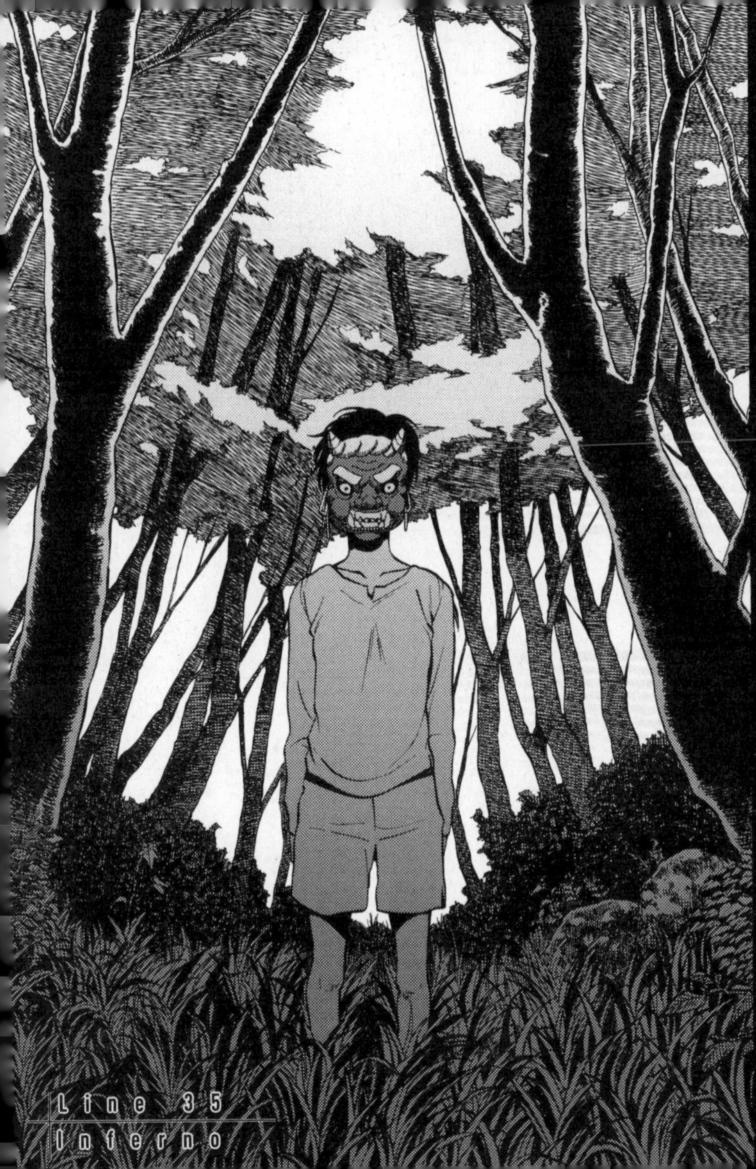
Line 35
Inferno

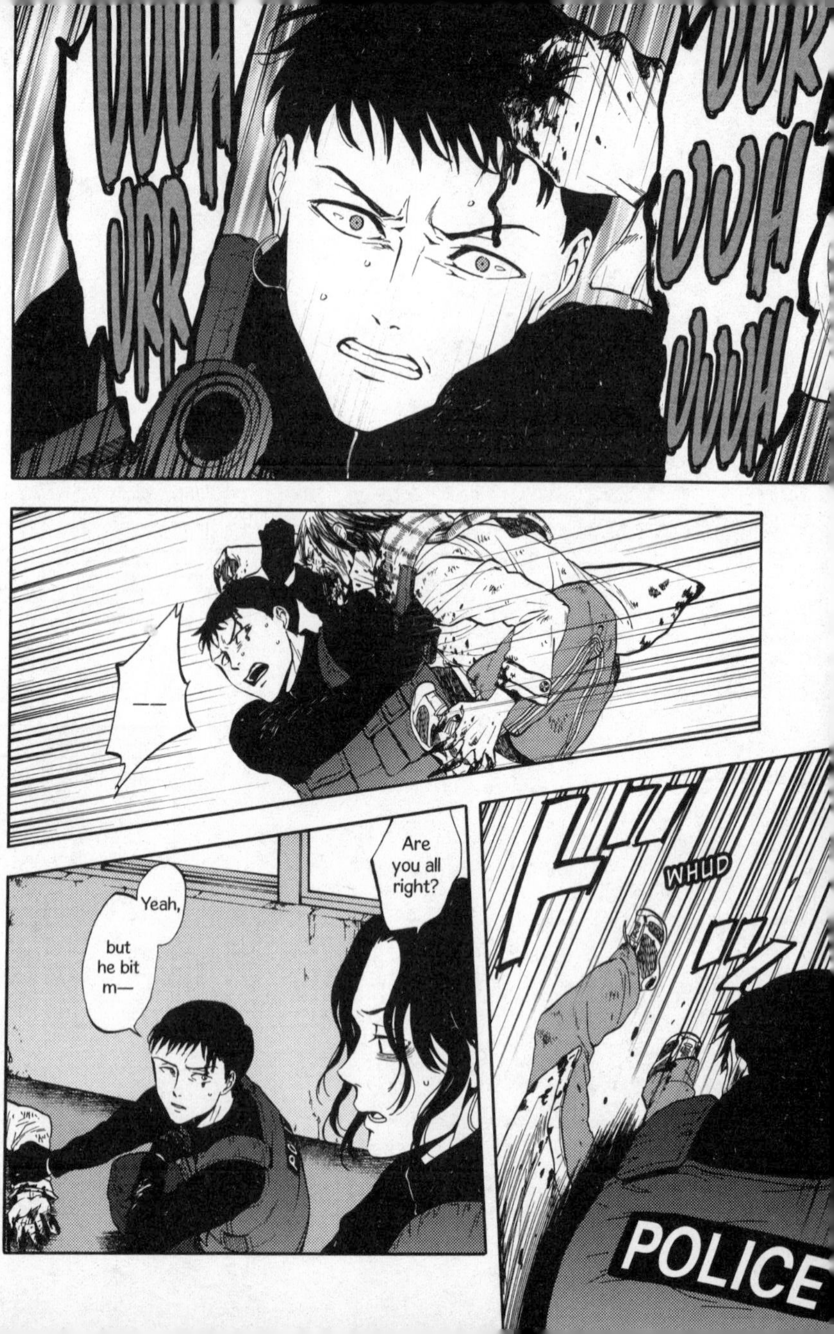
UUUH
UUUH URR
——
WHUD
POLICE
Are you all right?
Yeah, but he bit m—

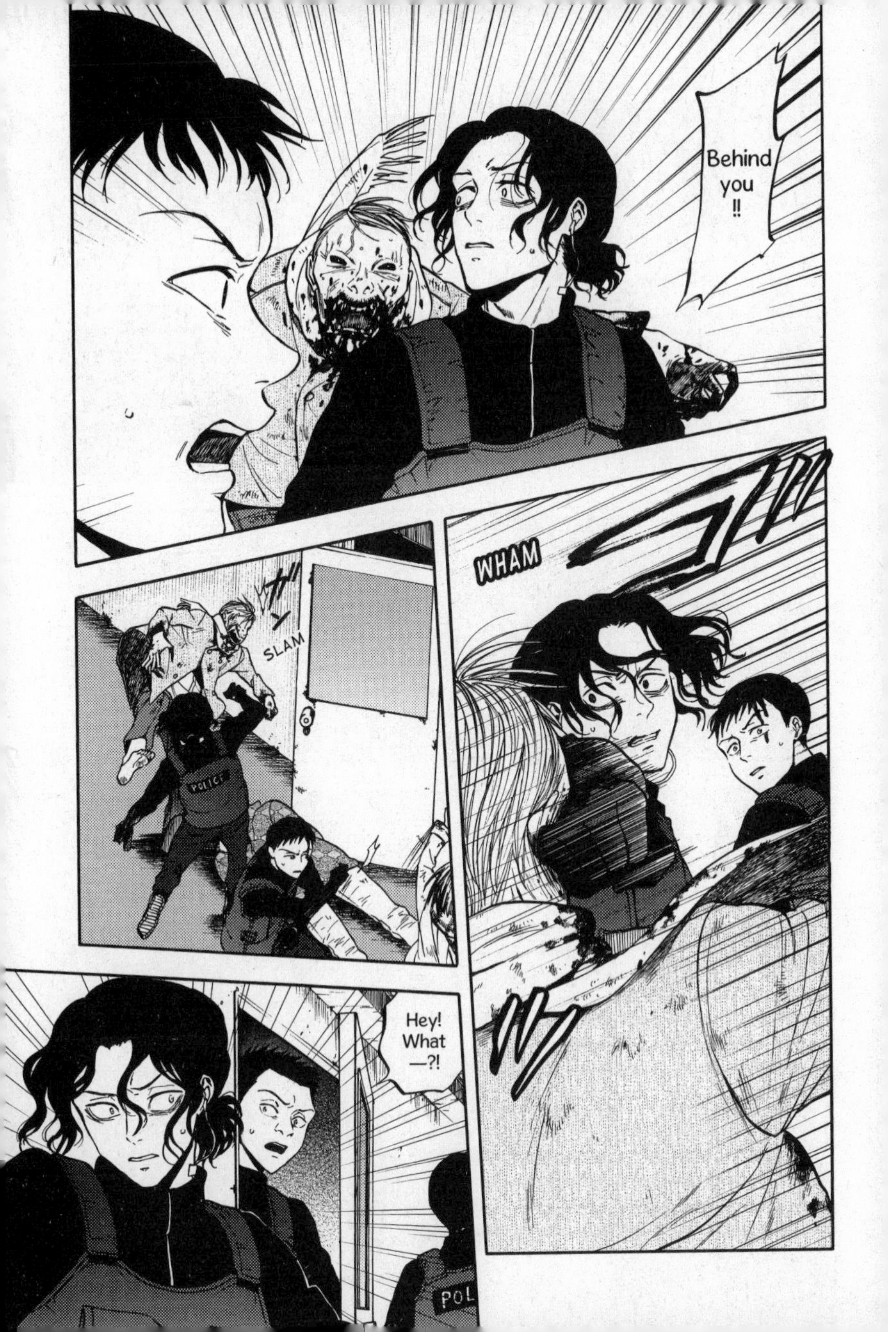
Behind you !!
WHAM
SLAM
Hey! What —?!
POL

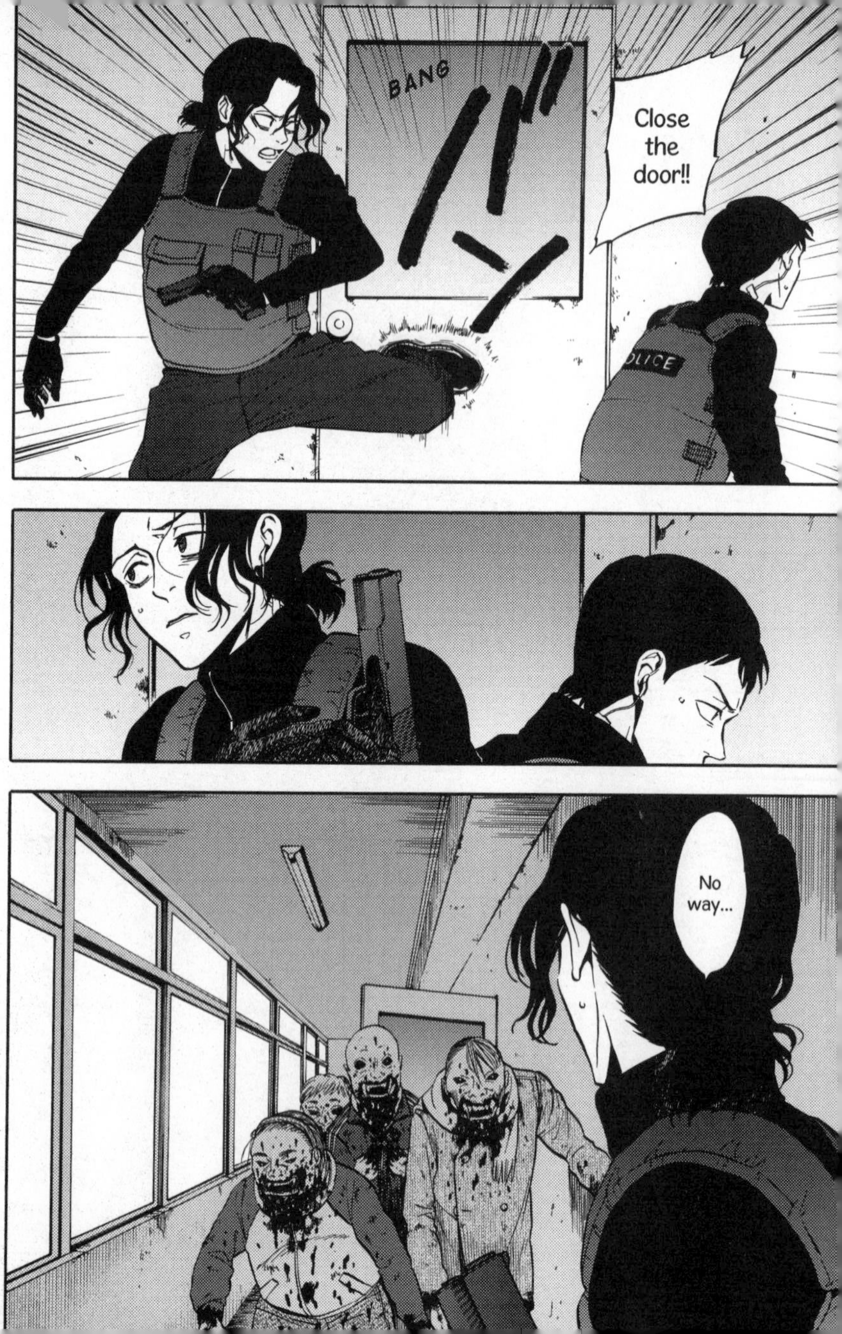
Close the door!!
BANG
POLICE
No way...

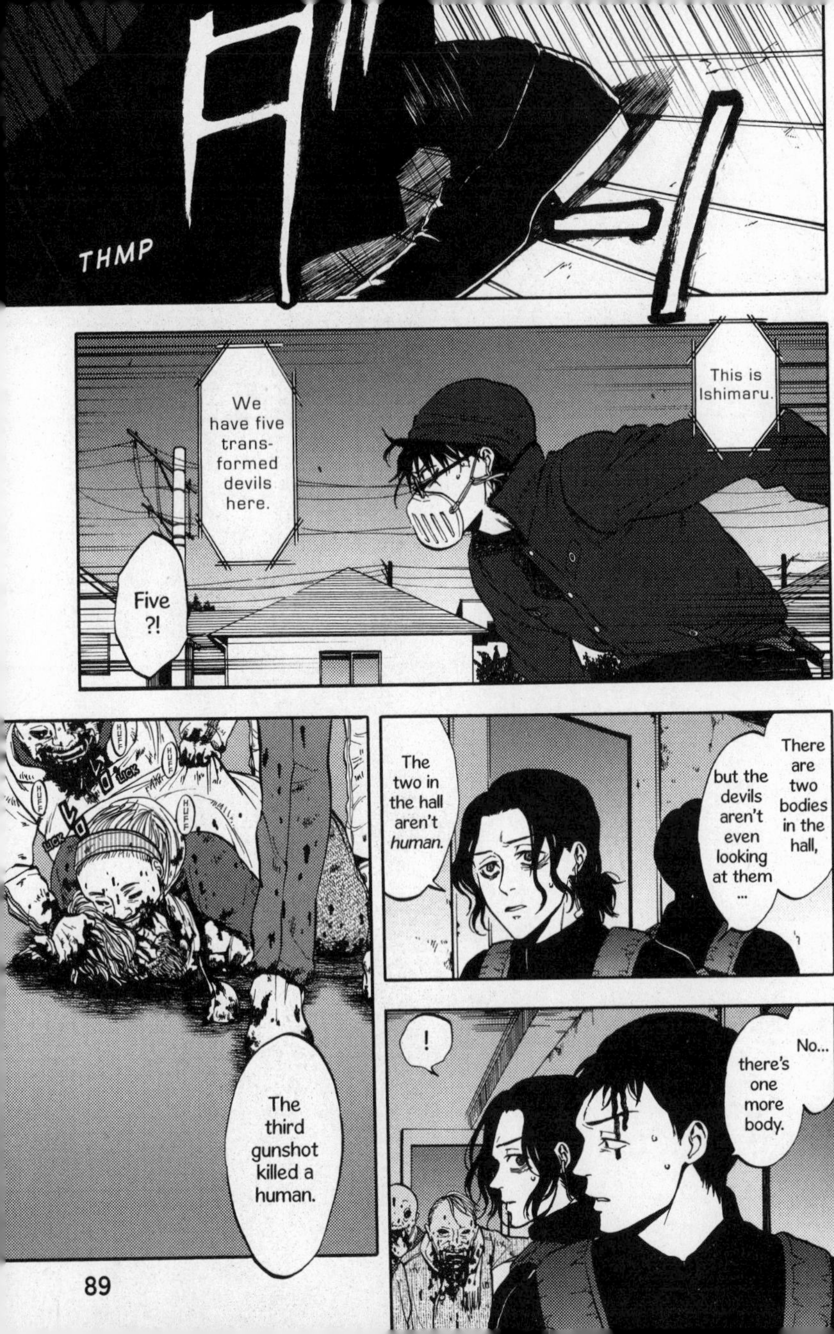
THMP
This is Ishimaru.
We have five transformed devils here.
Five ?!
There are two bodies in the hall,
but the devils aren't even looking at them ...
The two in the hall aren't *human*.
No... there's one more body.
!
HUFF
LICK
The third gunshot killed a human.

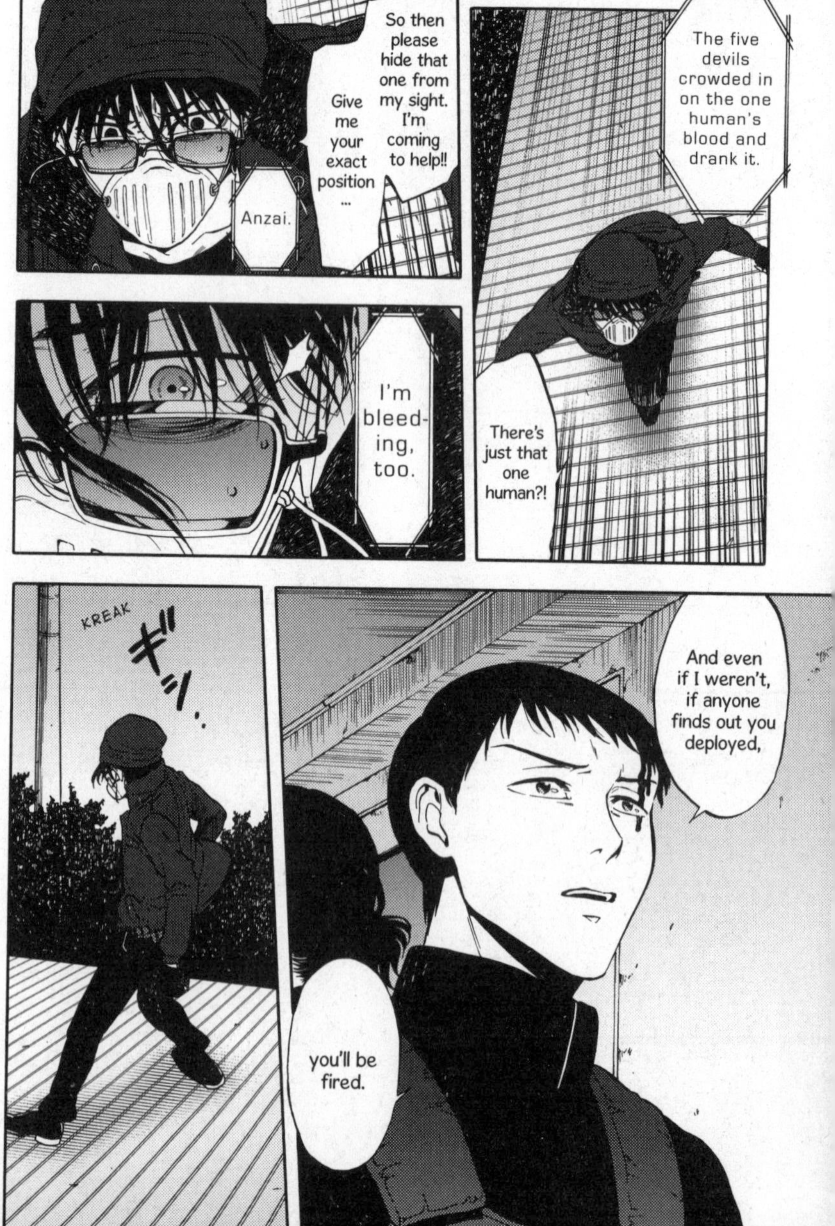
The five devils crowded in on the one human's blood and drank it.
There's just that one human?!
So then please hide that one from my sight. I'm coming to help!!
Give me your exact position ...
Anzai.
I'm bleeding, too.
And even if I weren't, if anyone finds out you deployed,
you'll be fired.
KREAK

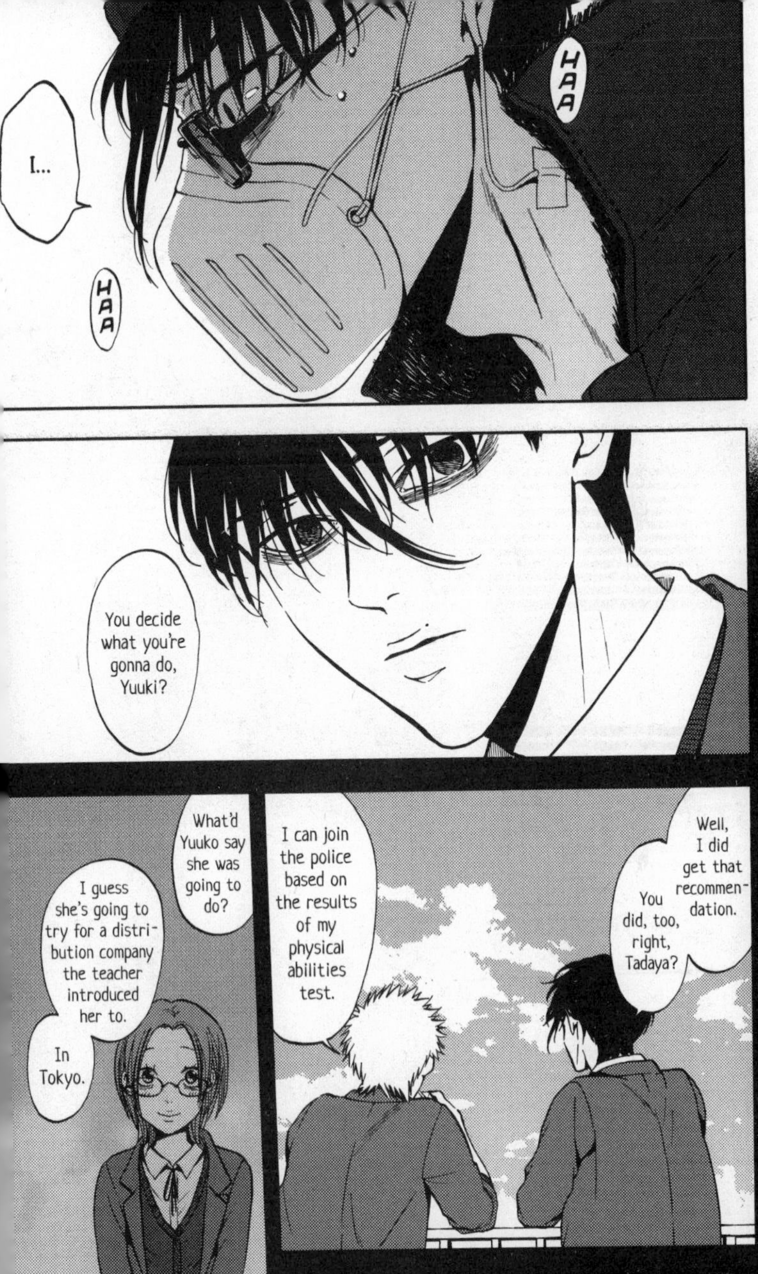
HAA
I...
HAA
You decide what you're gonna do, Yuuki?
Well, I did get that recommen-dation.
You did, too, right, Tadaya?
I can join the police based on the results of my physical abilities test.
What'd Yuuko say she was going to do?
I guess she's going to try for a distri-bution company the teacher introduced her to.
In Tokyo.

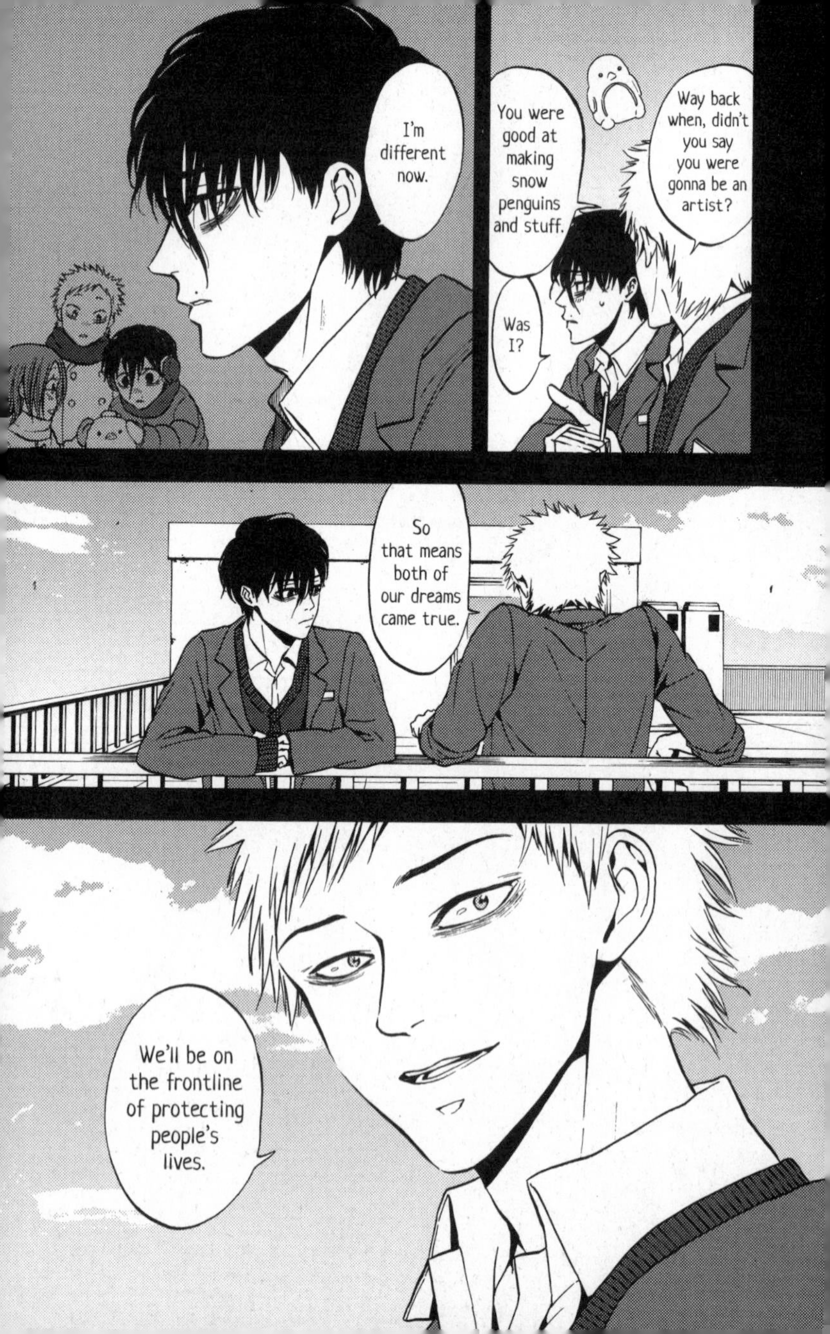
Way back when, didn't you say you were gonna be an artist?
You were good at making snow penguins and stuff.
Was I?
I'm different now.
So that means both of our dreams came true.
We'll be on the frontline of protecting people's lives.

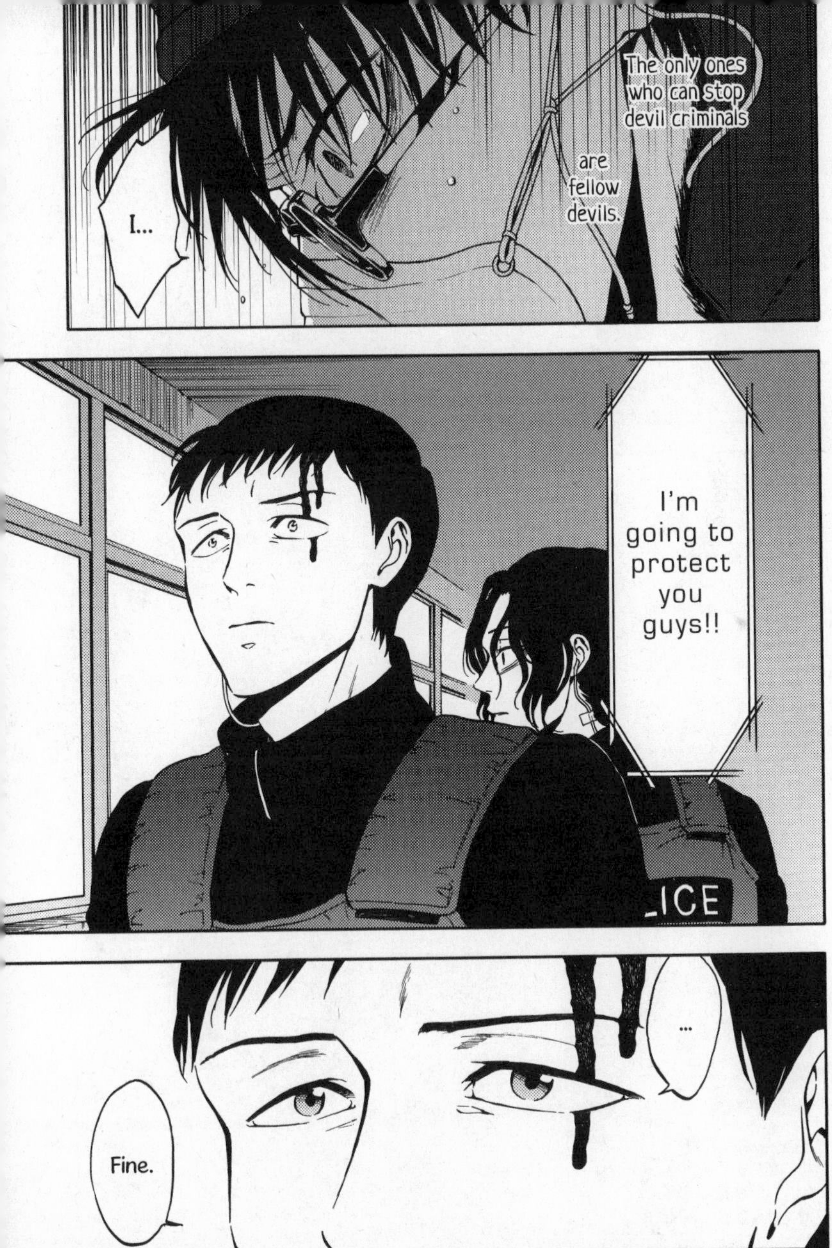
The only ones who can stop devil criminals
are fellow devils.
I...
I'm going to protect you guys!!
...
Fine.

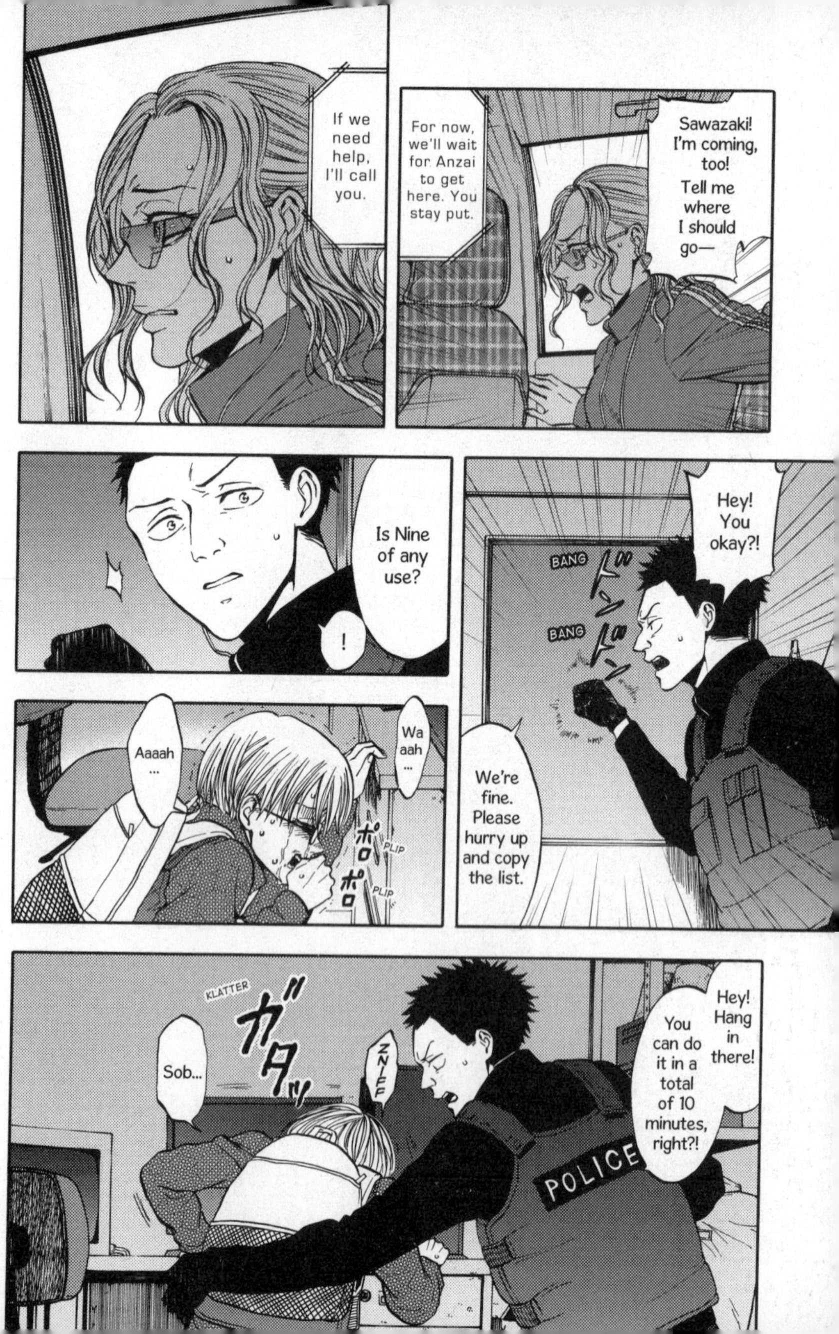
Sawazaki! I'm coming, too! Tell me where I should go—
For now, we'll wait for Anzai to get here. You stay put.
If we need help, I'll call you.
Hey! You okay?!
BANG
BANG
We're fine. Please hurry up and copy the list.
Is Nine of any use?
!
Wa aah ...
PLIP
PLIP
Aaaah ...
Hey! Hang in there!
You can do it in a total of 10 minutes, right?!
POLICE
ZNIFF
KLATTER
Sob...

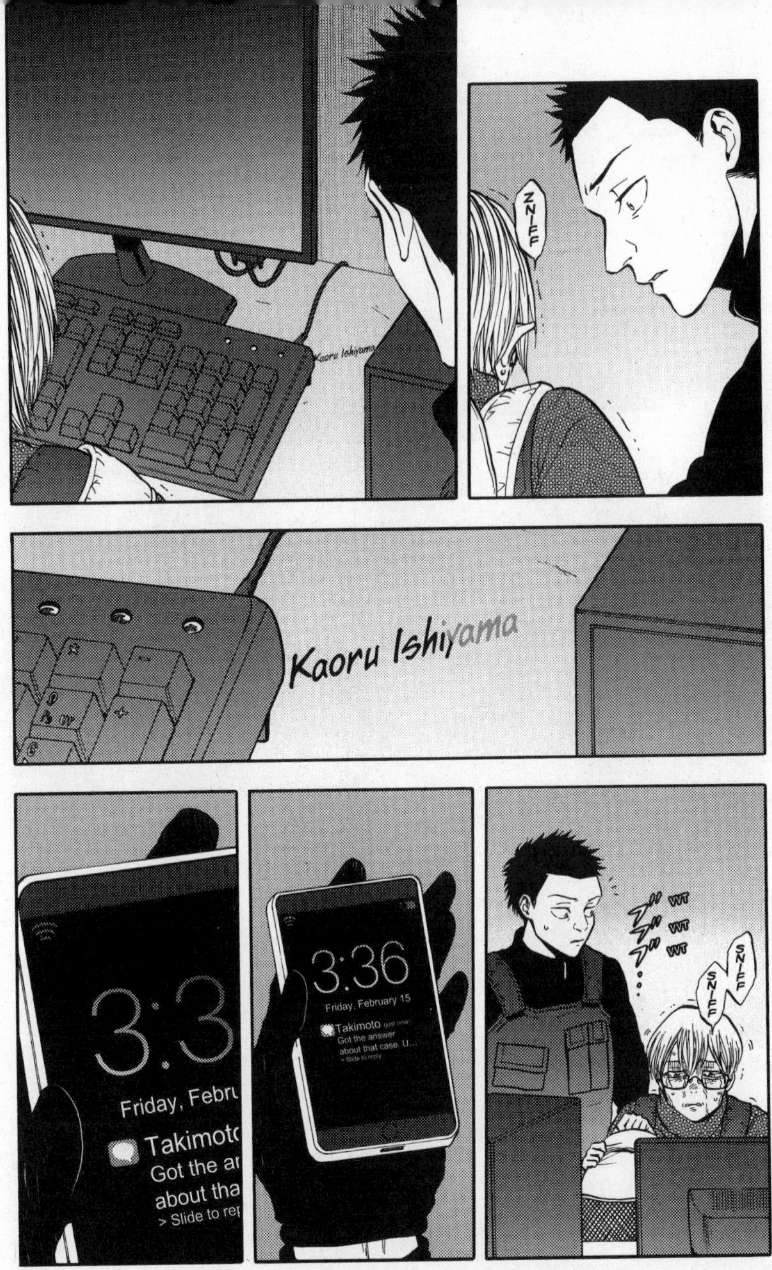
ZNIFF
Kaoru Ishiyama
Kaoru Ishiyama
SNIFF
SNIFF
VVT
VVT
VVT
3:36
Friday, February 15
Takimoto
Got the answer
about that case. U...
> Slide to reply
3:3
Friday, Febru
Takimoto
Got the ar
about tha
> Slide to rep

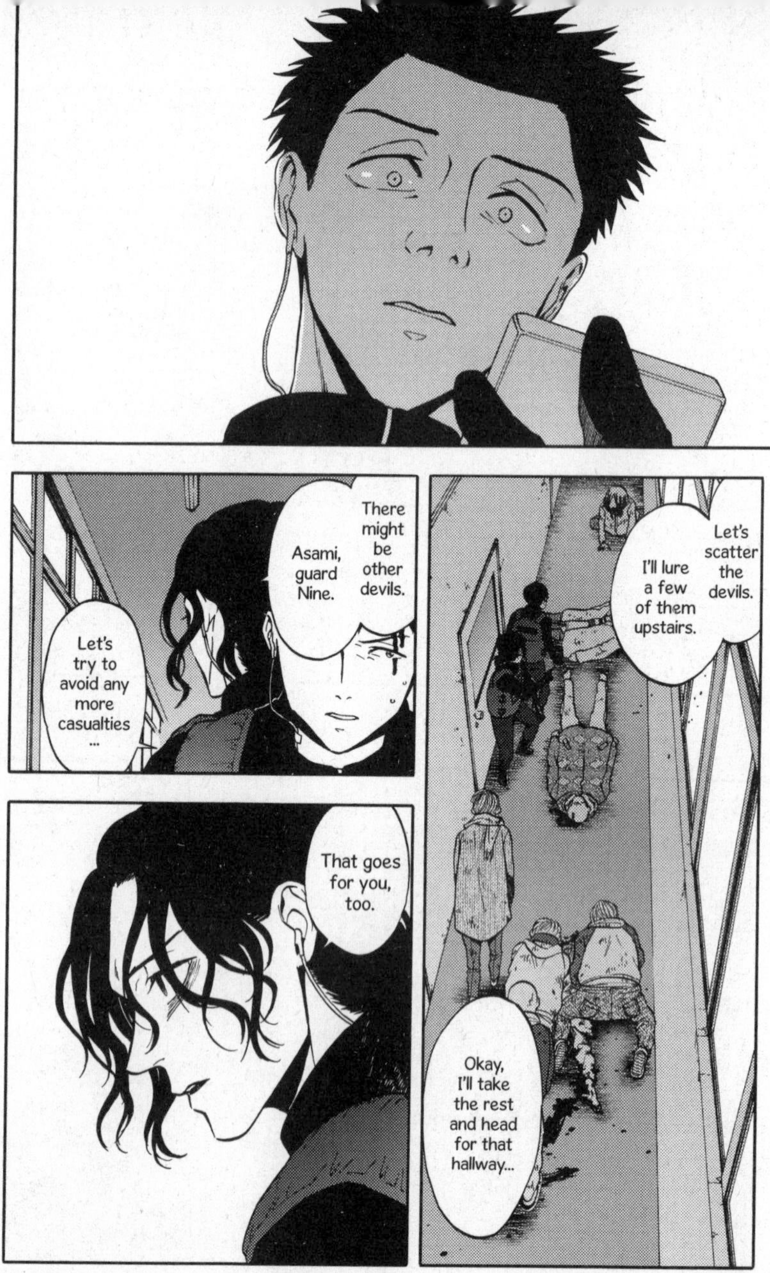
Let's scatter the devils.
I'll lure a few of them upstairs.
Okay, I'll take the rest and head for that hallway...
There might be other devils.
Asami, guard Nine.
Let's try to avoid any more casualties ...
That goes for you, too.

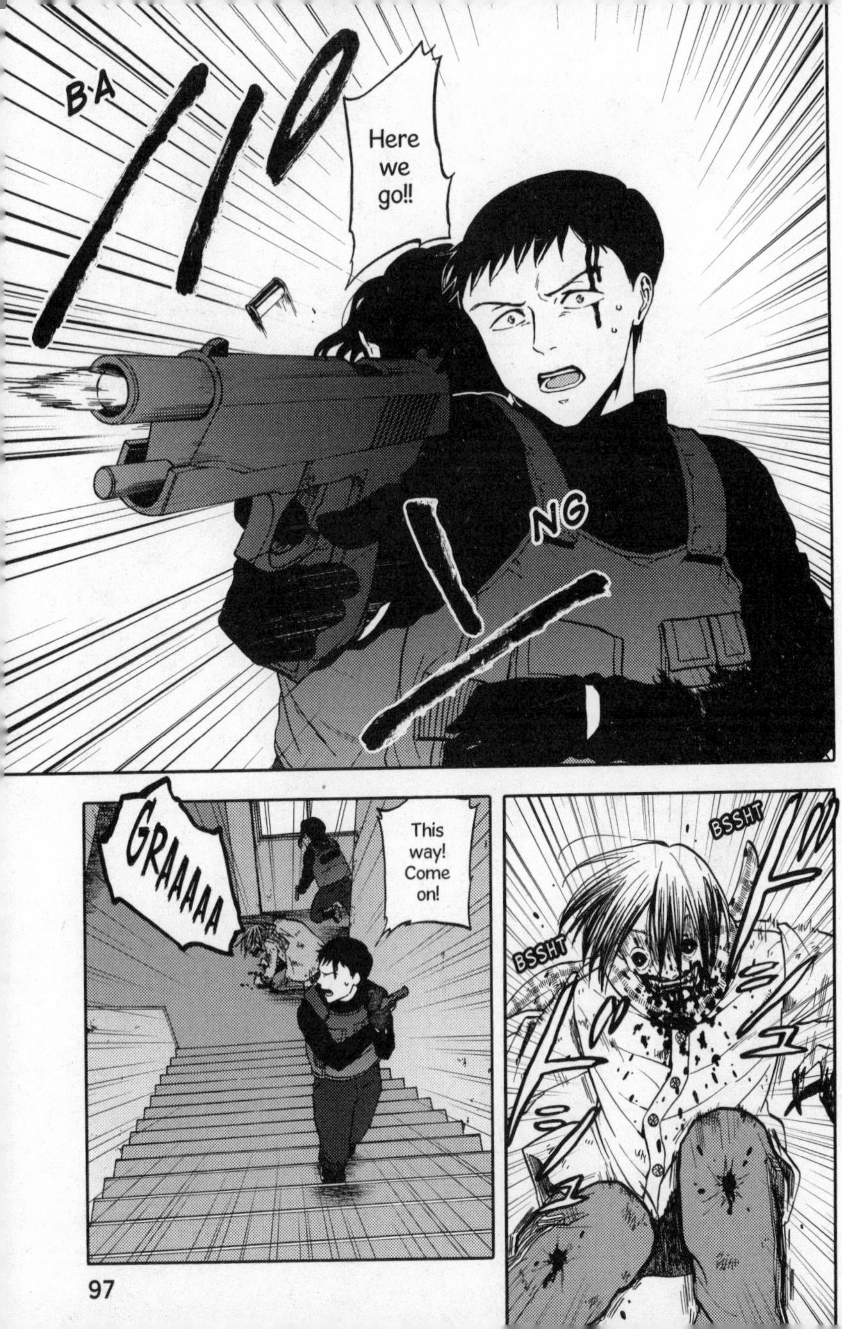
Here we go!!
B-A
NG
BSSHT
BSSHT
This way! Come on!
GRAAAAA

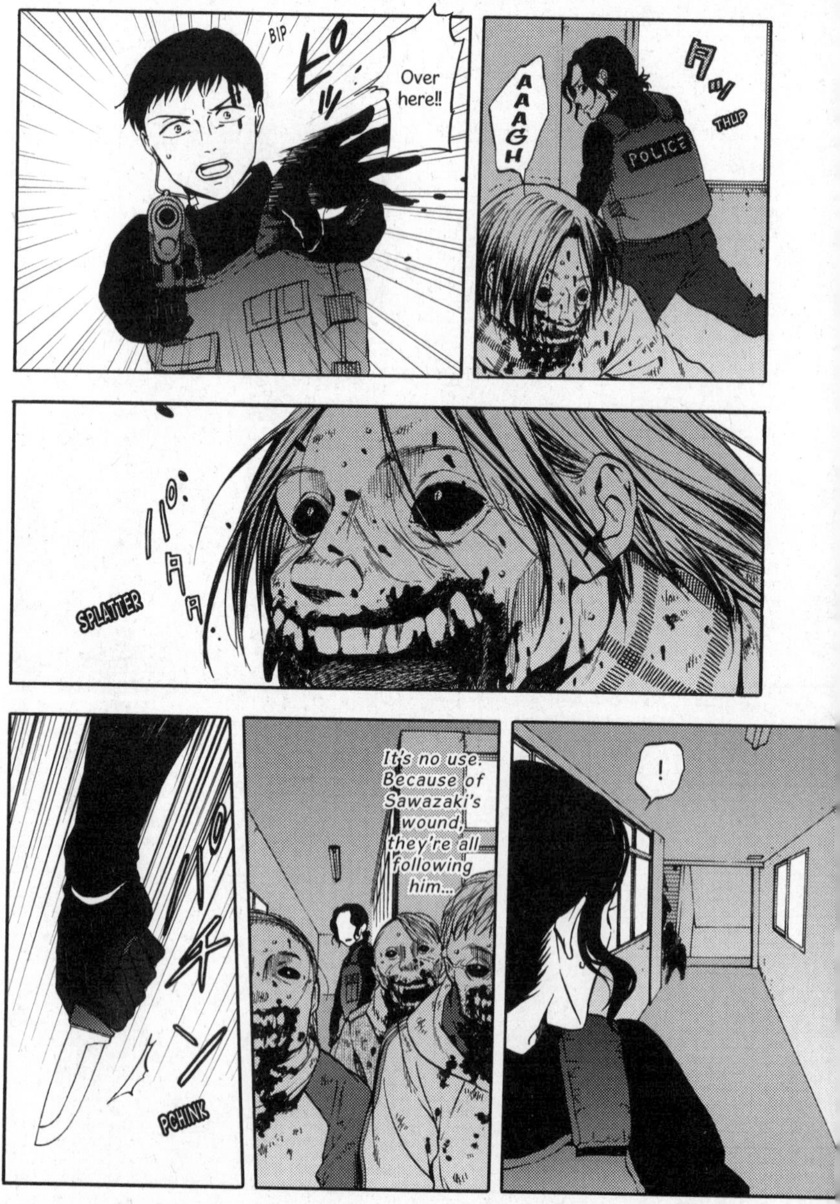
AAAGH
THUP
BIP
Over here!!
SPLATTER
!
It's no use. Because of Sawazaki's wound, they're all following him...
PCHINK

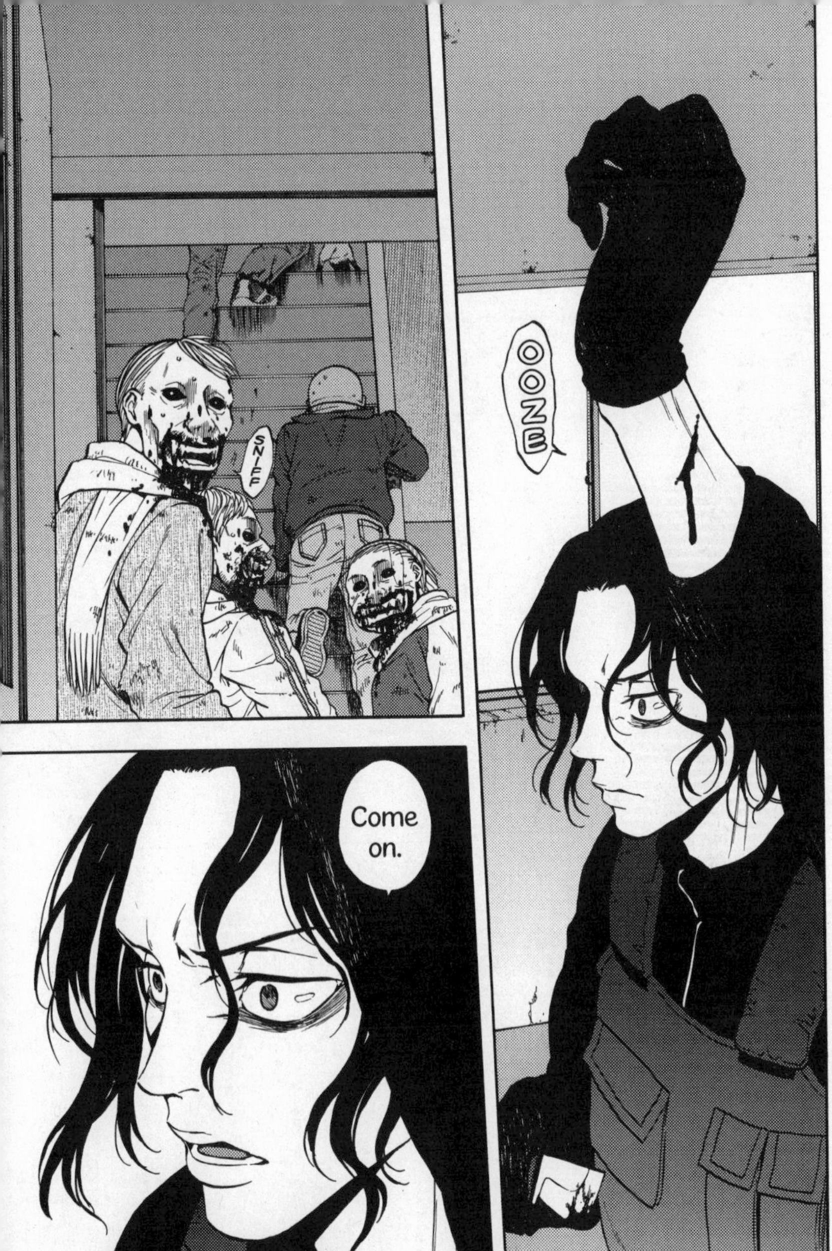
OOZE
SNIFF
Come on.

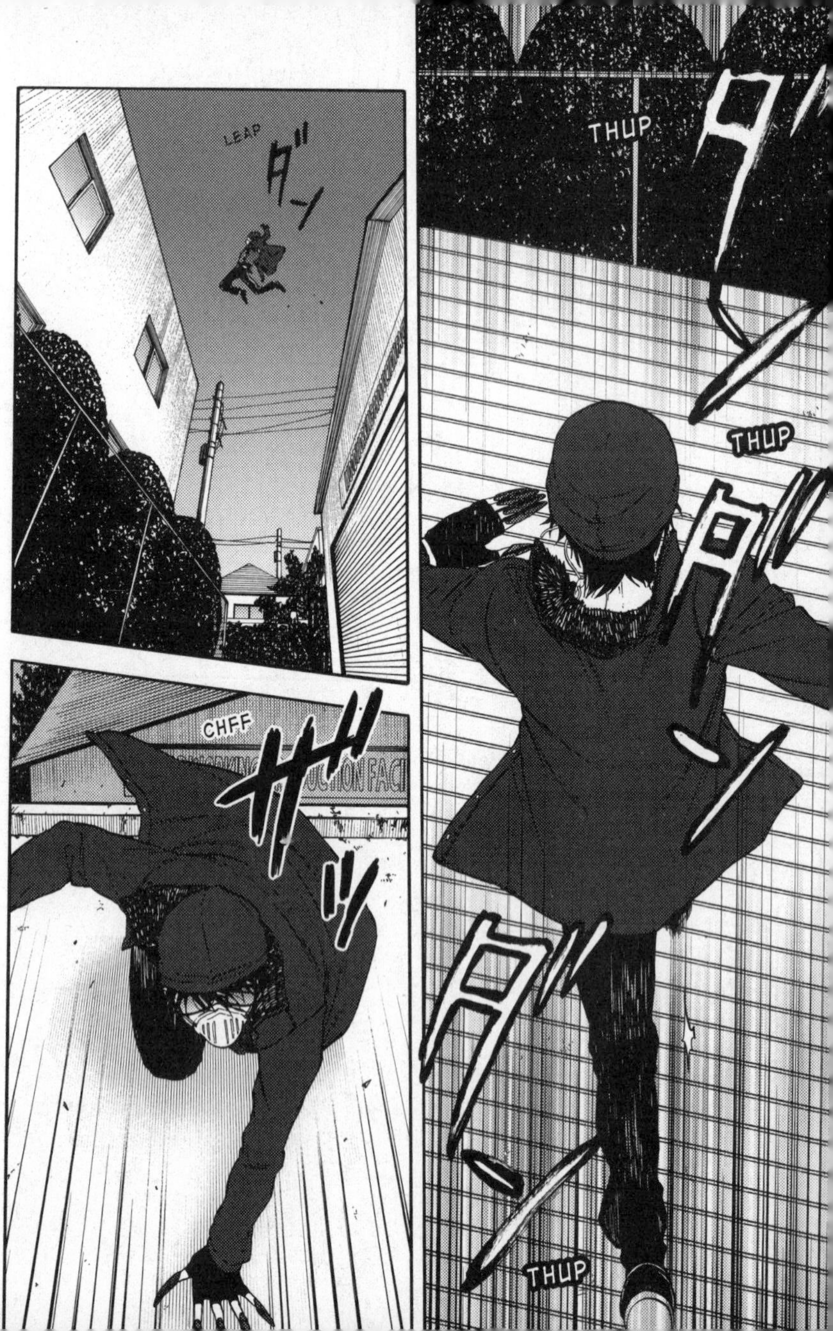
THUP
THUP
THUP
LEAP
CHFF

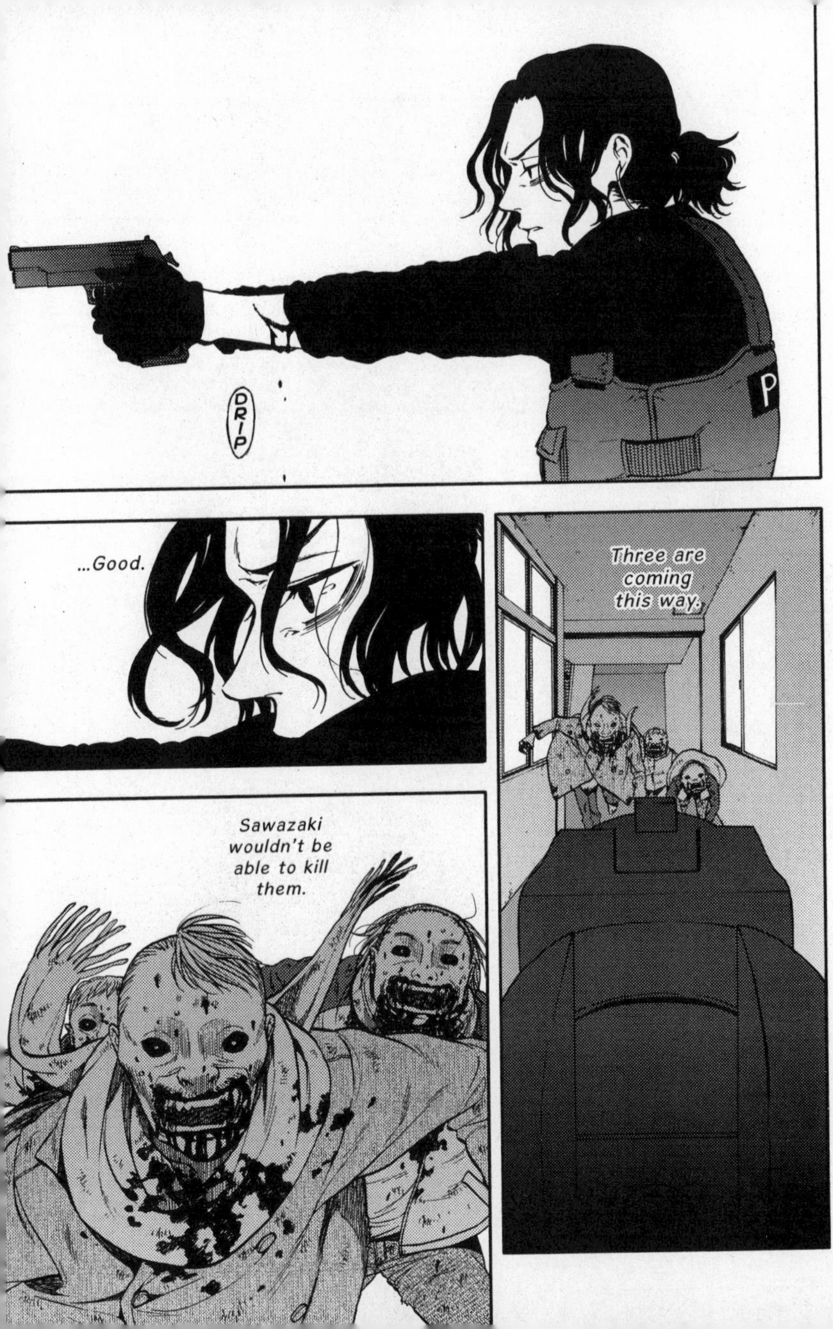
DRIP
Three are coming this way.
...Good.
Sawazaki wouldn't be able to kill them.

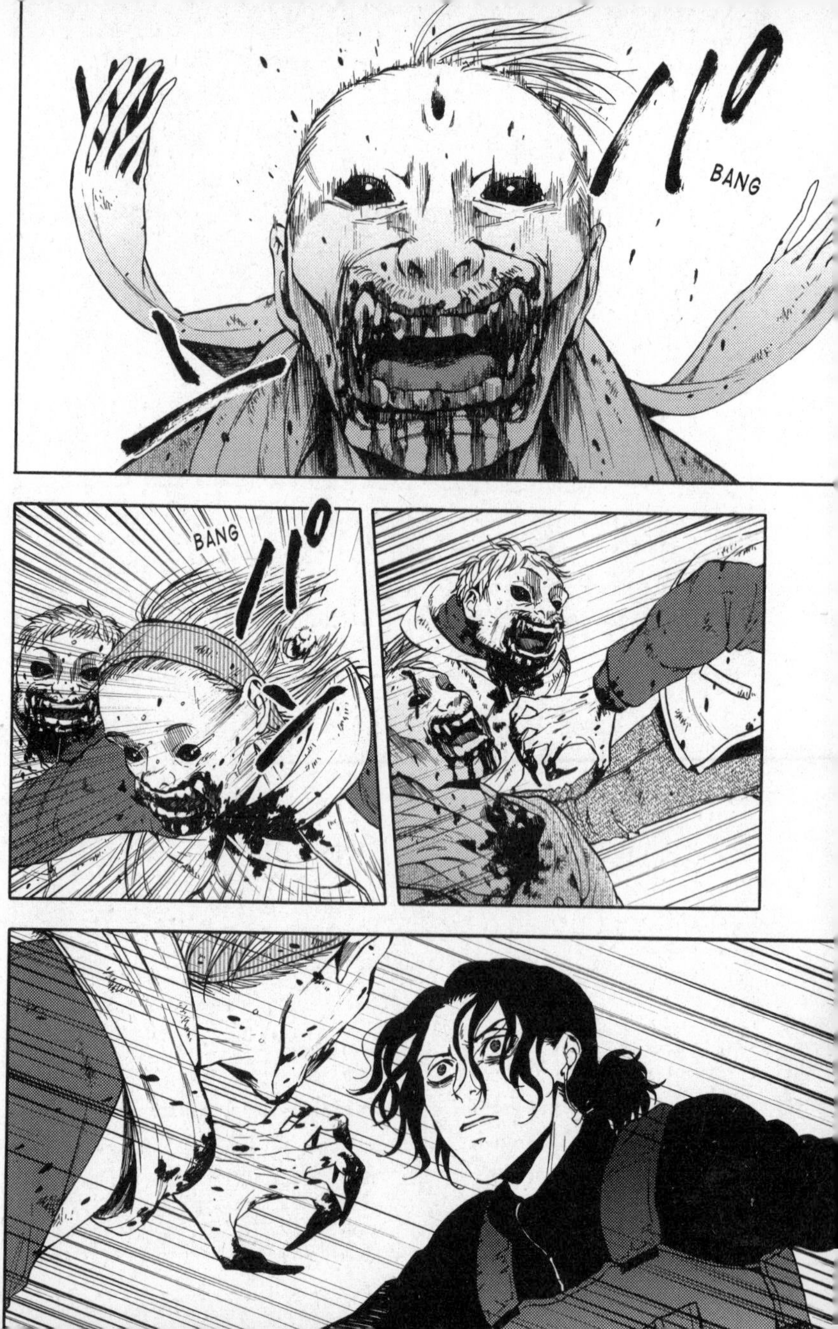
BANG
BANG

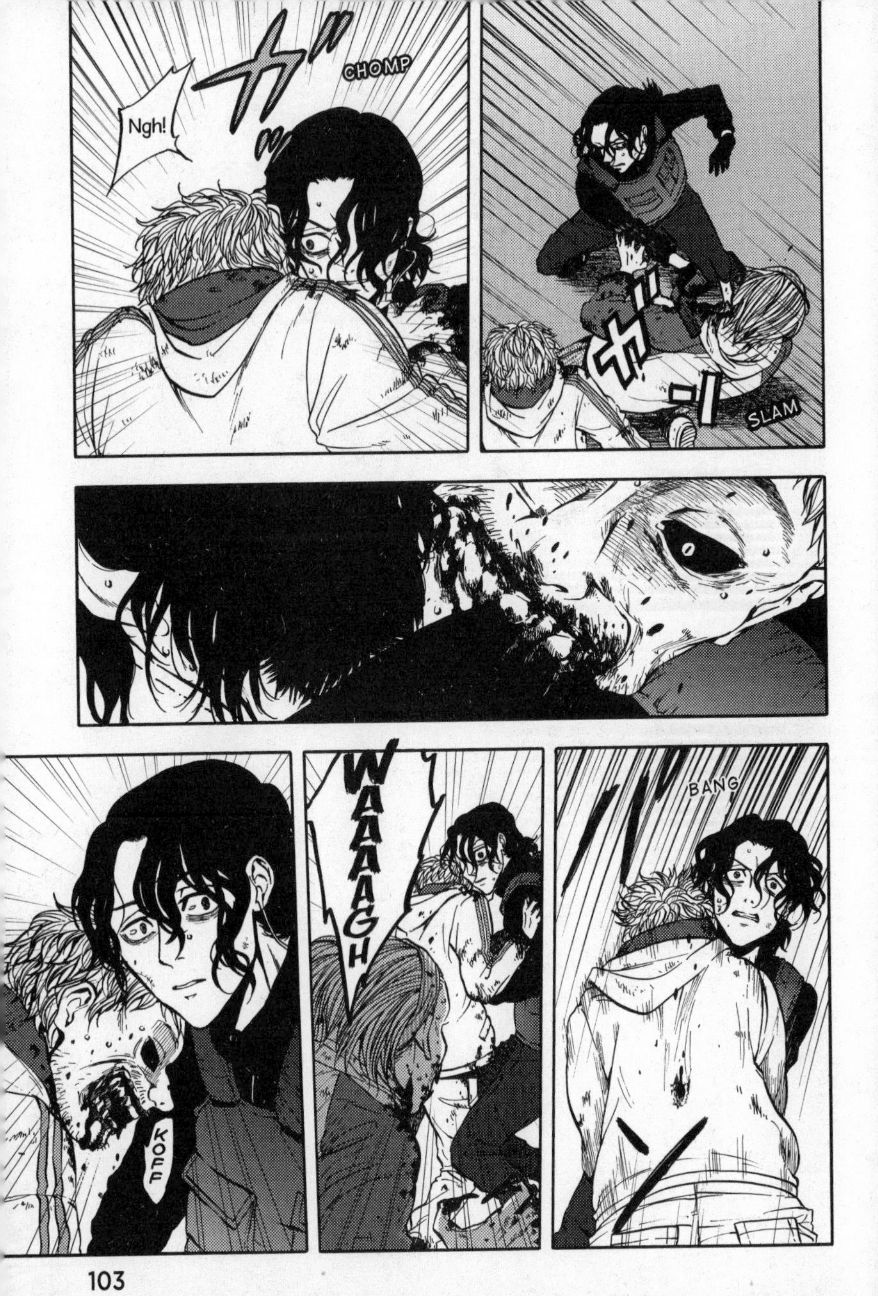

SLAM
Ngh!
CHOMP
BANG
WAAAAGH
KOFF

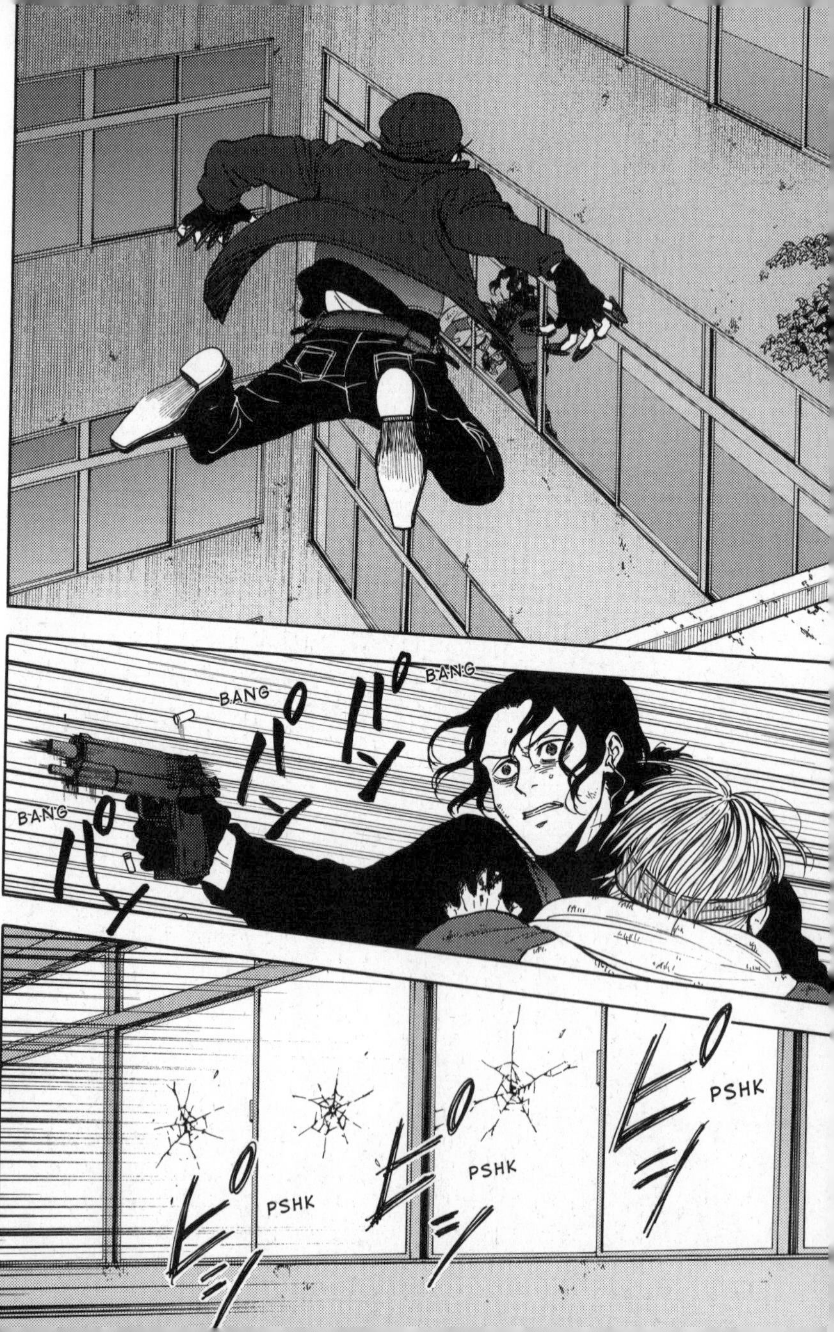
BANG
BANG
BANG
PSHK
PSHK
PSHK

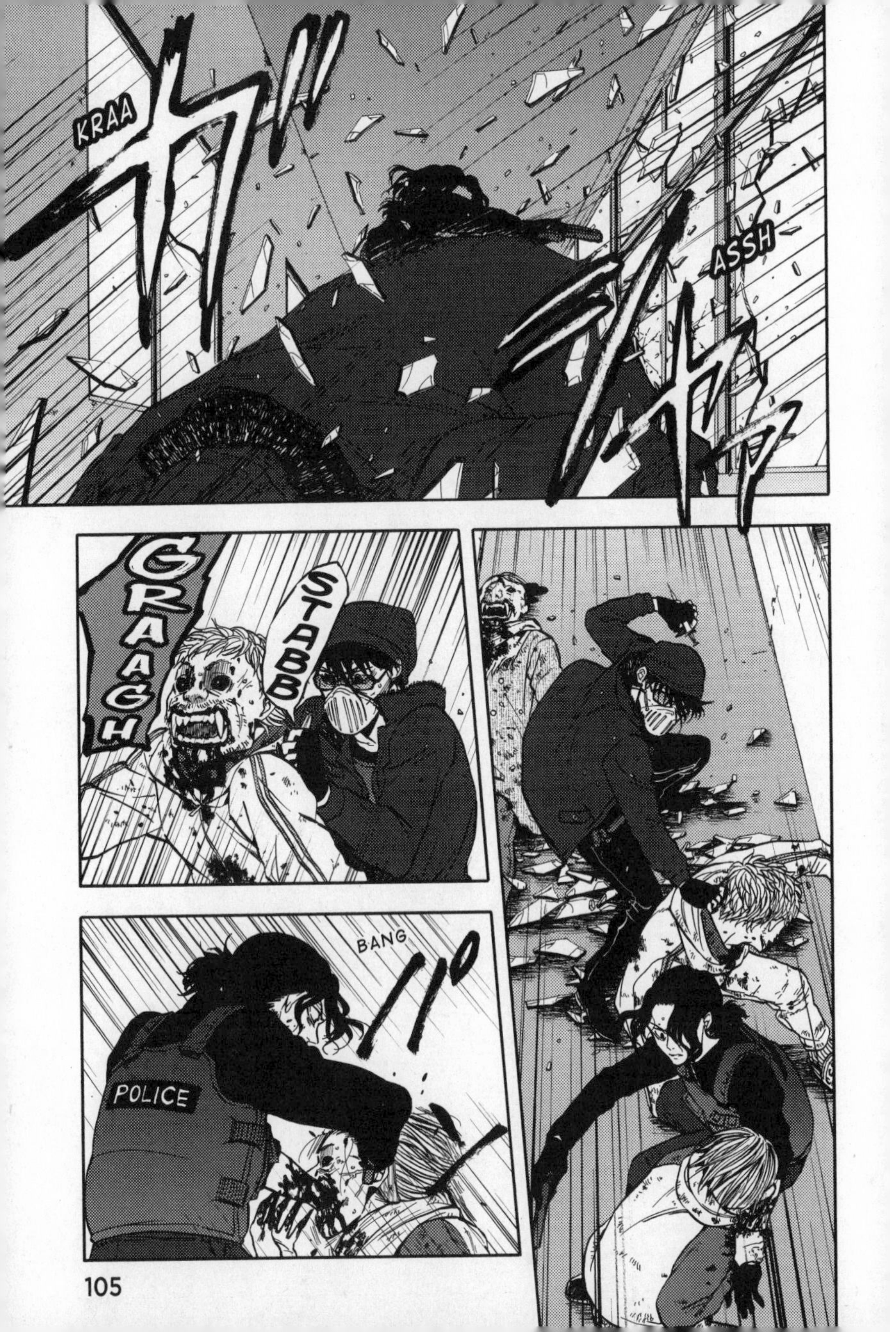
KRAA
ASSH
STABB
GRAAGH
BANG
POLICE

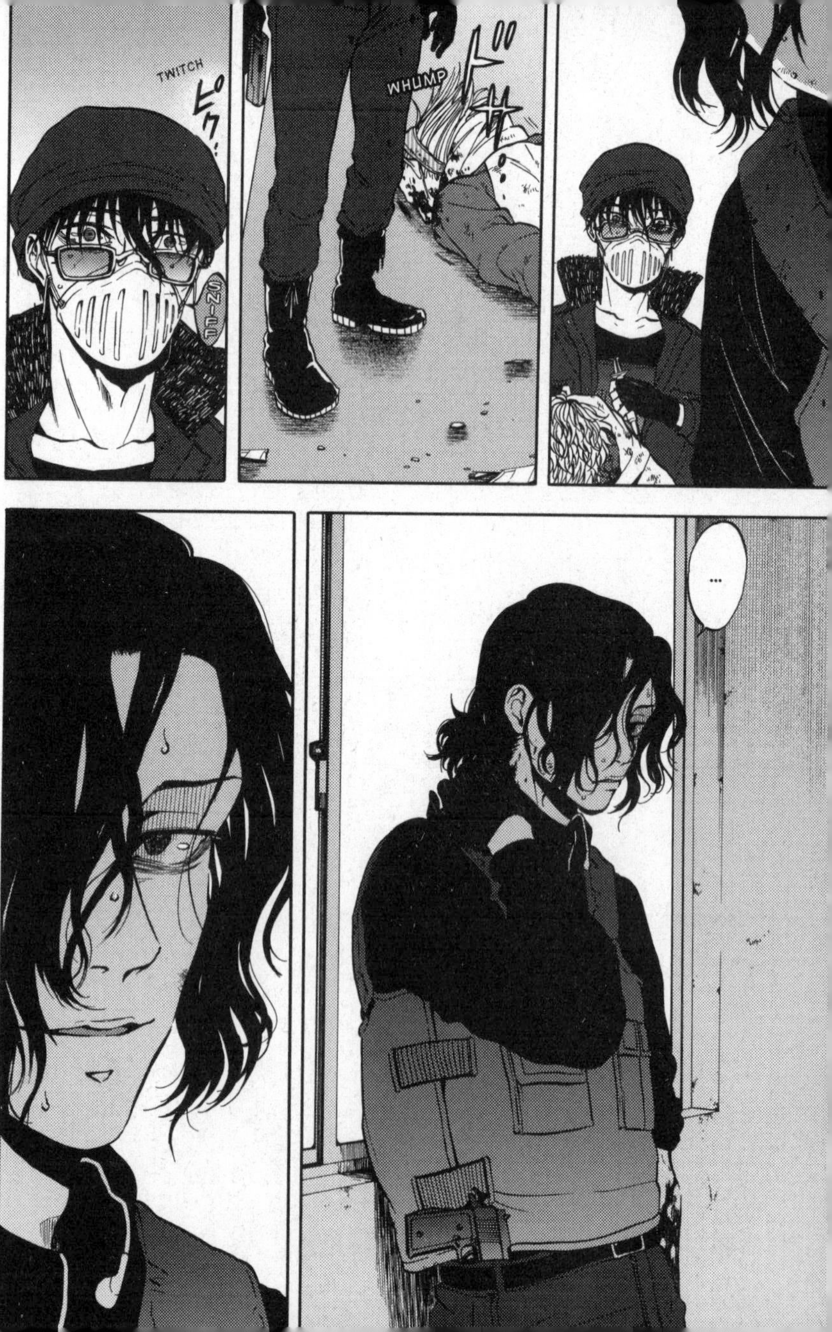
WHUMP
TWITCH
SNIFF
...

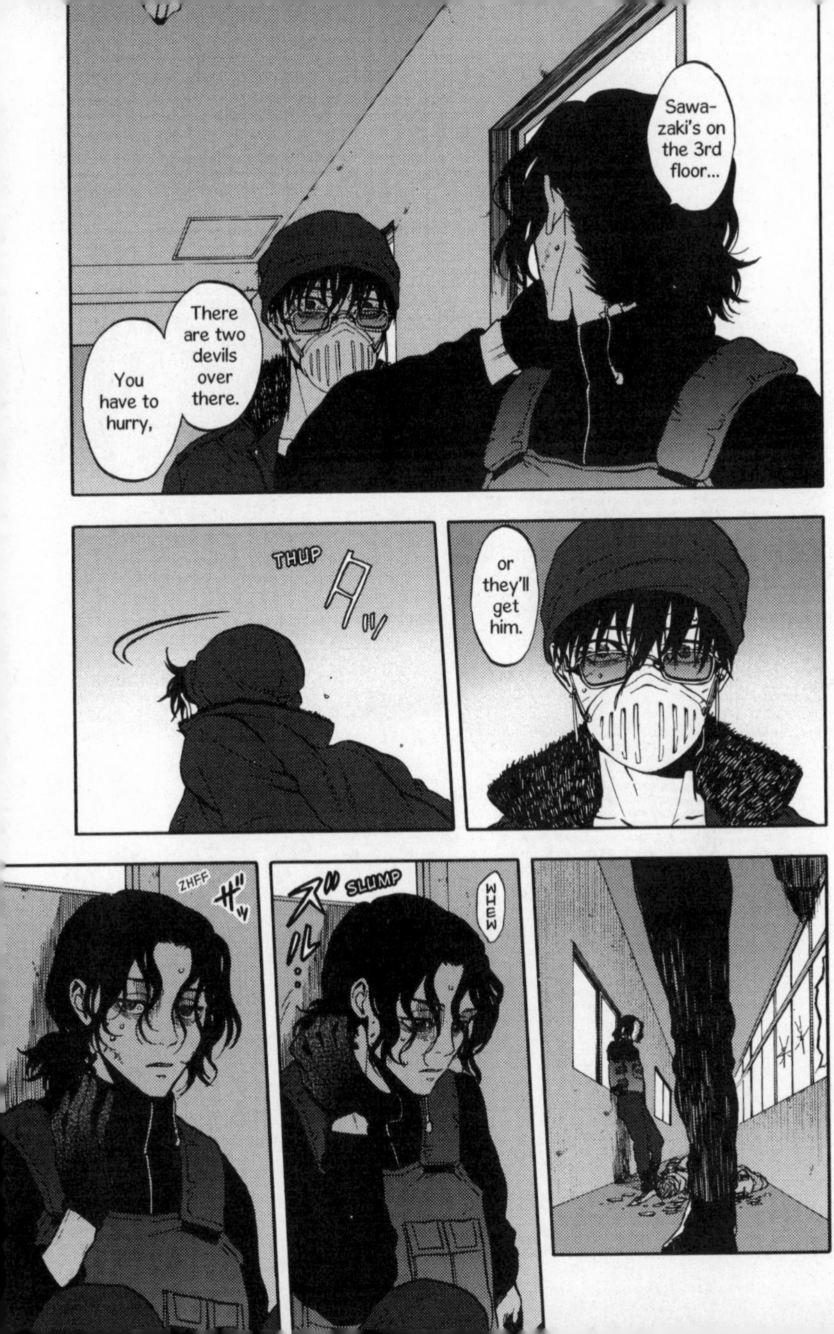
Sawa-zaki's on the 3rd floor...
There are two devils over there.
You have to hurry,
or they'll get him.
THUP
WHEW
SLUMP
ZHFF

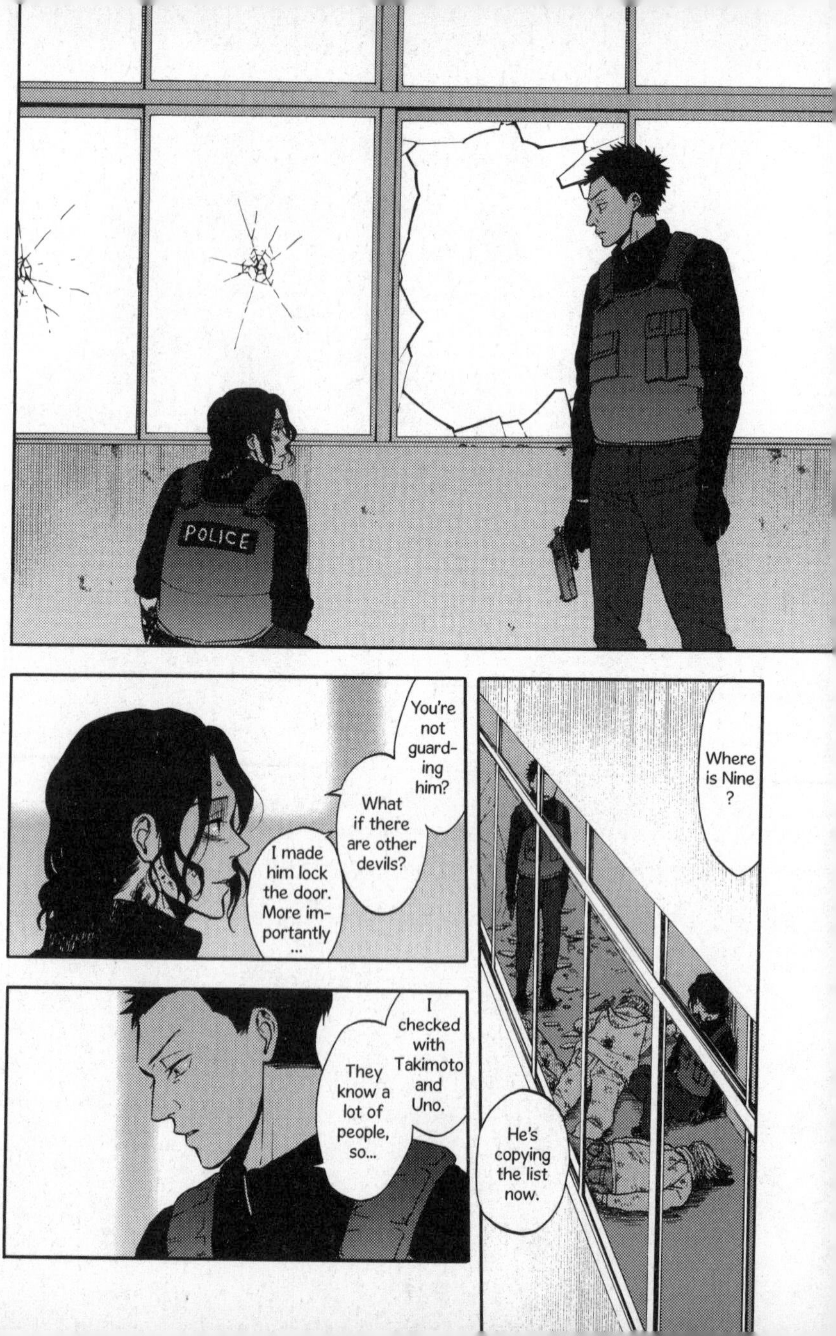
POLICE
Where is Nine?
He's copying the list now.
You're not guarding him? What if there are other devils?
I made him lock the door. More importantly...
I checked with Takimoto and Uno.
They know a lot of people, so...

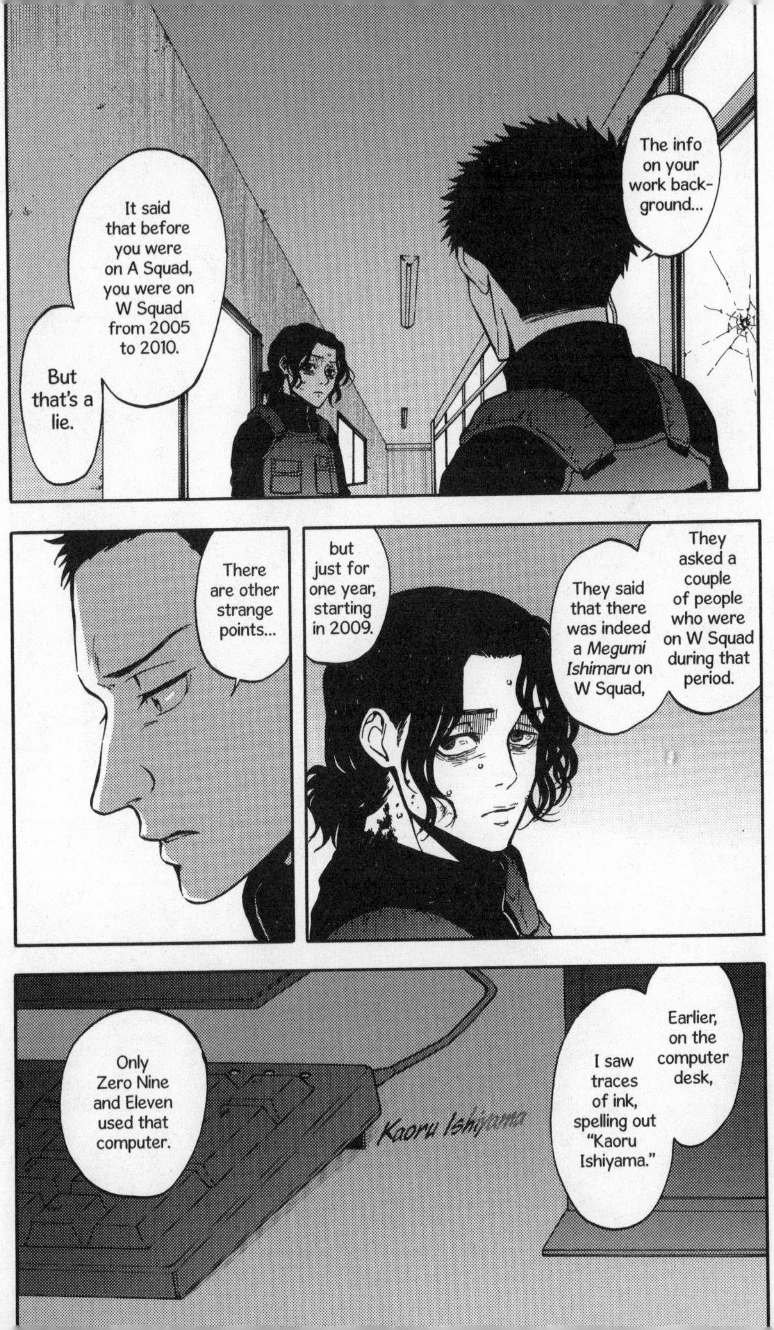
The info on your work back-ground...
It said that before you were on A Squad, you were on W Squad from 2005 to 2010.
But that's a lie.
They asked a couple of people who were on W Squad during that period.
They said that there was indeed a *Megumi Ishimaru* on W Squad,
but just for one year, starting in 2009.
There are other strange points...
Earlier, on the computer desk,
I saw traces of ink, spelling out "Kaoru Ishiyama."
Kaoru Ishiyama
Only Zero Nine and Eleven used that computer.

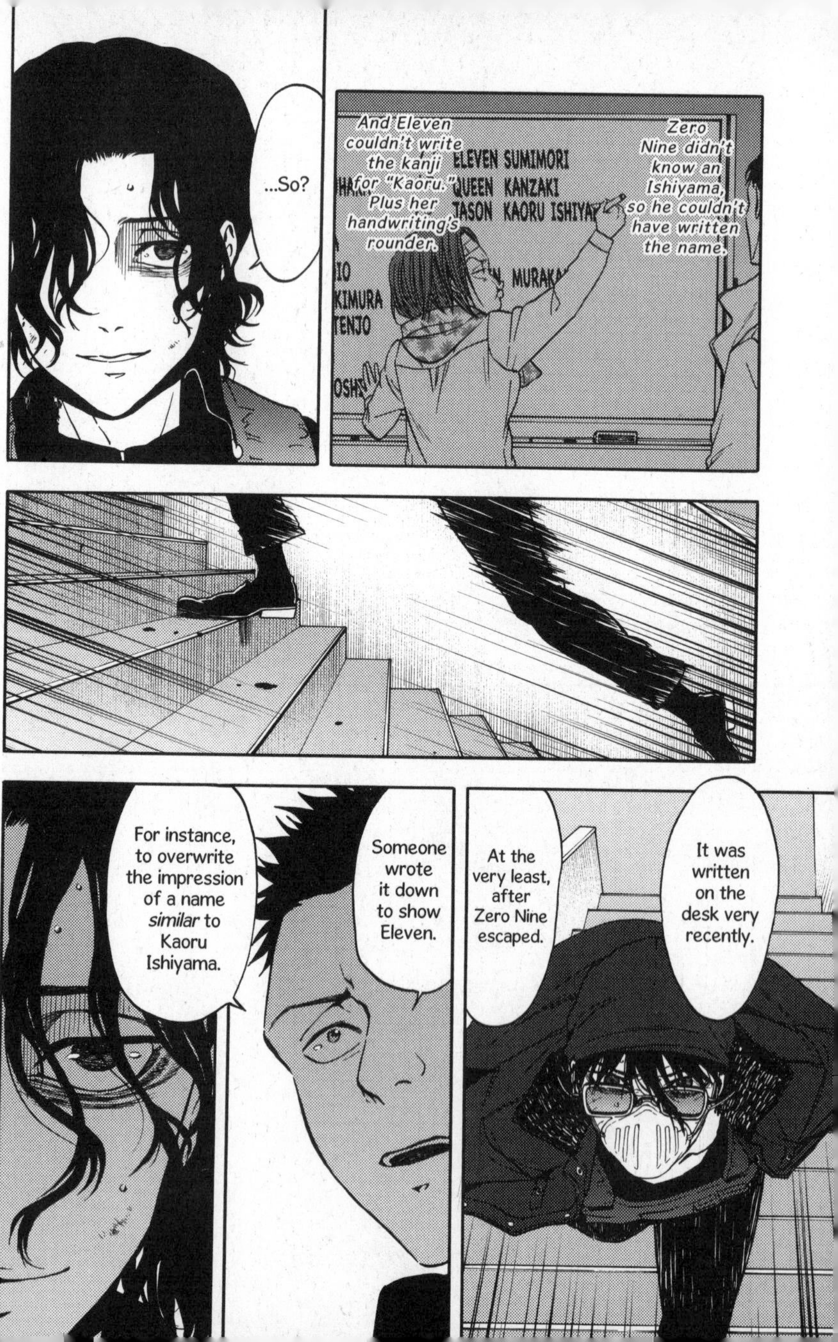
Zero Nine didn't know an Ishiyama, so he couldn't have written the name.
And Eleven couldn't write the kanji for "Kaoru." Plus her handwriting's rounder.
ELEVEN SUMIMORI
QUEEN KANZAKI
TASON KAORU ISHIYA
...So?
It was written on the desk very recently.
At the very least, after Zero Nine escaped.
Someone wrote it down to show Eleven.
For instance, to overwrite the impression of a name *similar* to Kaoru Ishiyama.

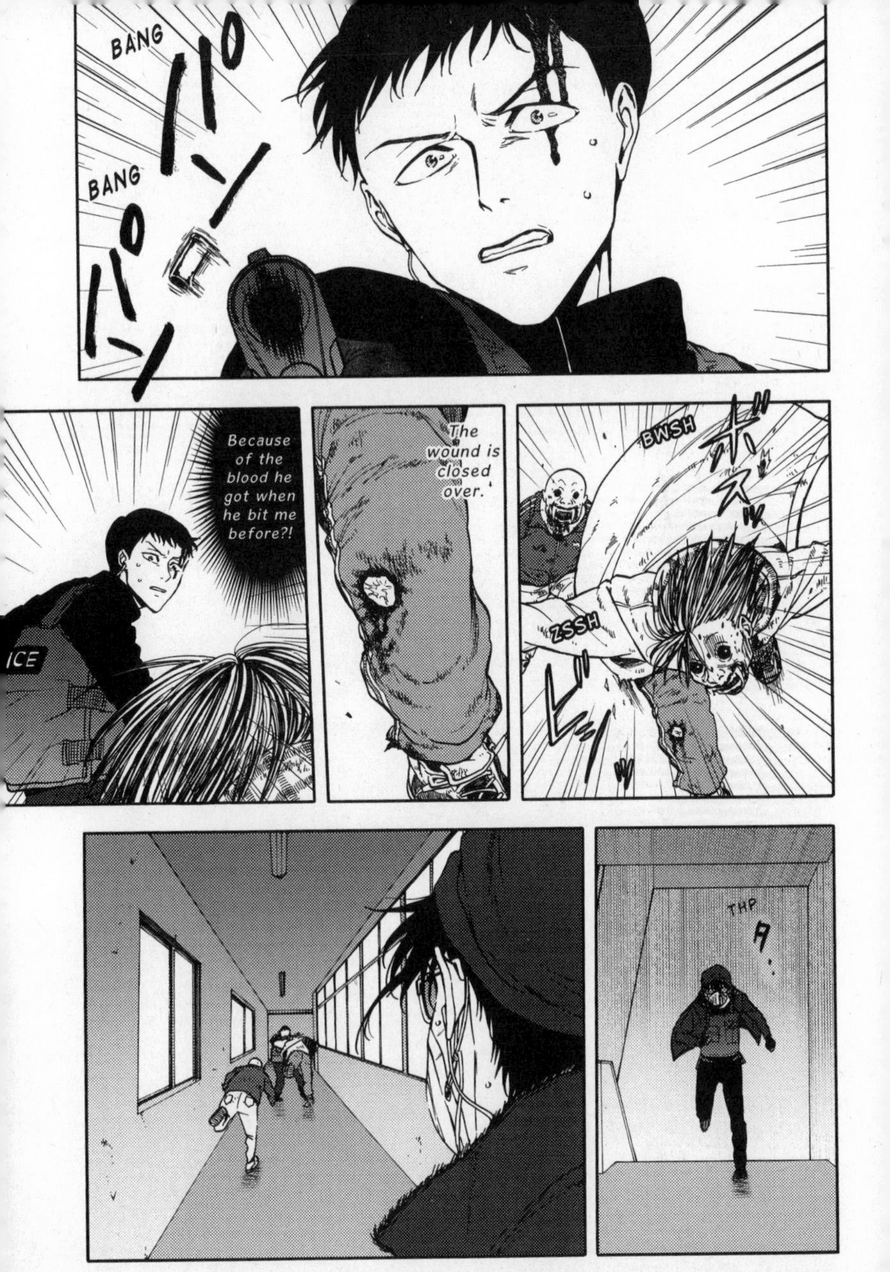
BANG
BANG
BWSH
ZSSH
The wound is closed over.
Because of the blood he got when he bit me before?!
ICE
THP

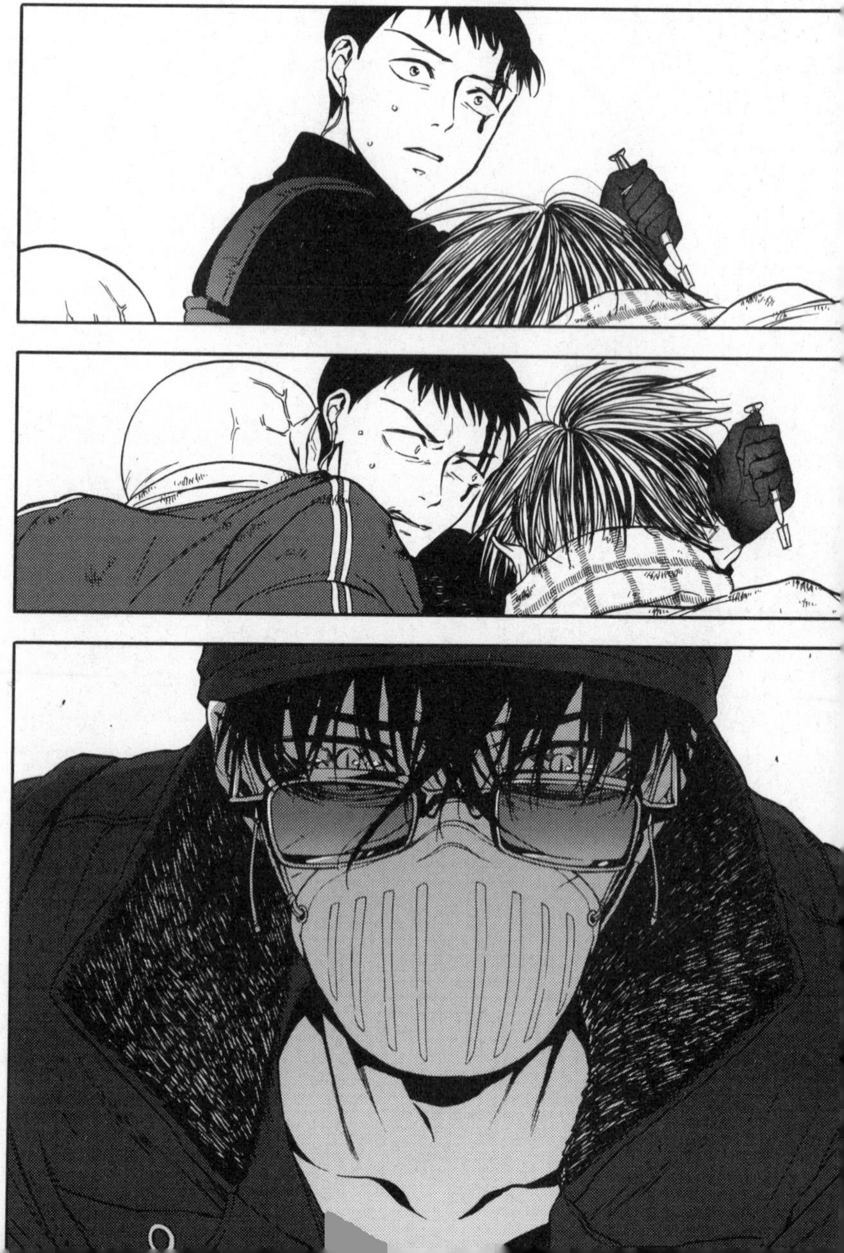

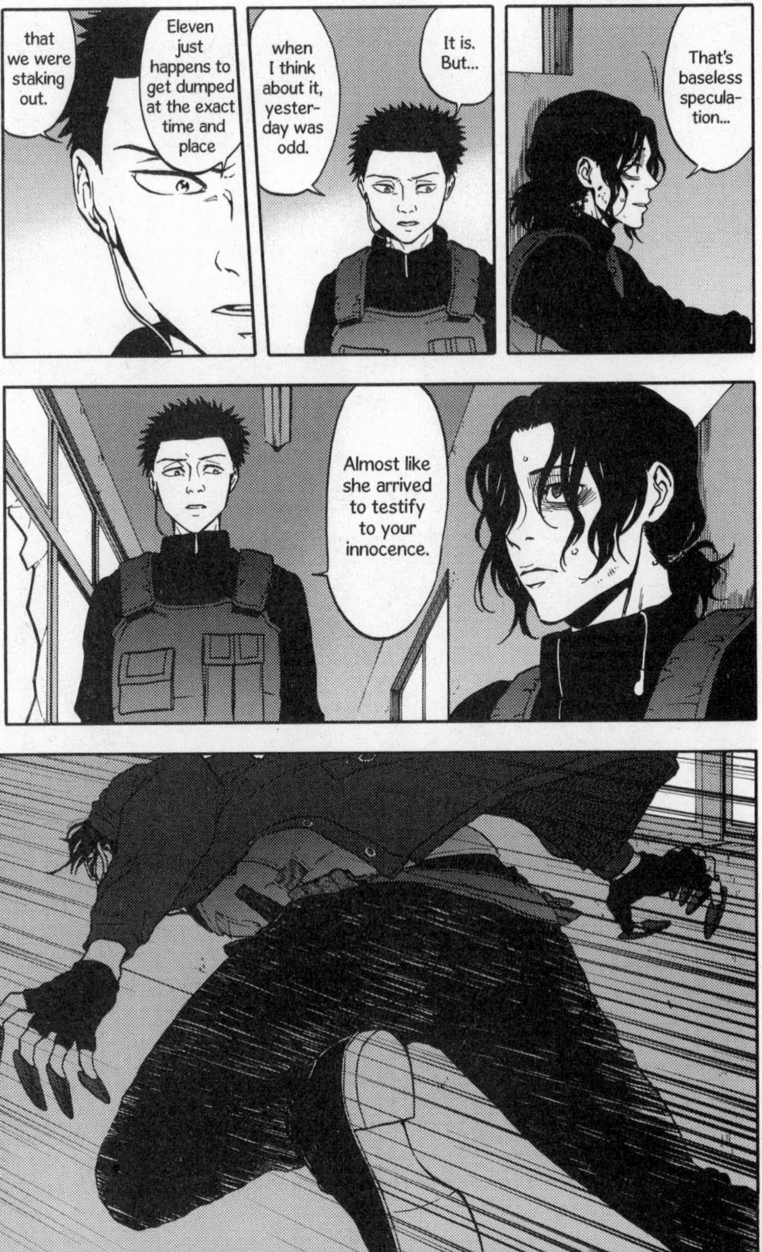
That's baseless speculation...
It is. But...
when I think about it, yesterday was odd.
Eleven just happens to get dumped at the exact time and place
that we were staking out.
Almost like she arrived to testify to your innocence.

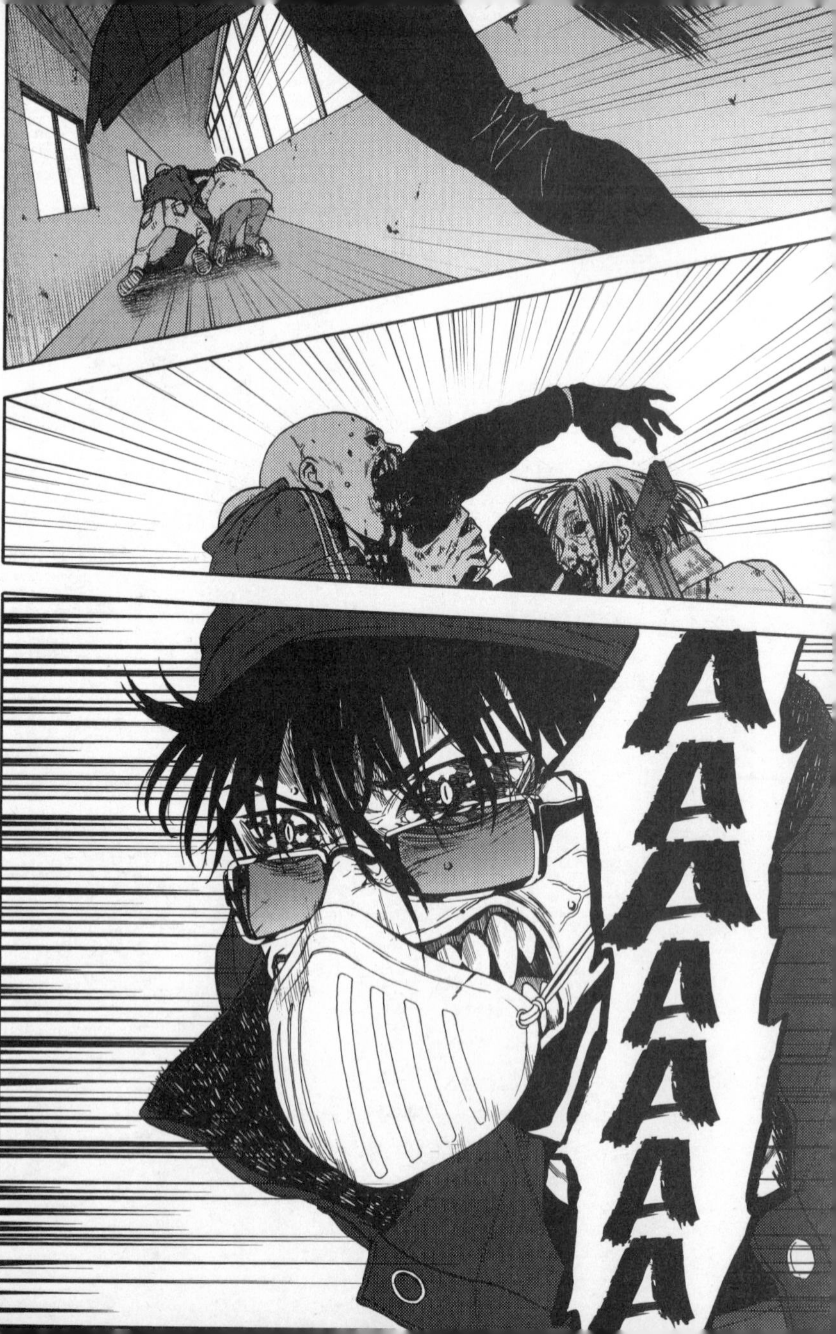
AAAAAAAAA

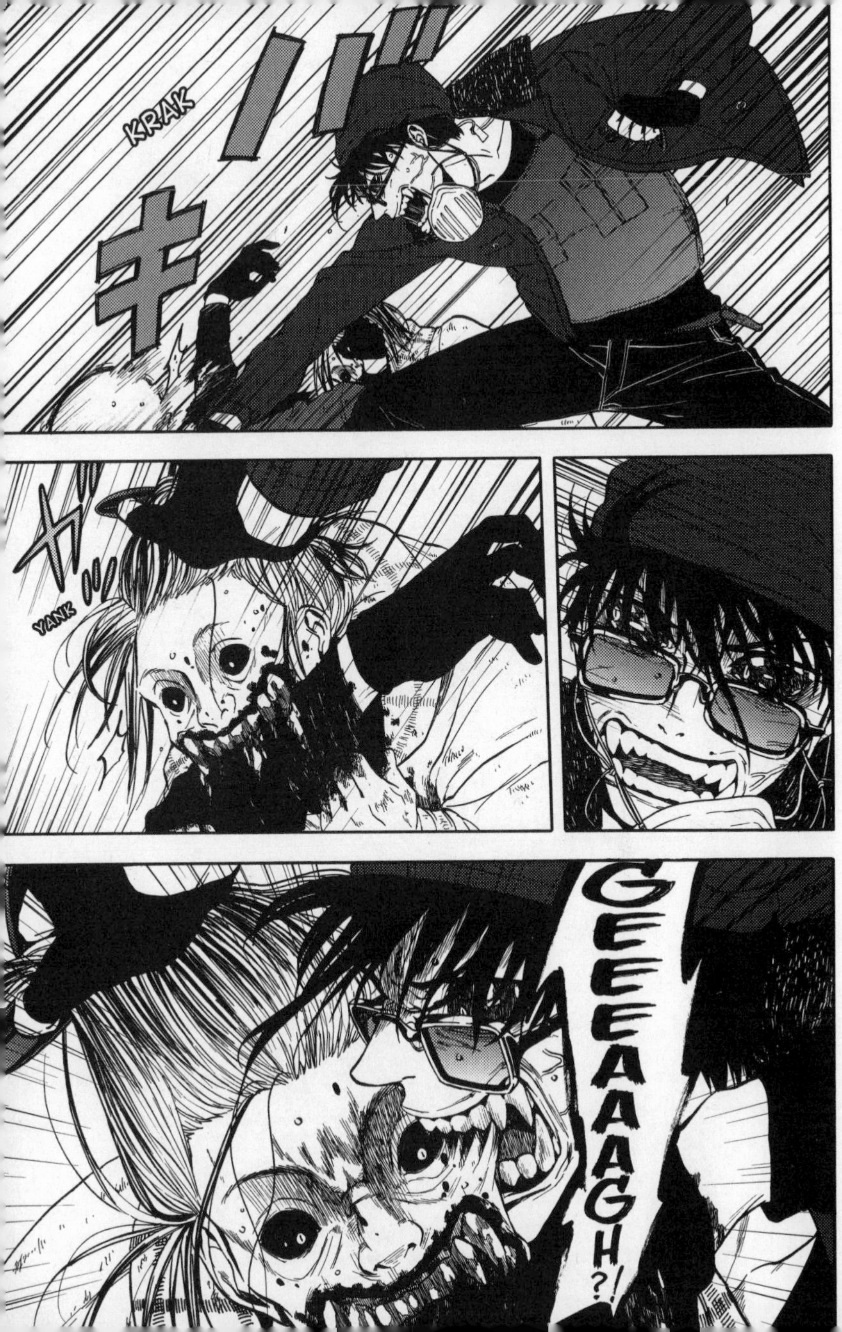
KRAK
YANK
GEEEAAAGH?!

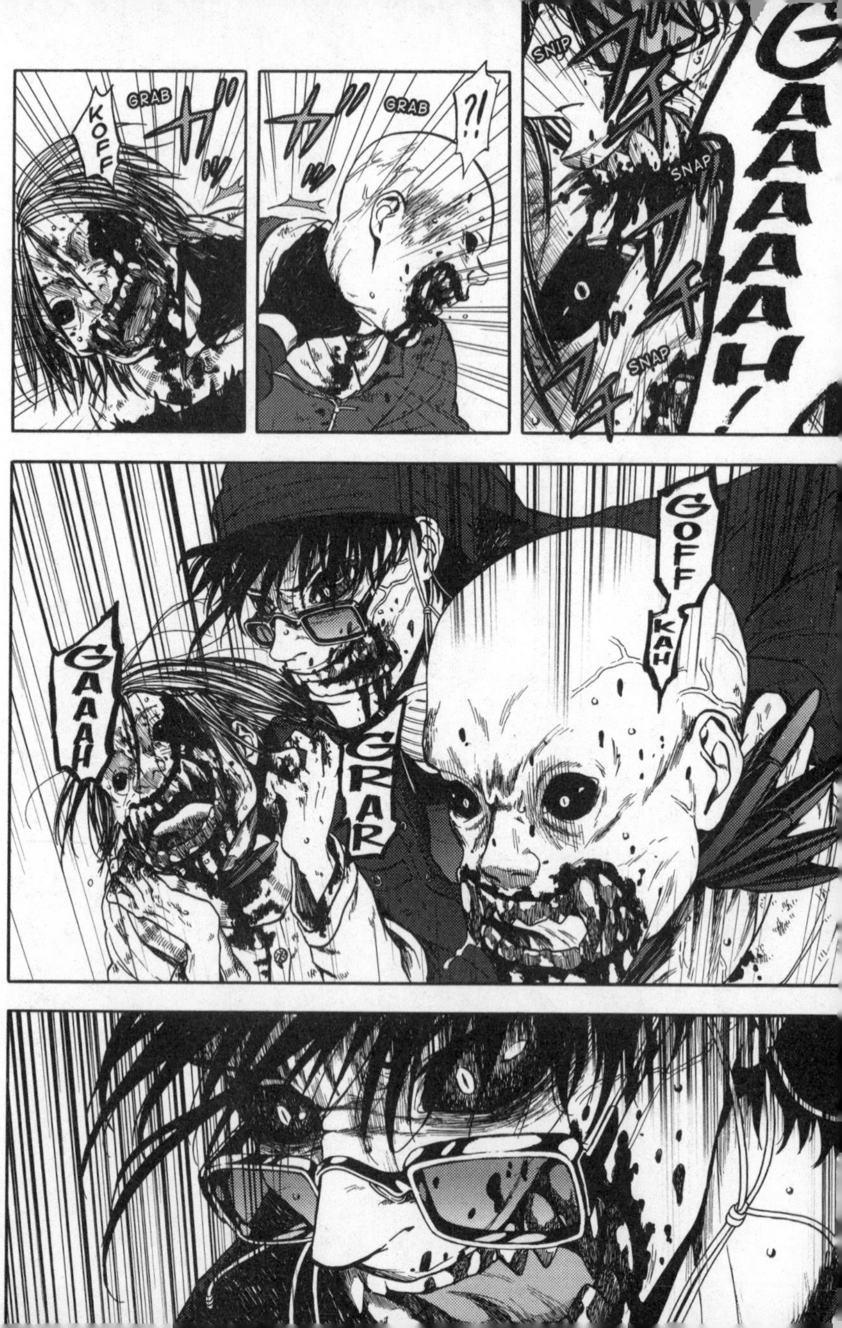
GAAAAAH!
SNIP
SNAP
SNAP
?!
GRAB
GRAB
KOFF
GOFF
KAH
GRAR
GAAAH

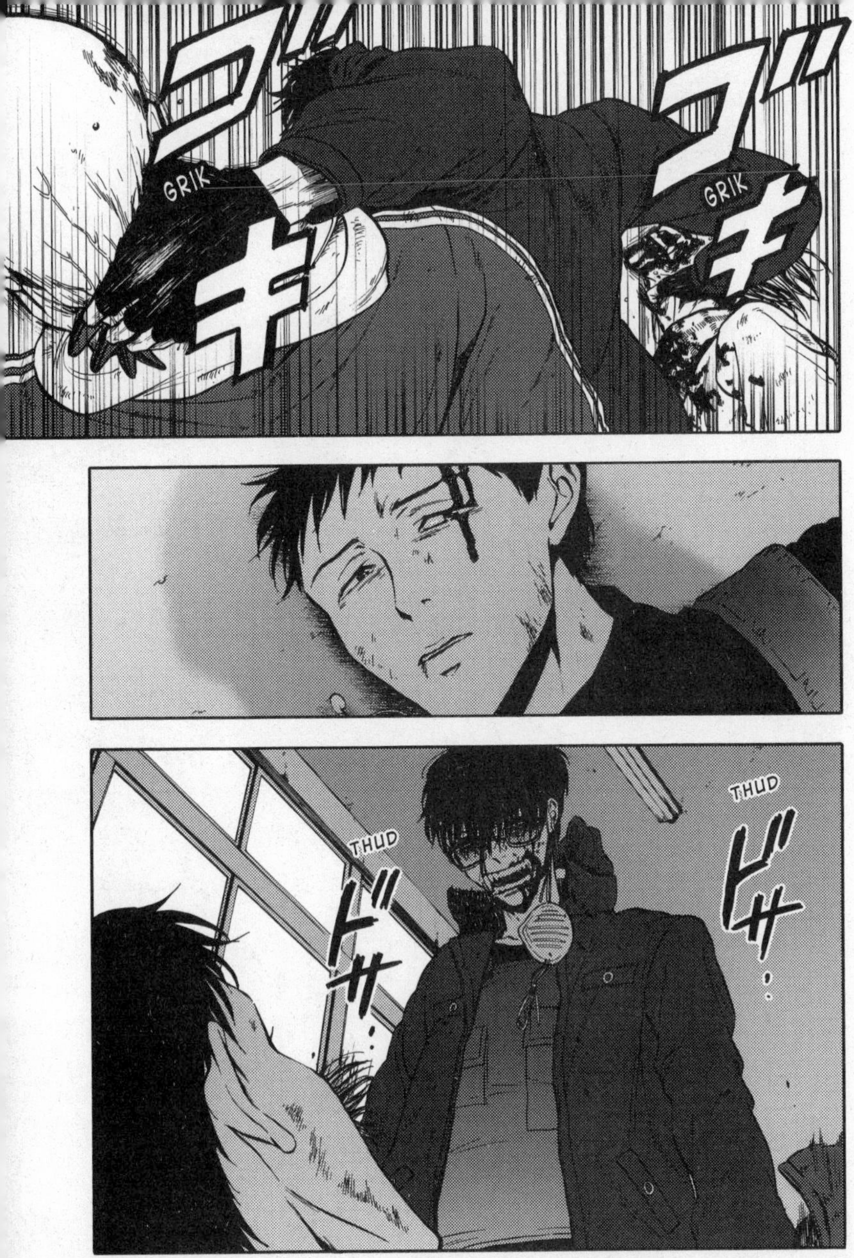
ゴキ
GRIK
GRIK
THUD
ドサ...
THUD
ドサ...

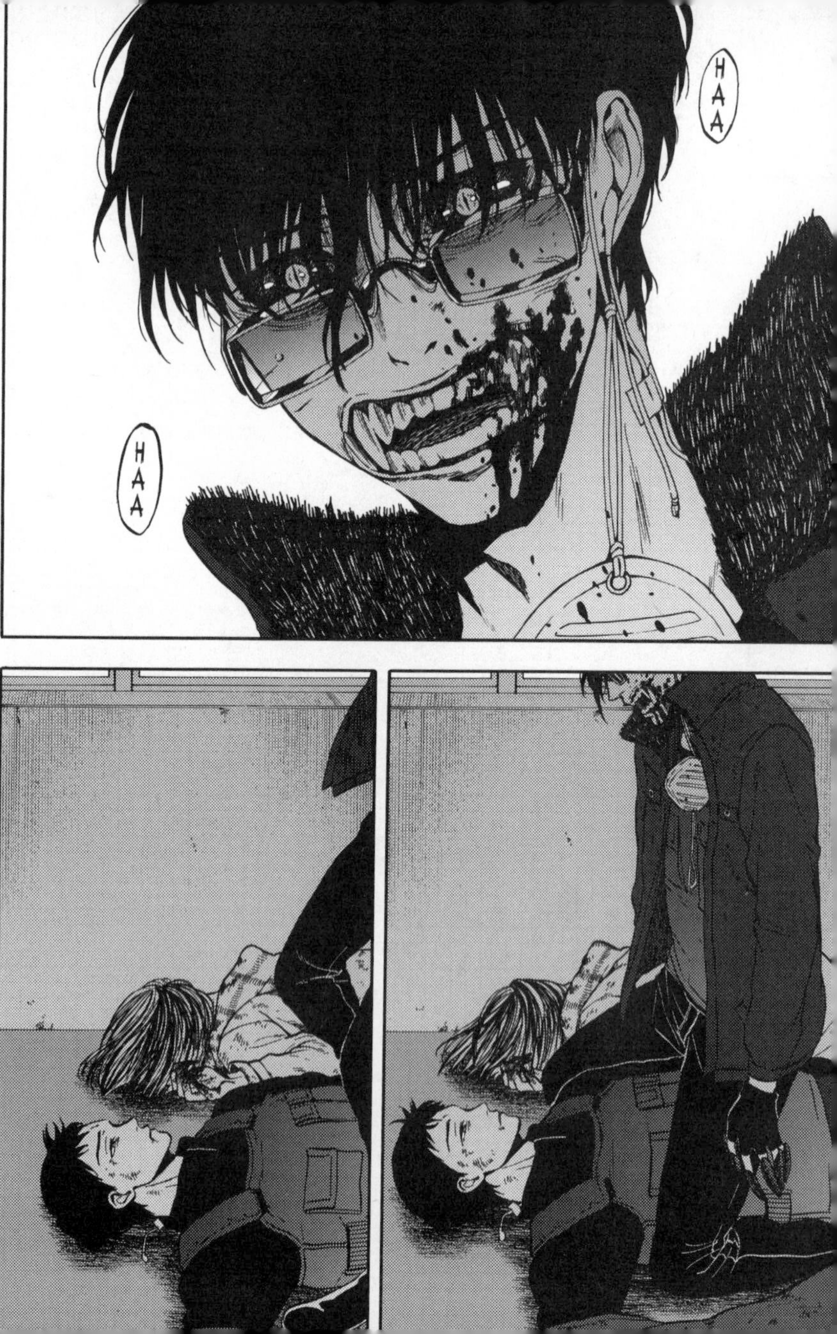
HAA
HAA

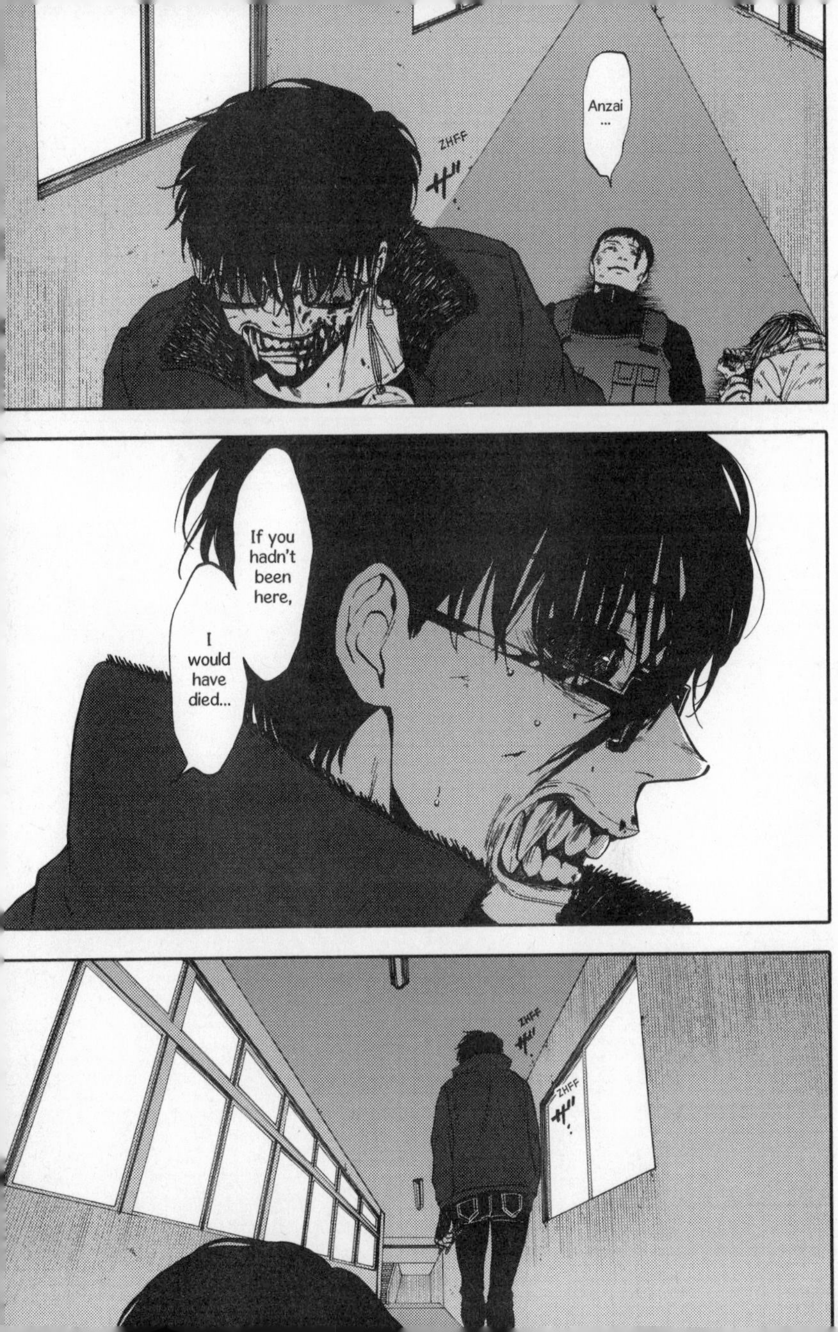
Anzai ...
ZHFF
If you hadn't been here,
I would have died...
ZHFF
ZHFF

"Let's try to avoid any more casualties..."
I should have killed them.
OOO
EEE
OOO
Emergency message for Public Safety Division 5 Squads L through N.
EEE

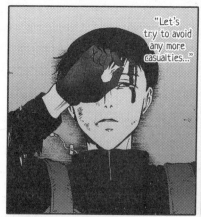

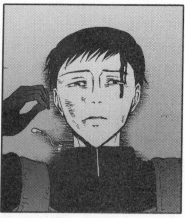

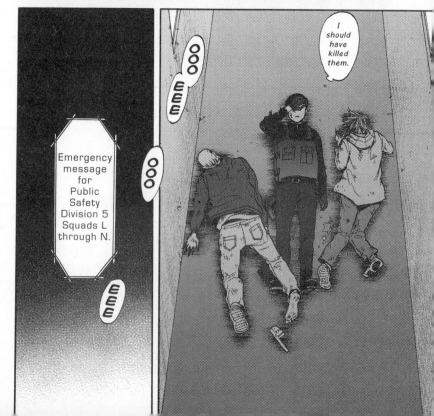

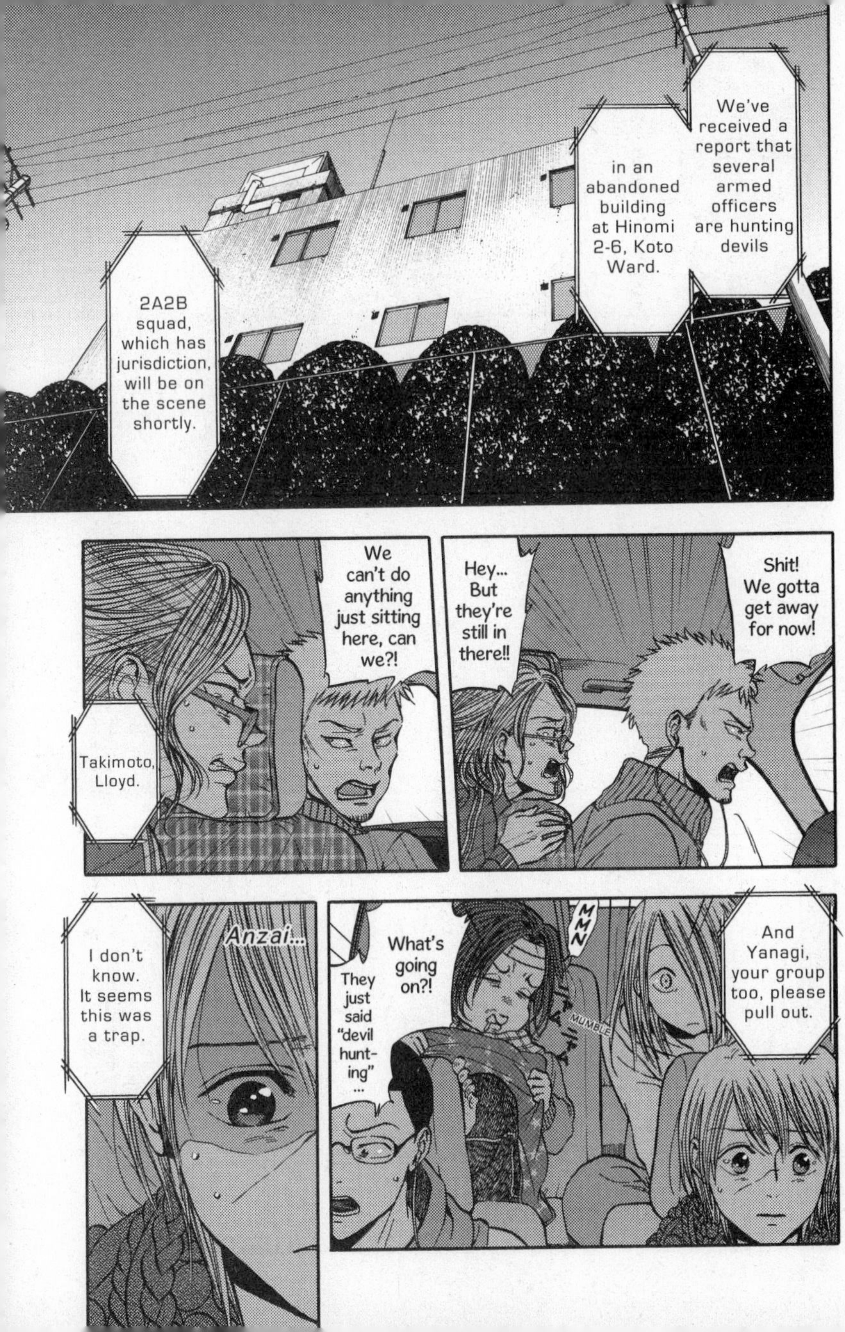
We've received a report that several armed officers are hunting devils
in an abandoned building at Hinomi 2-6, Koto Ward.
2A2B squad, which has jurisdiction, will be on the scene shortly.
Shit! We gotta get away for now!
Hey... But they're still in there!!
We can't do anything just sitting here, can we?!
Takimoto, Lloyd.
And Yanagi, your group too, please pull out.
MMN
MUMBLE
What's going on?!
They just said "devil hunting"...
Anzai...
I don't know. It seems this was a trap.

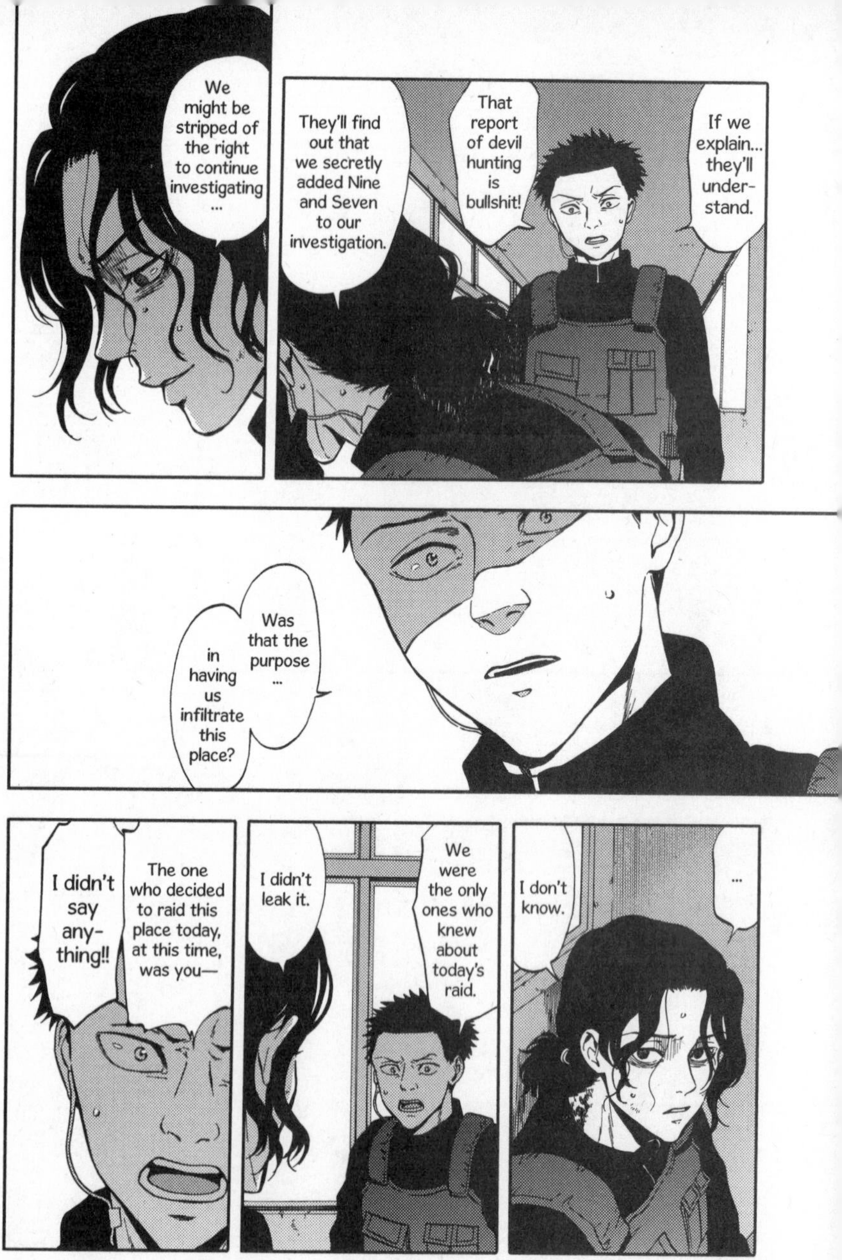
If we explain... they'll under-stand.
That report of devil hunting is bullshit!
They'll find out that we secretly added Nine and Seven to our investigation.
We might be stripped of the right to continue investigating ...
Was that the purpose ...
in having us infiltrate this place?
...
I don't know.
We were the only ones who knew about today's raid.
I didn't leak it.
The one who decided to raid this place today, at this time, was you—
I didn't say any-thing!!

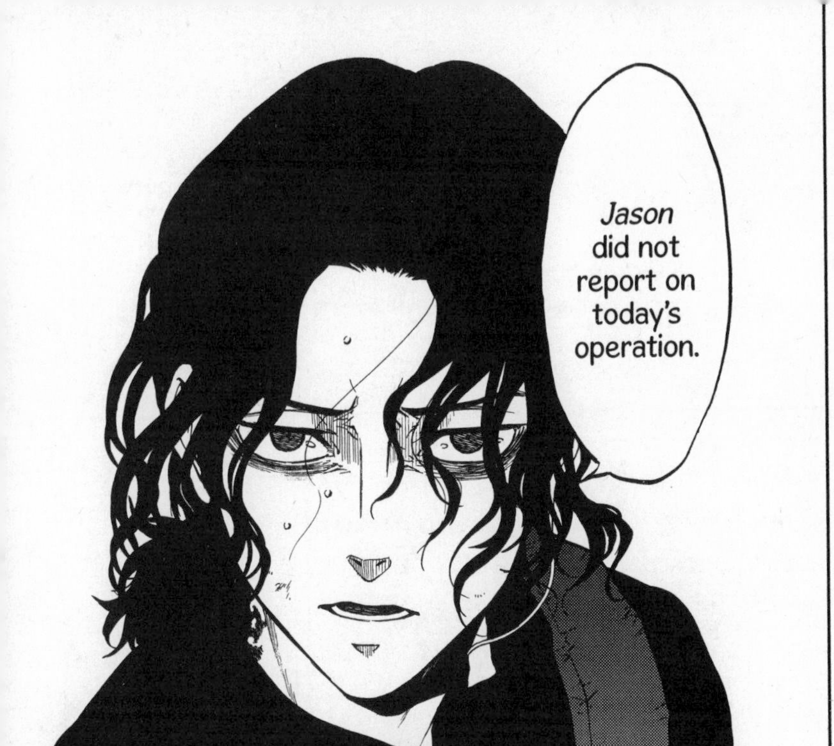
Jason did not report on today's operation.

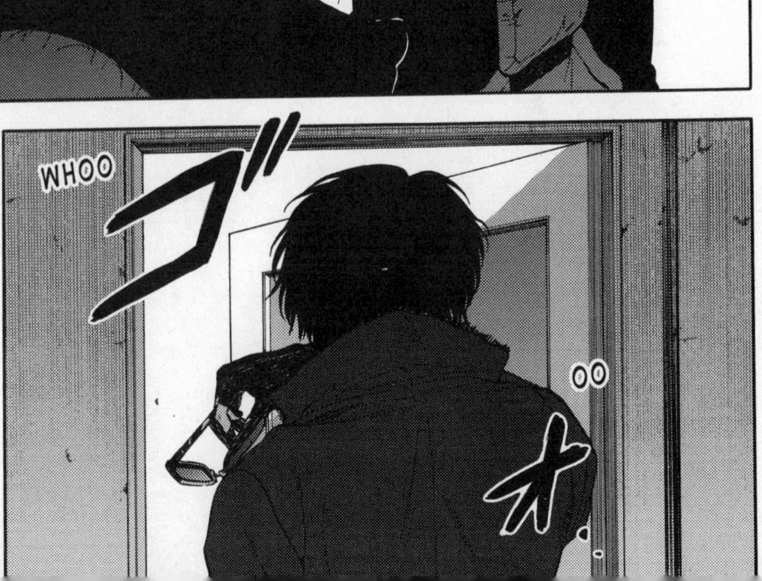
WHOO
ゴ
OO
オ

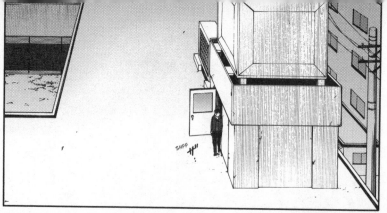

SHFF ﾂﾞ

SLIDE

ズル…

DRIP

DRIP

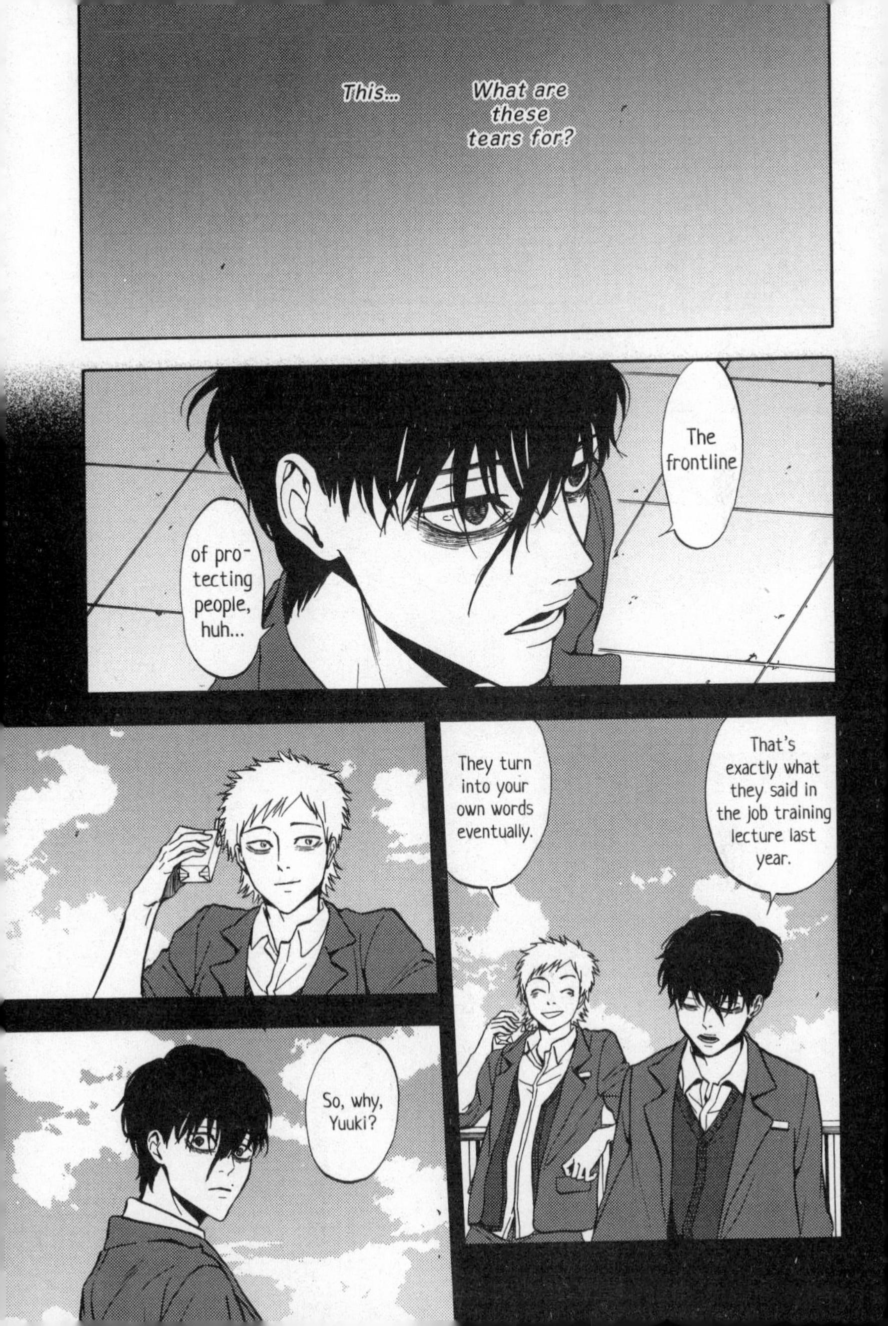
What are these tears for?
This...
The frontline
of protecting people, huh...
That's exactly what they said in the job training lecture last year.
They turn into your own words eventually.
So, why, Yuuki?

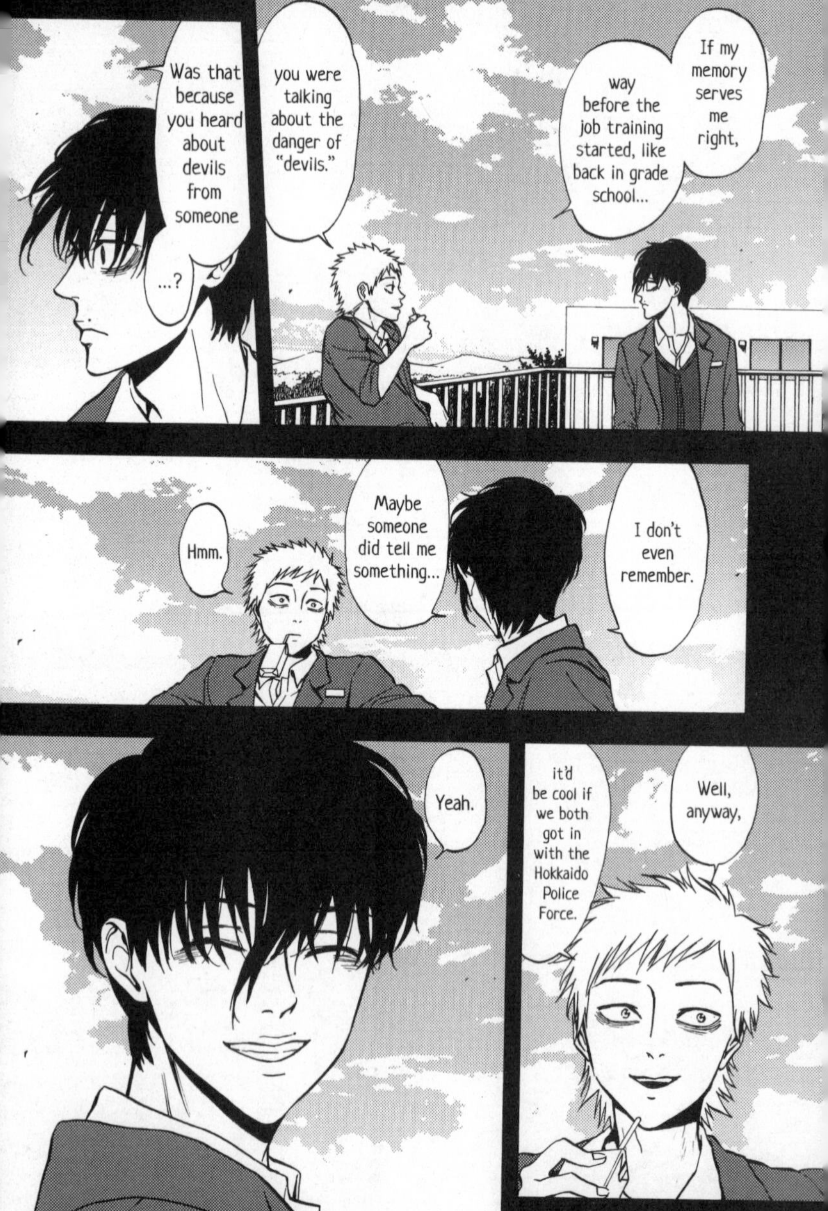
If my memory serves me right,
way before the job training started, like back in grade school...
you were talking about the danger of "devils."
Was that because you heard about devils from someone
...?
I don't even remember.
Maybe someone did tell me something...
Hmm.
Well, anyway,
it'd be cool if we both got in with the Hokkaido Police Force.
Yeah.

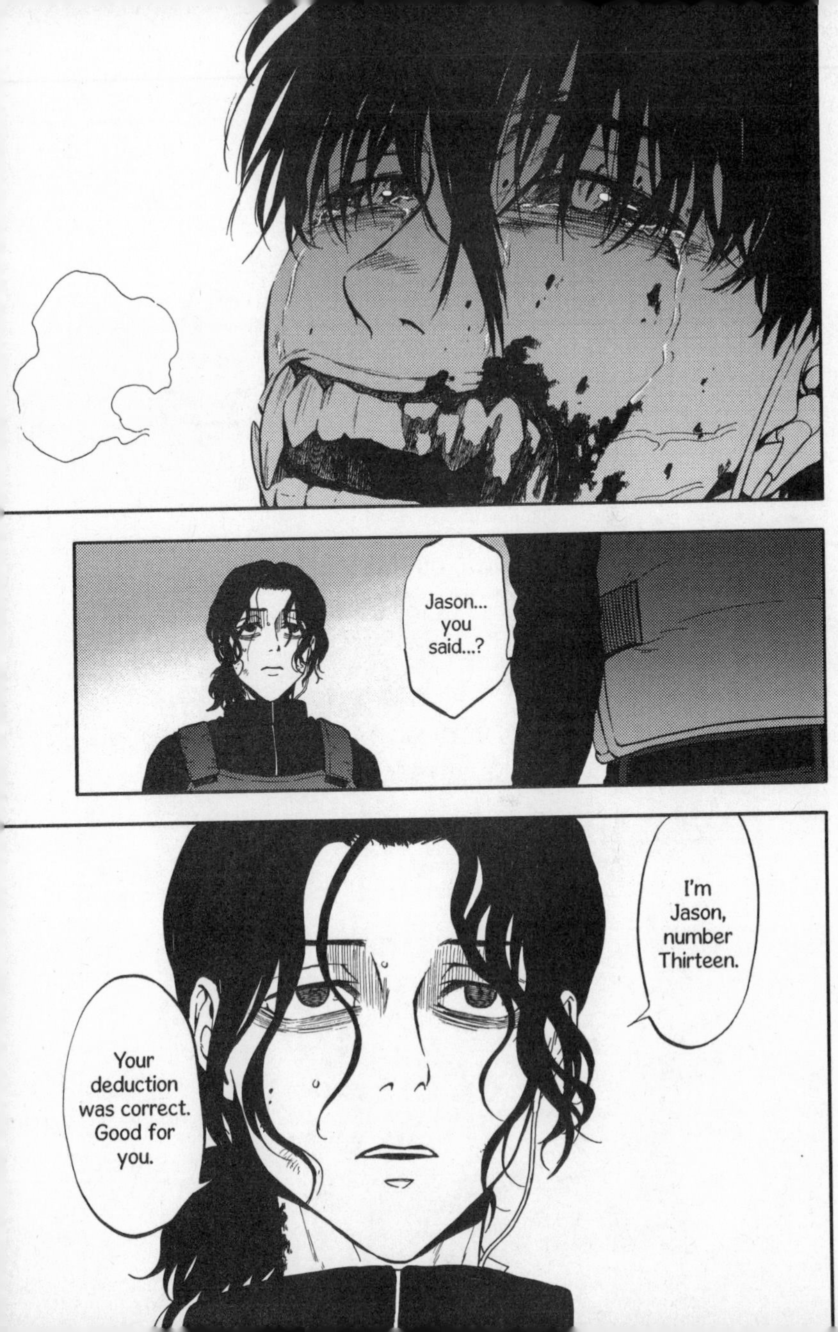
Jason... you said...?
I'm Jason, number Thirteen.
Your deduction was correct. Good for you.

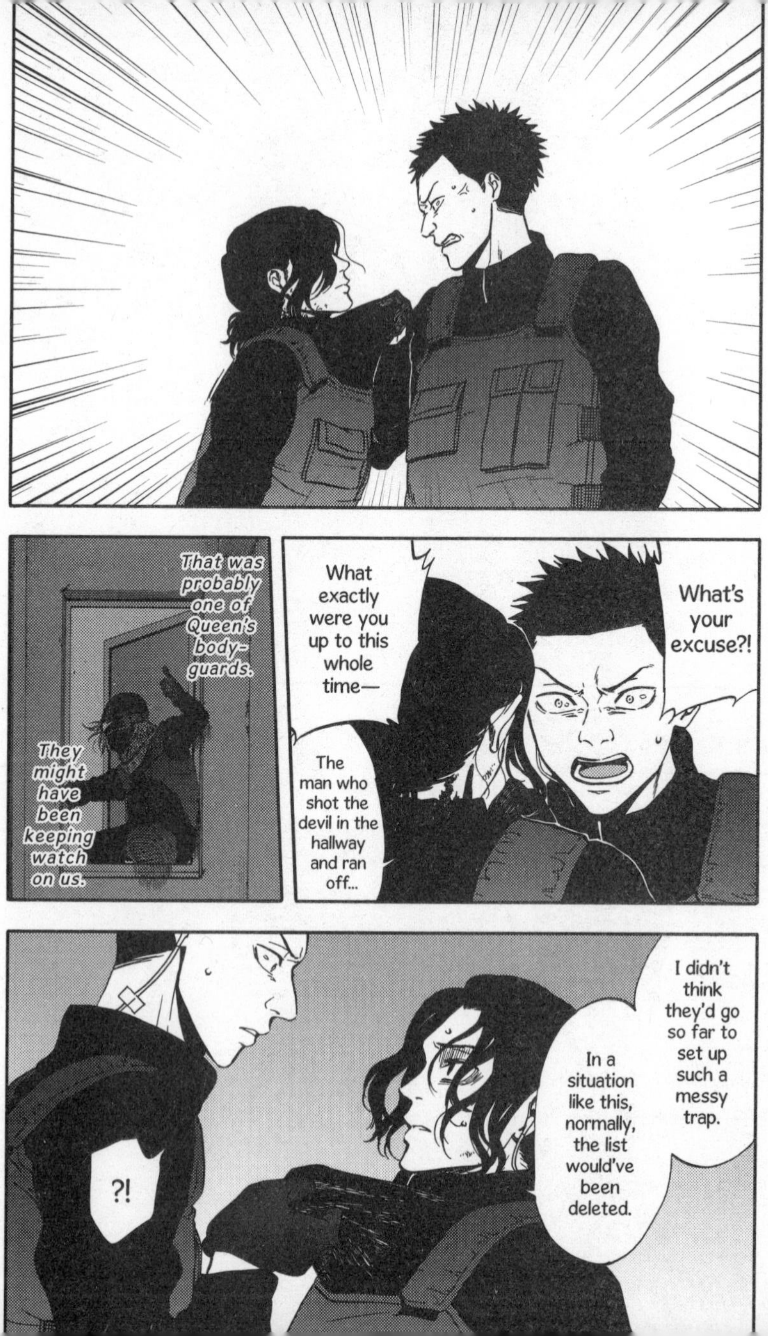

What's your excuse?!
What exactly were you up to this whole time—
The man who shot the devil in the hallway and ran off...
That was probably one of Queen's body-guards.
They might have been keeping watch on us.
I didn't think they'd go so far to set up such a messy trap.
In a situation like this, normally, the list would've been deleted.
?!

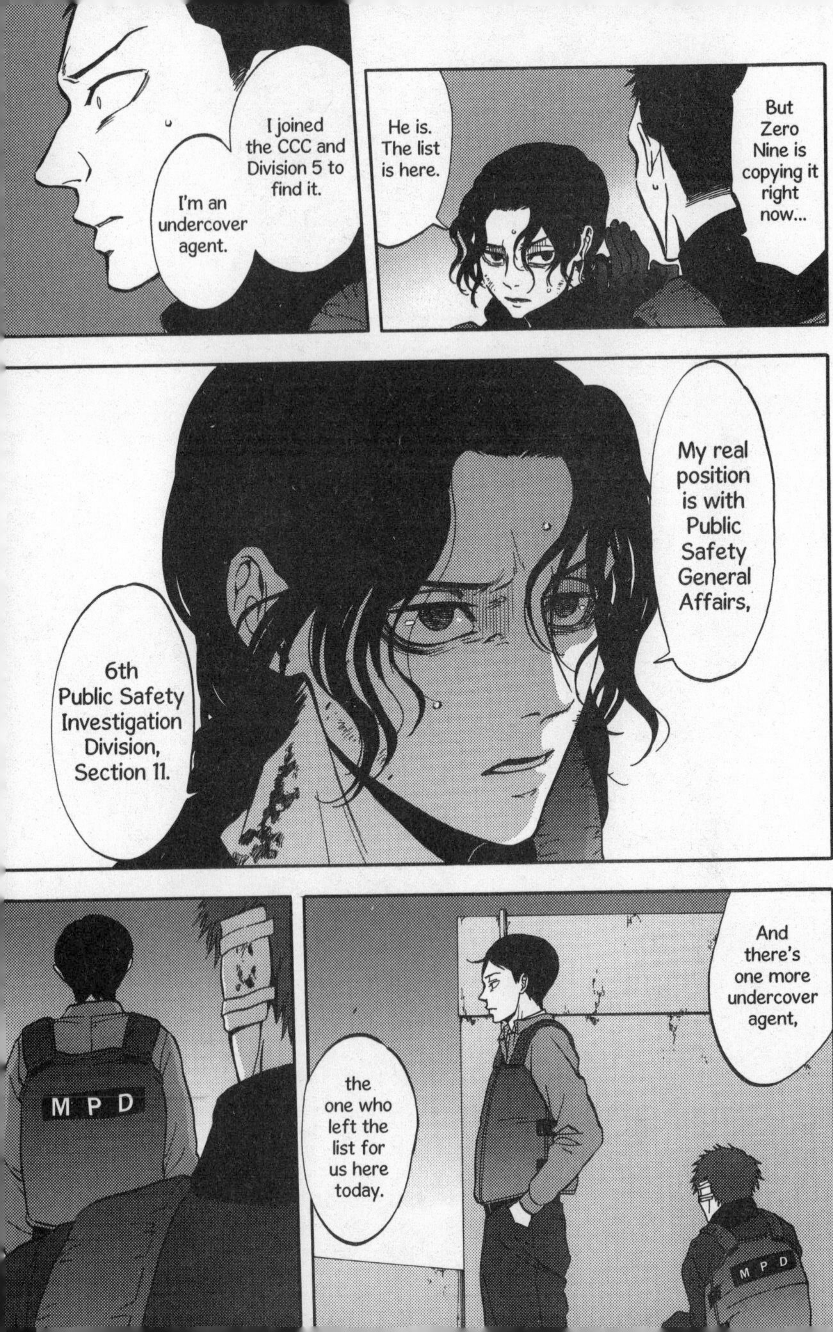

But Zero Nine is copying it right now...
He is. The list is here.
I joined the CCC and Division 5 to find it.
I'm an undercover agent.
My real position is with Public Safety General Affairs,
6th Public Safety Investigation Division, Section 11.
And there's one more undercover agent,
the one who left the list for us here today.
M P D
M P D

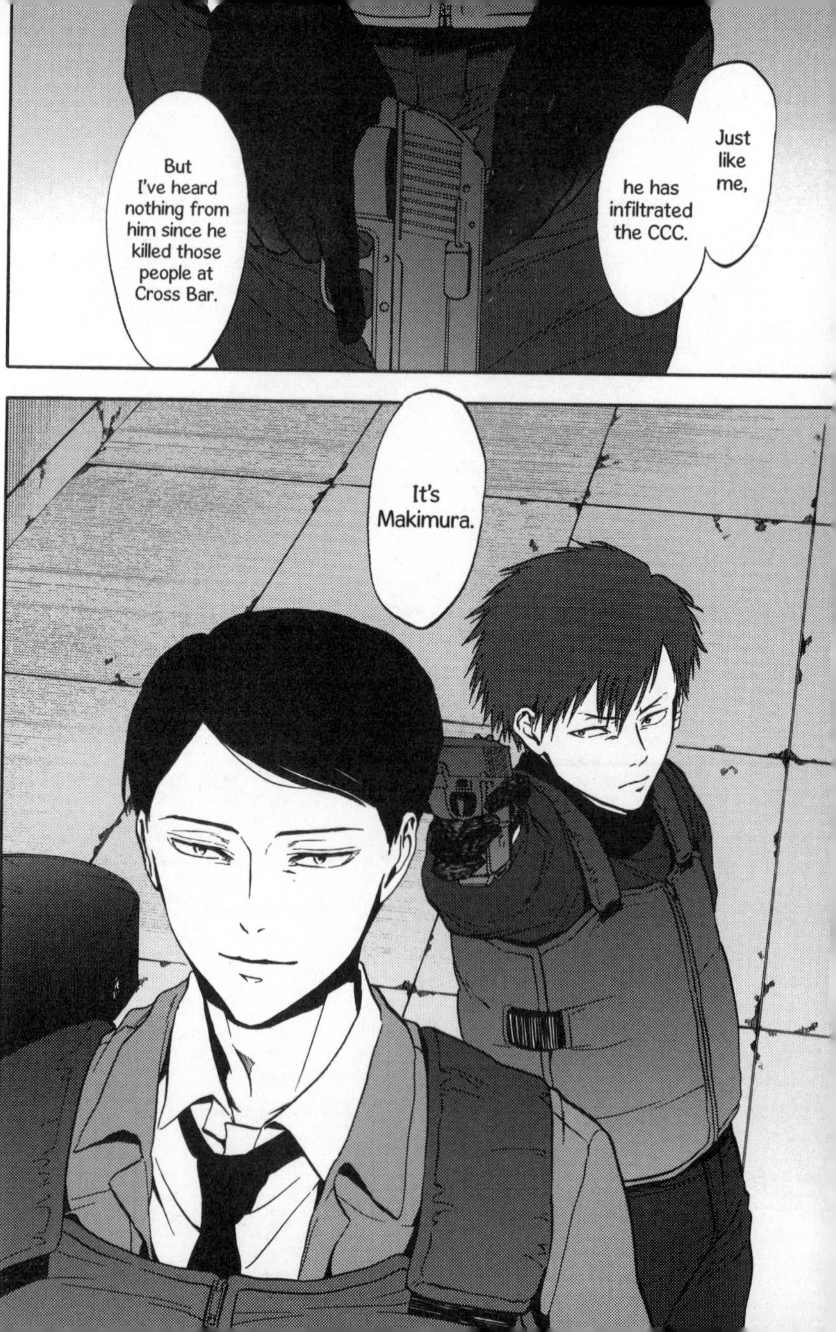
Just like me, he has infiltrated the CCC.
But I've heard nothing from him since he killed those people at Cross Bar.
It's Makimura.

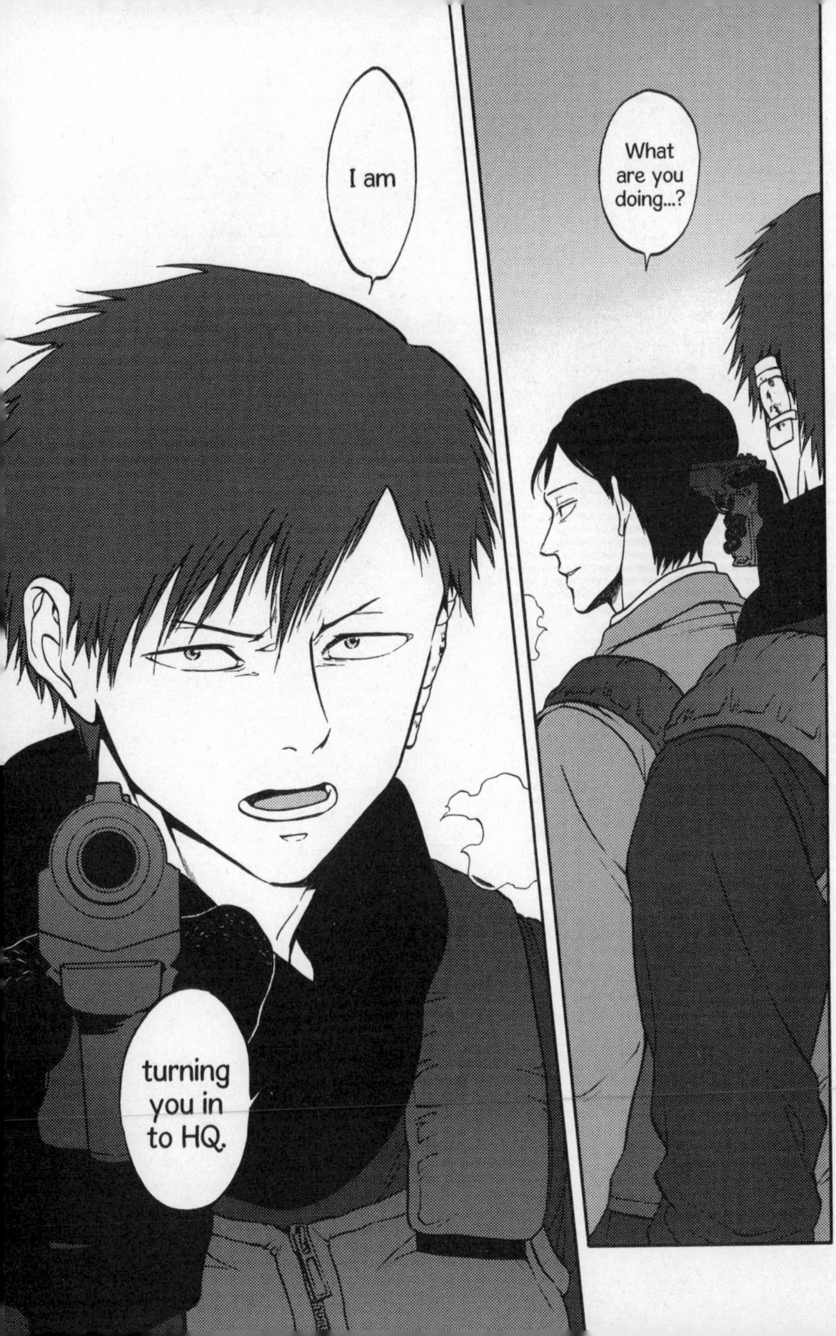
What are you doing...?
I am
turning you in to HQ.

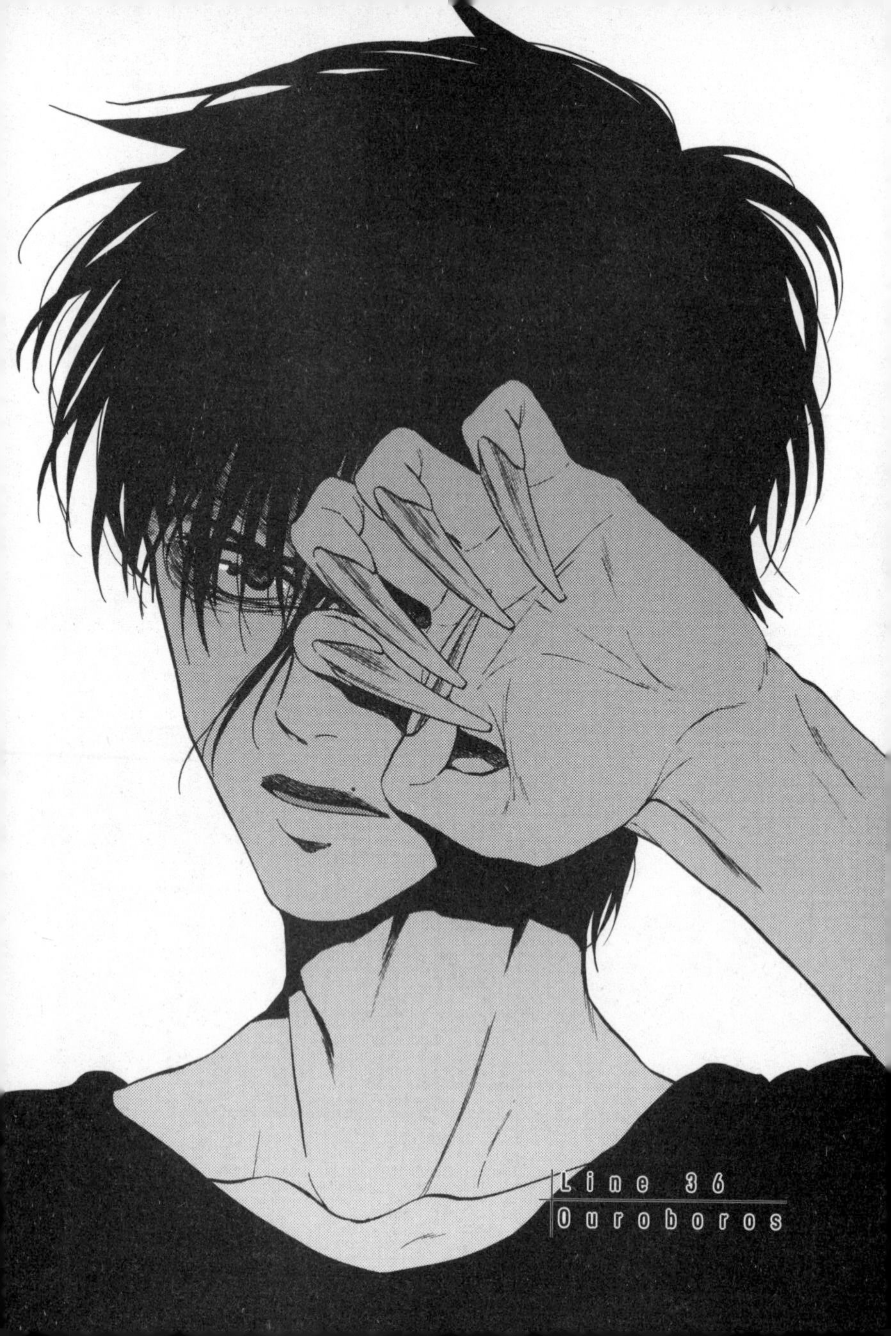
Line 36
Ouroboros

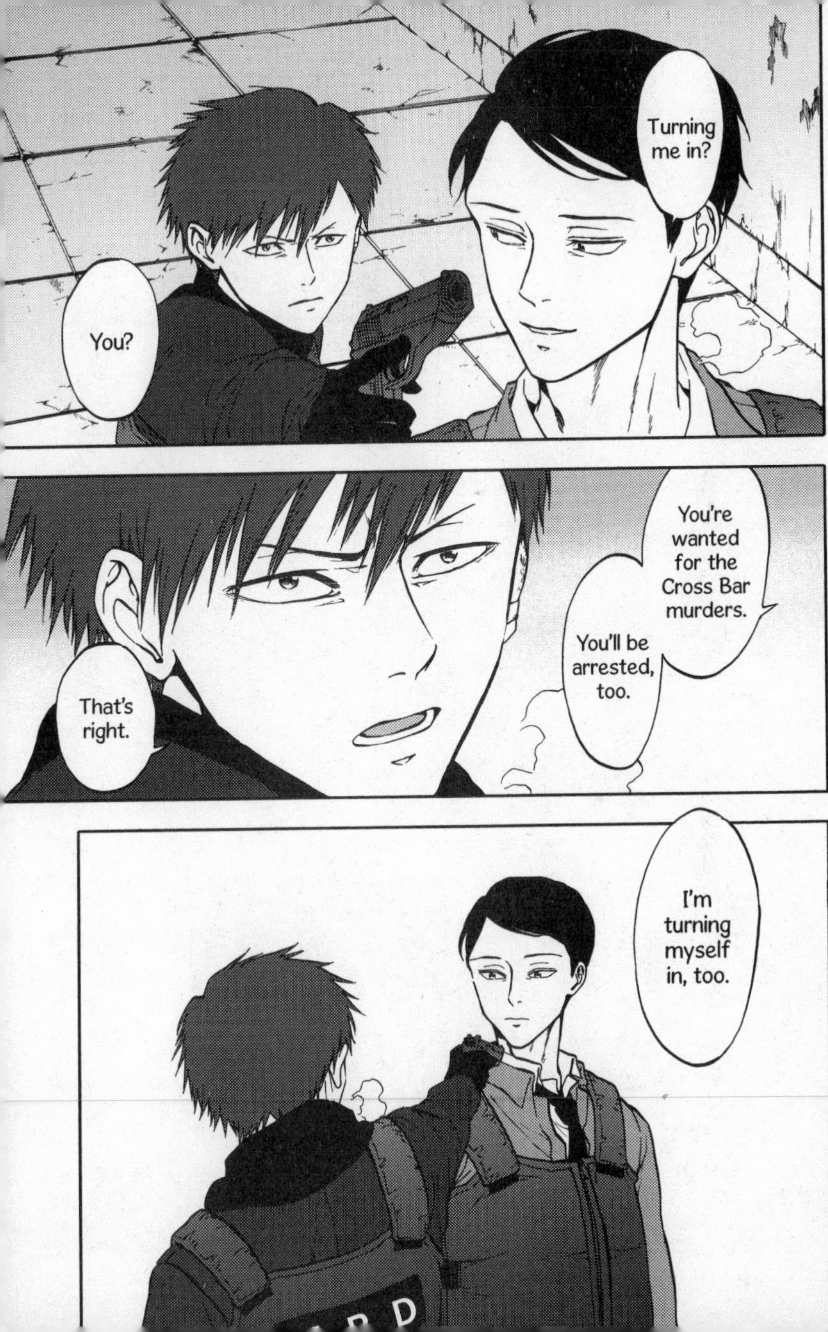
Turning me in?
You?
You're wanted for the Cross Bar murders.
You'll be arrested, too.
That's right.
I'm turning myself in, too.

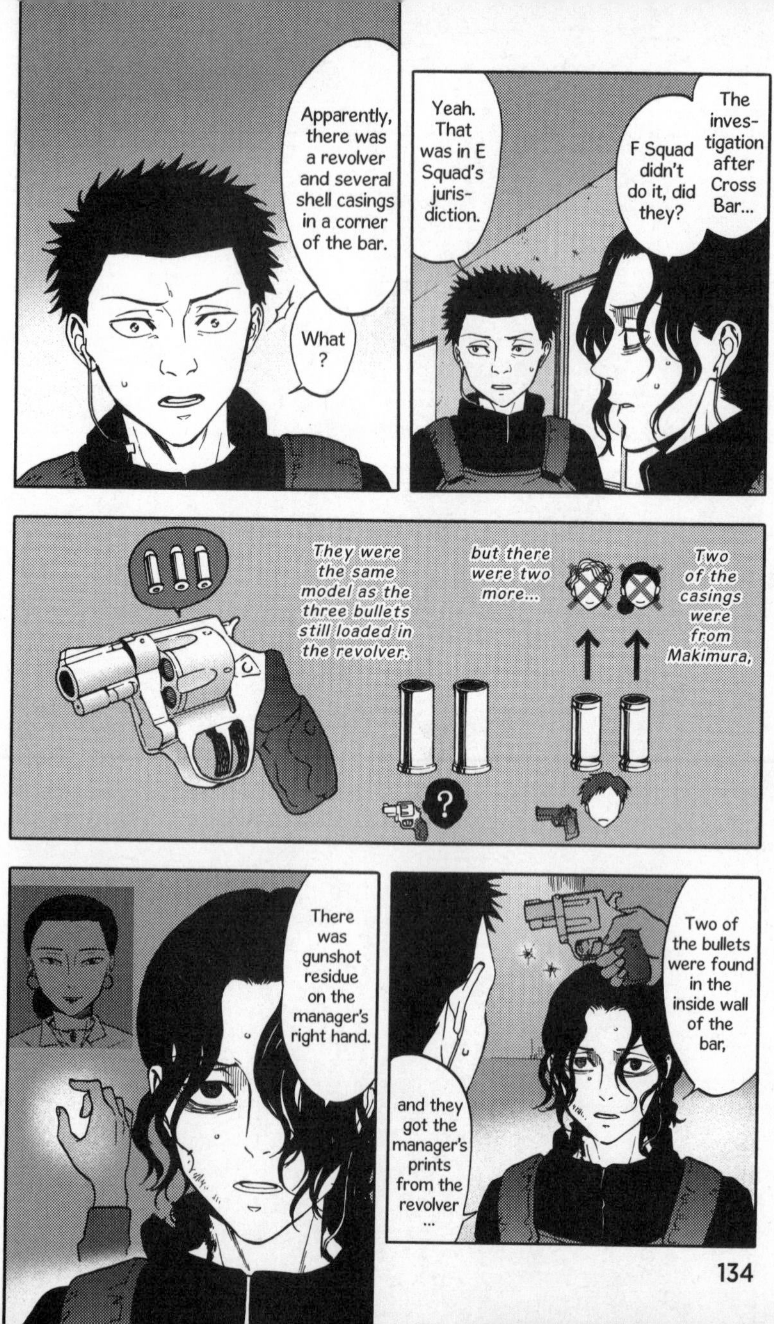
The investigation after Cross Bar...
F Squad didn't do it, did they?
Yeah. That was in E Squad's jurisdiction.
Apparently, there was a revolver and several shell casings in a corner of the bar.
What?
Two of the casings were from Makimura,
but there were two more...
They were the same model as the three bullets still loaded in the revolver.
Two of the bullets were found in the inside wall of the bar,
and they got the manager's prints from the revolver ...
There was gunshot residue on the manager's right hand.

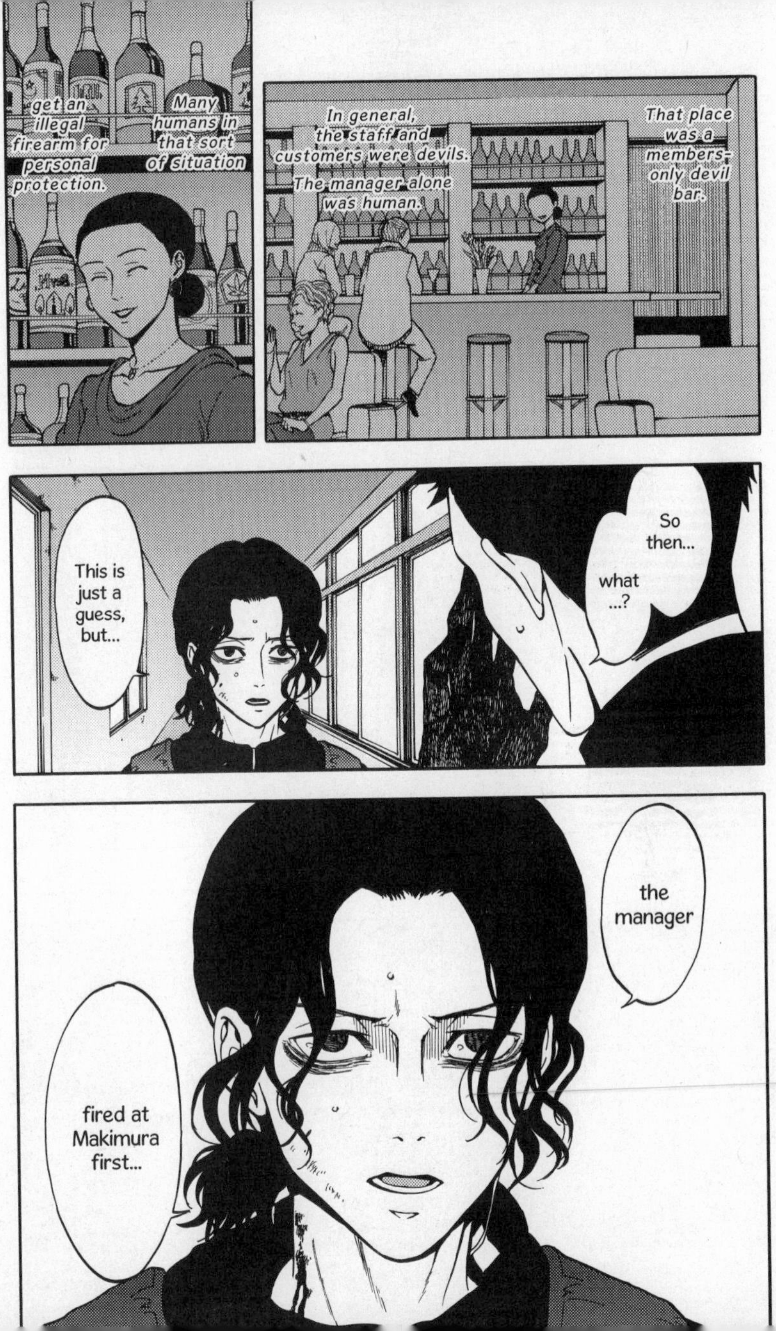
That place was a members-only devil bar.
In general, the staff and customers were devils.
The manager alone was human.
Many humans in that sort of situation
get an illegal firearm for personal protection.
So then... what ...?
This is just a guess, but...
the manager
fired at Makimura first...

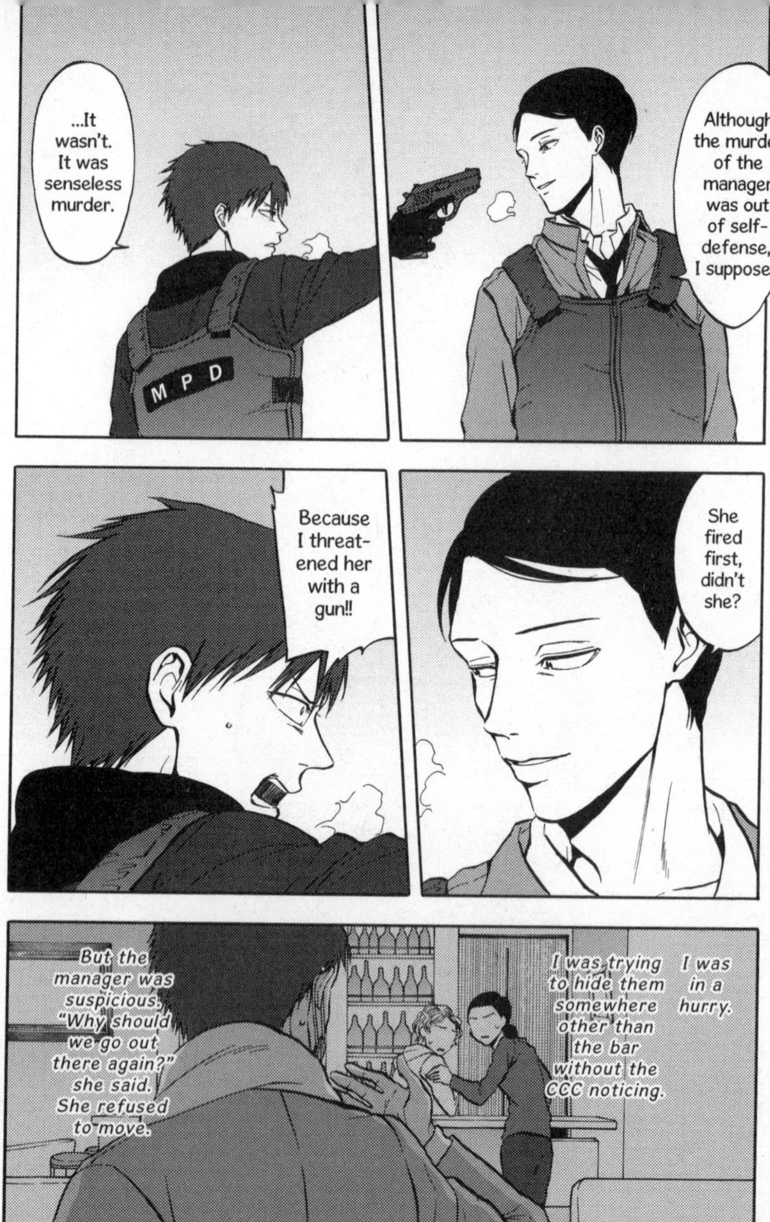
Although the murder of the manager was out of self-defense, I suppose.
...It wasn't. It was senseless murder.
M P D
She fired first, didn't she?
Because I threatened her with a gun!!
I was in a hurry.
I was trying to hide them somewhere other than the bar without the CCC noticing.
But the manager was suspicious. "Why should we go out there again?" she said. She refused to move.

So I pointed my gun at her. "Do it now," I said.

Then she suddenly took out a gun...

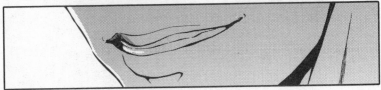

LOOM

What a laugh.

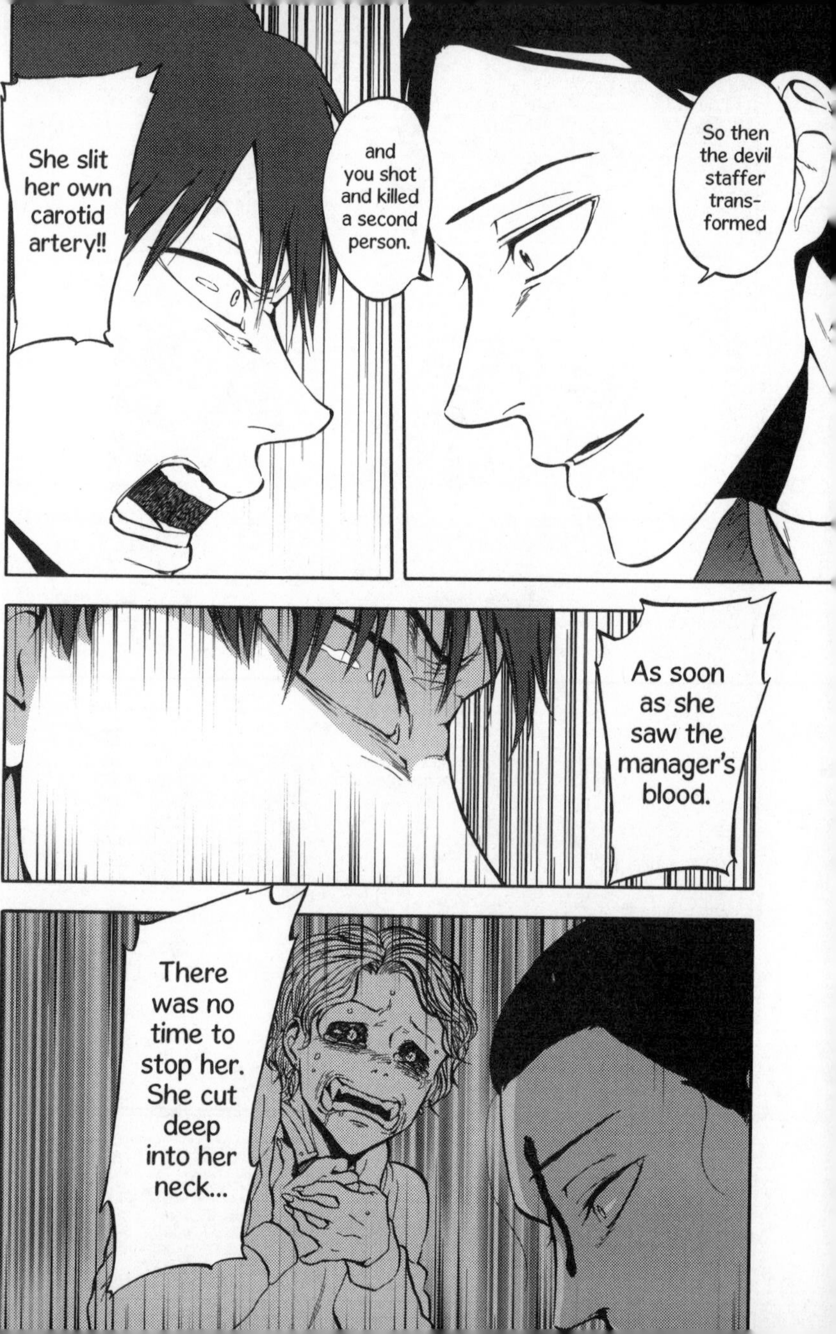
So then the devil staffer trans-formed
and you shot and killed a second person.
She slit her own carotid artery!!
As soon as she saw the manager's blood.
There was no time to stop her. She cut deep into her neck...

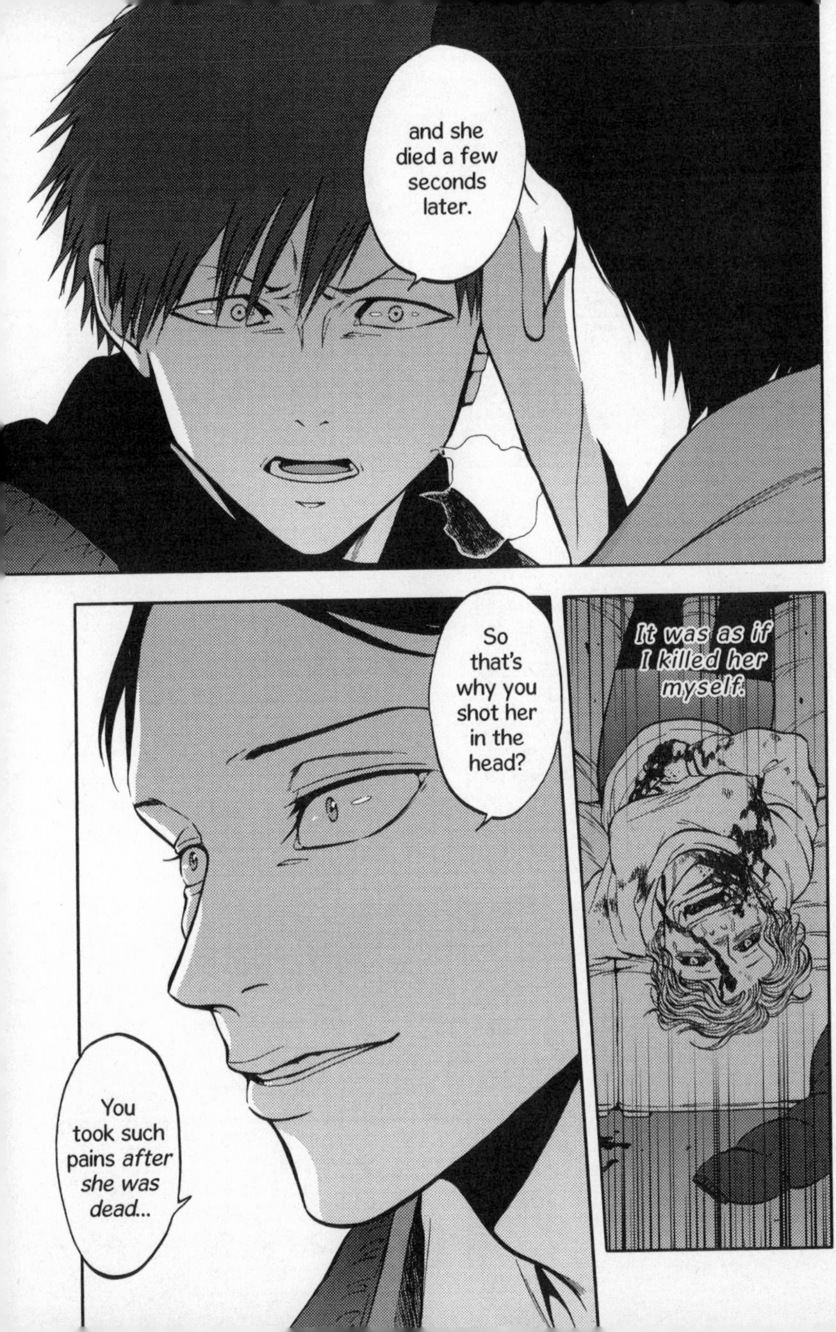
and she died a few seconds later.
It was as if I killed her myself.
So that's why you shot her in the head?
You took such pains *after* she was dead...

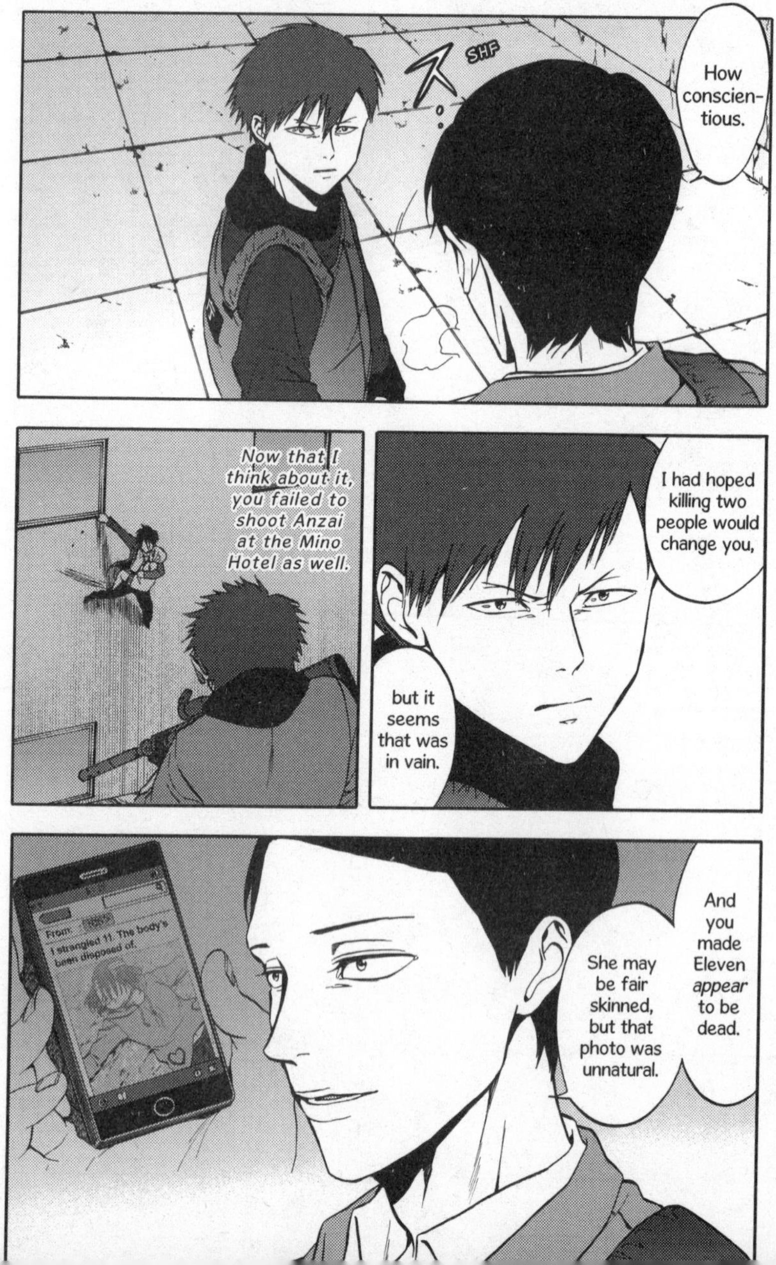
How conscientious.
SHF
I had hoped killing two people would change you,
but it seems that was in vain.
Now that I think about it, you failed to shoot Anzai at the Mino Hotel as well.
And you made Eleven *appear* to be dead.
She may be fair skinned, but that photo was unnatural.
From:
I strangled 11. The body's been disposed of.

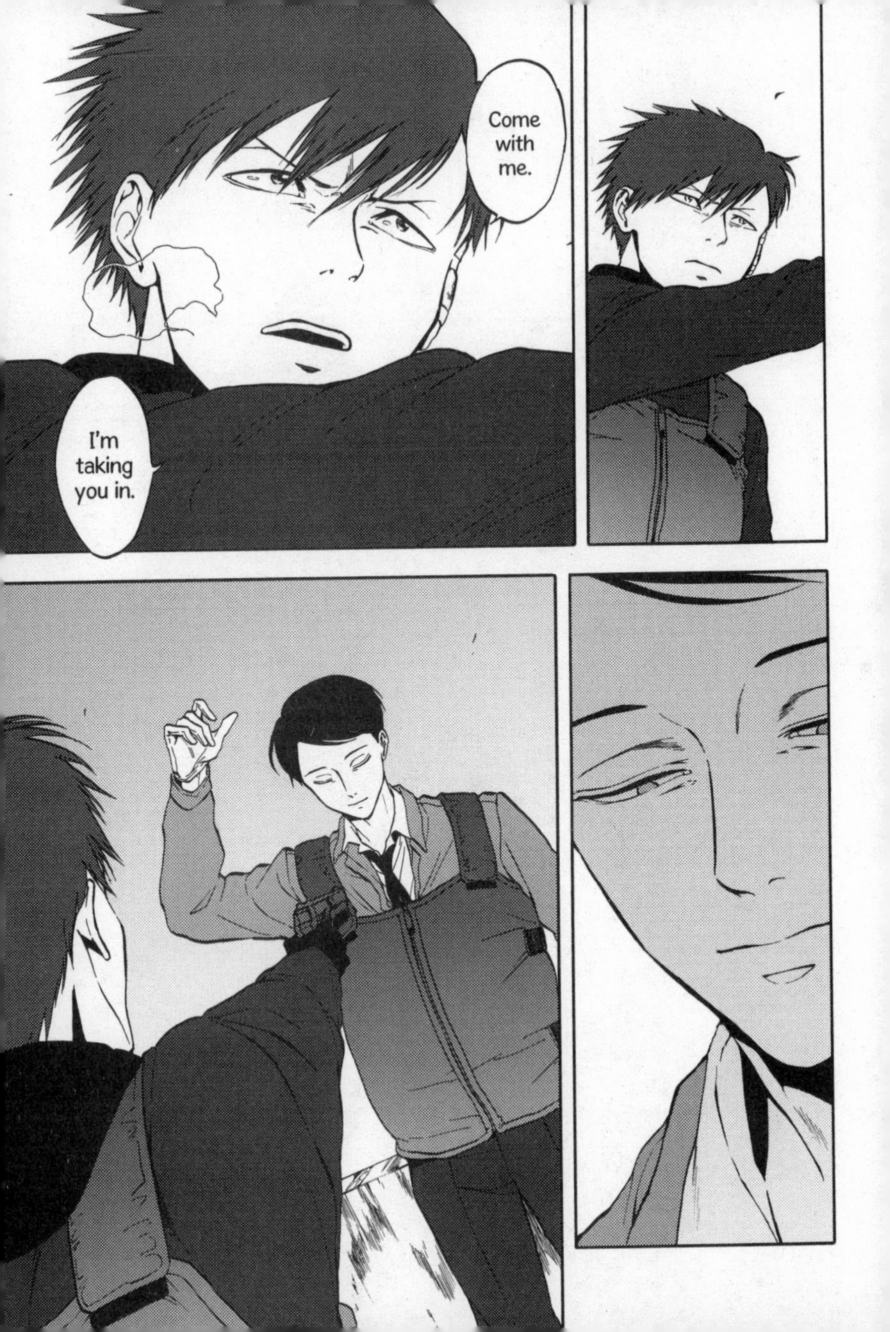
Come with me.
I'm taking you in.

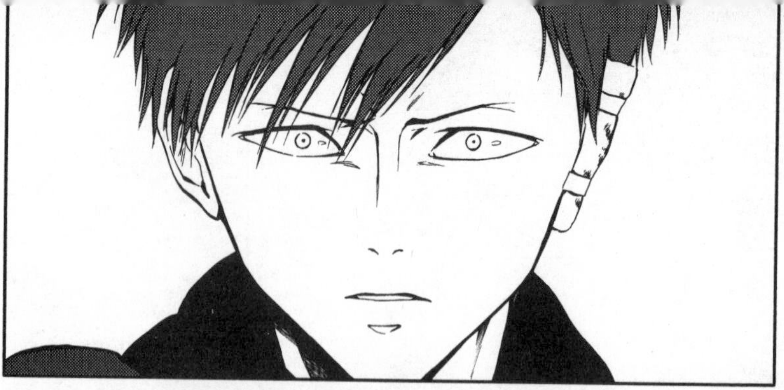
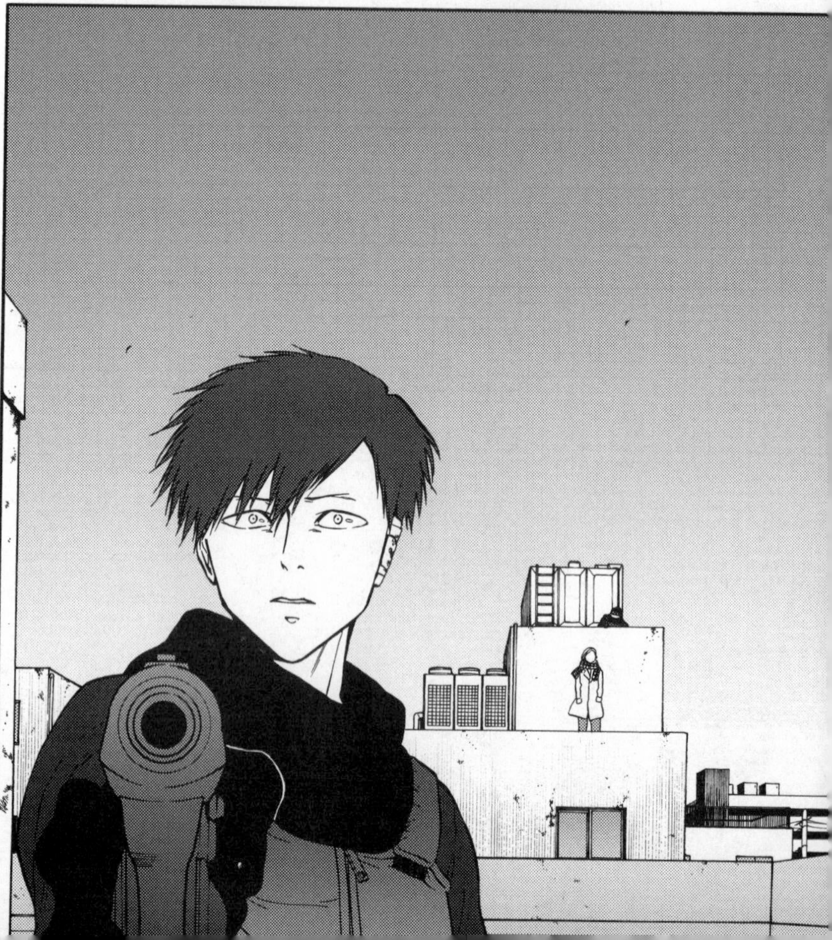

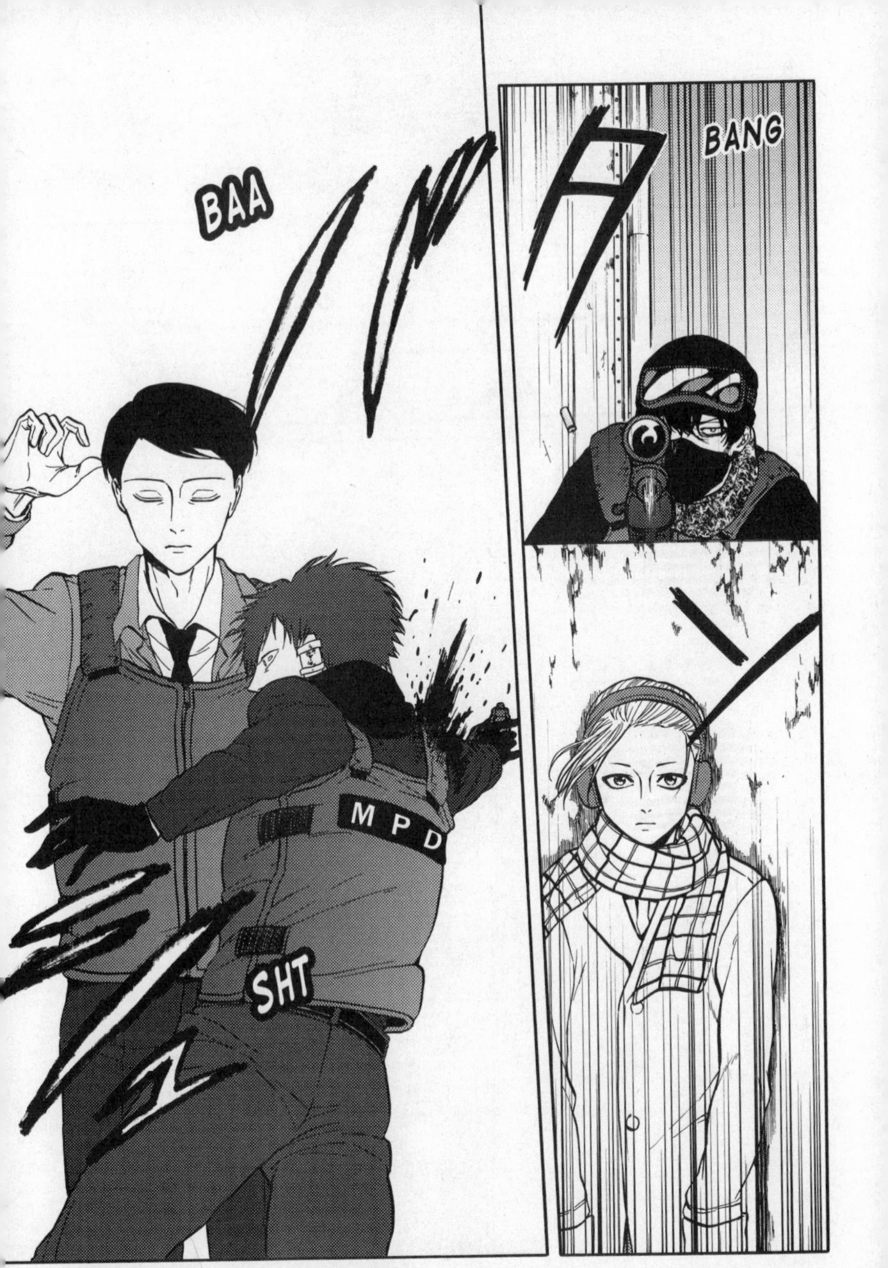
BANG
BAA
MPD
SHT

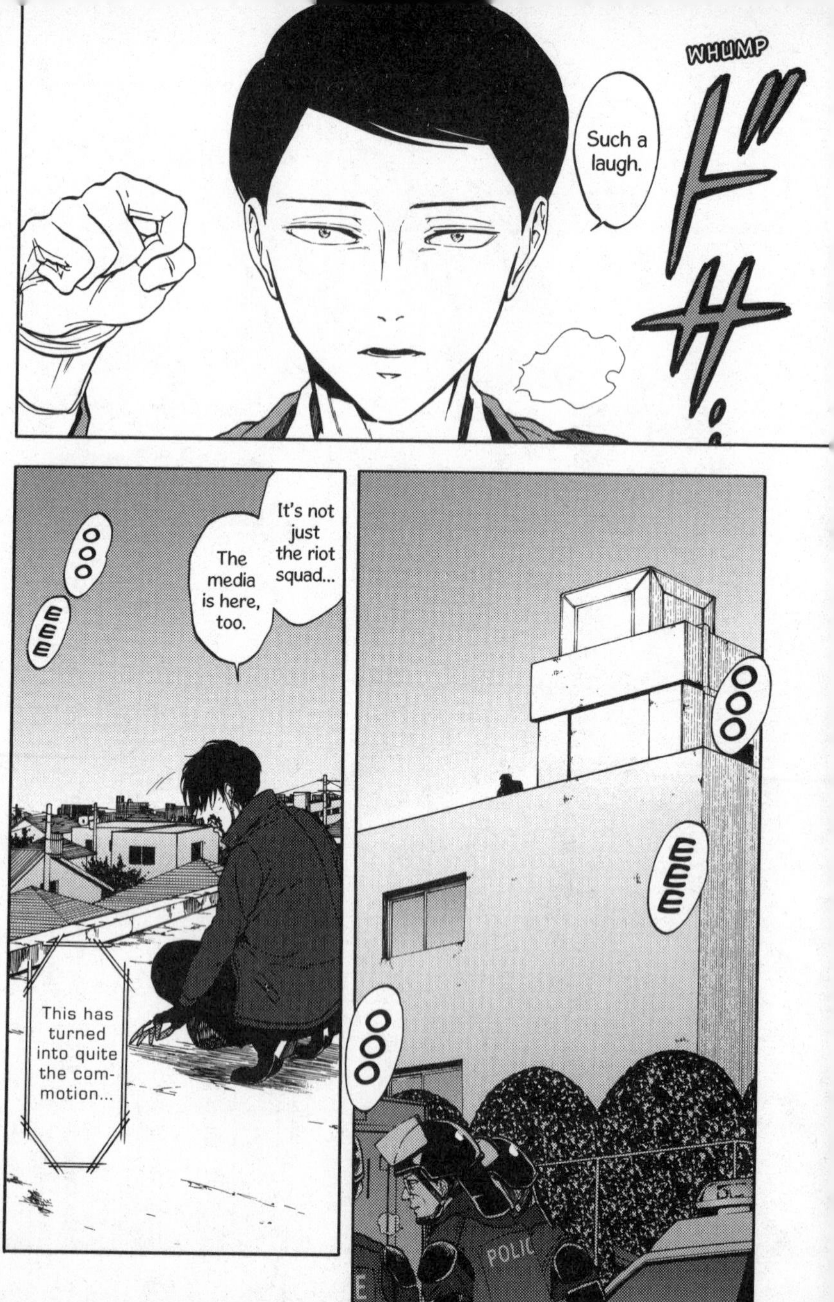
WHUMP
Such a laugh.
OOO
EEE
OOO
It's not just the riot squad...
The media is here, too.
OOO
EEE
This has turned into quite the commotion...
POLIC

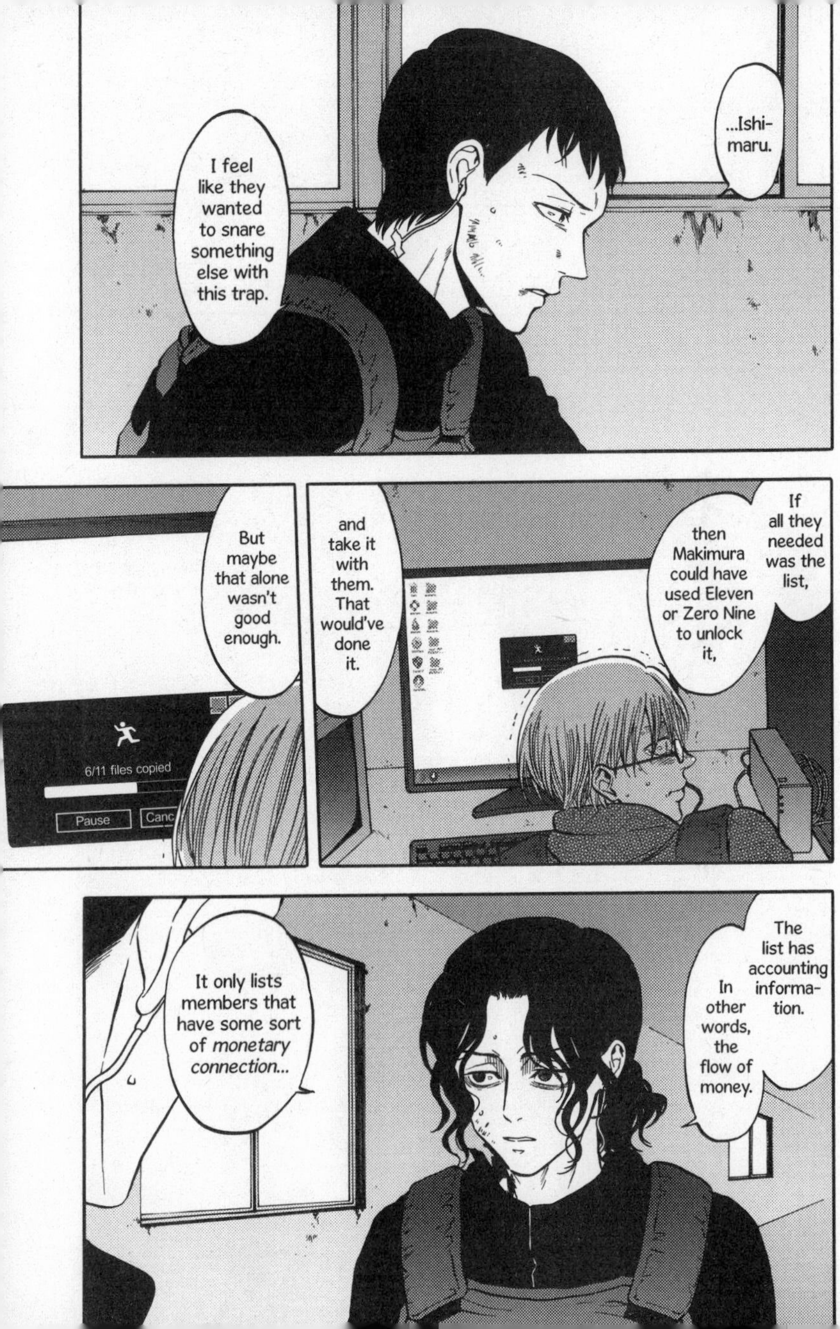
...Ishi-maru.
I feel like they wanted to snare something else with this trap.
If all they needed was the list,
then Makimura could have used Eleven or Zero Nine to unlock it,
and take it with them. That would've done it.
6/11 files copied
Pause
But maybe that alone wasn't good enough.
The list has accounting information.
In other words, the flow of money.
It only lists members that have some sort of *monetary connection...*

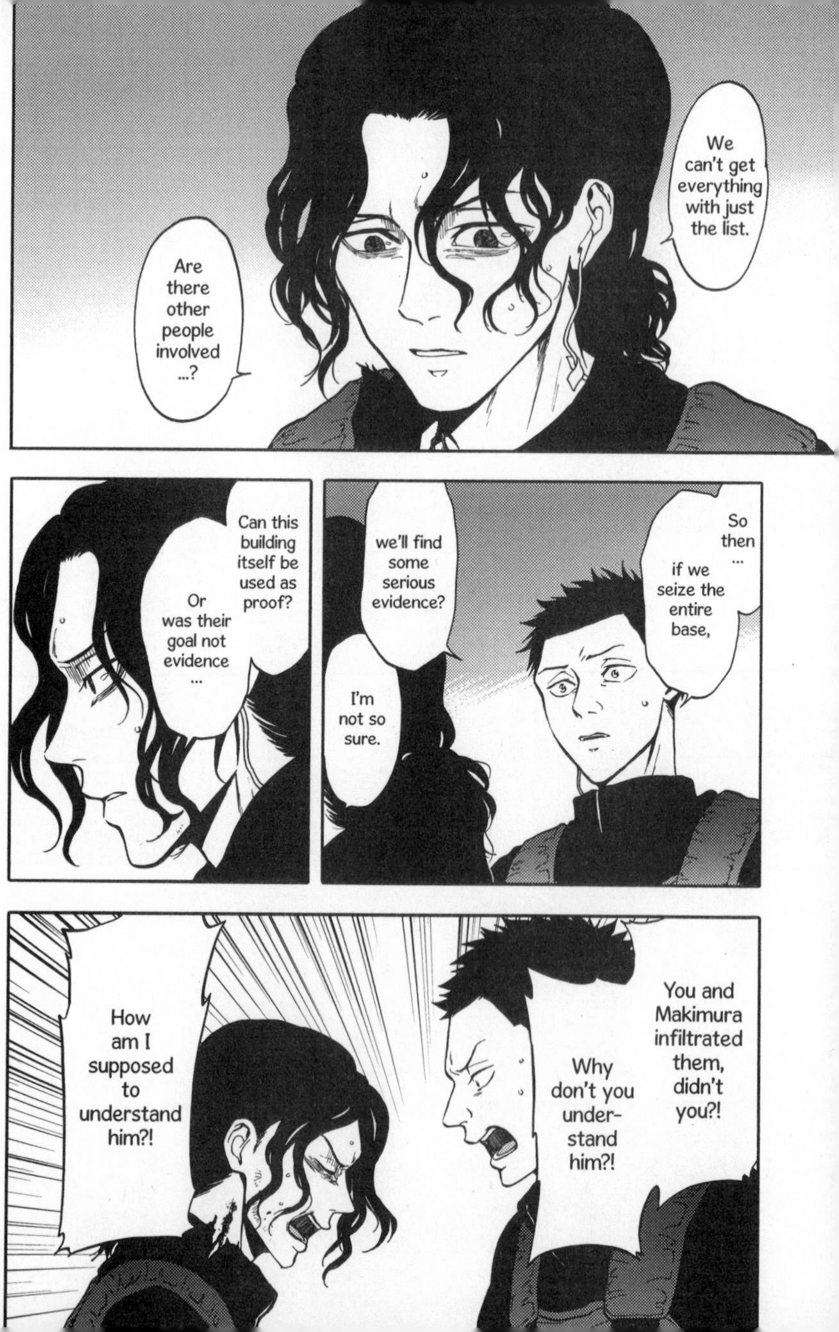
We can't get everything with just the list.
Are there other people involved ...?
So then ...
if we seize the entire base,
we'll find some serious evidence?
I'm not so sure.
Can this building itself be used as proof?
Or was their goal not evidence ...
You and Makimura infiltrated them, didn't you?!
Why don't you under-stand him?!
How am I supposed to understand him?!

The moment he killed someone and tossed his police ID,
Section 11 took Makimura off the case.
How can you count on a pawn who isn't under your control?!
... Then at least ...
you could have told us earlier that you'd infiltrated—
Told you?
Would anything be different if I had told you sooner?
You didn't notice my falsified work history until recently.
I'm not counting on F Squad's investi-gative abilities.

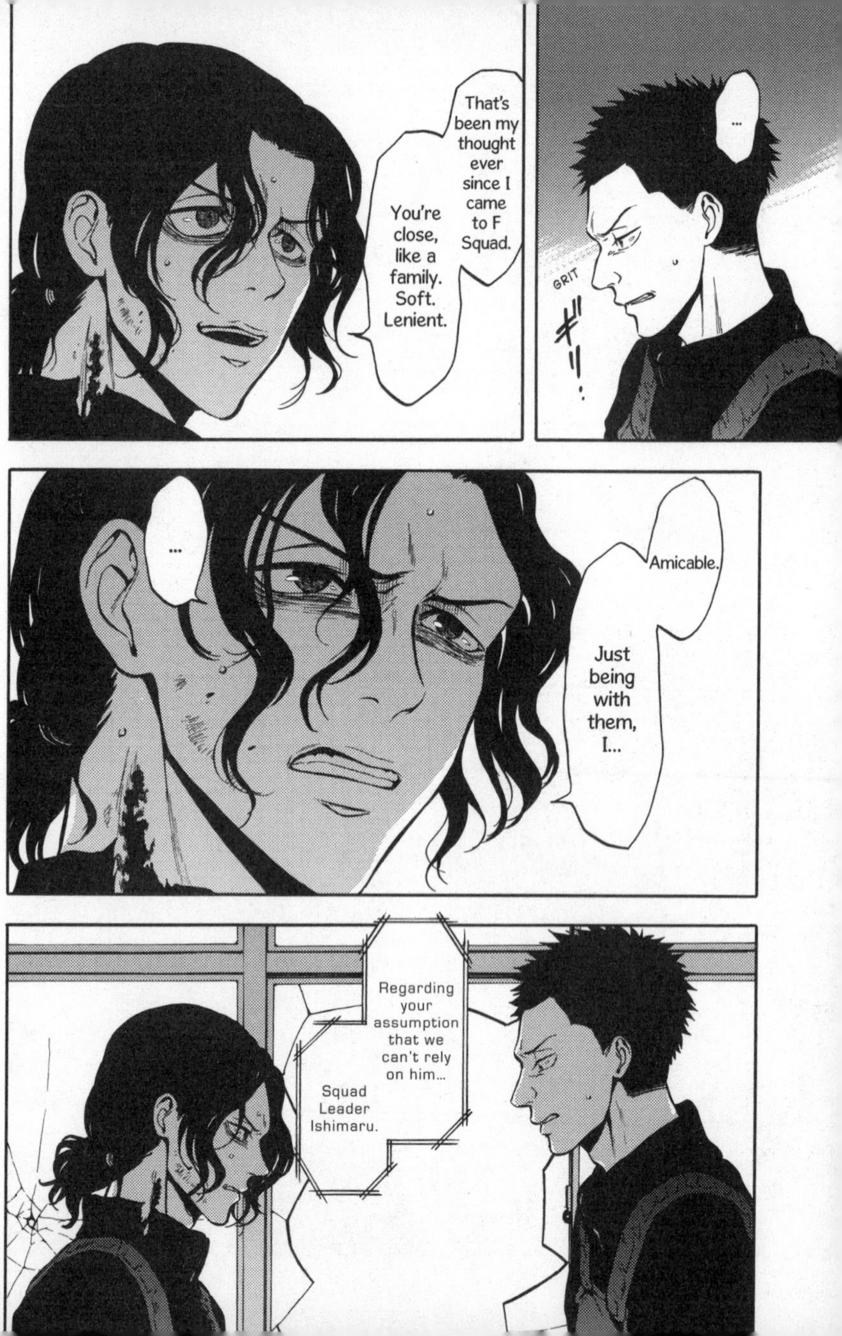
...
GRIT
That's been my thought ever since I came to F Squad.
You're close, like a family. Soft. Lenient.
Amicable.
Just being with them, I...
...
Regarding your assumption that we can't rely on him...
Squad Leader Ishimaru.

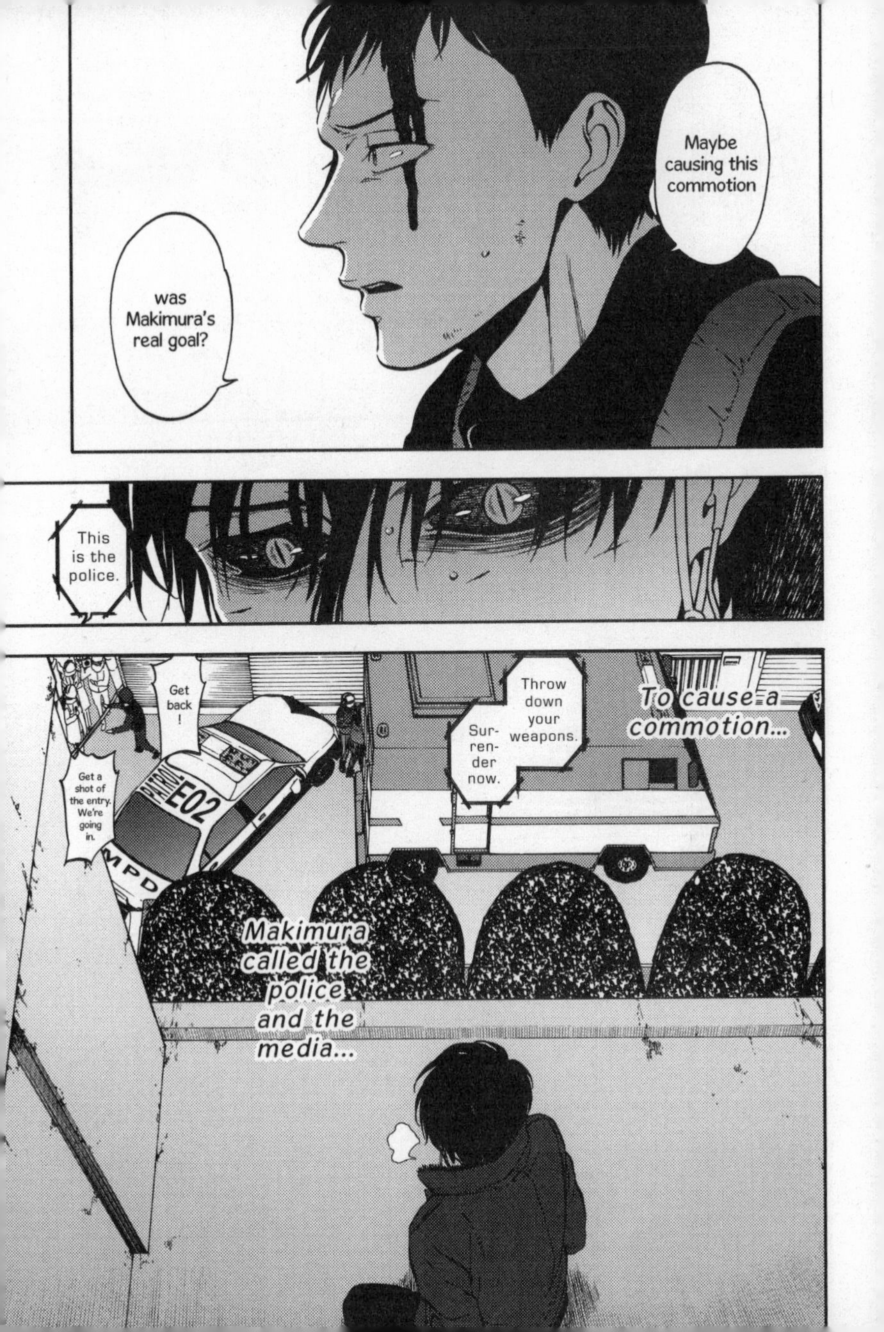
Maybe causing this commotion
was Makimura's real goal?
This is the police.
To cause a commotion...
Throw down your weapons.
Sur-ren-der now.
Get back!
Get a shot of the entry. We're going in.
Makimura called the police and the media...

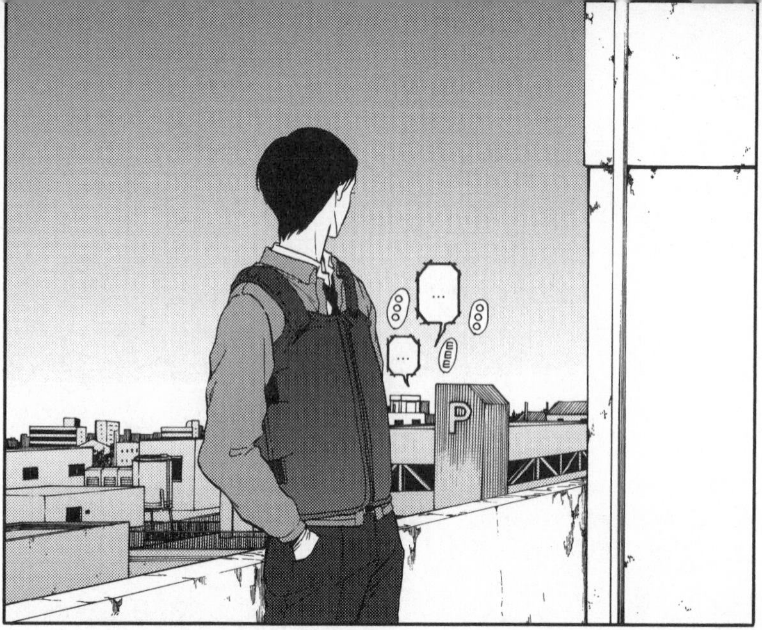
...
...

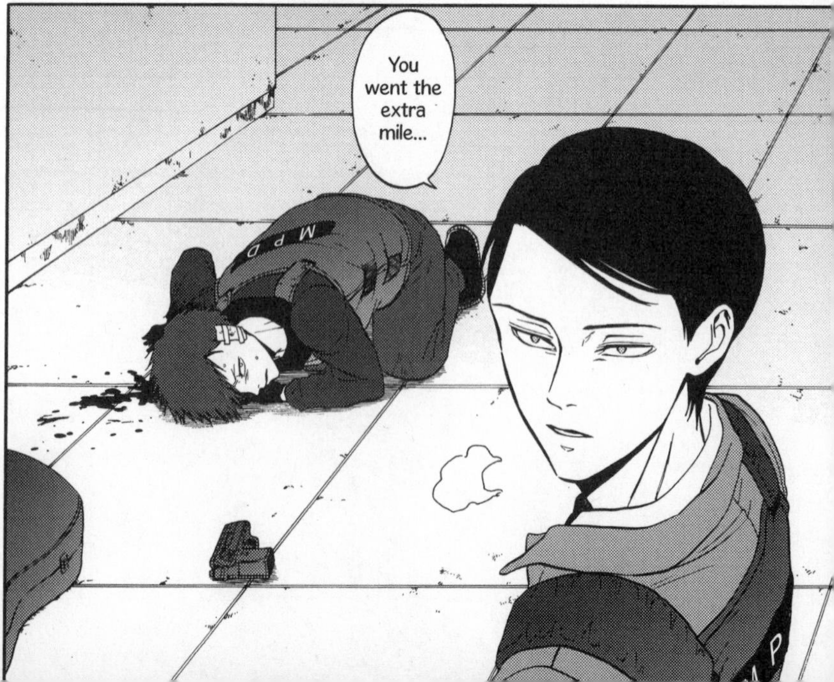
You went the extra mile...
MPD

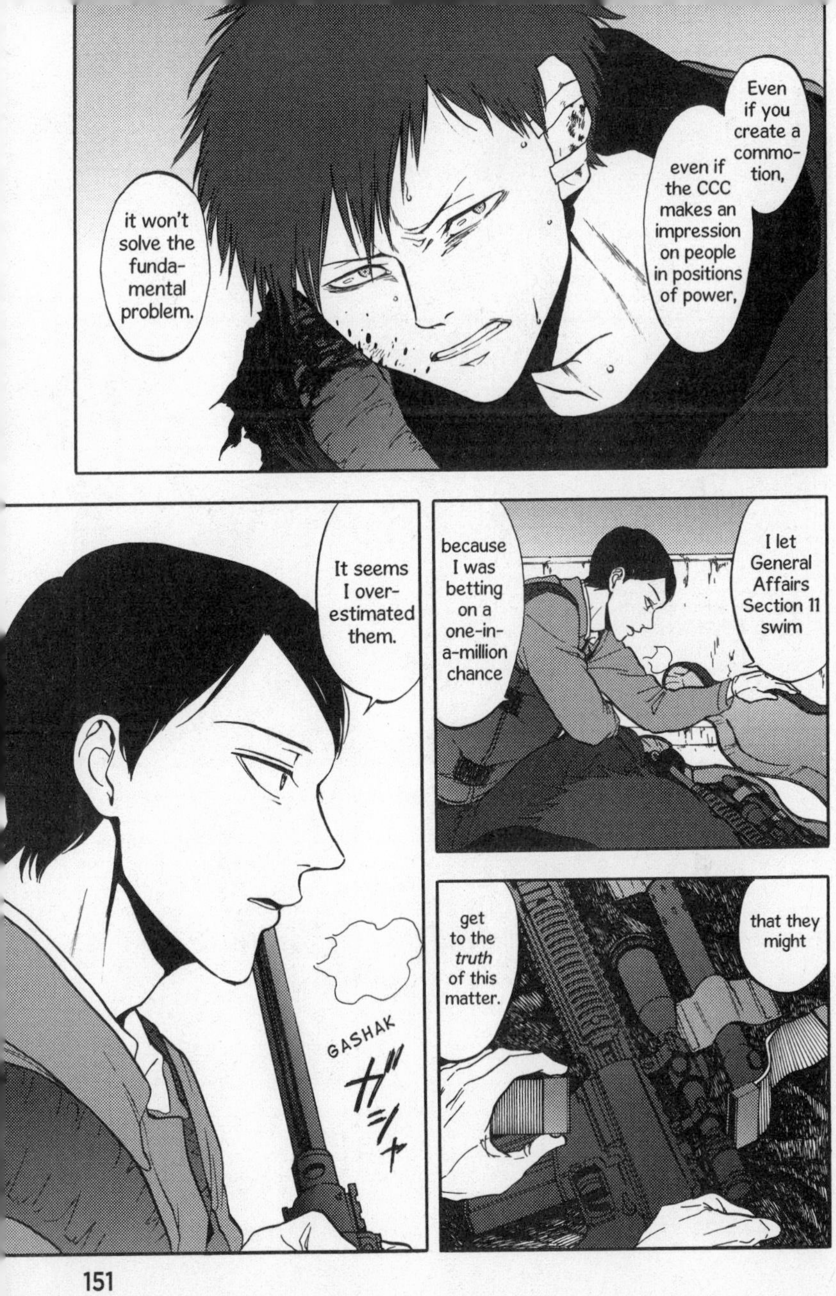

Even if you create a commotion,
even if the CCC makes an impression on people in positions of power,
it won't solve the fundamental problem.
I let General Affairs Section 11 swim
because I was betting on a one-in-a-million chance
that they might
get to the *truth* of this matter.
It seems I overestimated them.
GASHAK

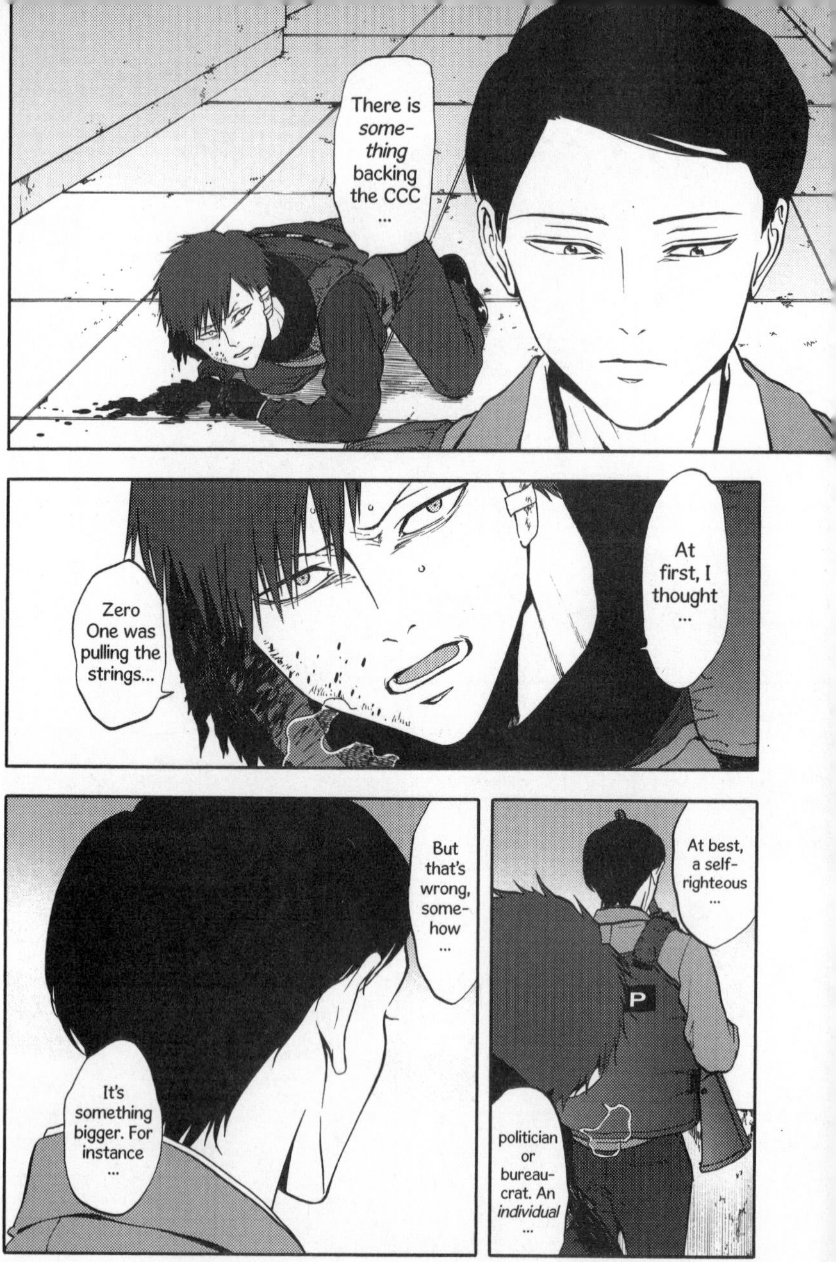
There is *something* backing the CCC...
At first, I thought...
Zero One was pulling the strings...
At best, a self-righteous...
politician or bureaucrat. An *individual*...
But that's wrong, somehow...
It's something bigger. For instance...

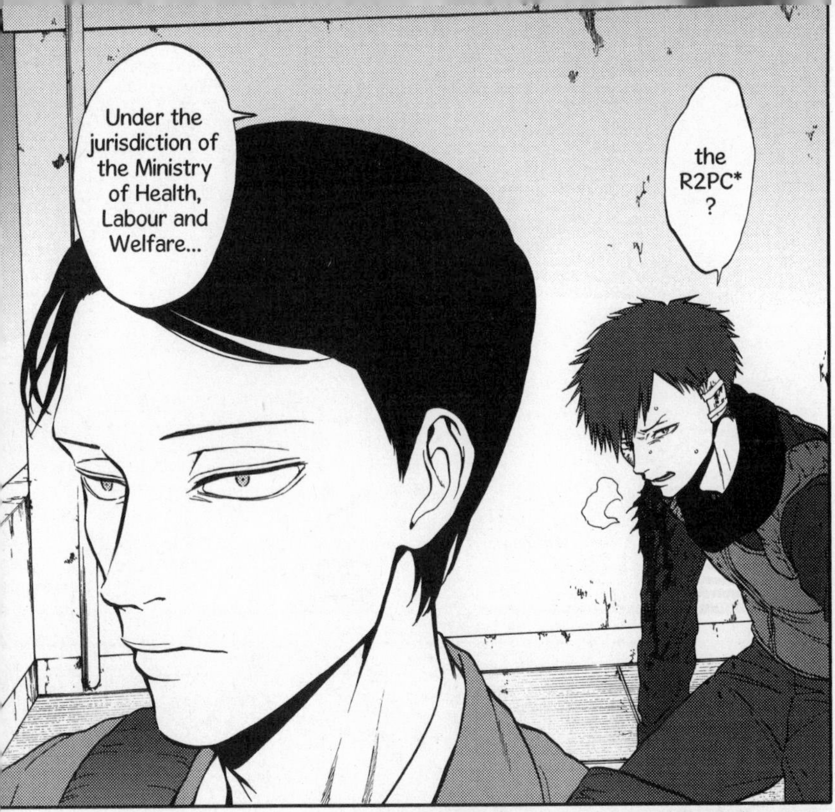
the R2PC* ?
Under the jurisdiction of the Ministry of Health, Labour and Welfare...

※ R2PC: Redeye Rights Protection Committee

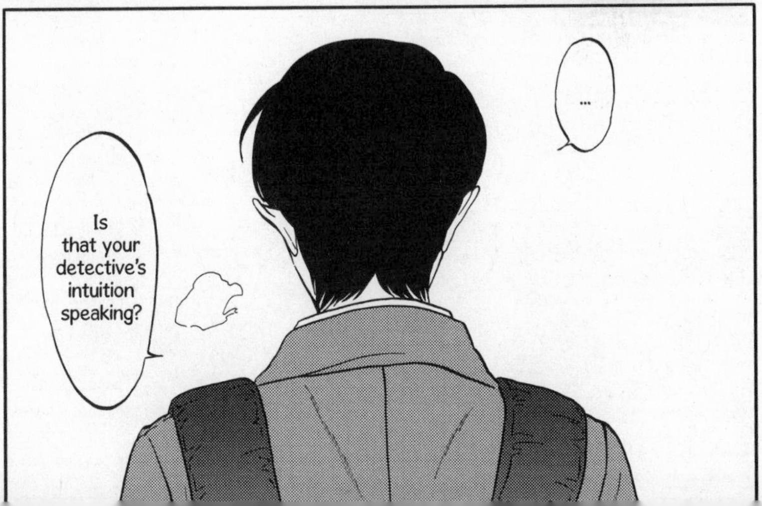
...
Is that your detective's intuition speaking?

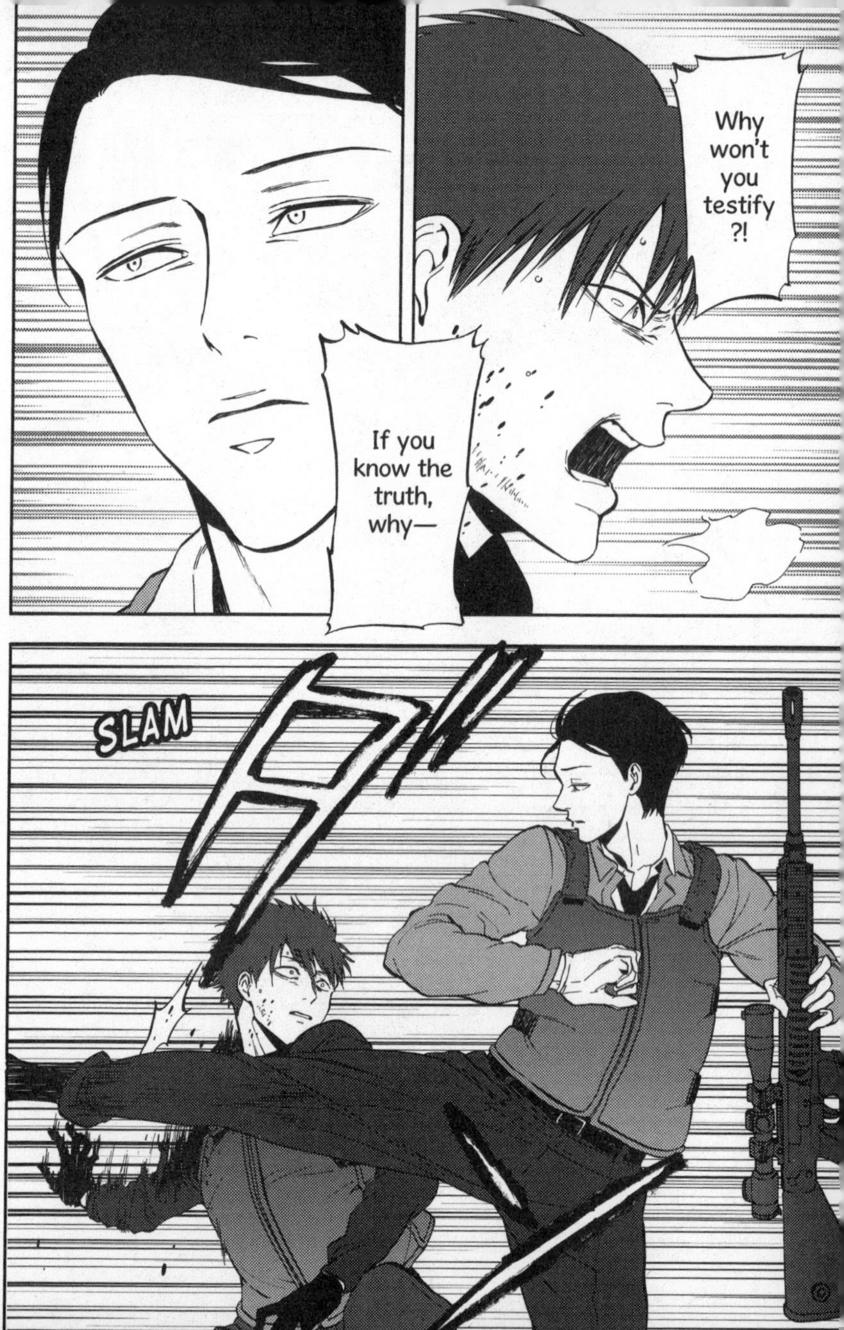
Why won't you testify?!
If you know the truth, why—
SLAM

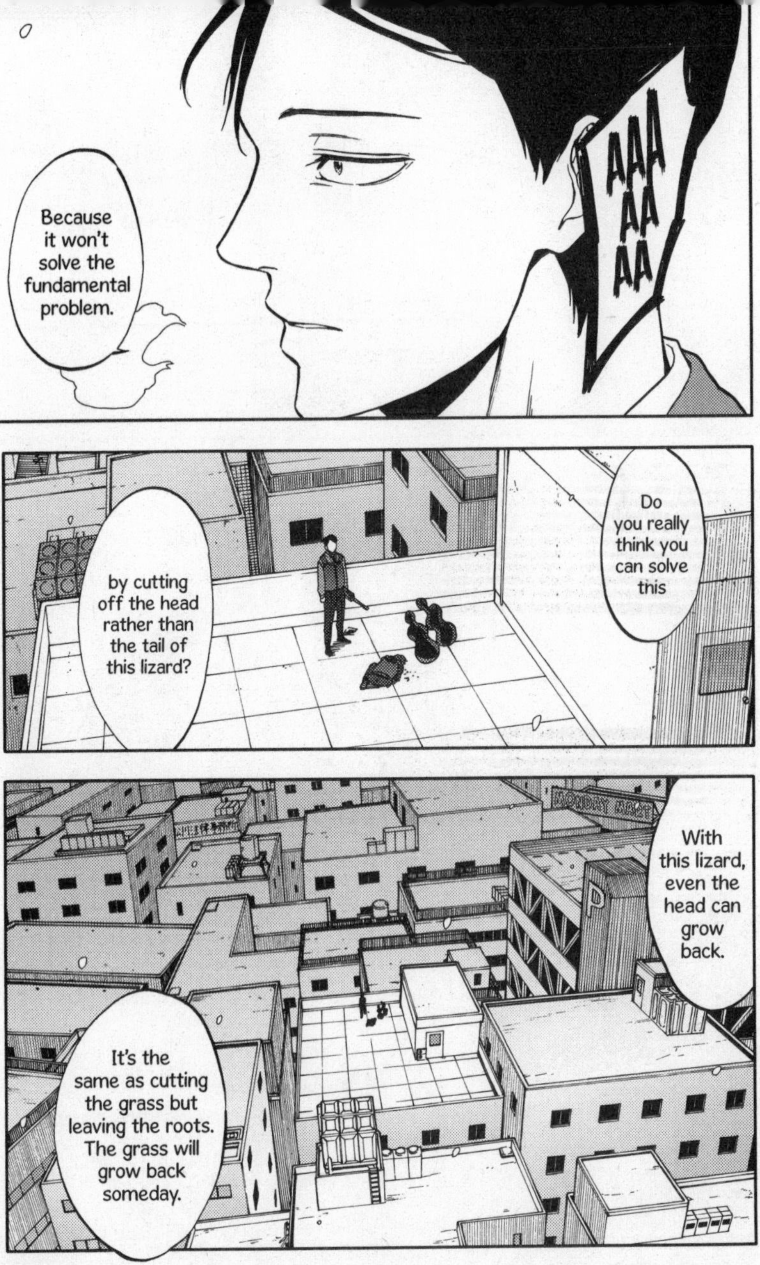
AAA AA AA
Because it won't solve the fundamental problem.
Do you really think you can solve this
by cutting off the head rather than the tail of this lizard?
With this lizard, even the head can grow back.
It's the same as cutting the grass but leaving the roots. The grass will grow back someday.

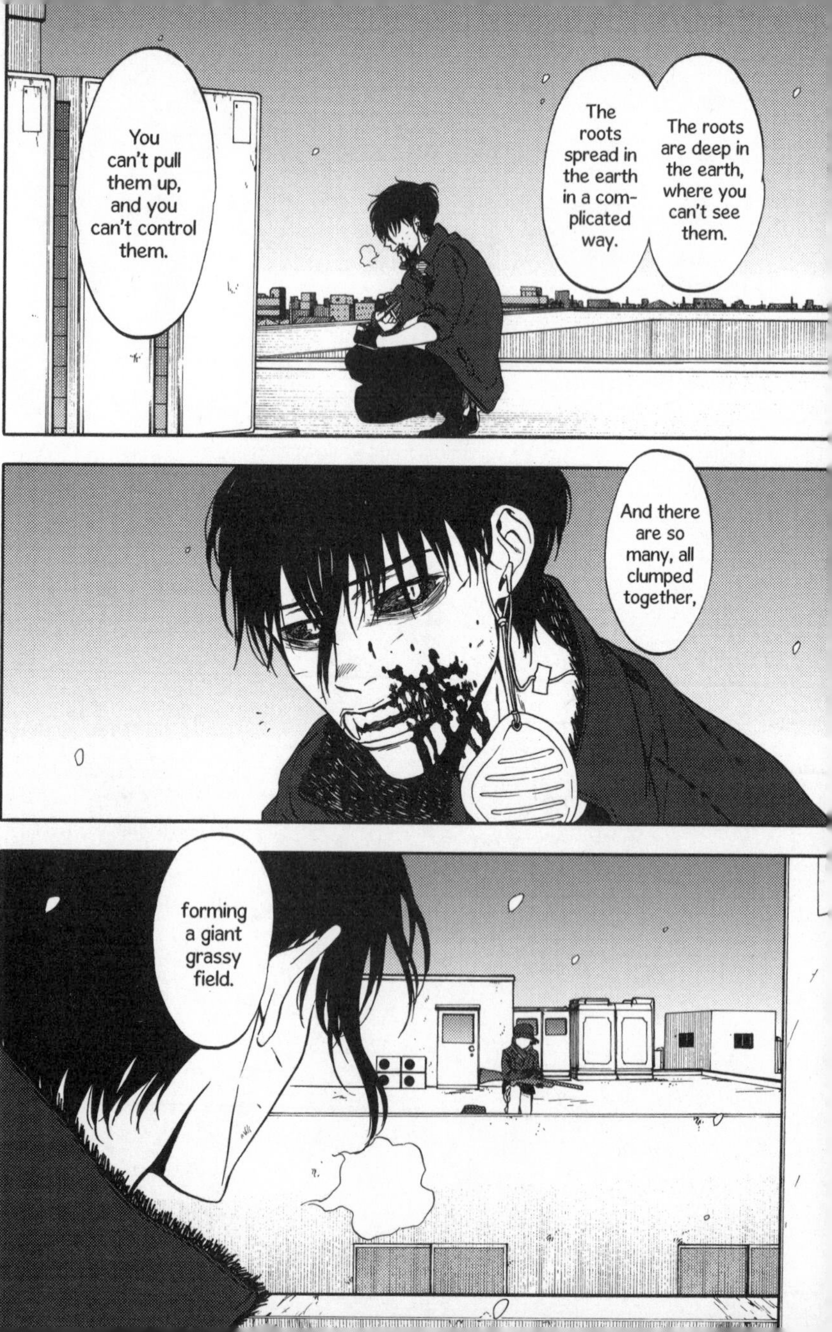
The roots are deep in the earth, where you can't see them.
The roots spread in the earth in a com-plicated way.
You can't pull them up, and you can't control them.
And there are so many, all clumped together,
forming a giant grassy field.

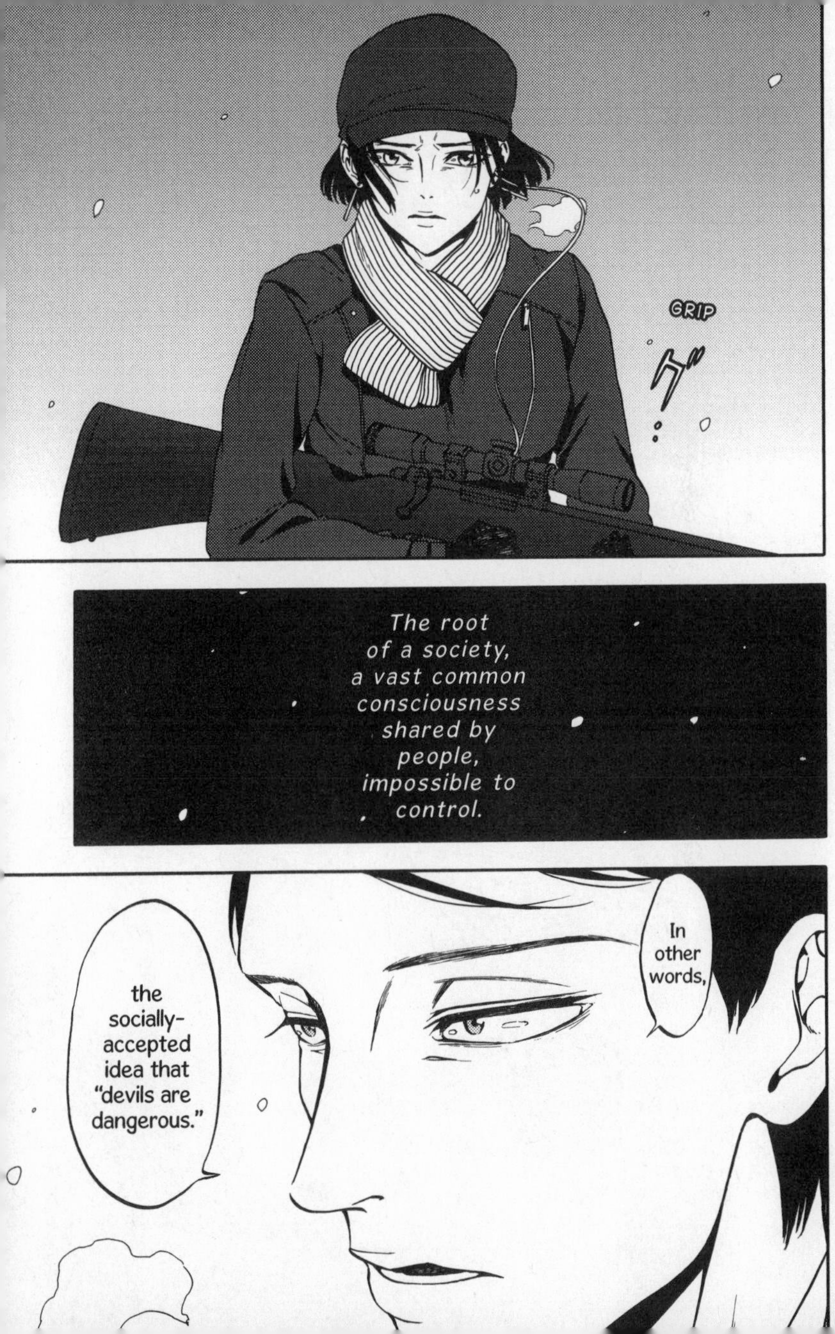
GRIP
The root of a society, a vast common consciousness shared by people, impossible to control.
In other words,
the socially-accepted idea that "devils are dangerous."

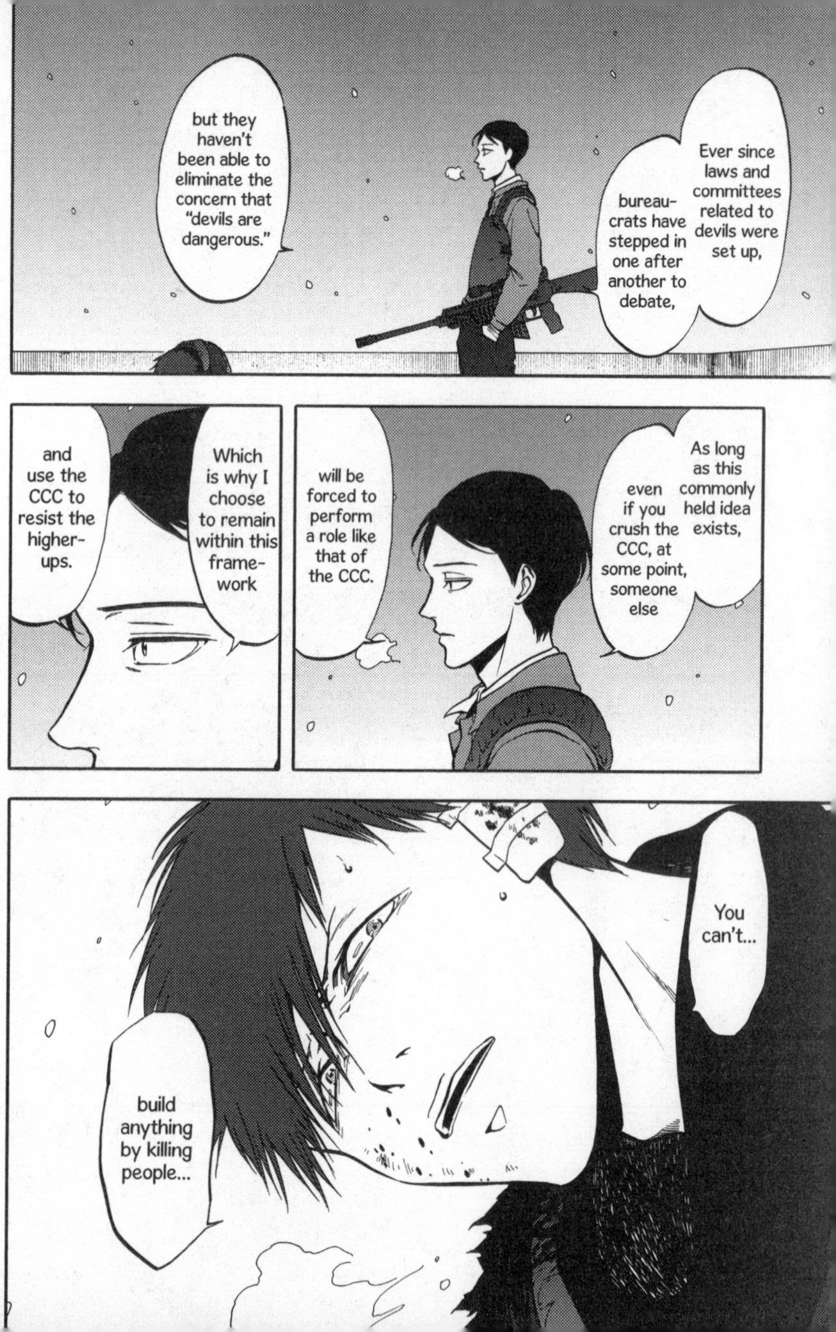
Ever since laws and committees related to devils were set up,
bureaucrats have stepped in one after another to debate,
but they haven't been able to eliminate the concern that "devils are dangerous."
As long as this commonly held idea exists,
even if you crush the CCC, at some point, someone else
will be forced to perform a role like that of the CCC.
Which is why I choose to remain within this framework
and use the CCC to resist the higher-ups.
You can't...
build anything by killing people...

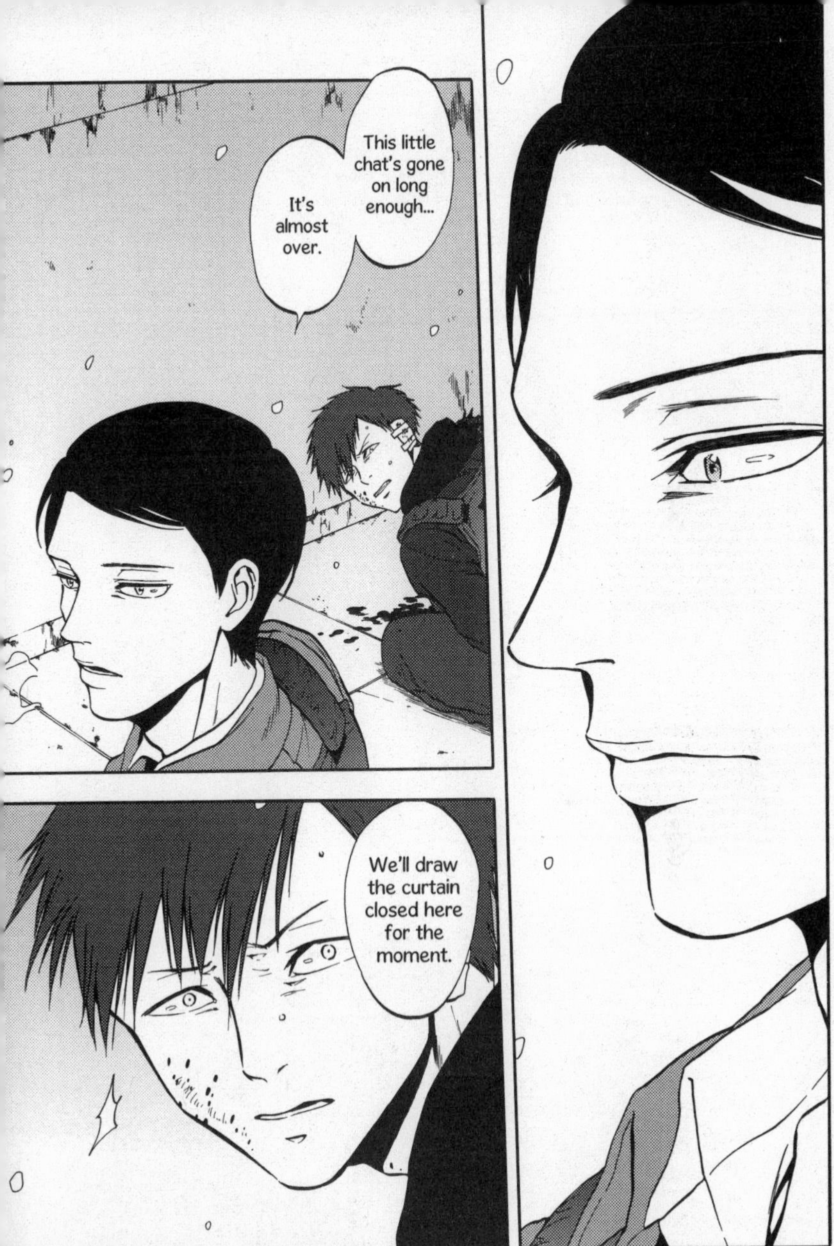
This little chat's gone on long enough...
It's almost over.
We'll draw the curtain closed here for the moment.

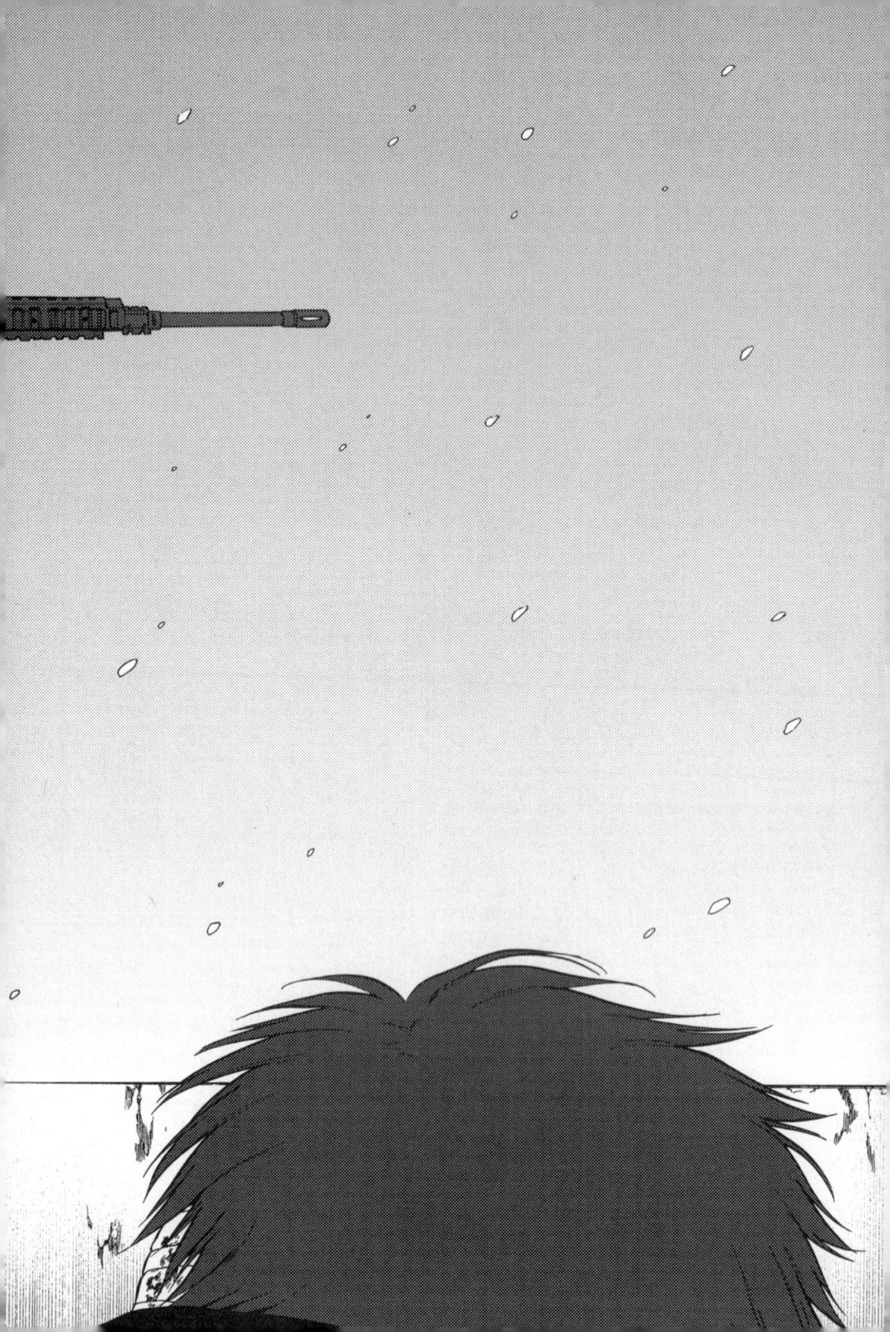

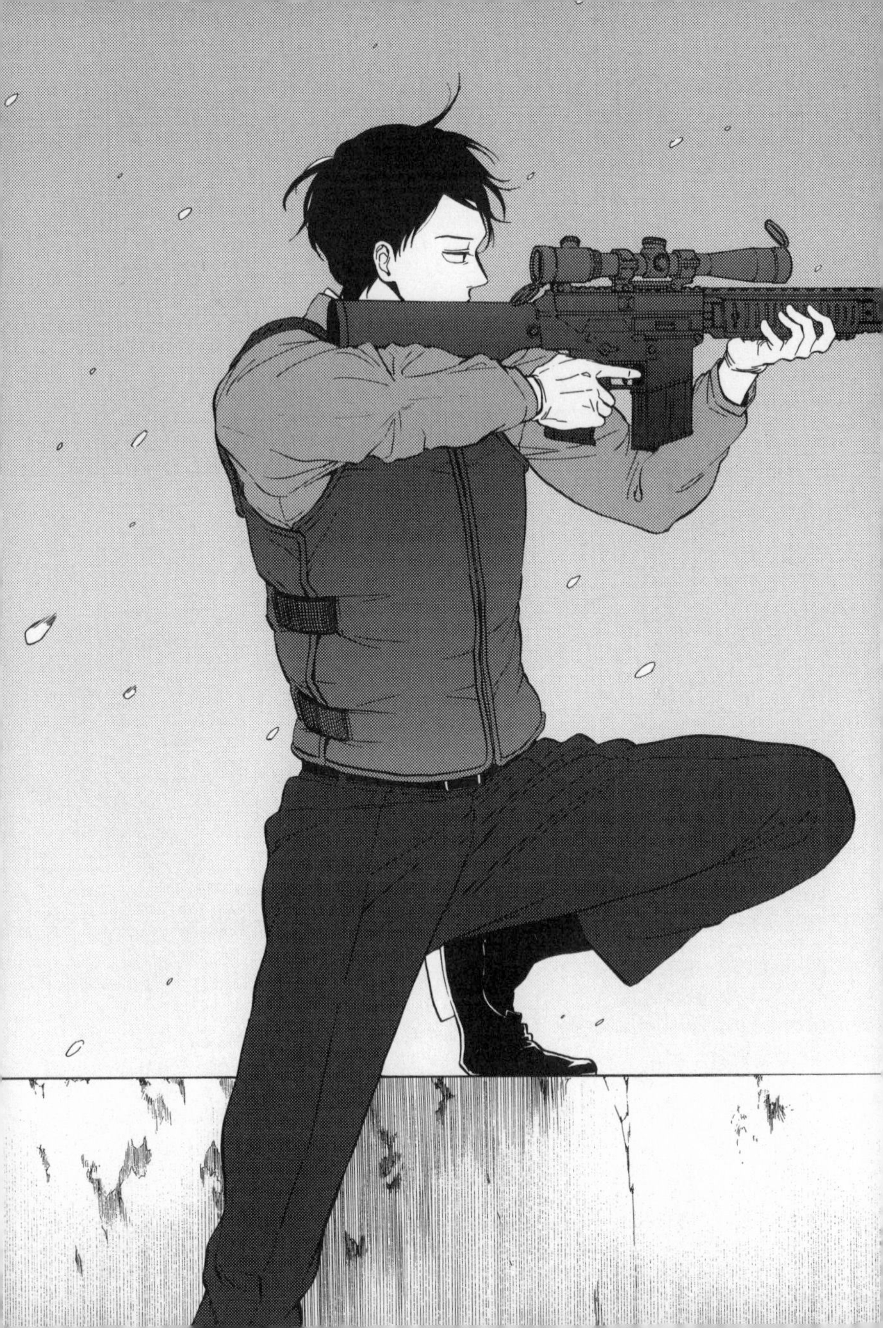

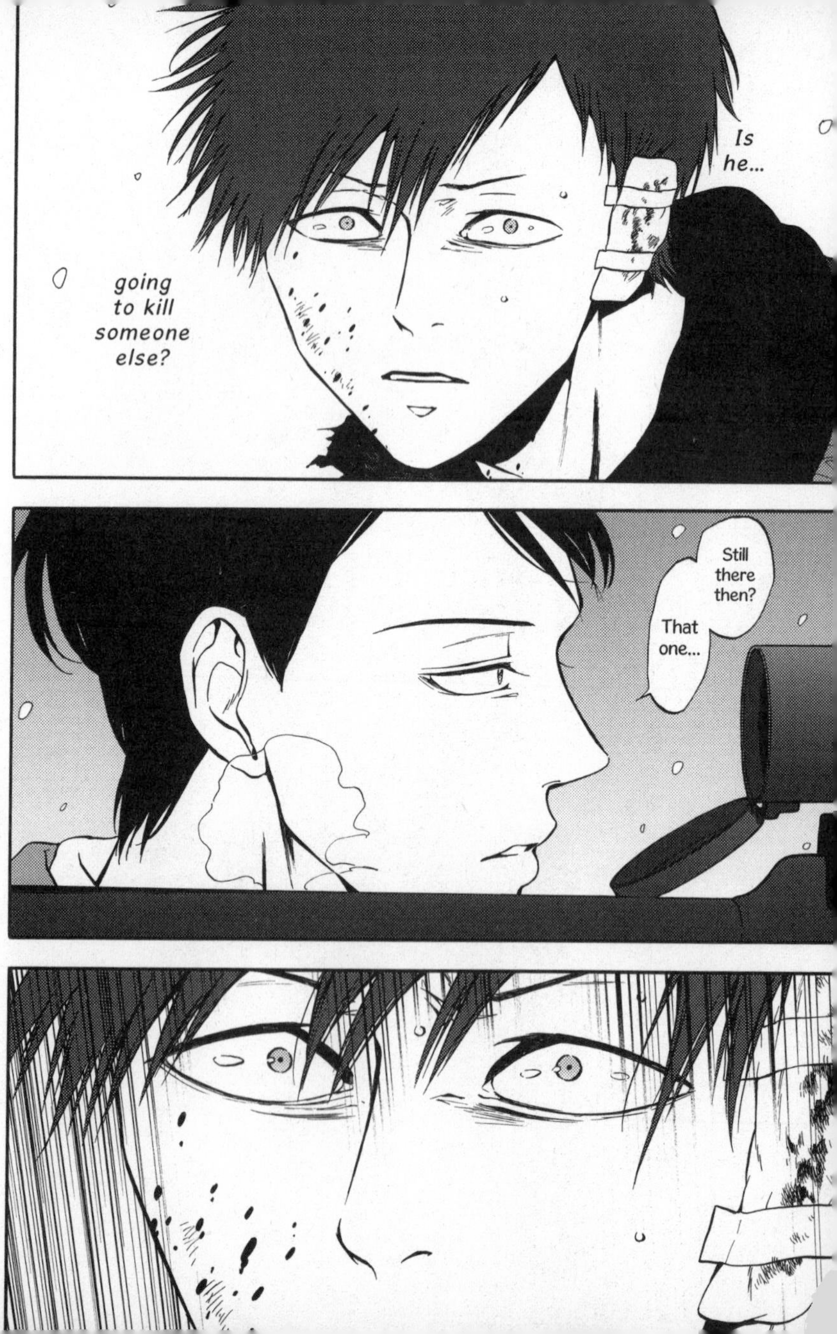
Is he...
going to kill someone else?
Still there then?
That one...

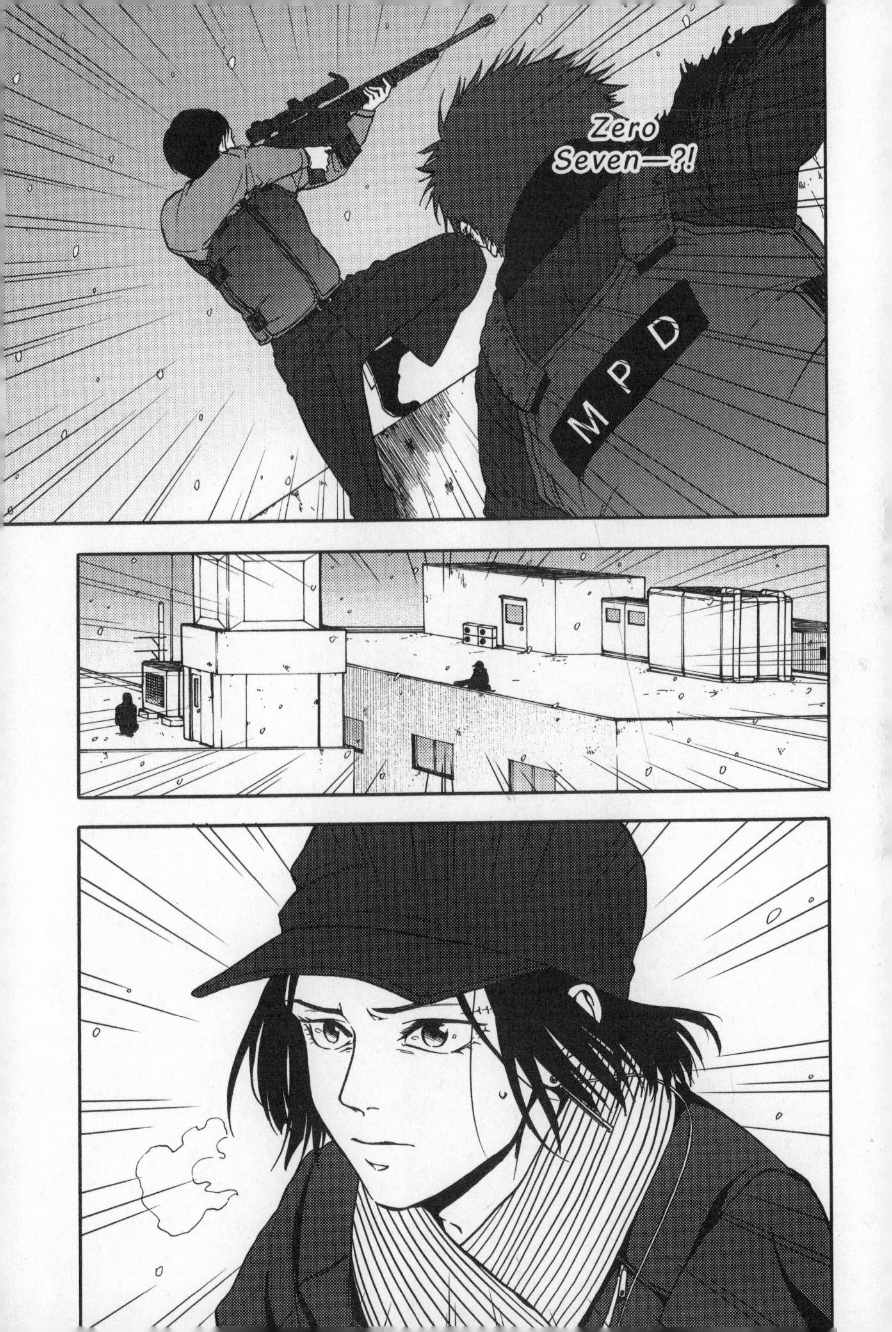
Zero Seven—?!
MPD

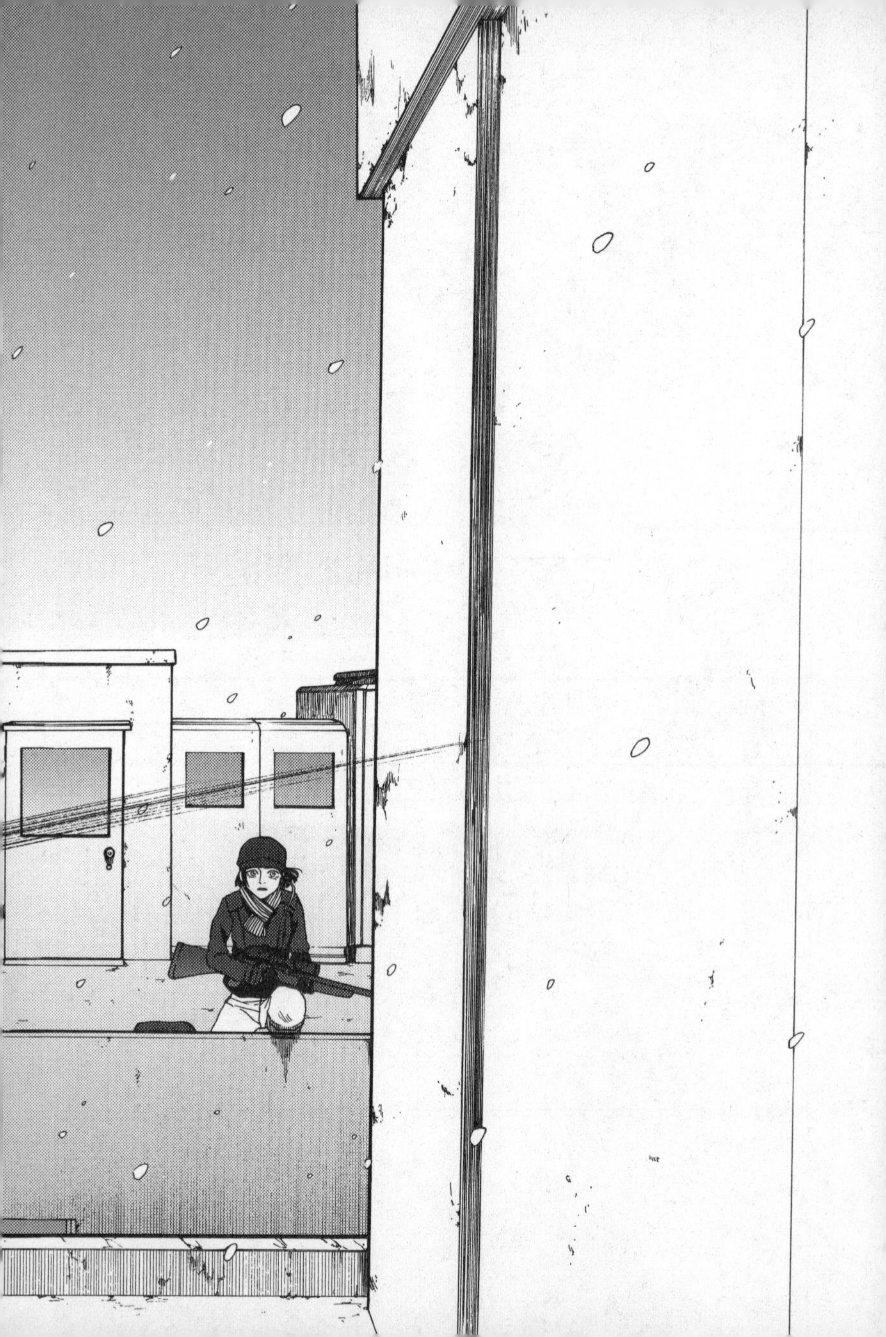

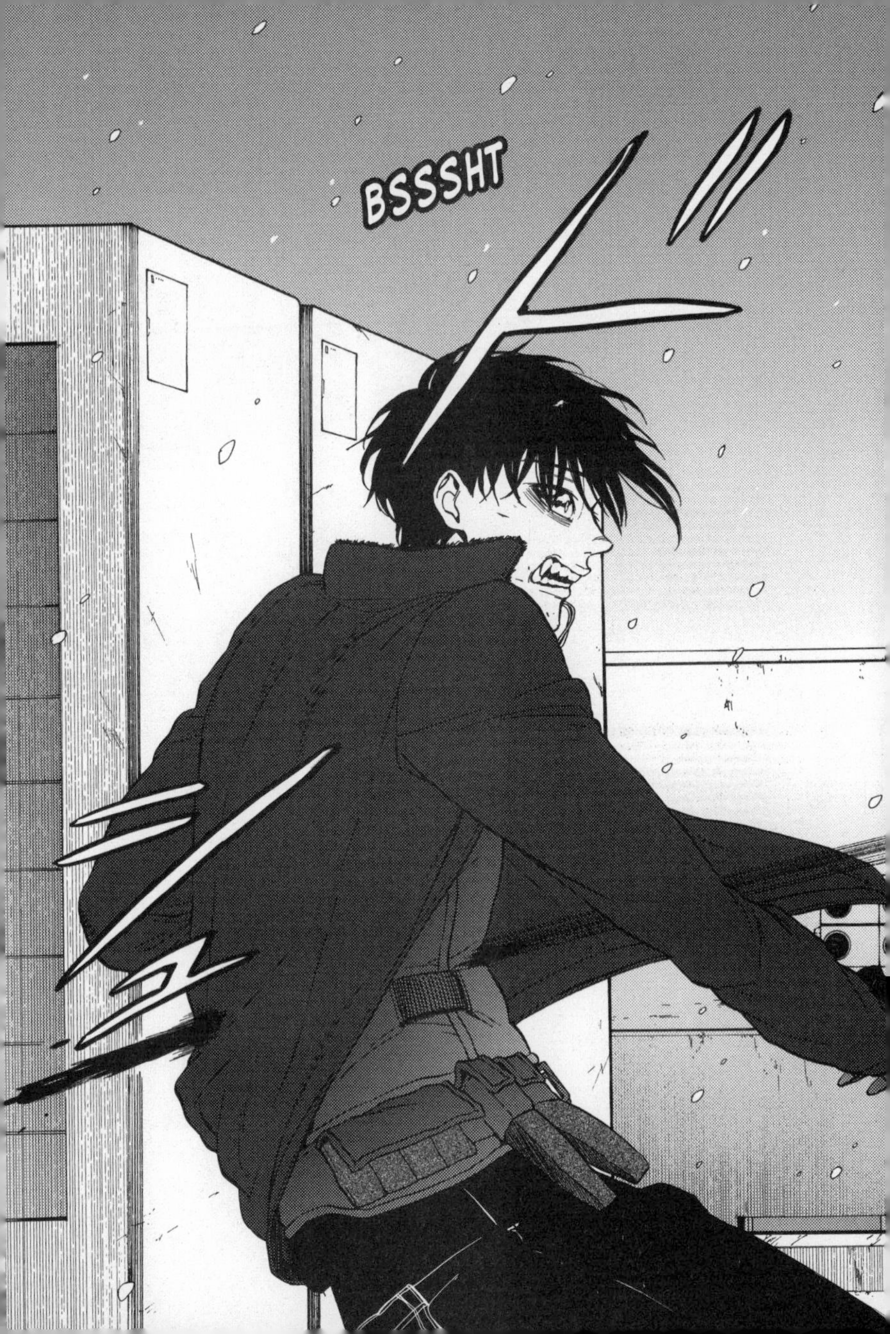
BSSSHT

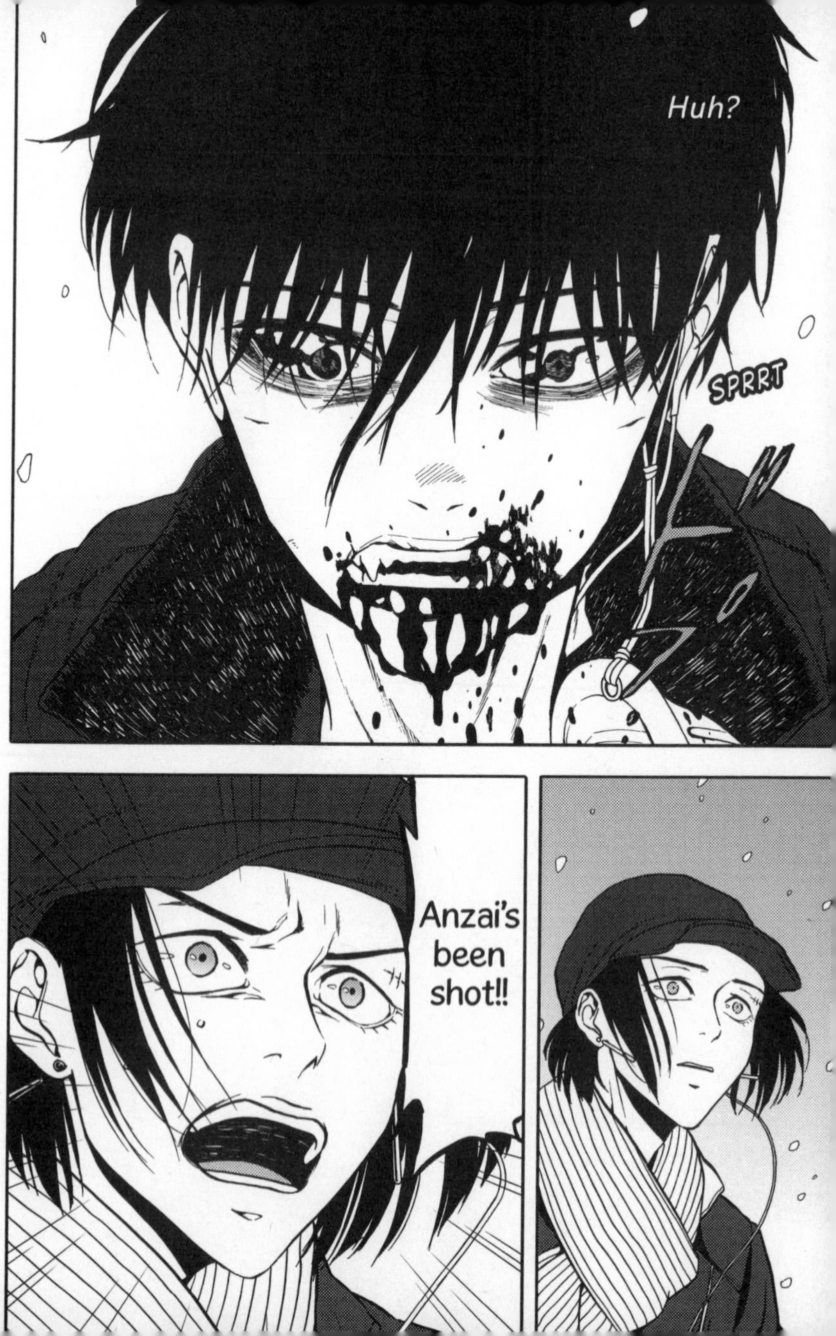
Huh?
SPRRT
Anzai's been shot!!

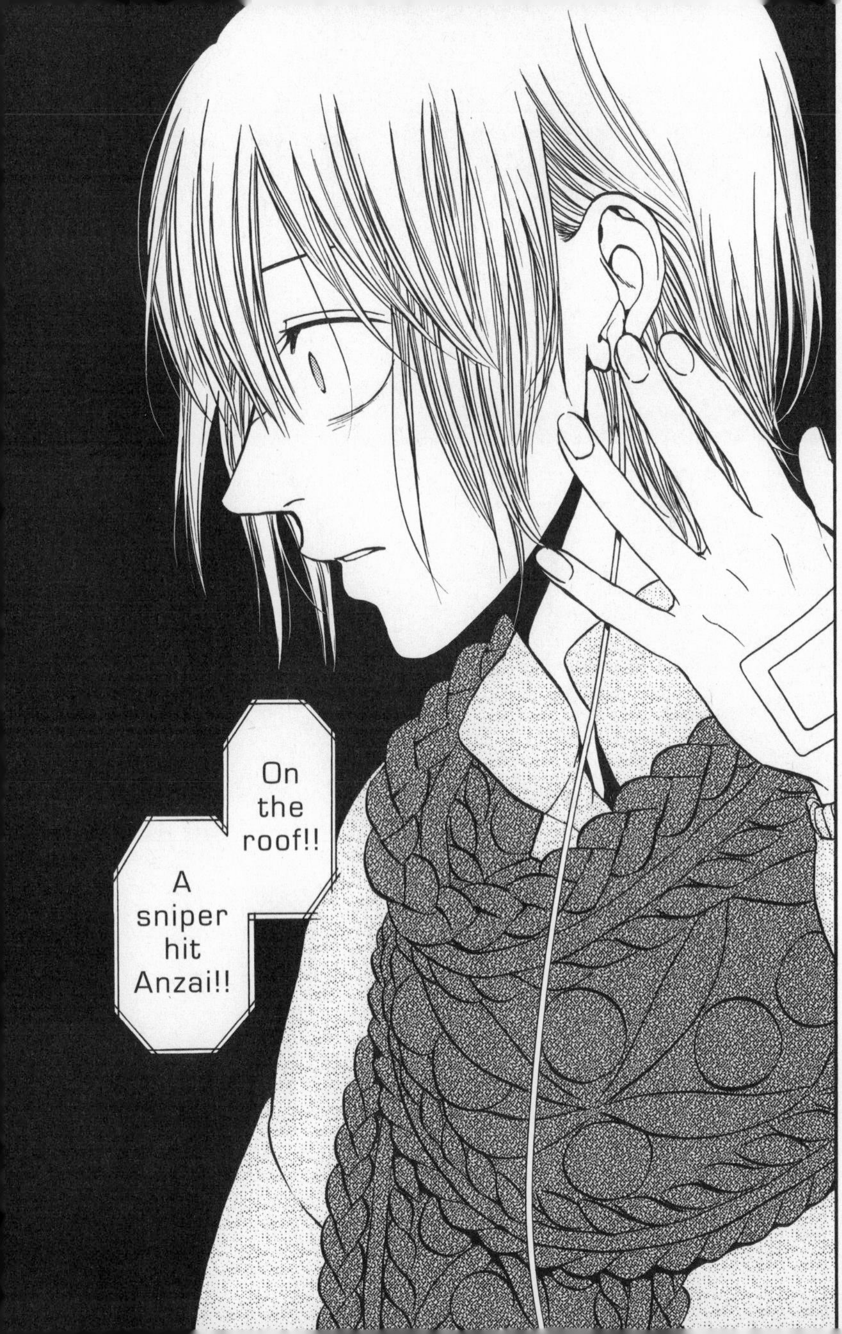
On the roof!!
A sniper hit Anzai!!

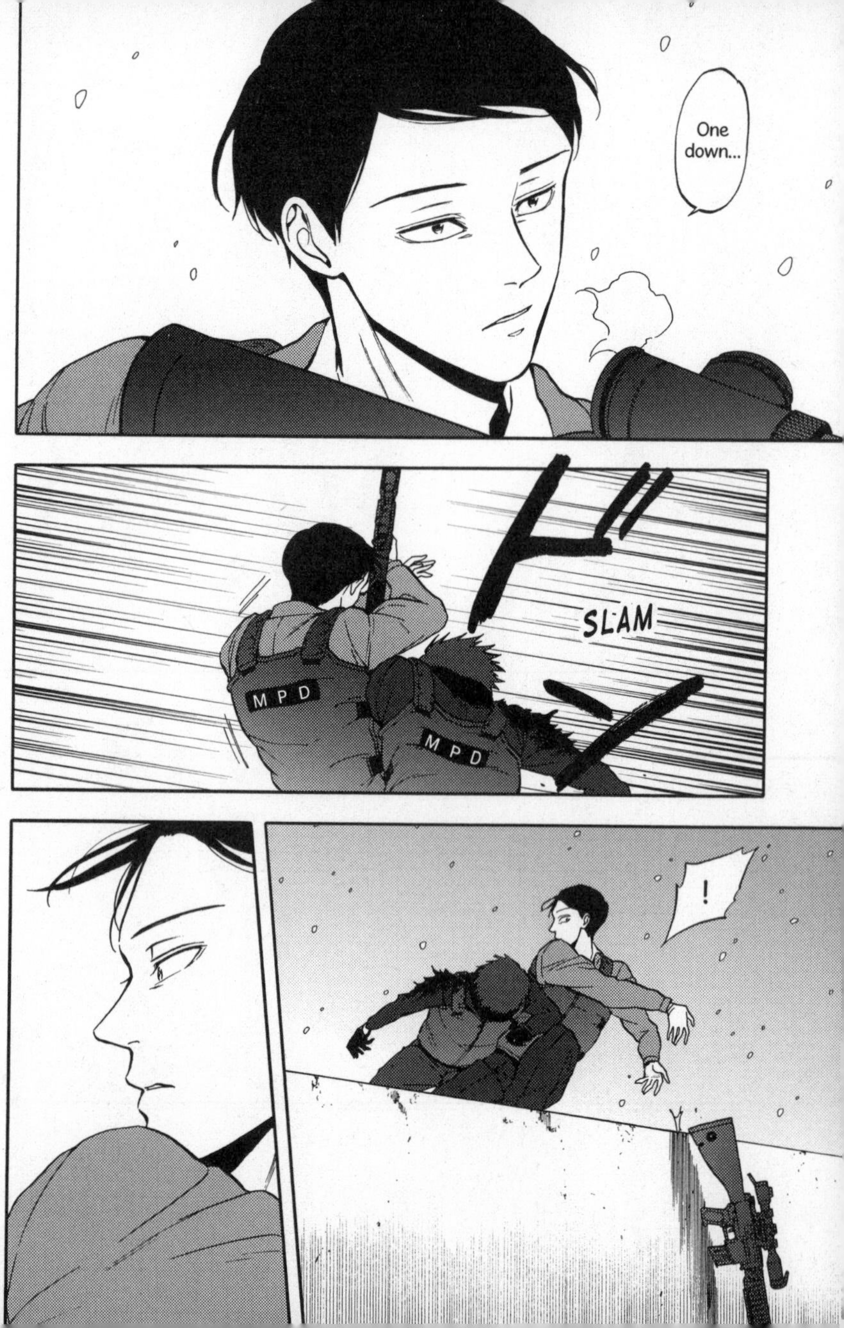
One down...
SLAM
!

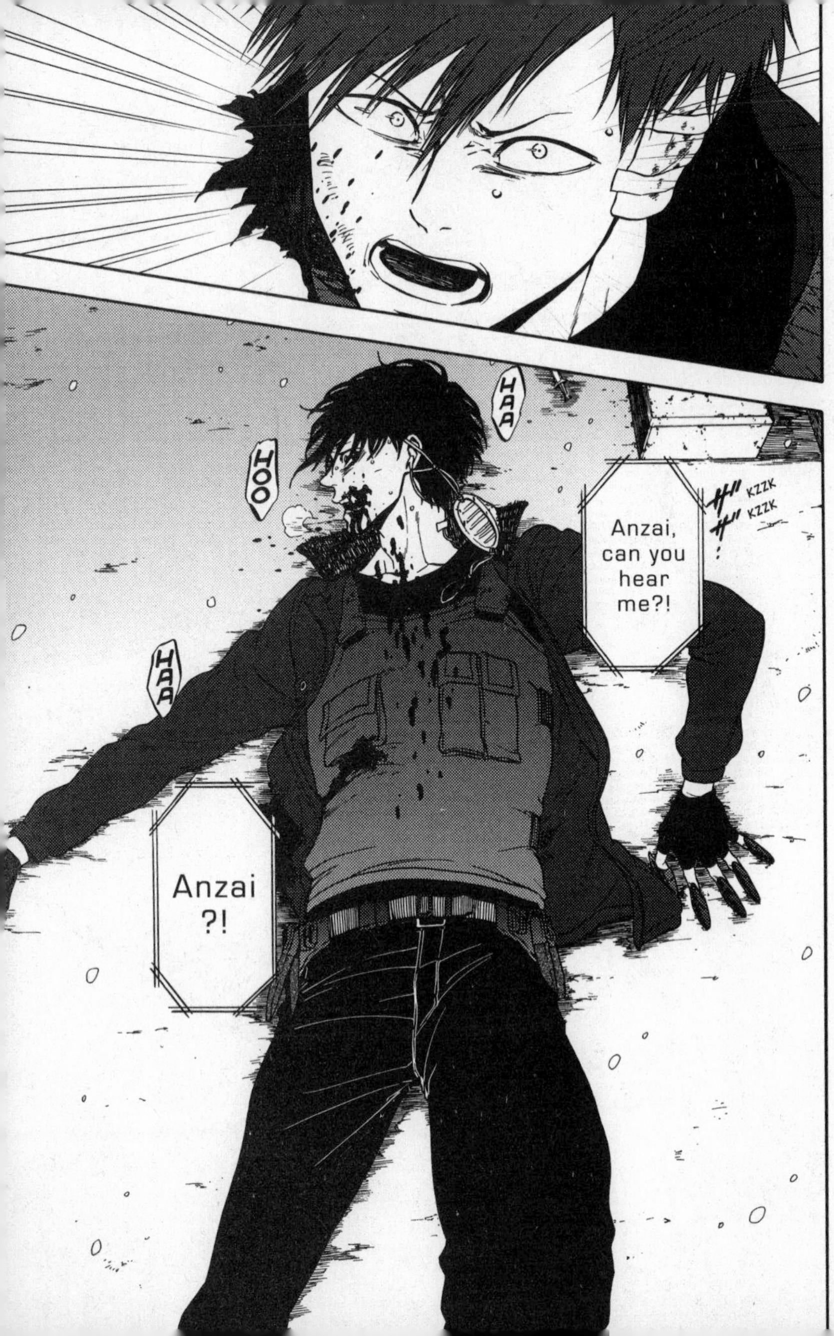
KZZK KZZK
Anzai, can you hear me?!
HAA
HOO
HAA
Anzai ?!

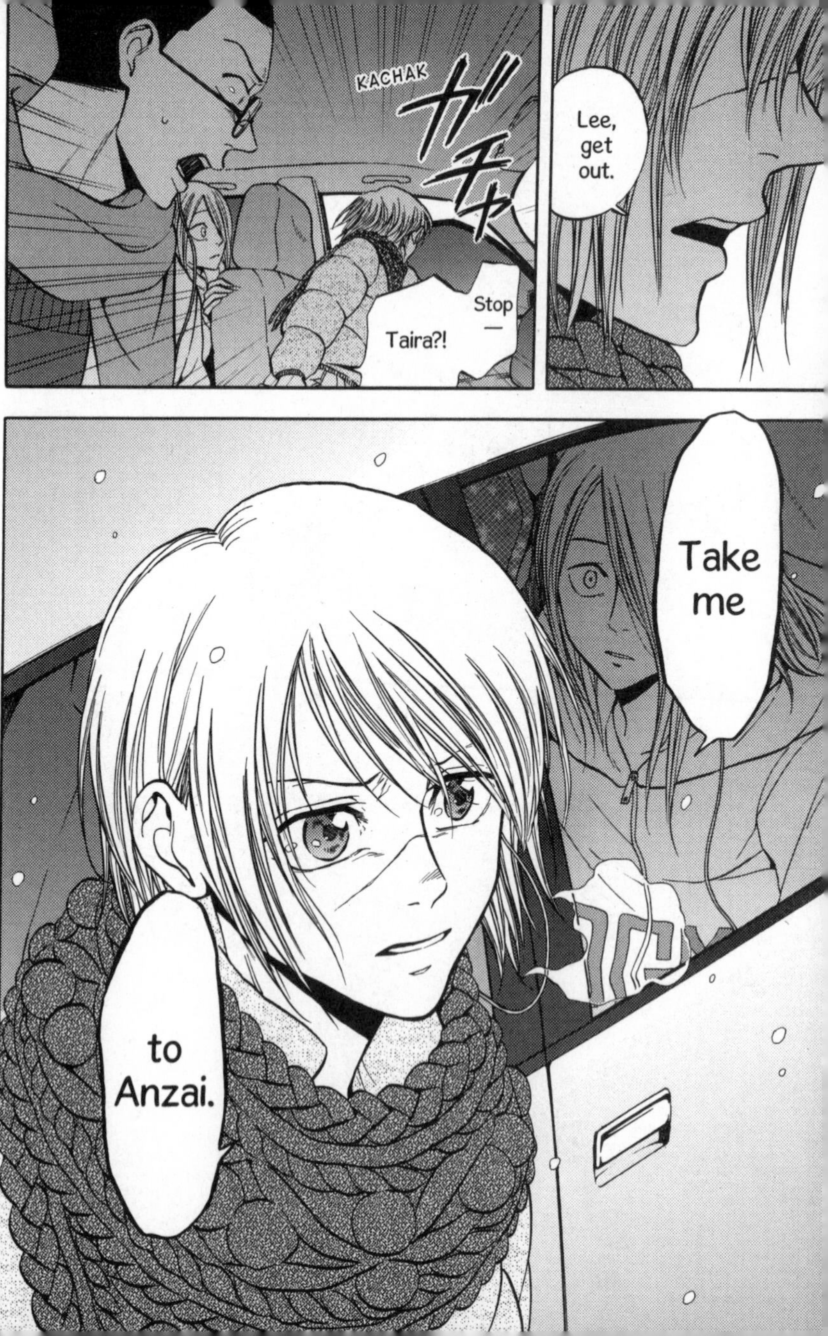
Lee, get out.
ガチャ
KACHAK
Stop —
Taira?!
Take me
to Anzai.

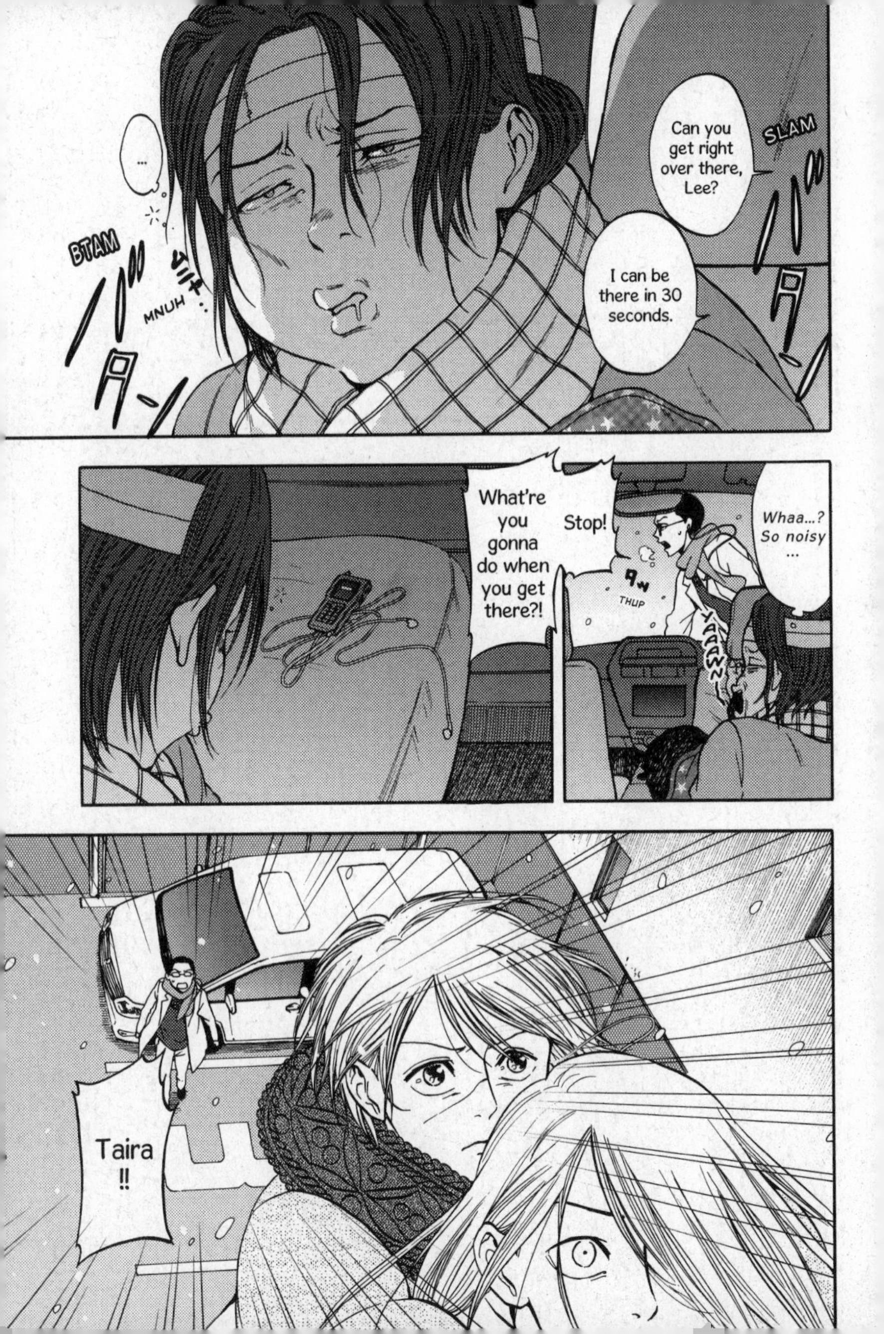
SLAM
Can you get right over there, Lee?
I can be there in 30 seconds.
...
BTAM
MNUH
Whaa...? So noisy ...
Stop!
THUP
YAAAWN
What're you gonna do when you get there?!
Taira !!

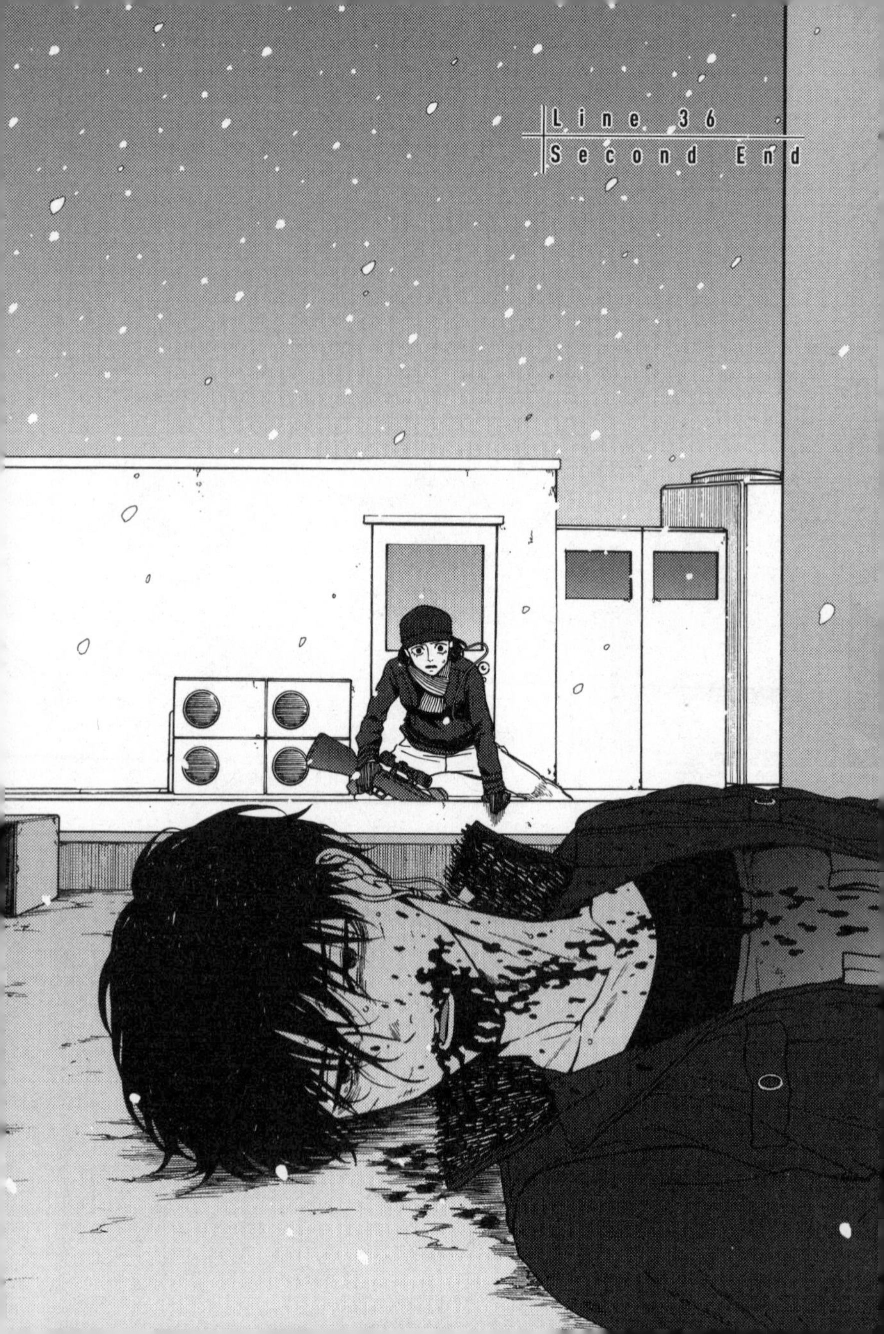
Line 36
Second End

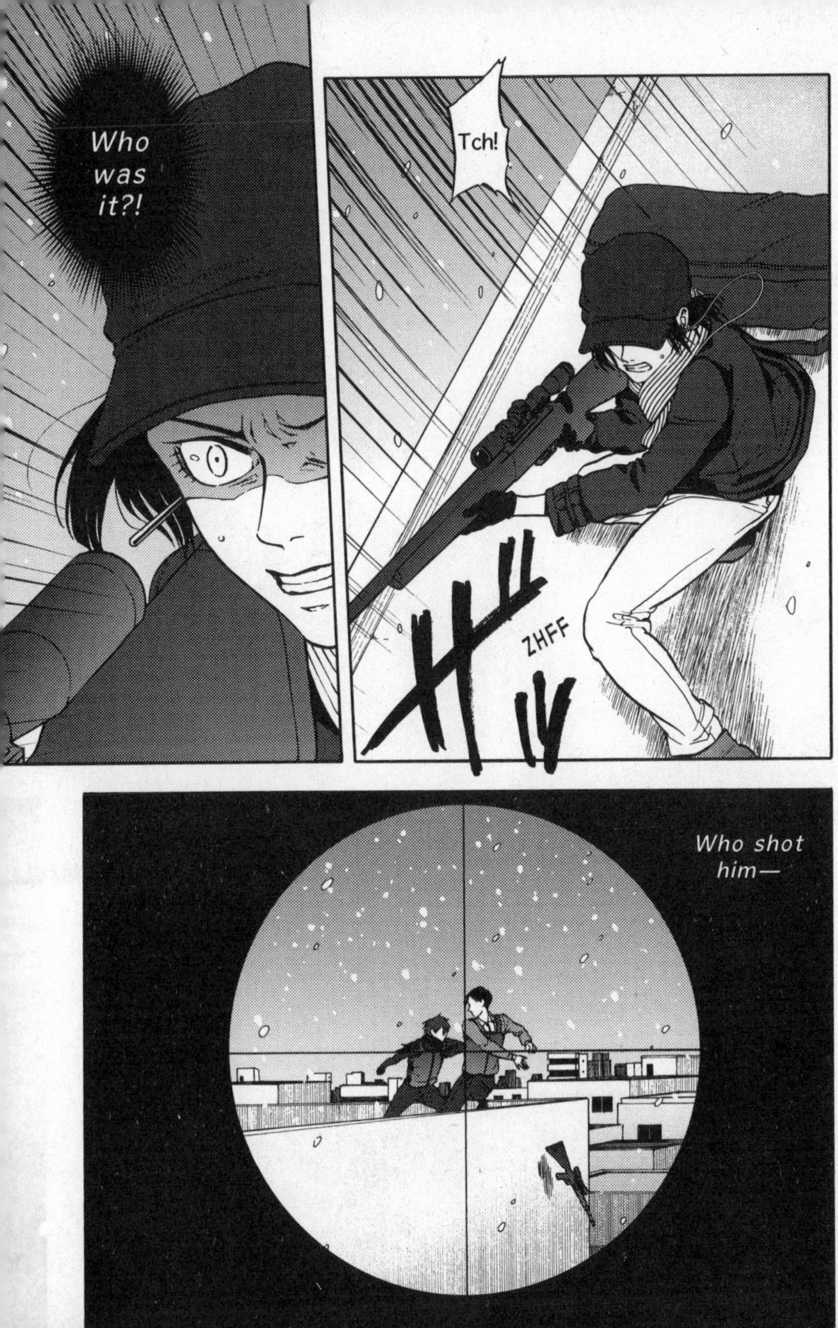
Tch!
ZHFF
Who was it?!
Who shot him—

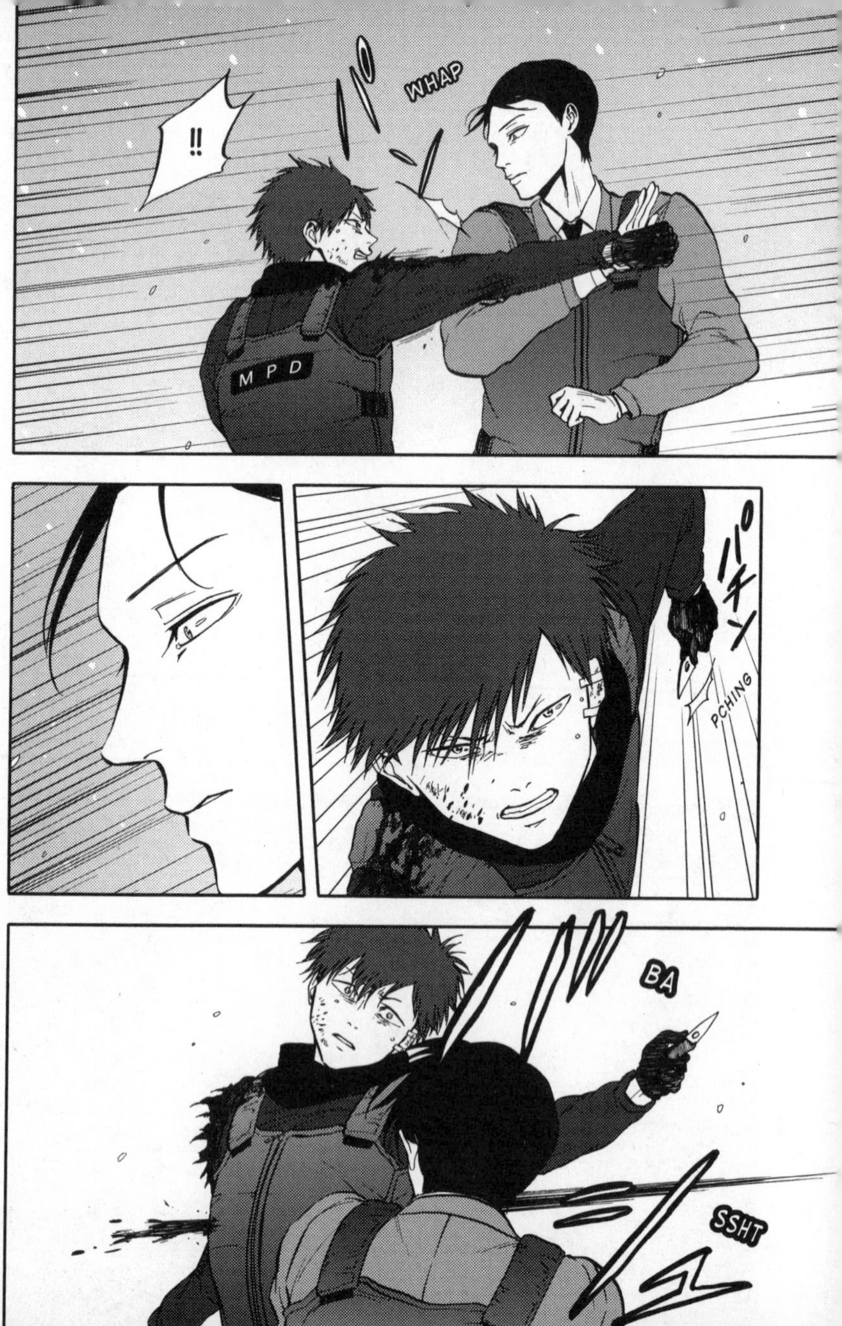
!!
WHAP
パチン
PCHING
BA
SSHT

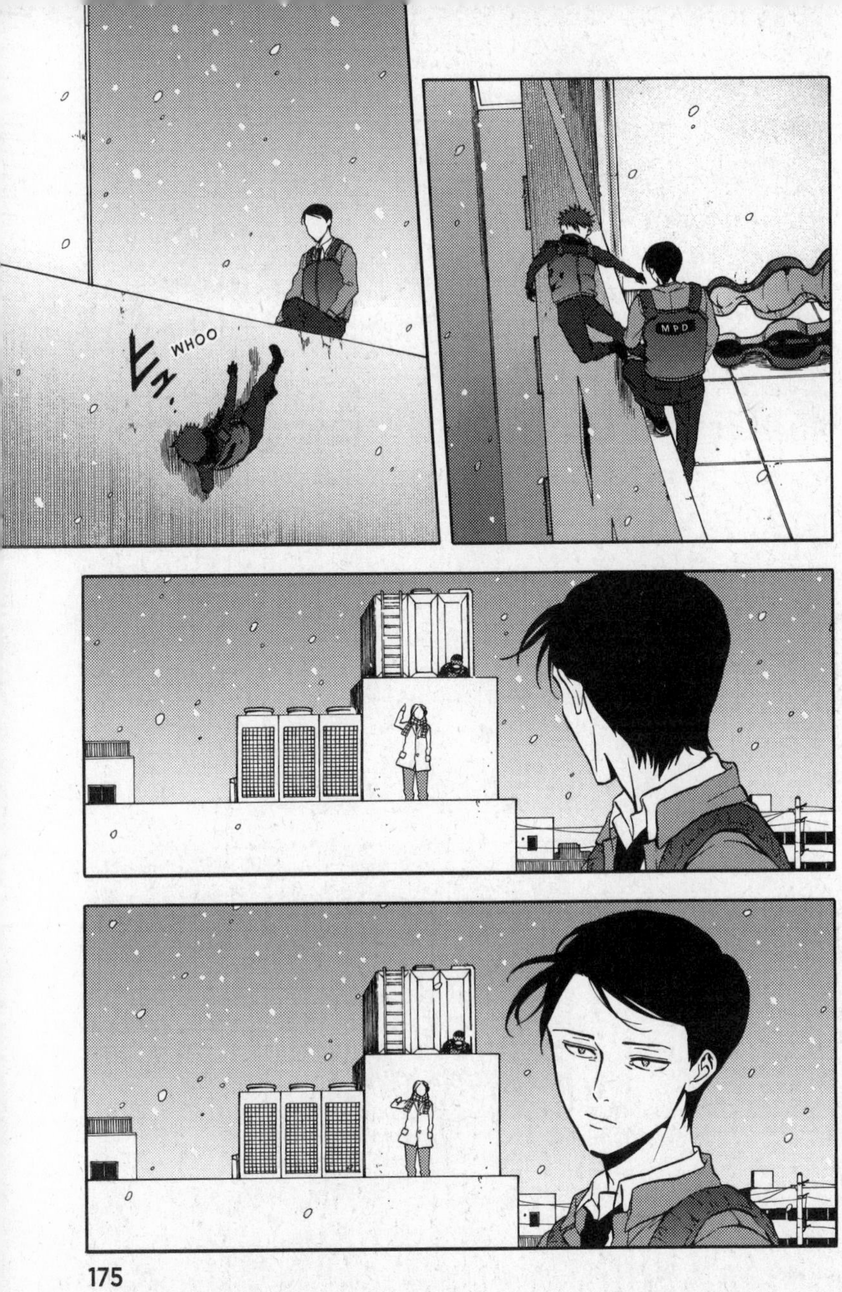
ヒュ
WHOO

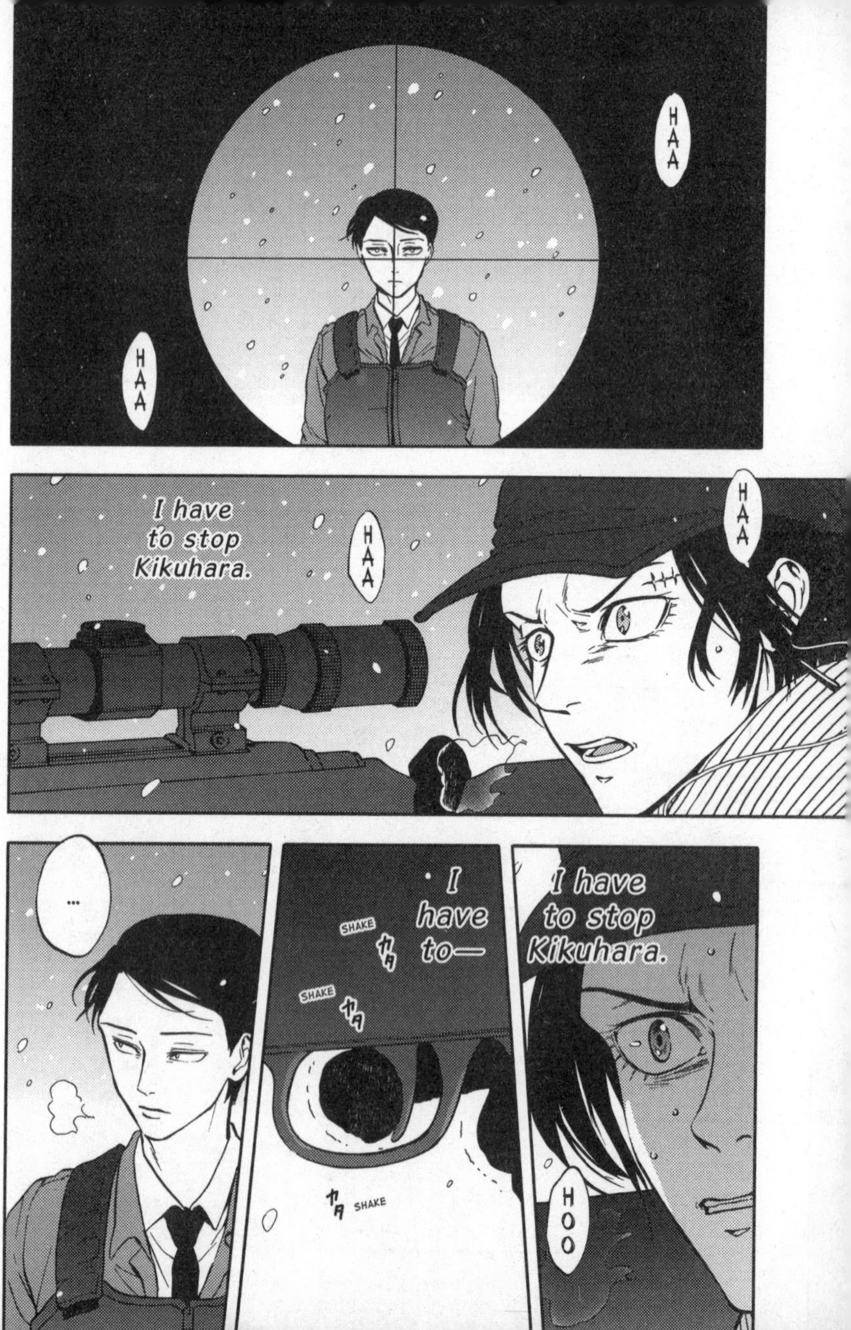
HAA
HAA
HAA
HAA
I have to stop Kikuhara.
I have to stop Kikuhara.
HOO
I have to—
SHAKE カタ
SHAKE カタ
カタ SHAKE
...

You can't shoot me, can you?

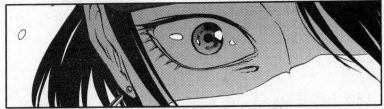

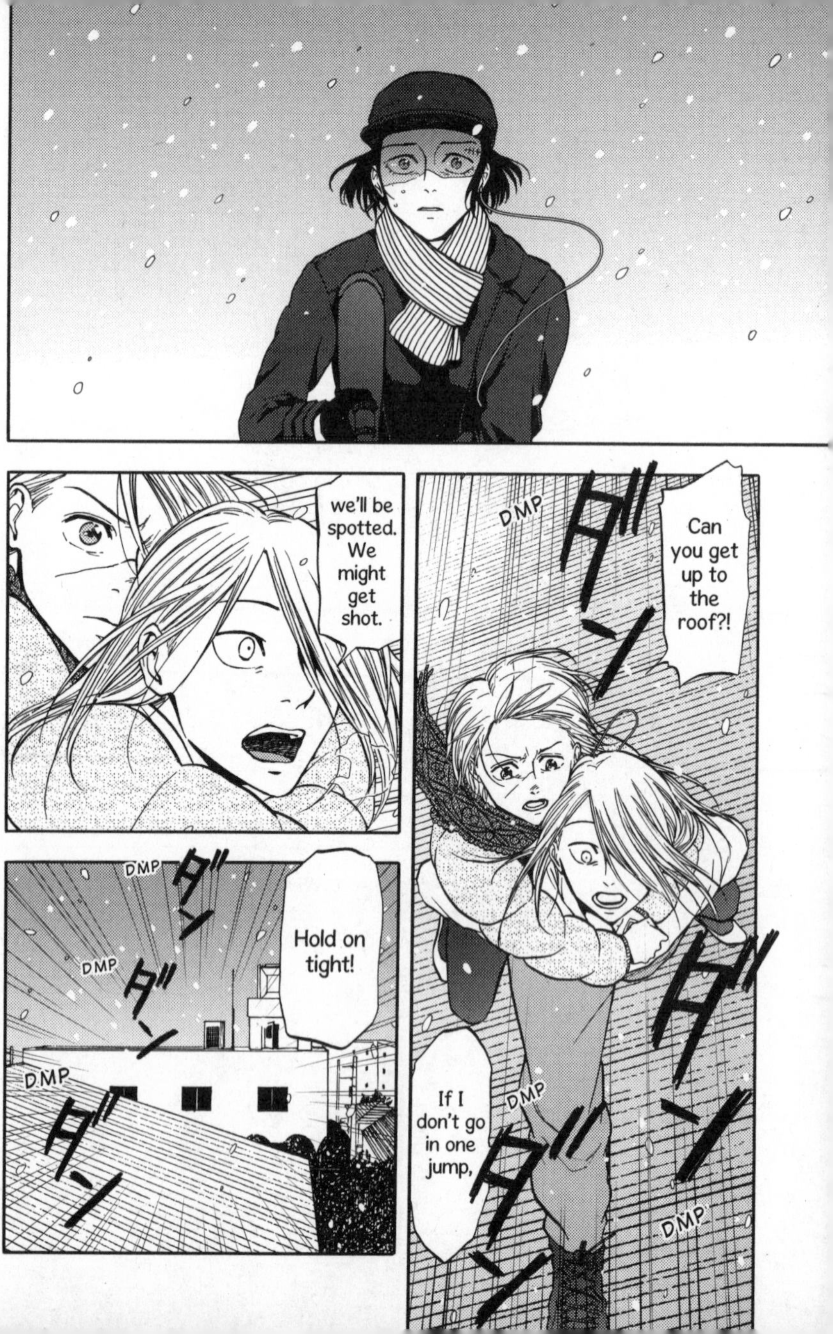
DMP
Can you get up to the roof?!
If I don't go in one jump,
DMP
DMP
we'll be spotted. We might get shot.
DMP
Hold on tight!
DMP
DMP

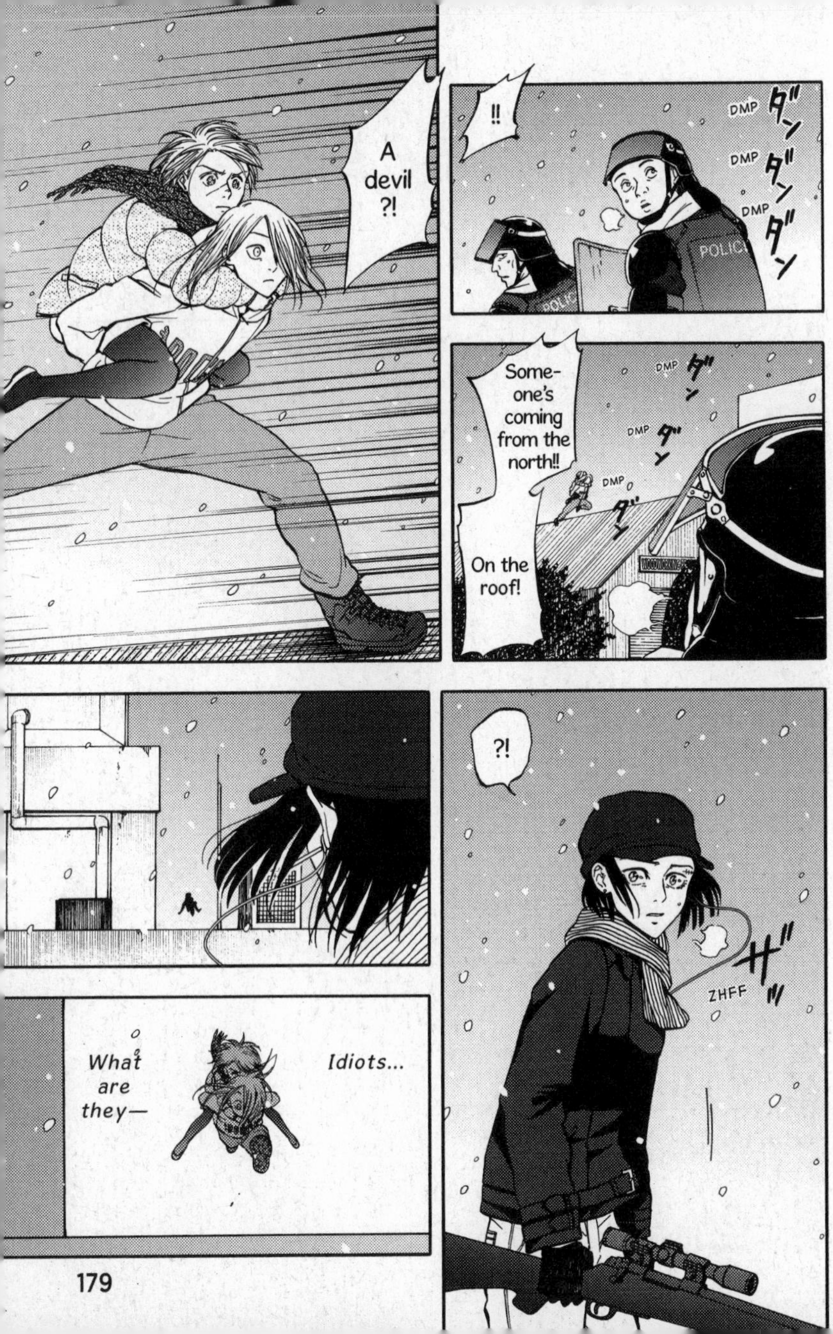
!!
DMP ダン
DMP ダン
DMP ダン
Some-one's coming from the north!!
On the roof!
DMP ダン
DMP ダン
DMP ダン
A devil ?!
?!
ZHFF ザッ
Idiots...
What are they—

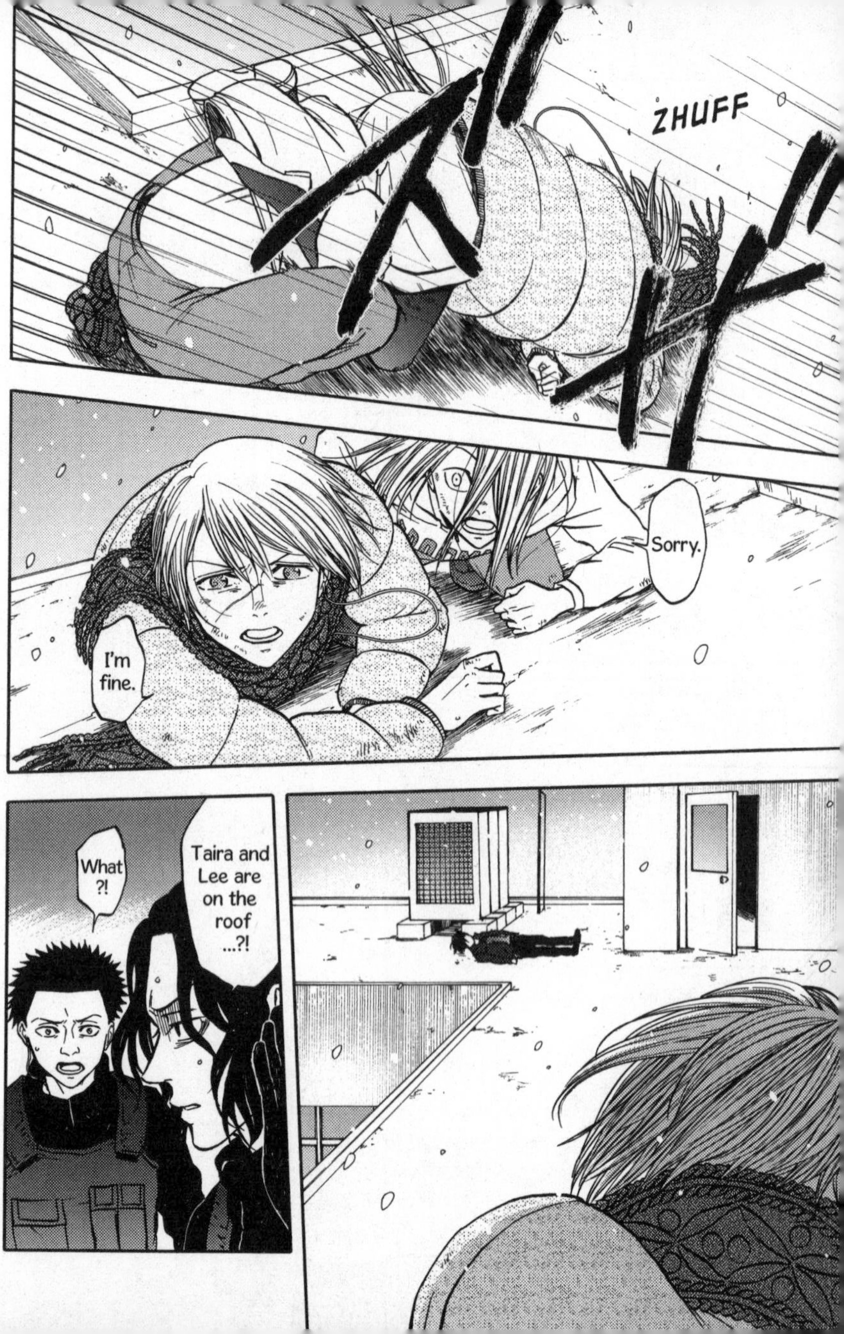
ZHUFF
Sorry.
I'm fine.
Taira and Lee are on the roof ...?!
What ?!

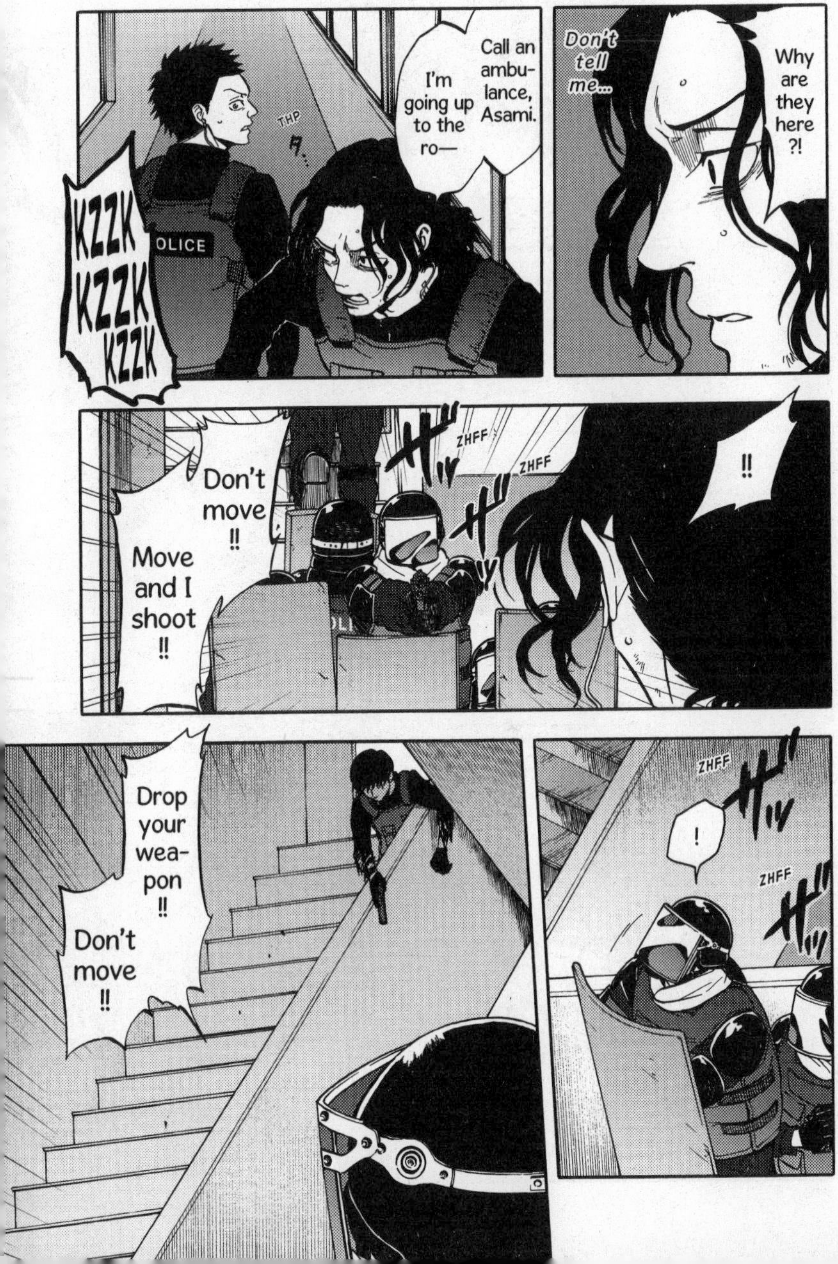
Why are they here?!
Don't tell me...
Call an ambulance, Asami. I'm going up to the ro—
THP
KZZK KZZK KZZK
!!
ZHFF
ZHFF
Don't move!! Move and I shoot!!
ZHFF
!
ZHFF
Drop your weapon!! Don't move!!

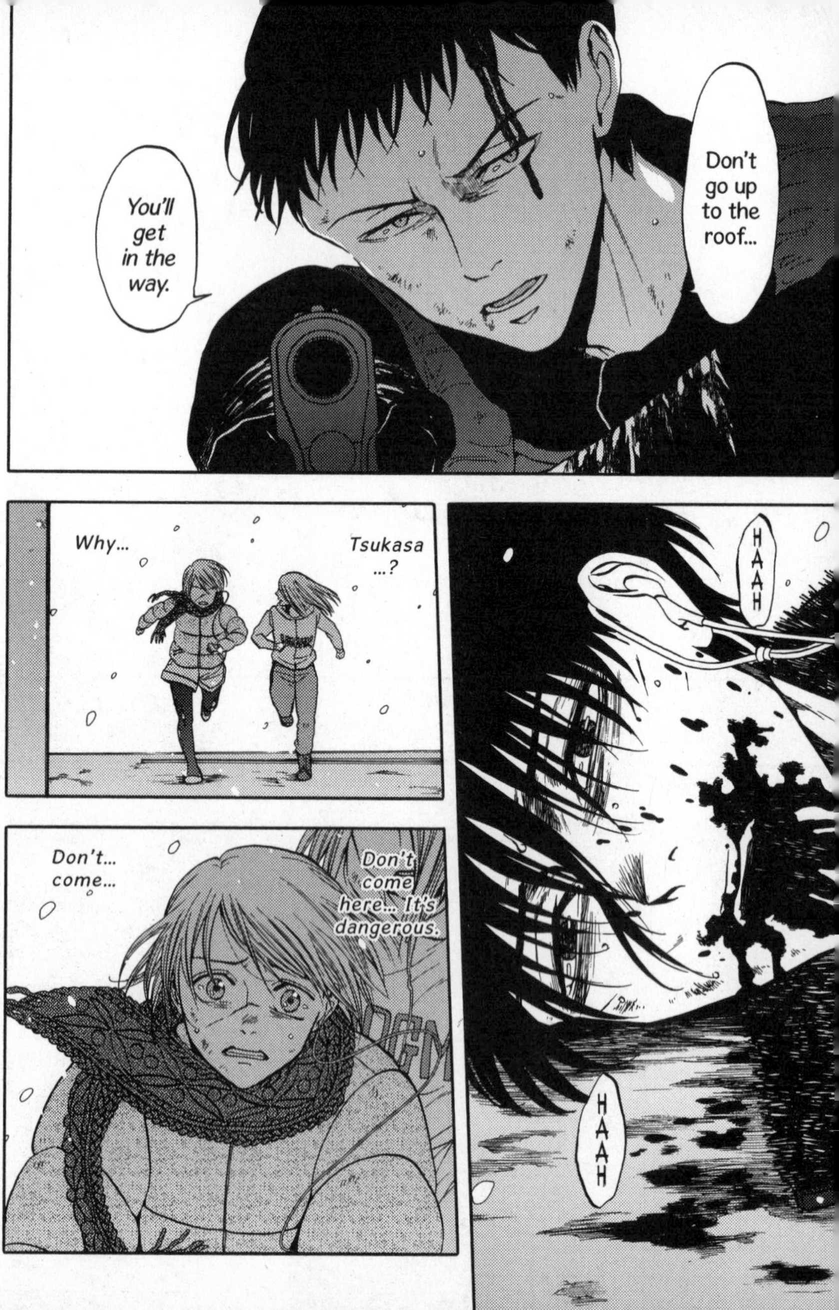
Don't go up to the roof...
You'll get in the way.
HAAH
HAAH
Why...
Tsukasa ...?
Don't come here... It's dangerous.
Don't... come...

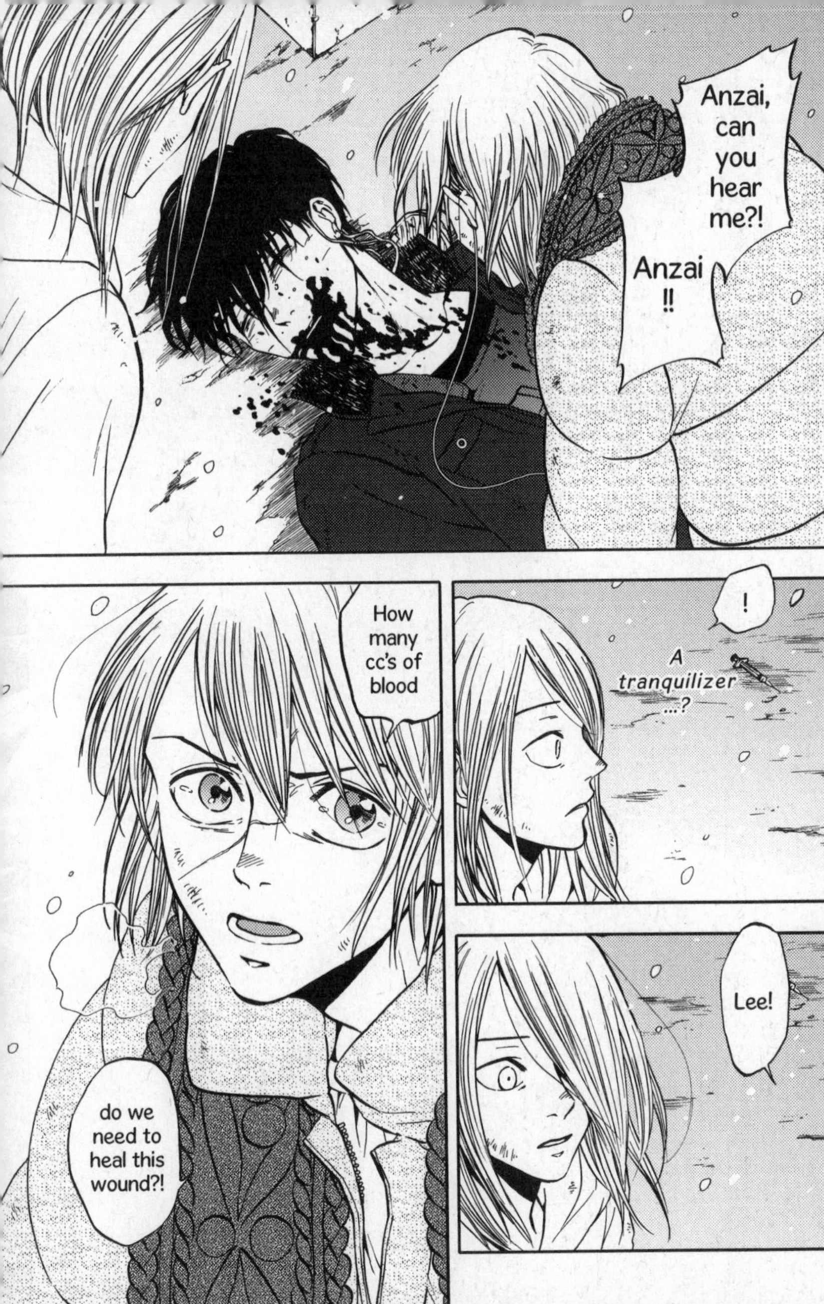
Anzai, can you hear me?!
Anzai!!
!
A tranquilizer ...?
Lee!
How many cc's of blood
do we need to heal this wound?!

So that is why they came...

...

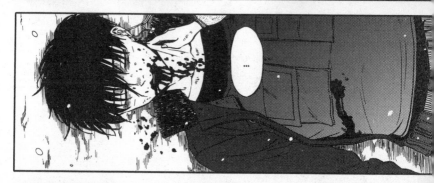

...

For just the wound and lost blood, 200 cc.

But right now he needs 400 cc.

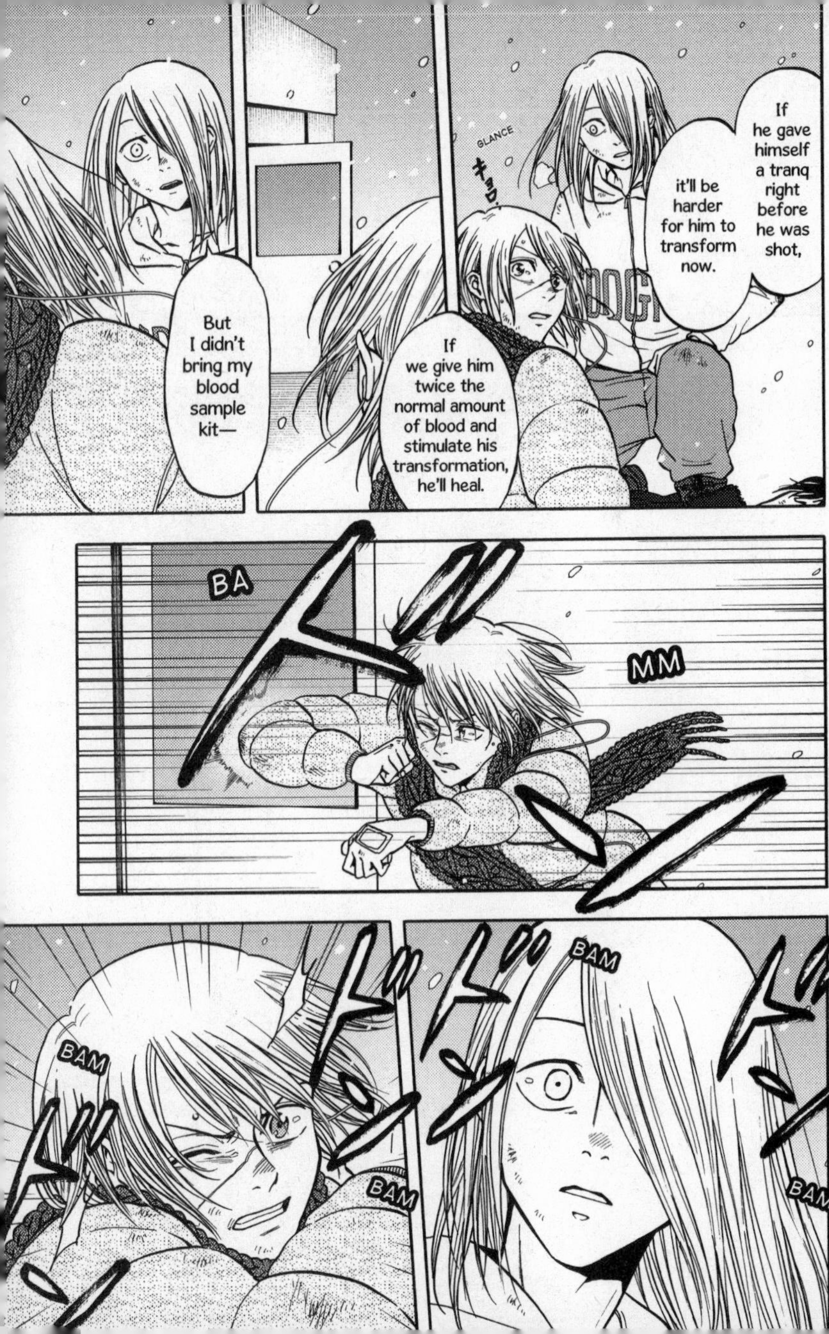
If he gave himself a tranq right before he was shot,
it'll be harder for him to transform now.
GLANCE
If we give him twice the normal amount of blood and stimulate his transformation, he'll heal.
But I didn't bring my blood sample kit—
BA
MM
BAM
BAM
BAM
BAM

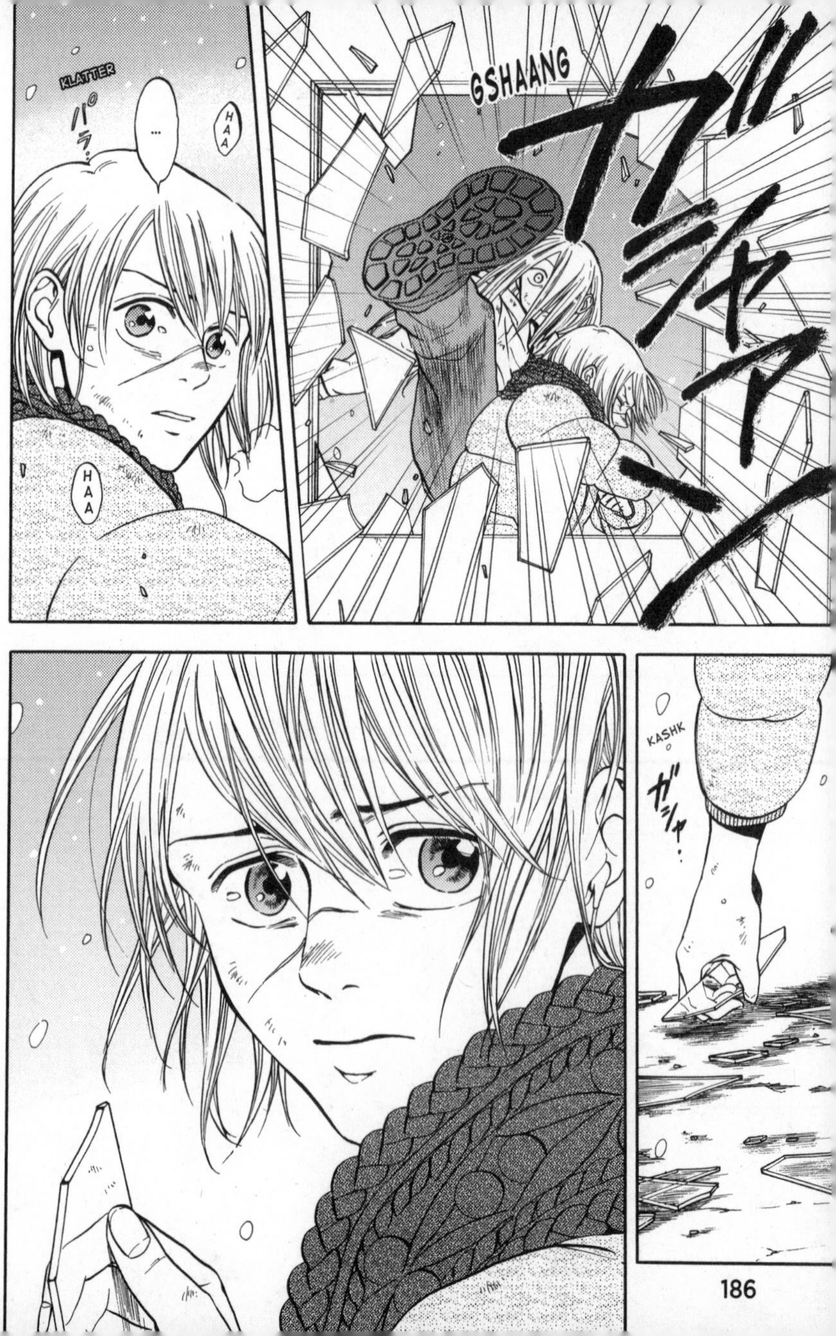
GSHAANG
ガシャーン
KLATTER
パラ
HAA
...
HAA
KASHK
ガシャ

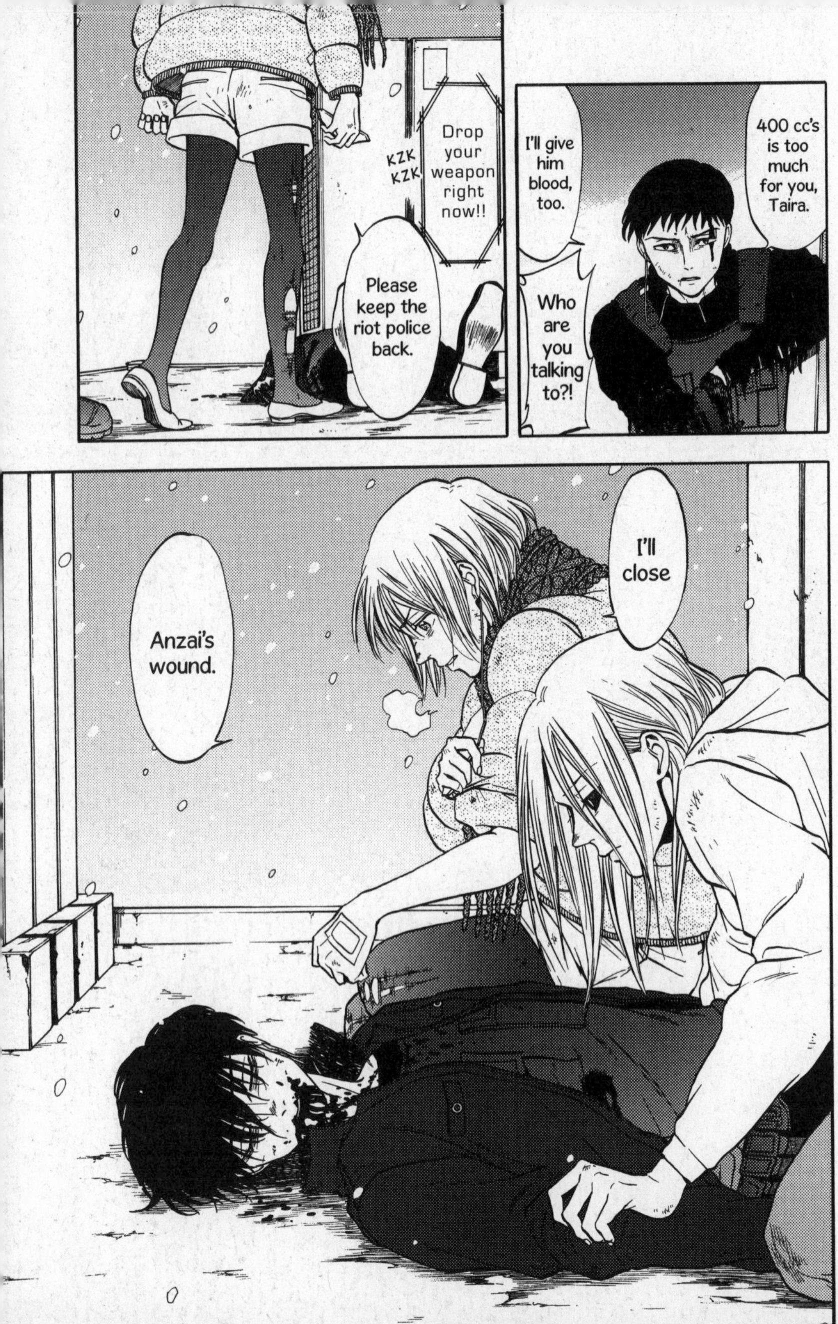
400 cc's is too much for you, Taira.
I'll give him blood, too.
Who are you talking to?!
Drop your weapon right now!!
KZK KZK
Please keep the riot police back.
I'll close
Anzai's wound.

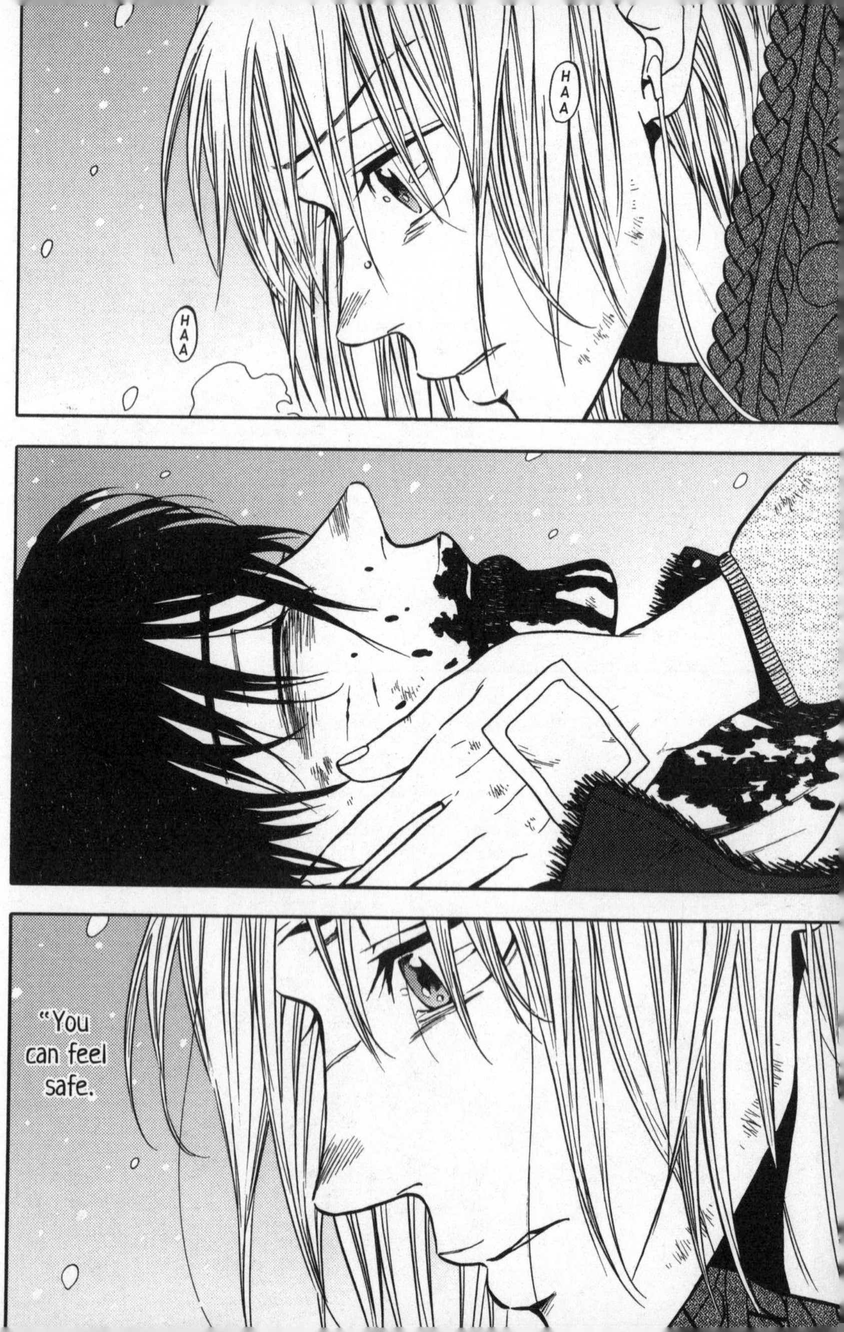
HAA
HAA
"You can feel safe.

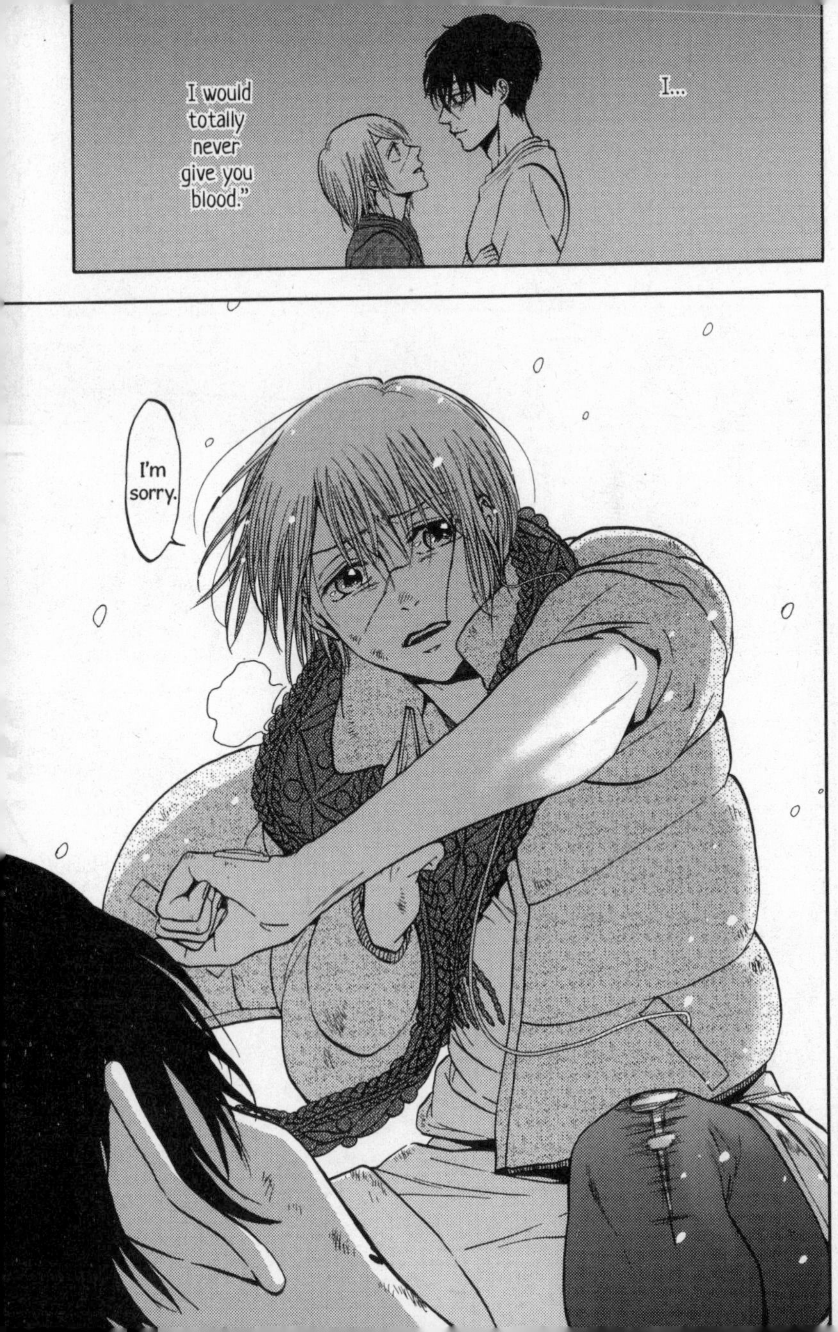
I...
I would totally never give you blood."
I'm sorry.

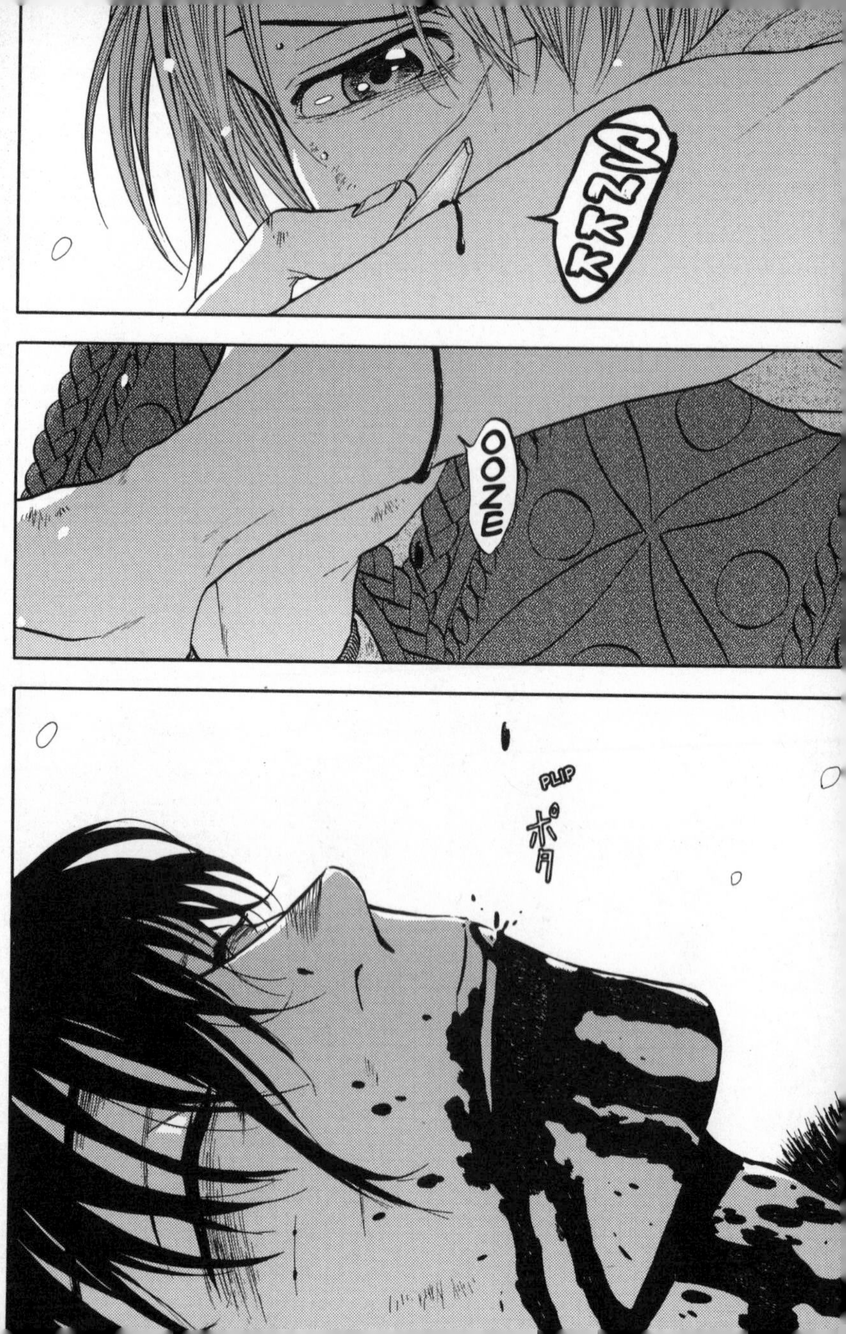
SLKK
OOZE
PLIP
ポタ

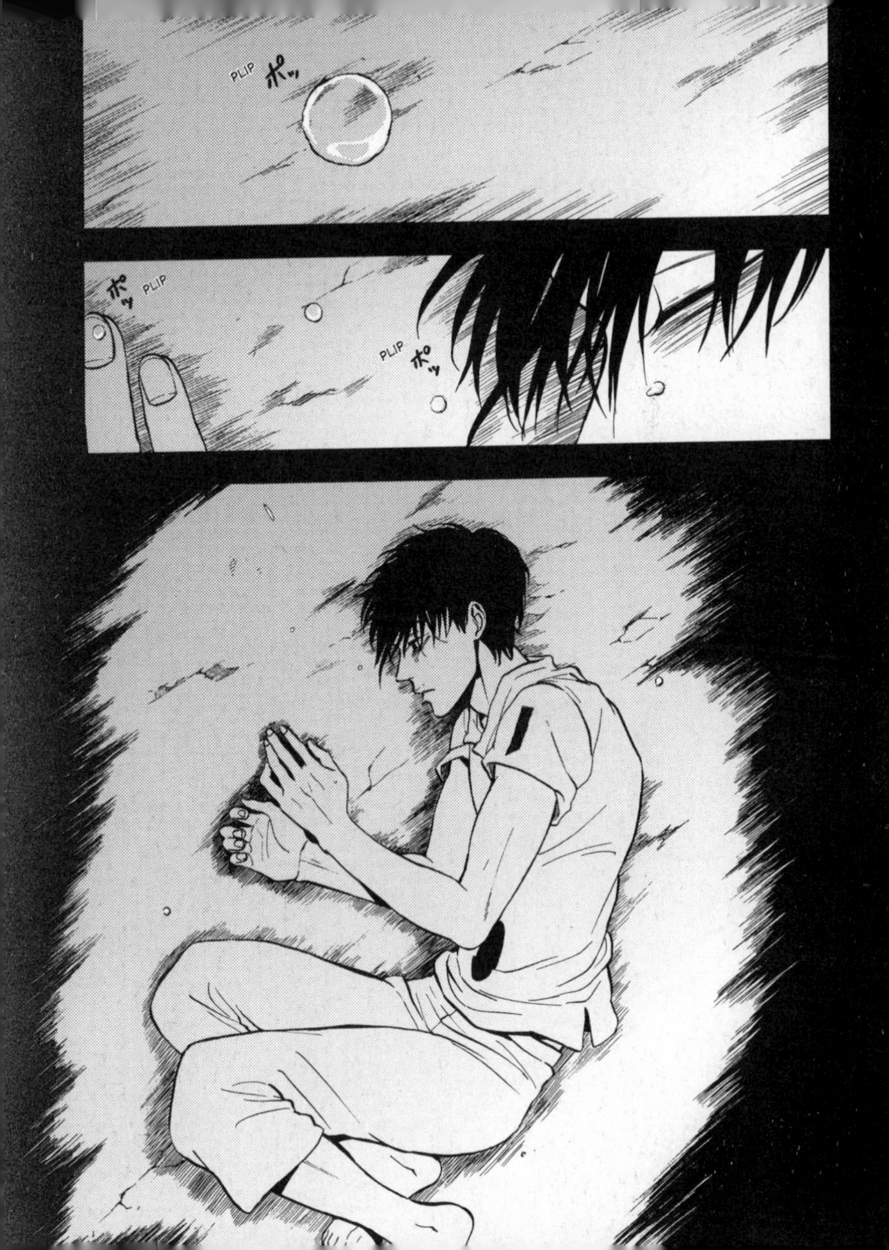
PLIP
ポッ
PLIP
ポッ
ポッ
PLIP

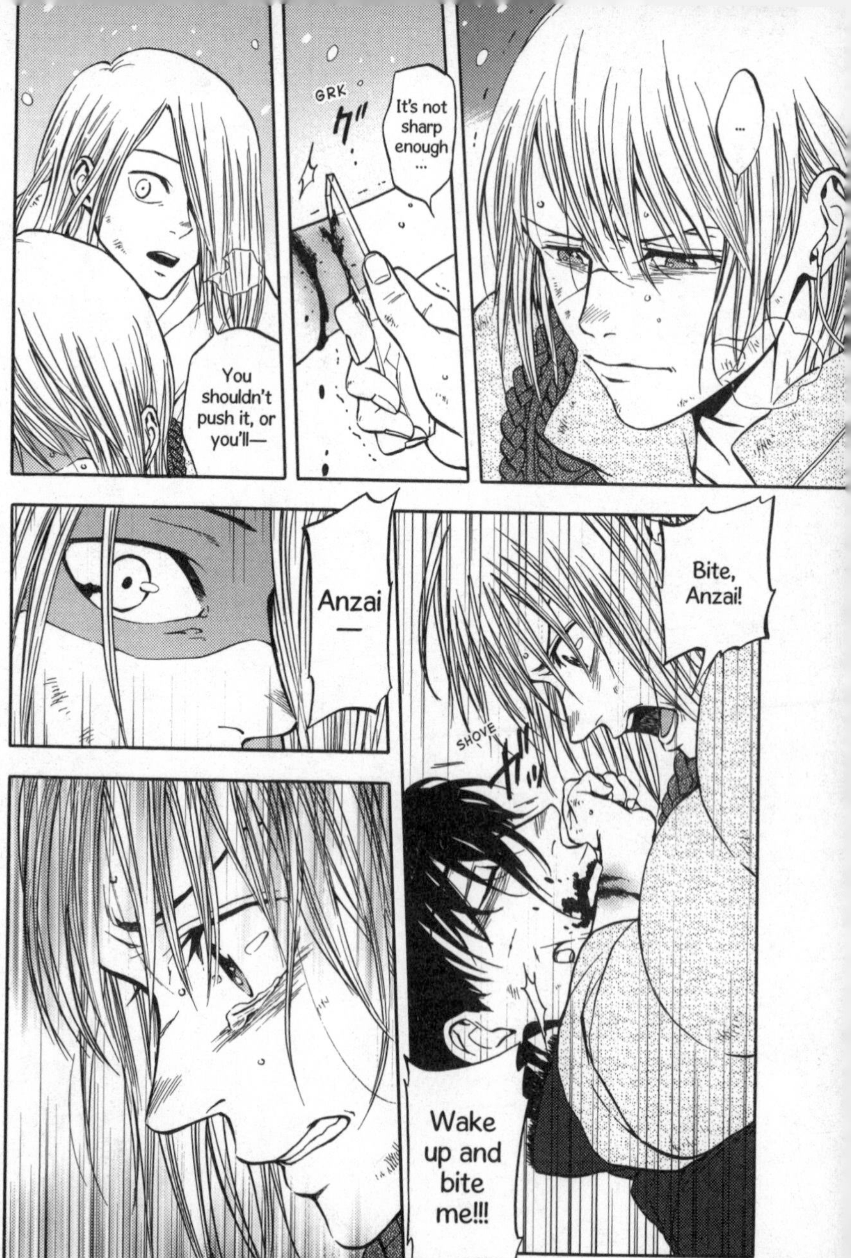
...
GRK
It's not sharp enough ...
You shouldn't push it, or you'll—
Bite, Anzai!
SHOVE
Wake up and bite me!!!
Anzai —

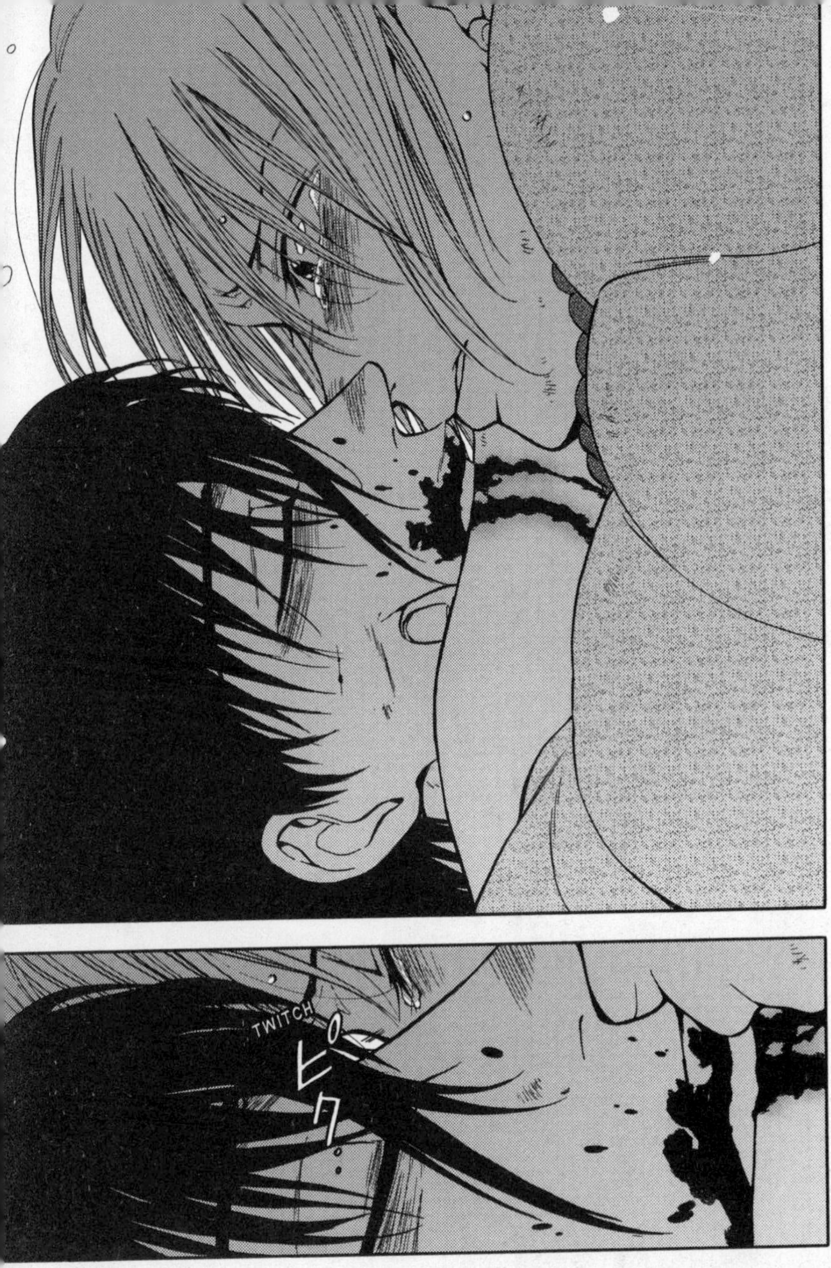
TWITCH
ピク

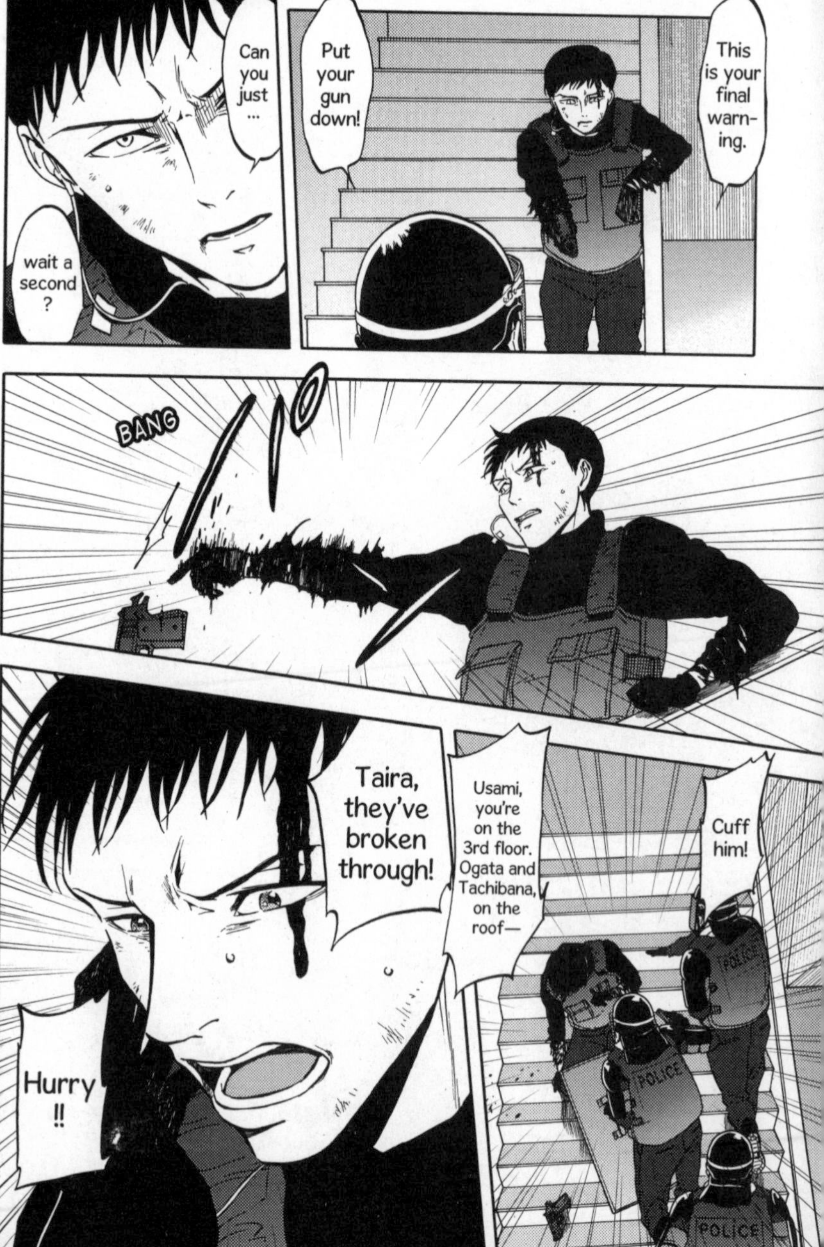
This is your final warn-ing.
Put your gun down!
Can you just ...
wait a second ?
BANG
Cuff him!
Usami, you're on the 3rd floor. Ogata and Tachibana, on the roof—
Taira, they've broken through!
Hurry !!

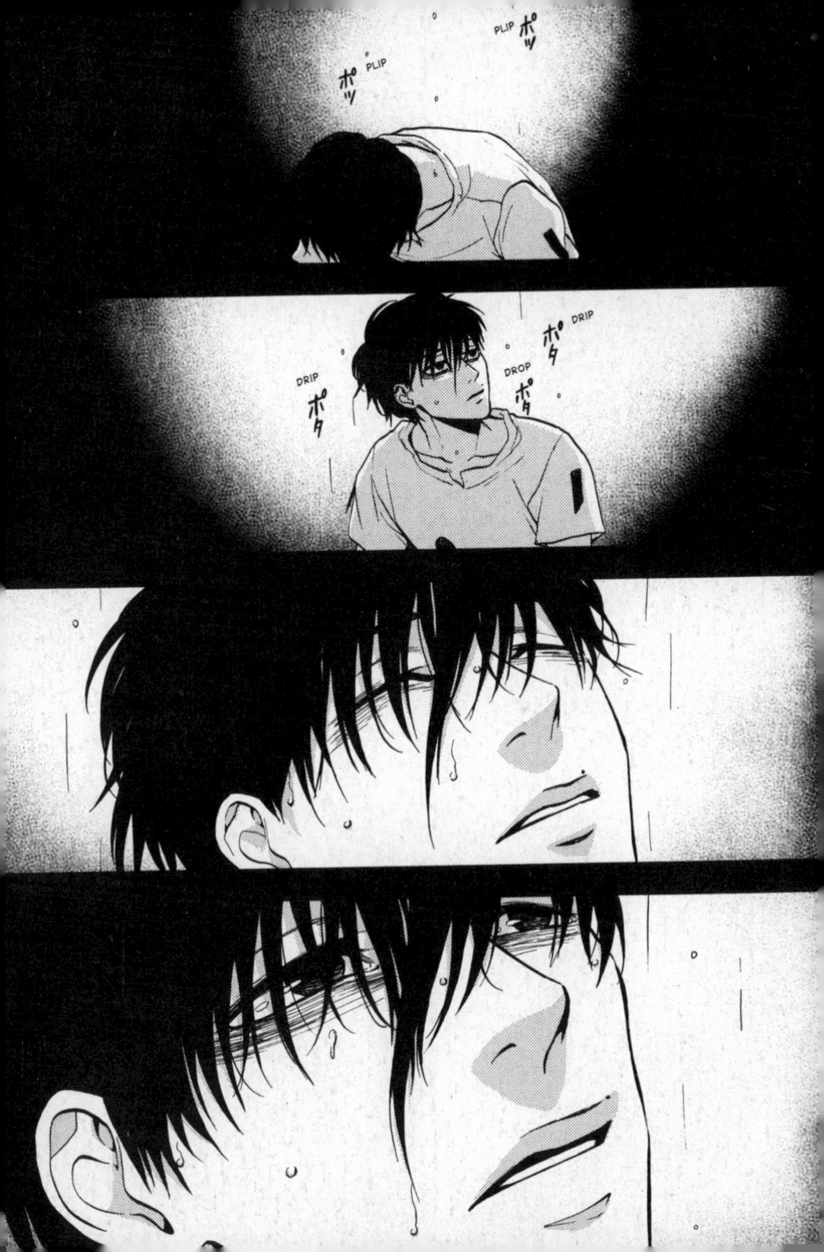
PLIP ポッ
ポッ PLIP
ポタ DRIP
ポタ DROP
ポタ DRIP

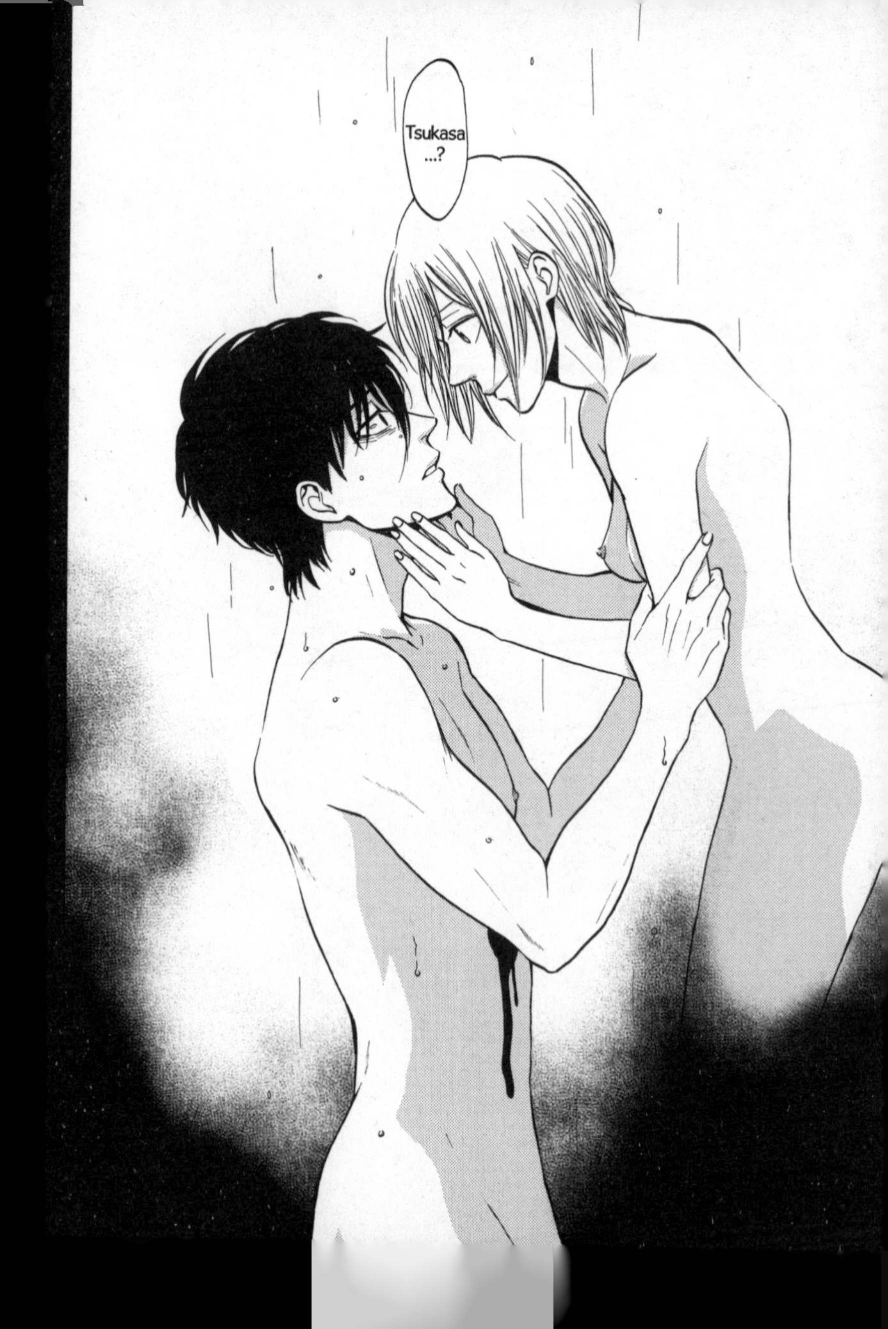
Tsukasa ...?

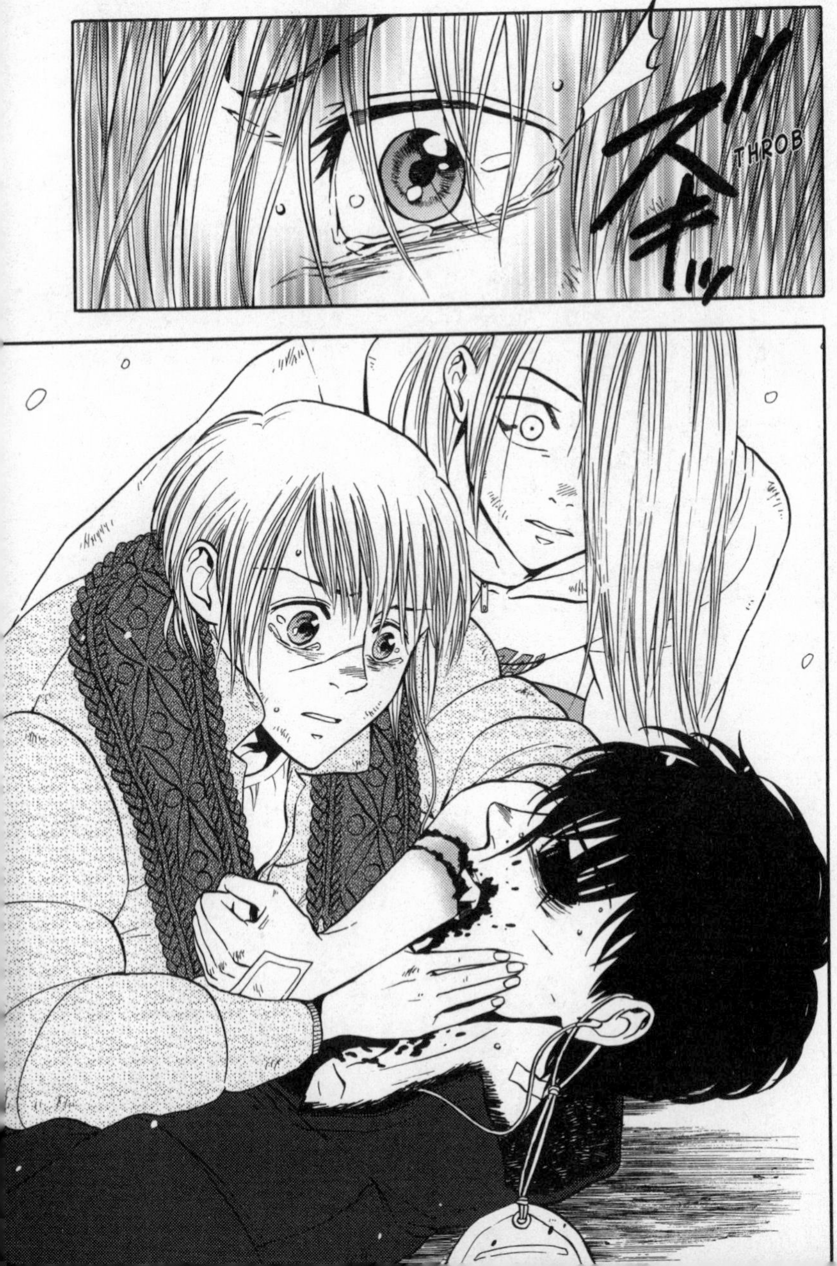
ズキッ
THROB

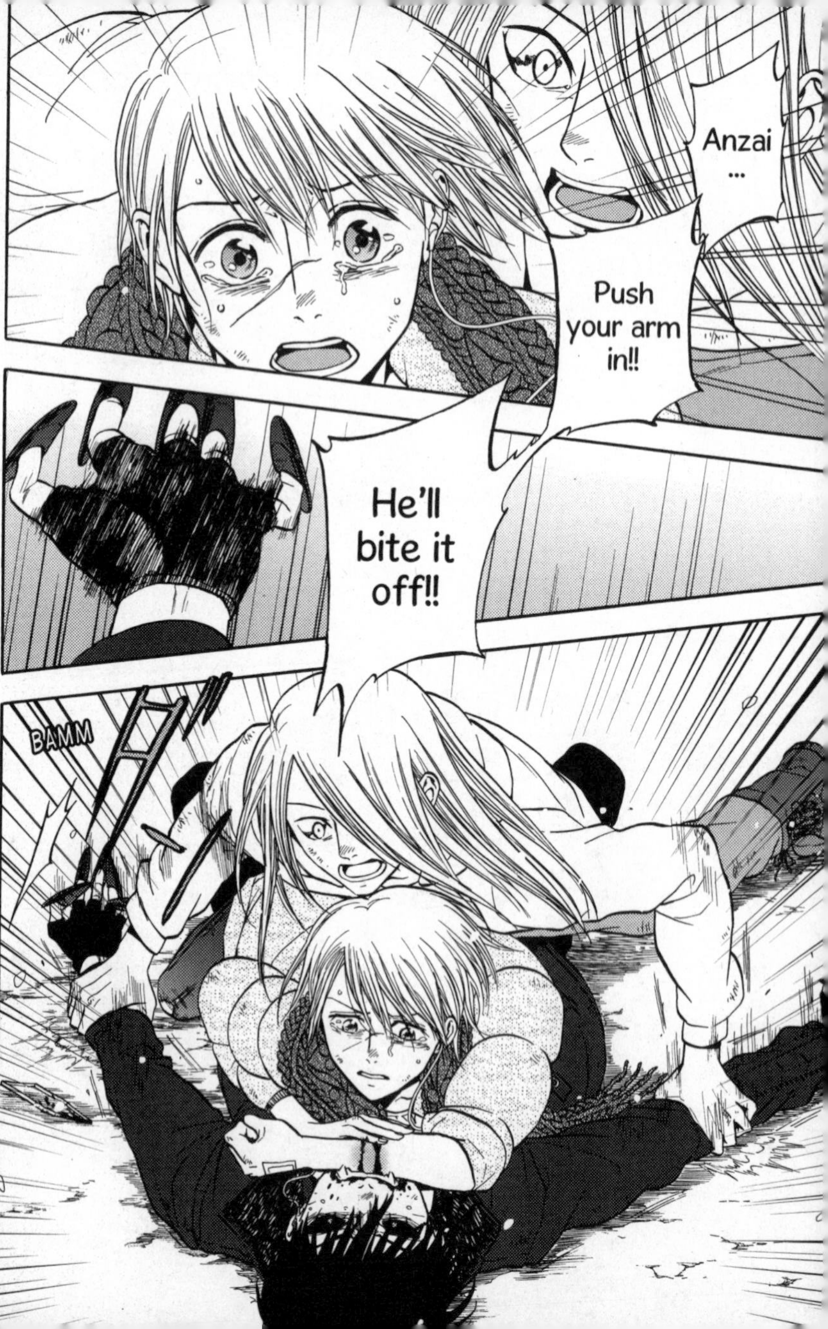
Anzai ...
Push your arm in!!
He'll bite it off!!
BAMM

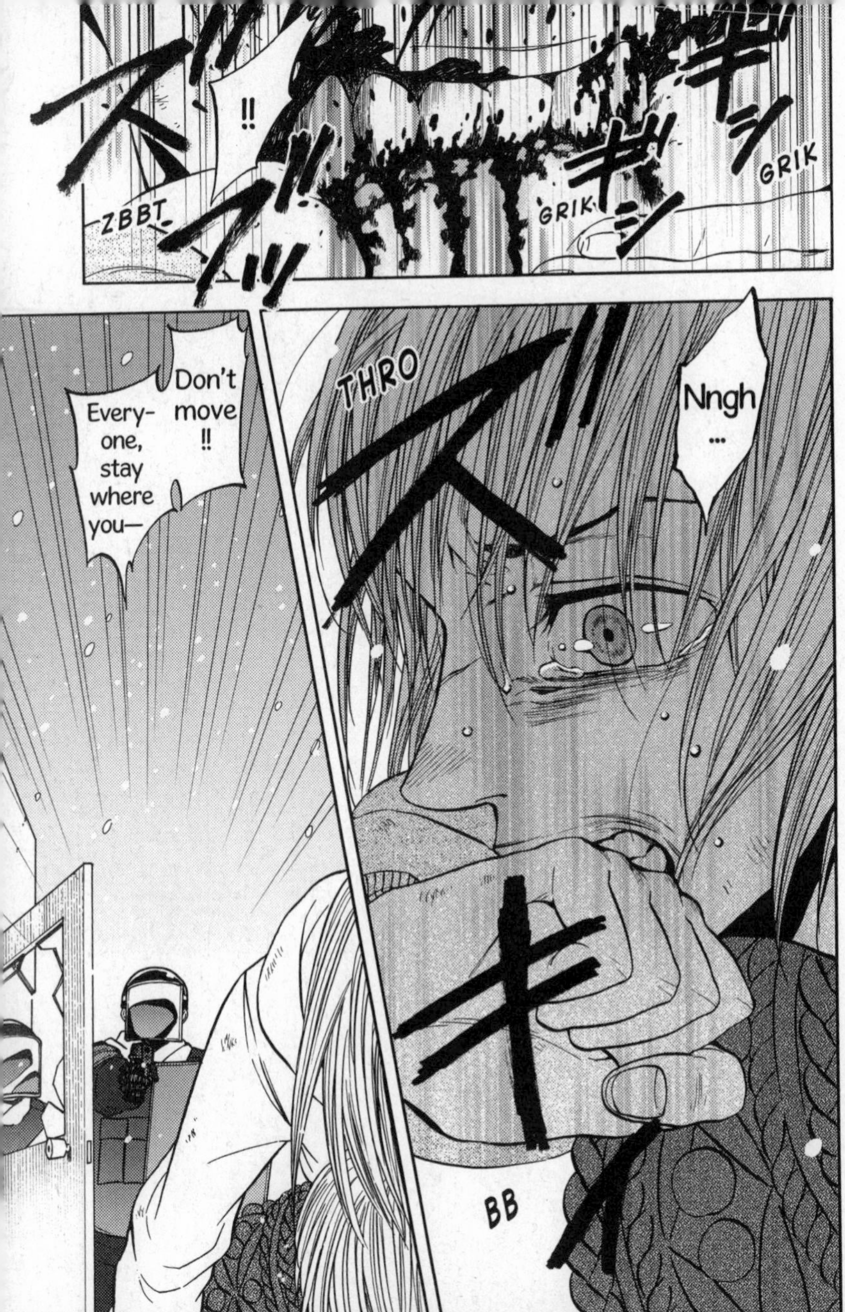
GRIK
GRIK
!!
ZBBT
THRO
Nngh…
BB
Don't move!!
Every-one, stay where you—

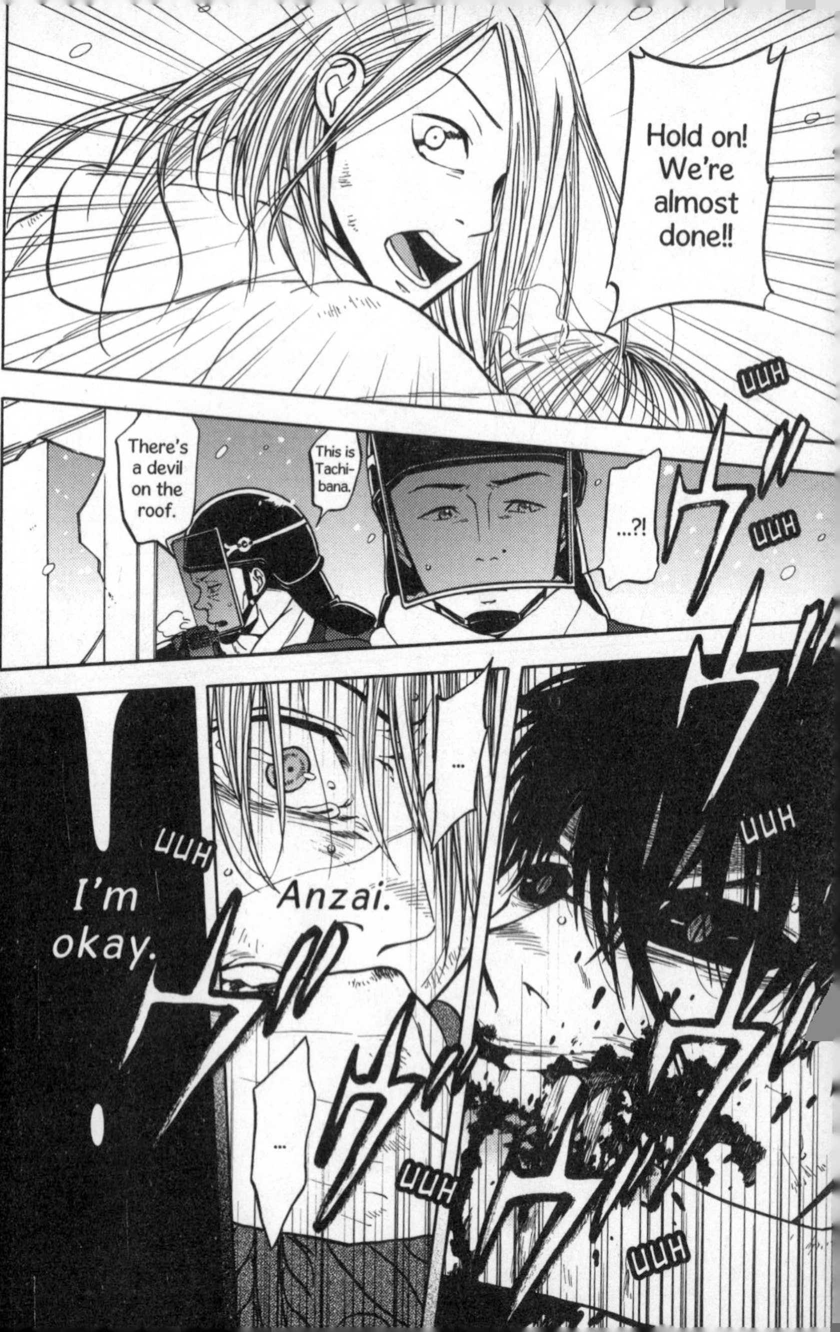
Hold on! We're almost done!!
UUH
...?!
UUH
This is Tachibana.
There's a devil on the roof.
UUH
...
Anzai.
UUH
I'm okay.
...
UUH
UUH

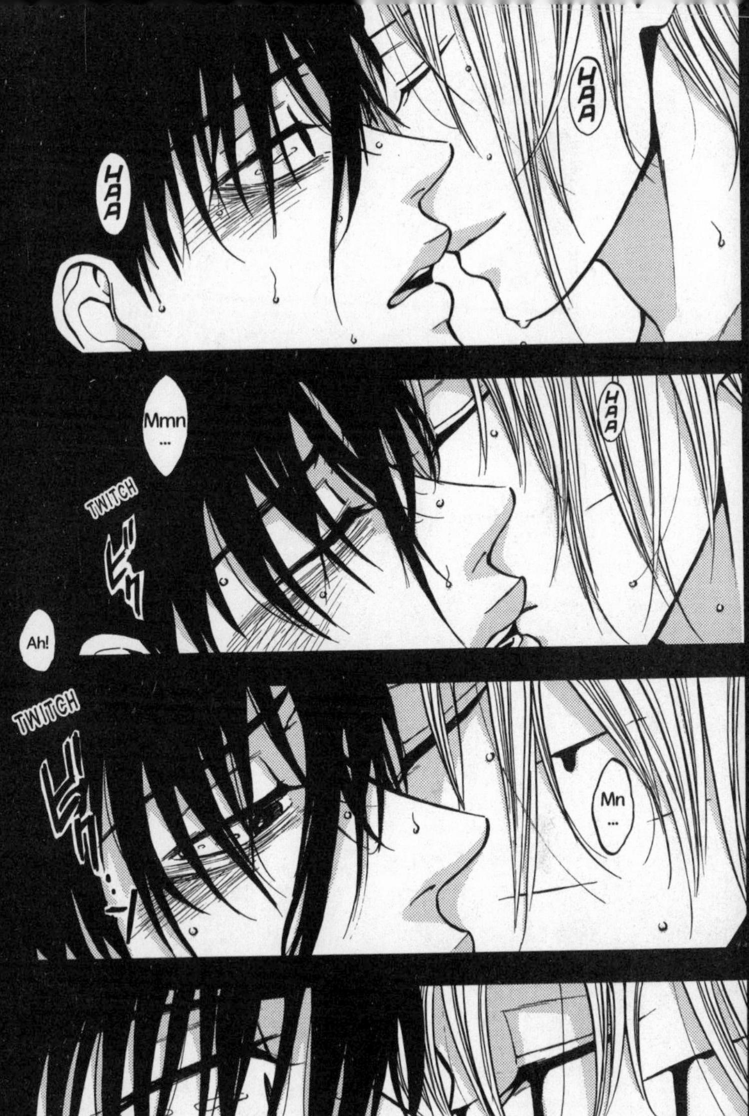
HAA
HAA
HAA
Mmn...
TWITCH
Ah!
Mn...
TWITCH

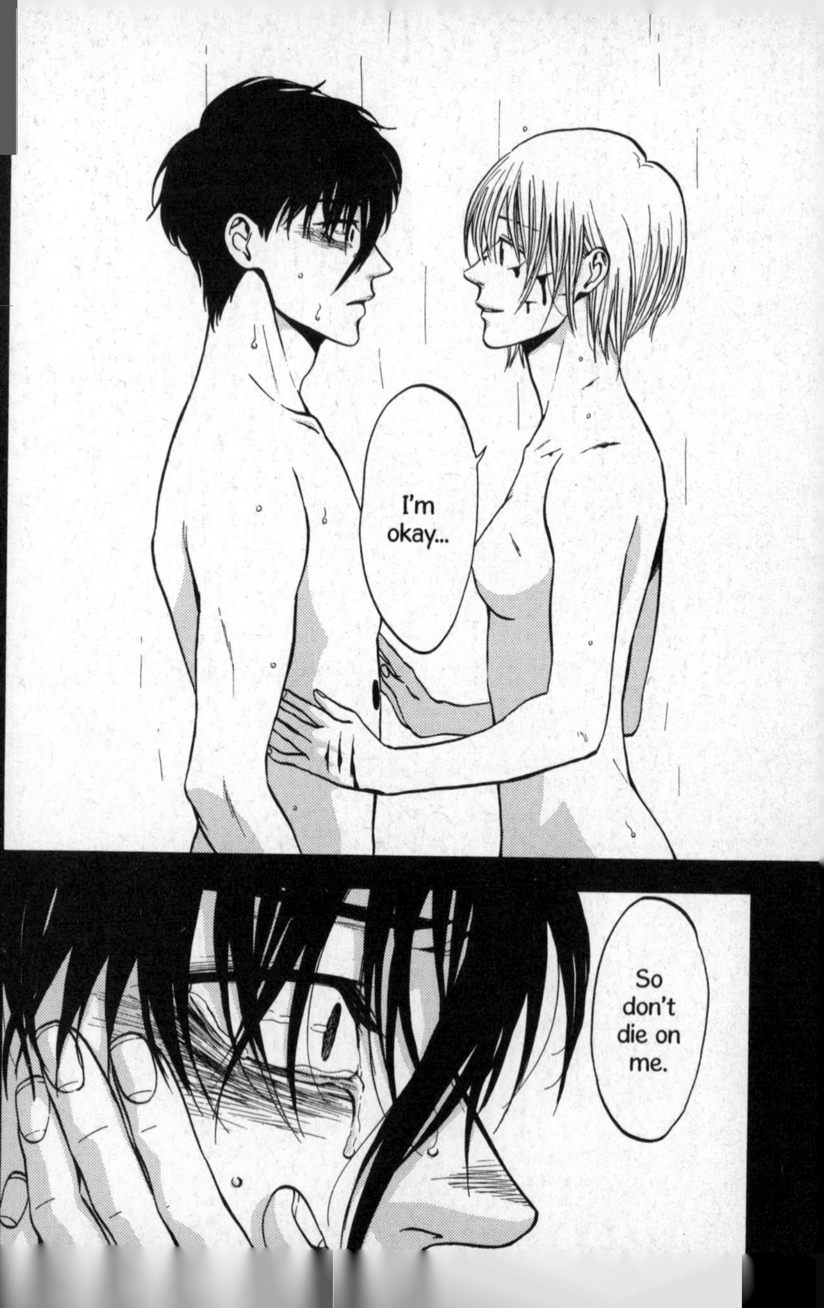
I'm okay...
So don't die on me.

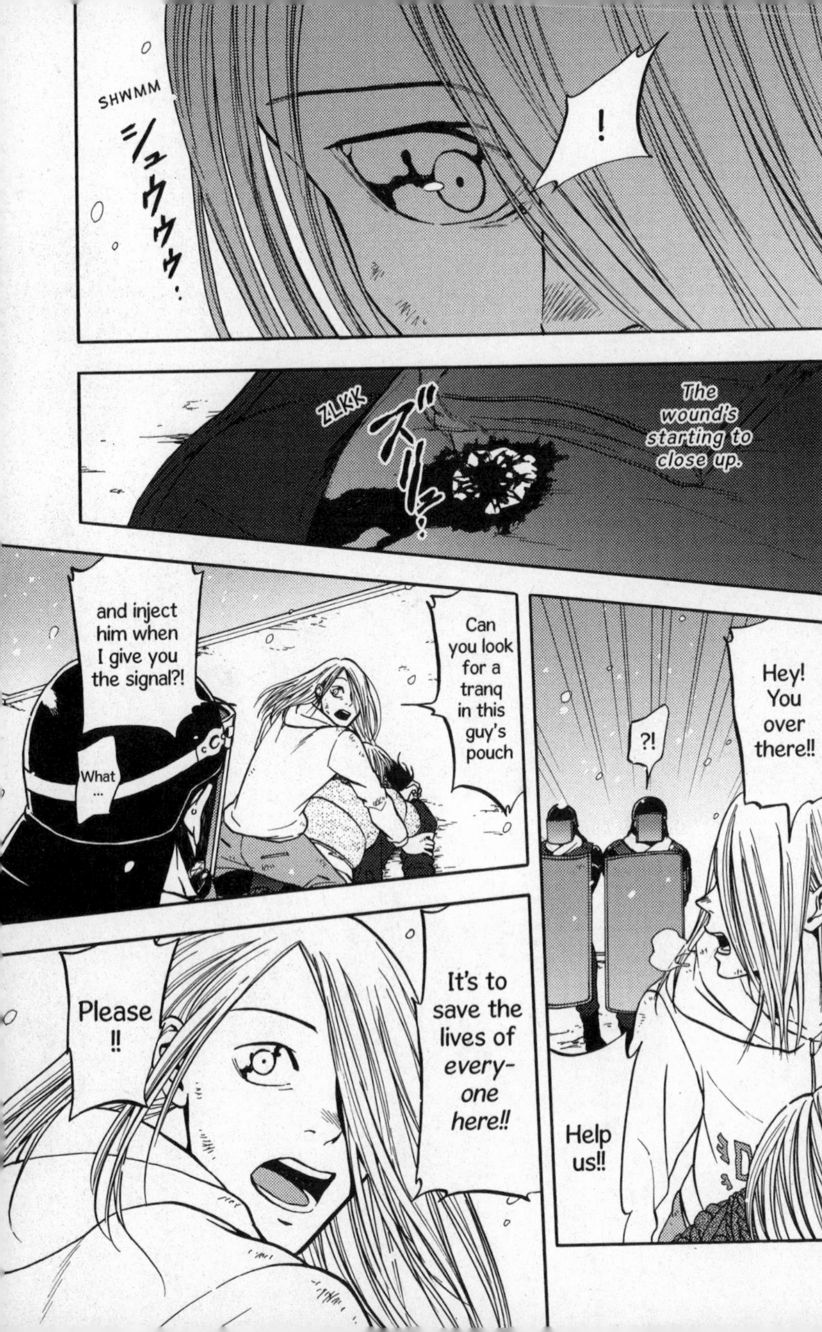
!
SHWMM
シュウウウ‥
The wound's starting to close up.
ZLKK
ズリュ‥
Hey! You over there!!
?!
Help us!!
Can you look for a tranq in this guy's pouch
and inject him when I give you the signal?!
What ...
It's to save the lives of *every-one here!!*
Please !!

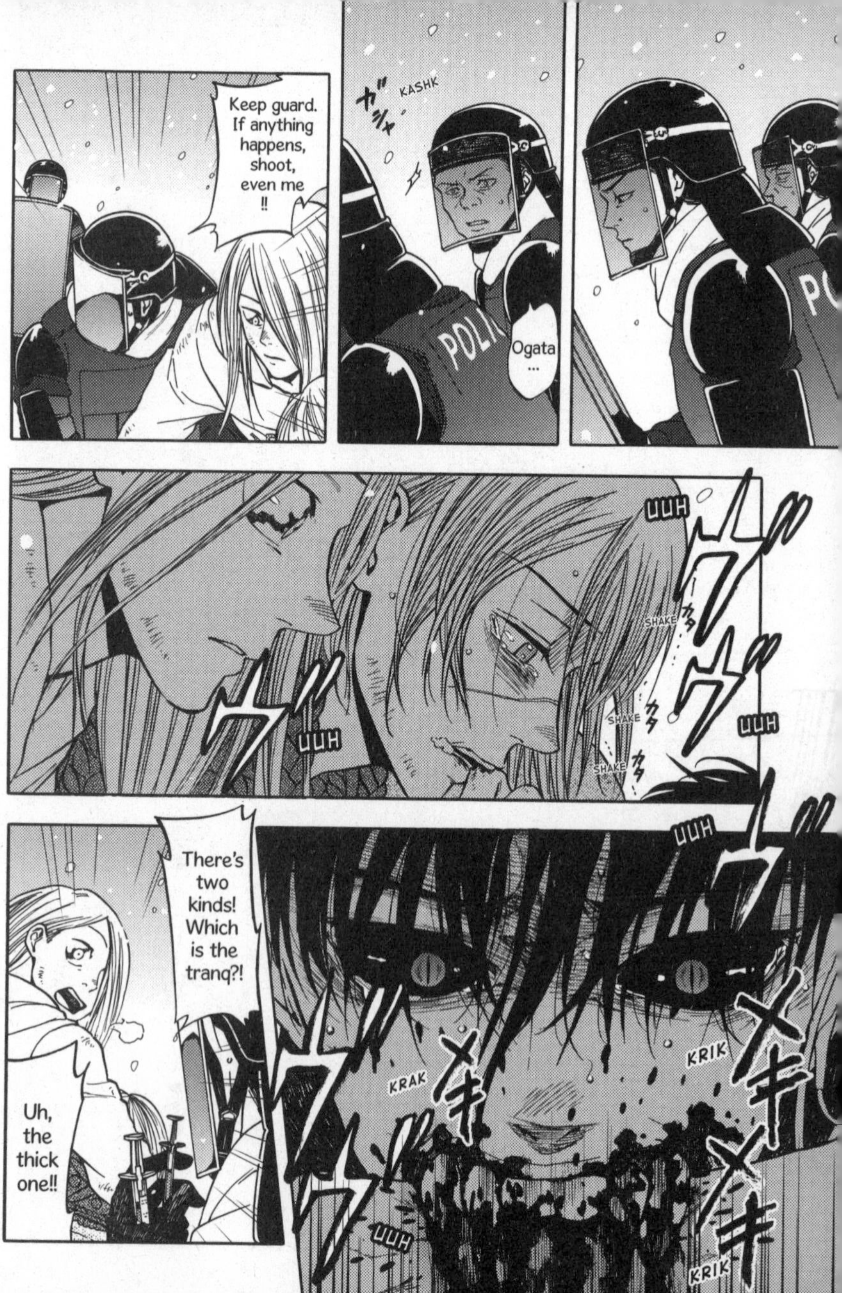
KASHK
Ogata ...
Keep guard. If anything happens, shoot, even me !!
UUH
SHAKE
SHAKE
SHAKE
UUH
UUH
UUH
KRIK
KRAK
KRIK
UUH
There's two kinds! Which is the tranq?!
Uh, the thick one!!

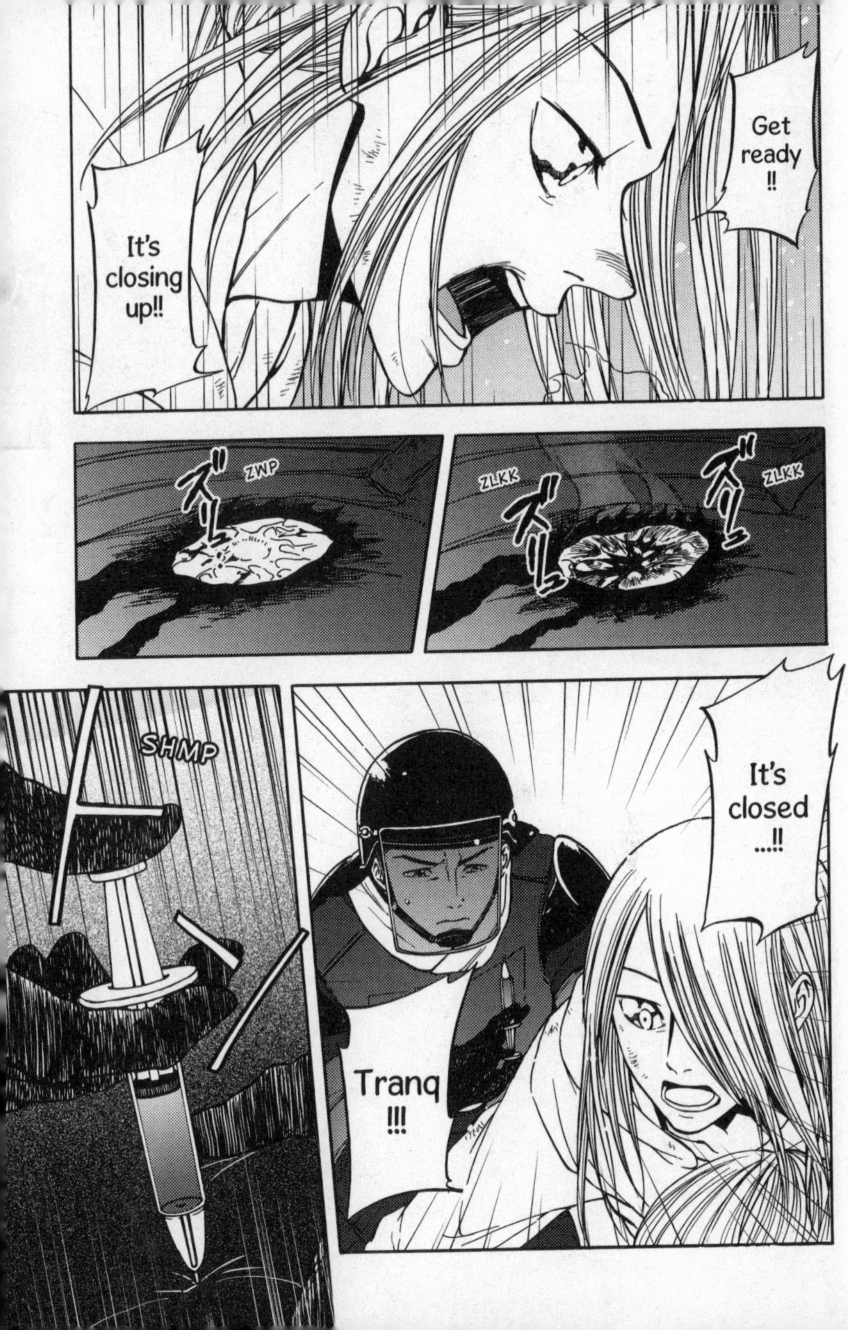
Get ready !!
It's closing up!!
ZLKK
ZLKK
ZWP
It's closed ...!!
Tranq !!!
SHMP

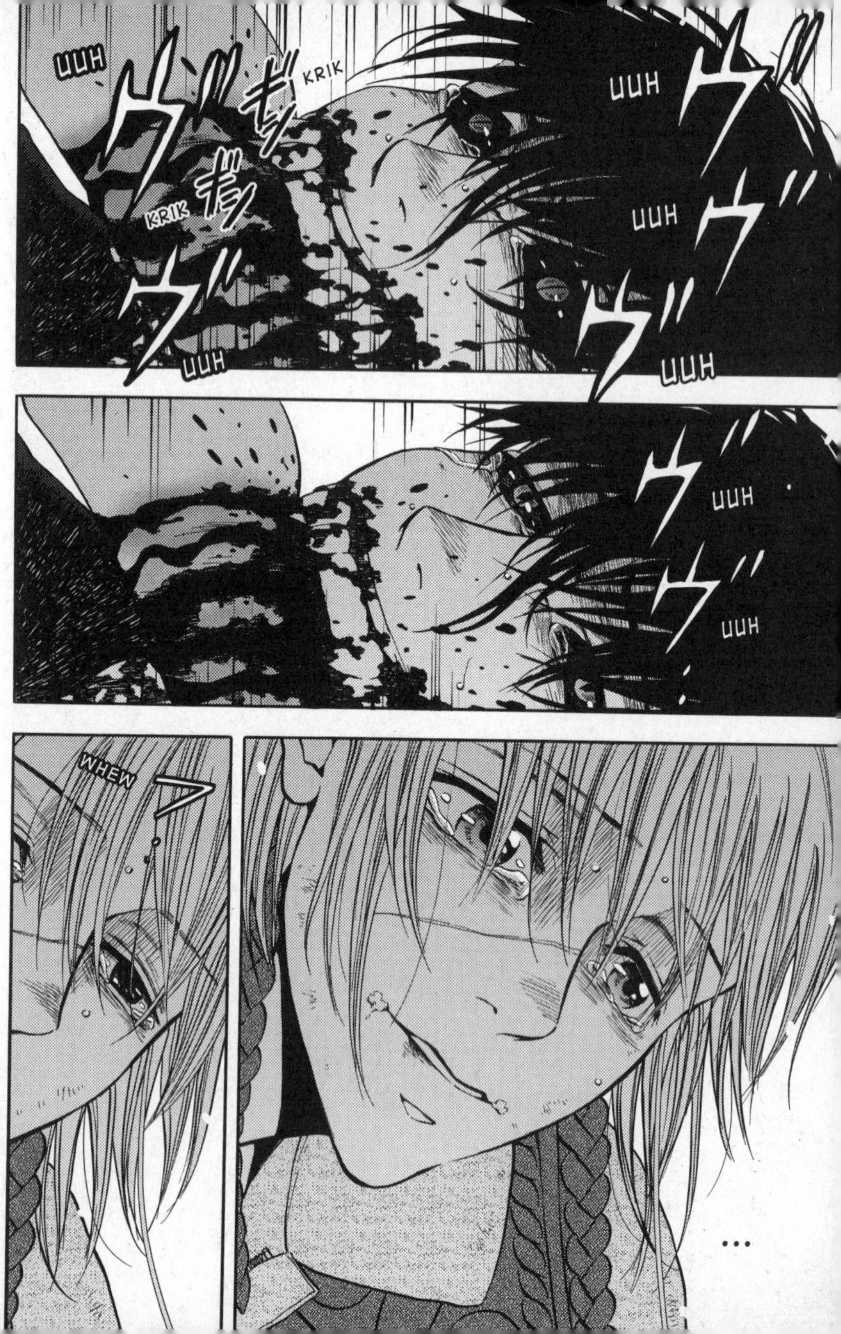
UUH
KRIK
UUH
KRIK
UUH
UUH
UUH
UUH
UUH
...
WHEW

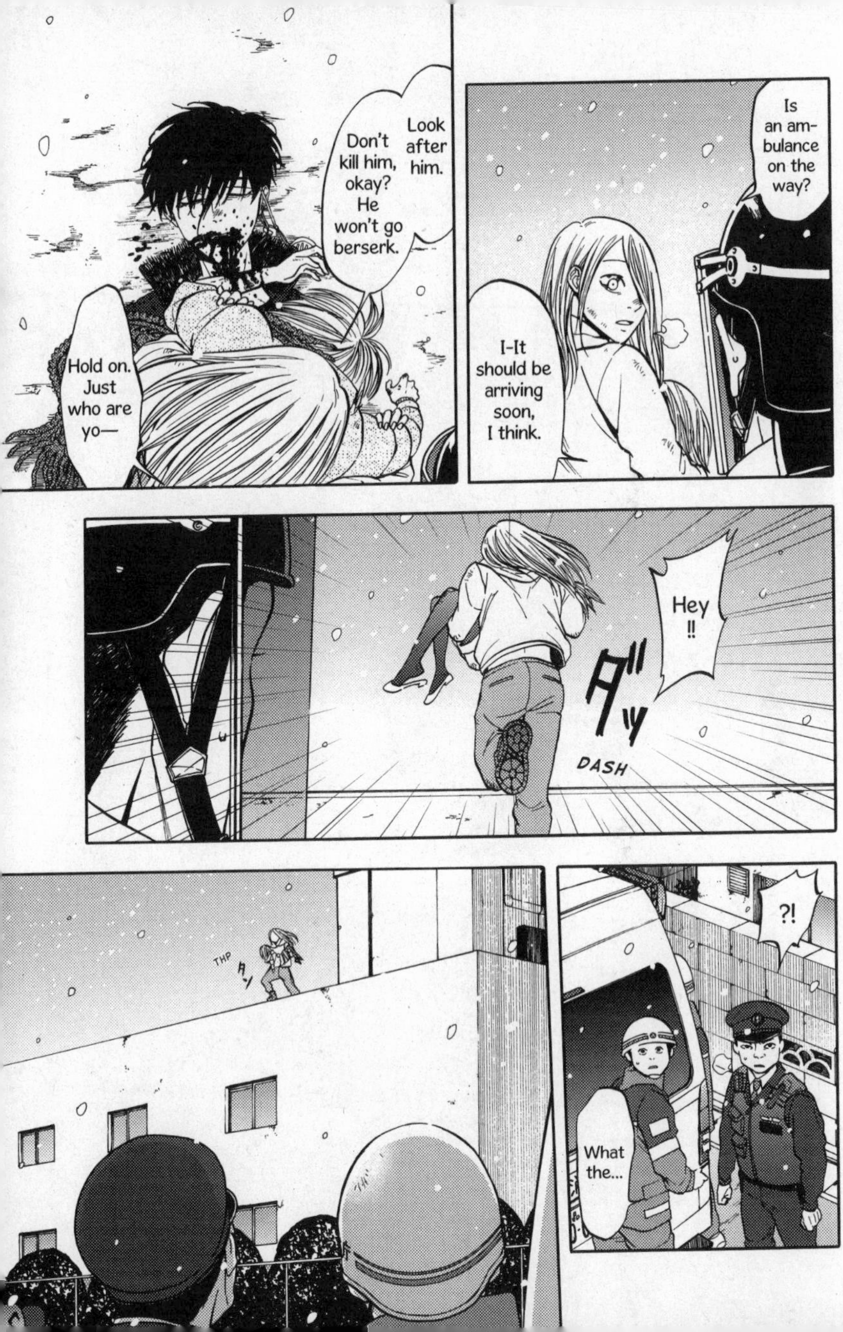
Is an ambulance on the way?
I-It should be arriving soon, I think.
Look after him.
Don't kill him, okay? He won't go berserk.
Hold on. Just who are yo—
Hey!!
ダッ
DASH
?!
What the...
THP

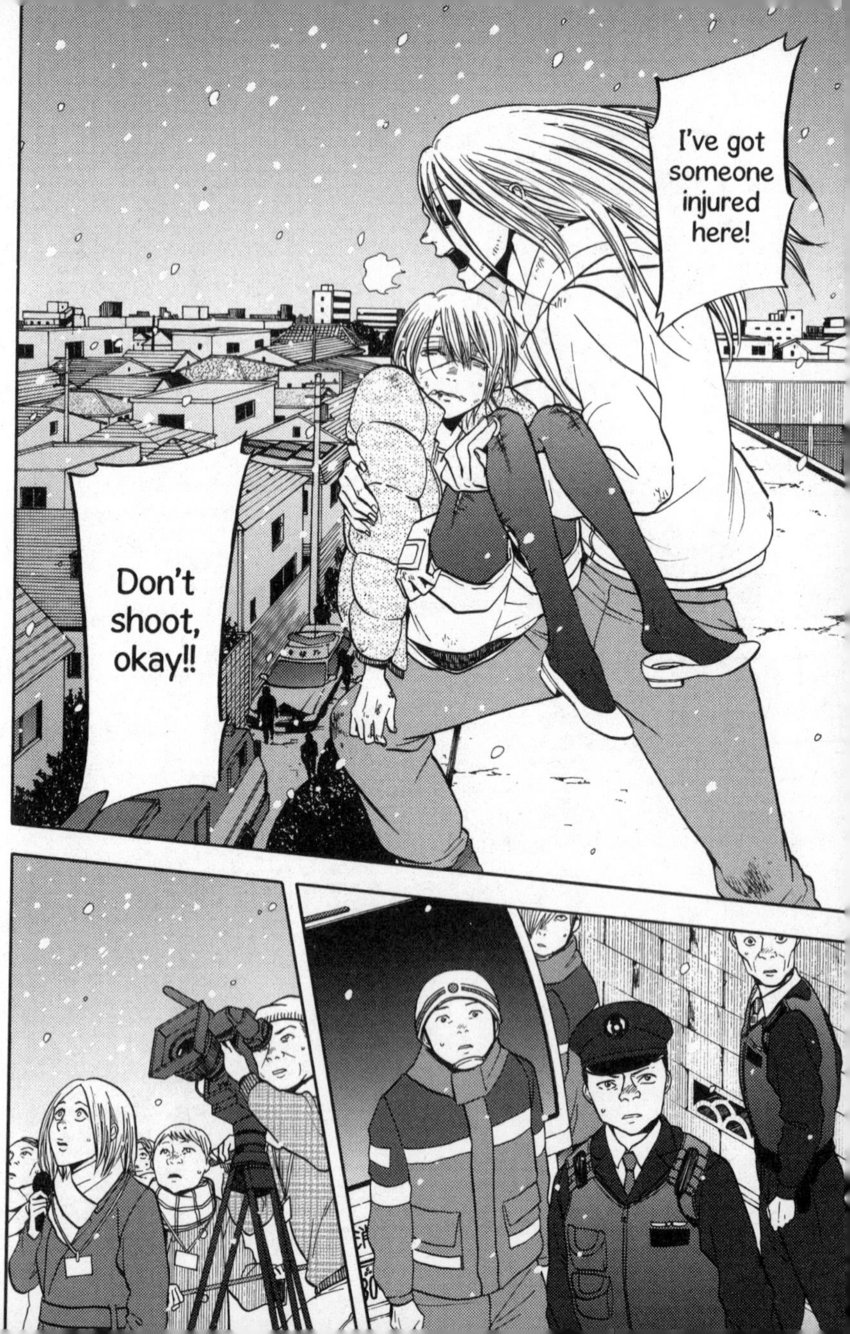
I've got someone injured here!
Don't shoot, okay!!

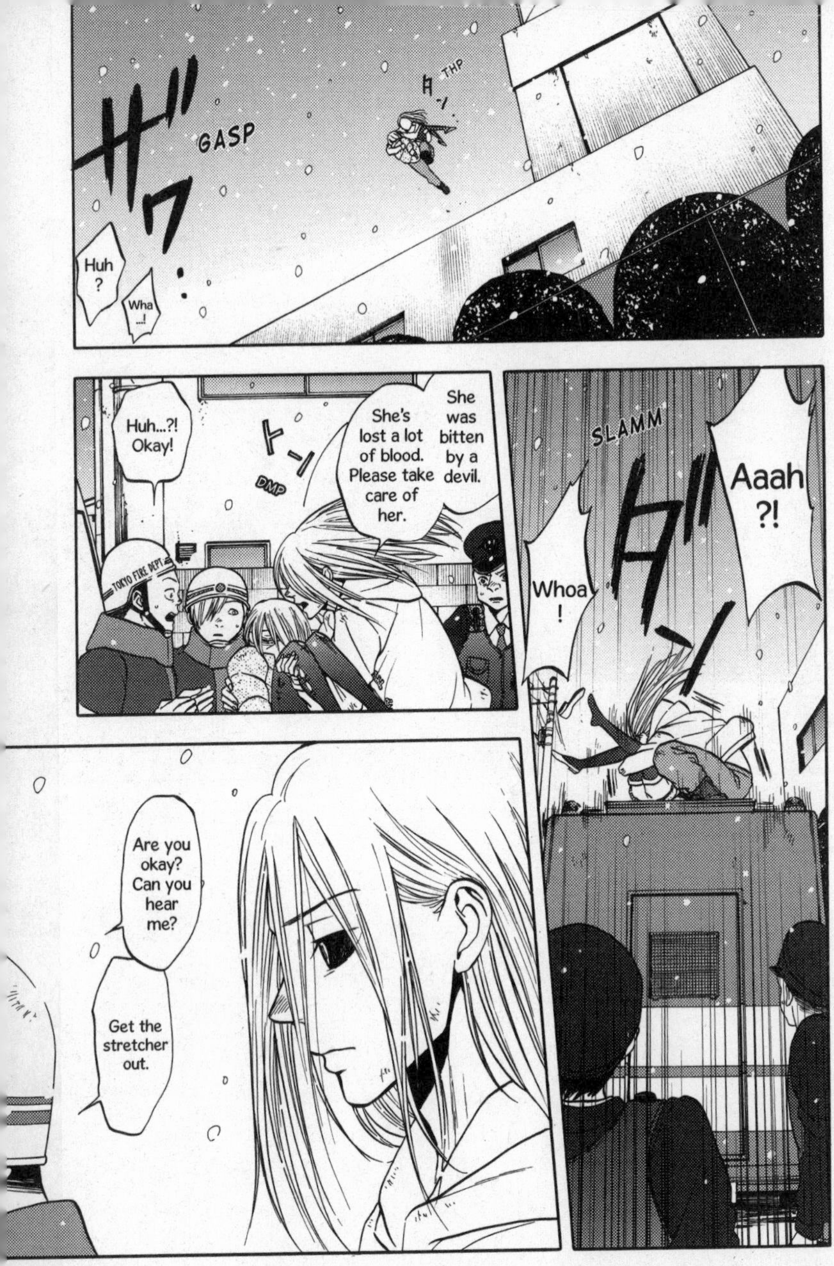
THP
GASP
Huh?
Wha...!
SLAMM
Aaah?!
Whoa!
She was bitten by a devil.
She's lost a lot of blood. Please take care of her.
DMP
Huh...?! Okay!
Are you okay? Can you hear me?
Get the stretcher out.

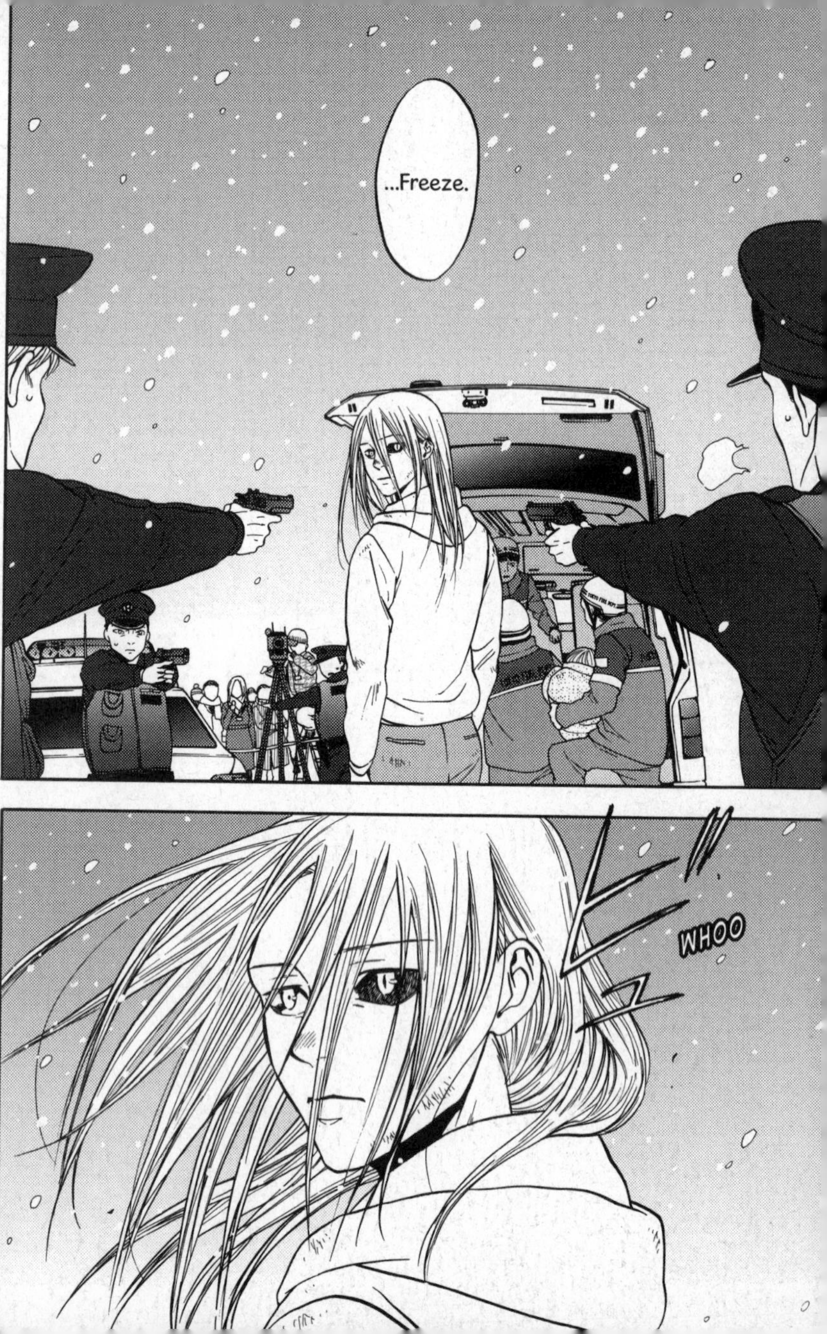
...Freeze.
WHOO

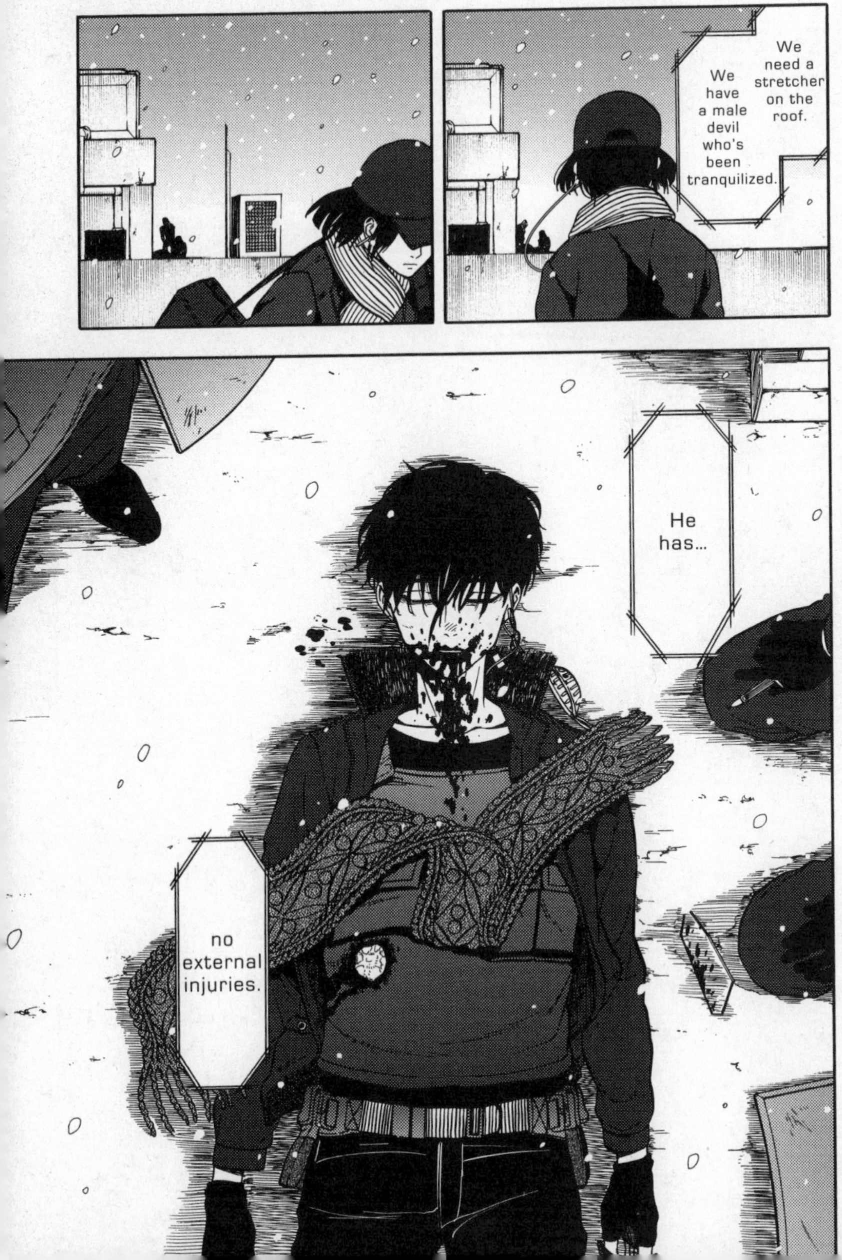
We need a stretcher on the roof.
We have a male devil who's been tranquilized.
He has...
no external injuries.

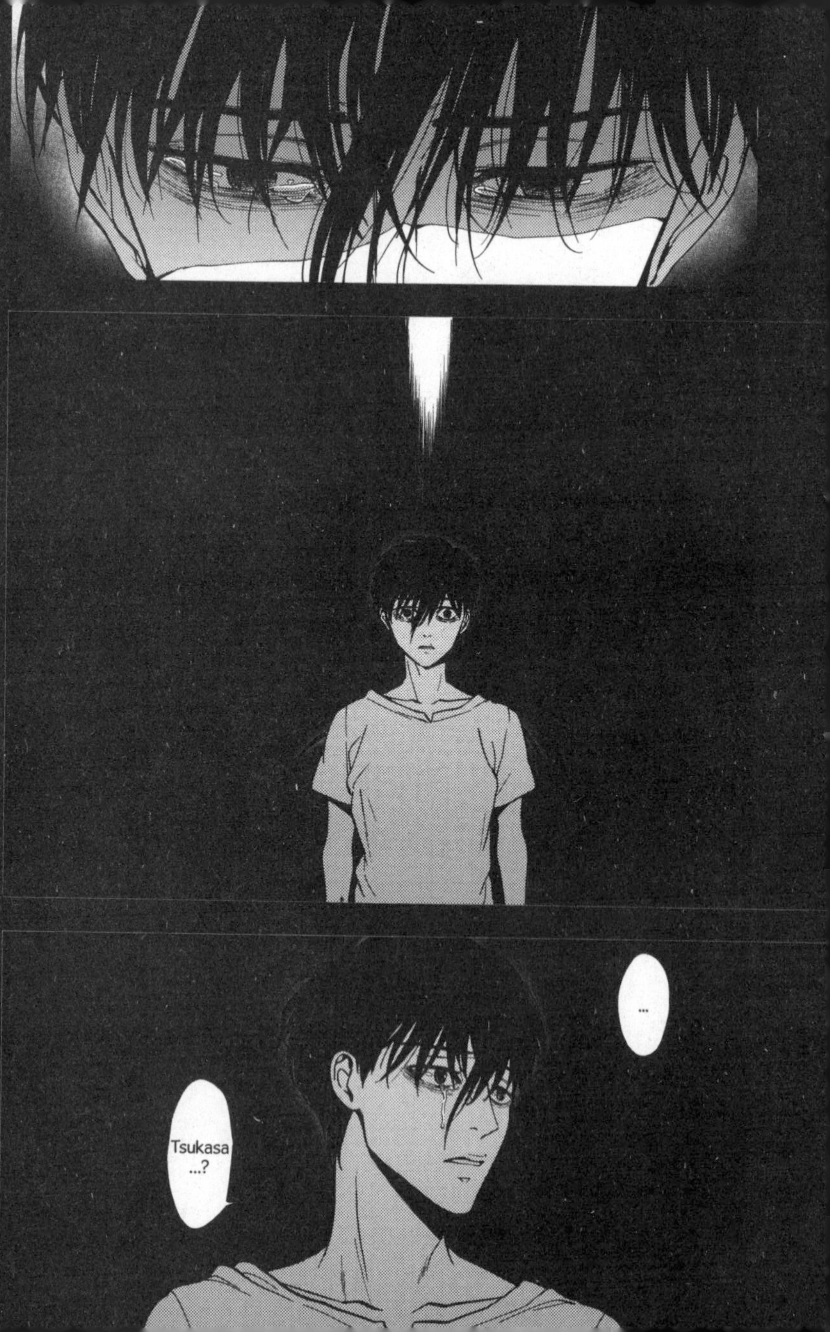
...
Tsukasa ...?

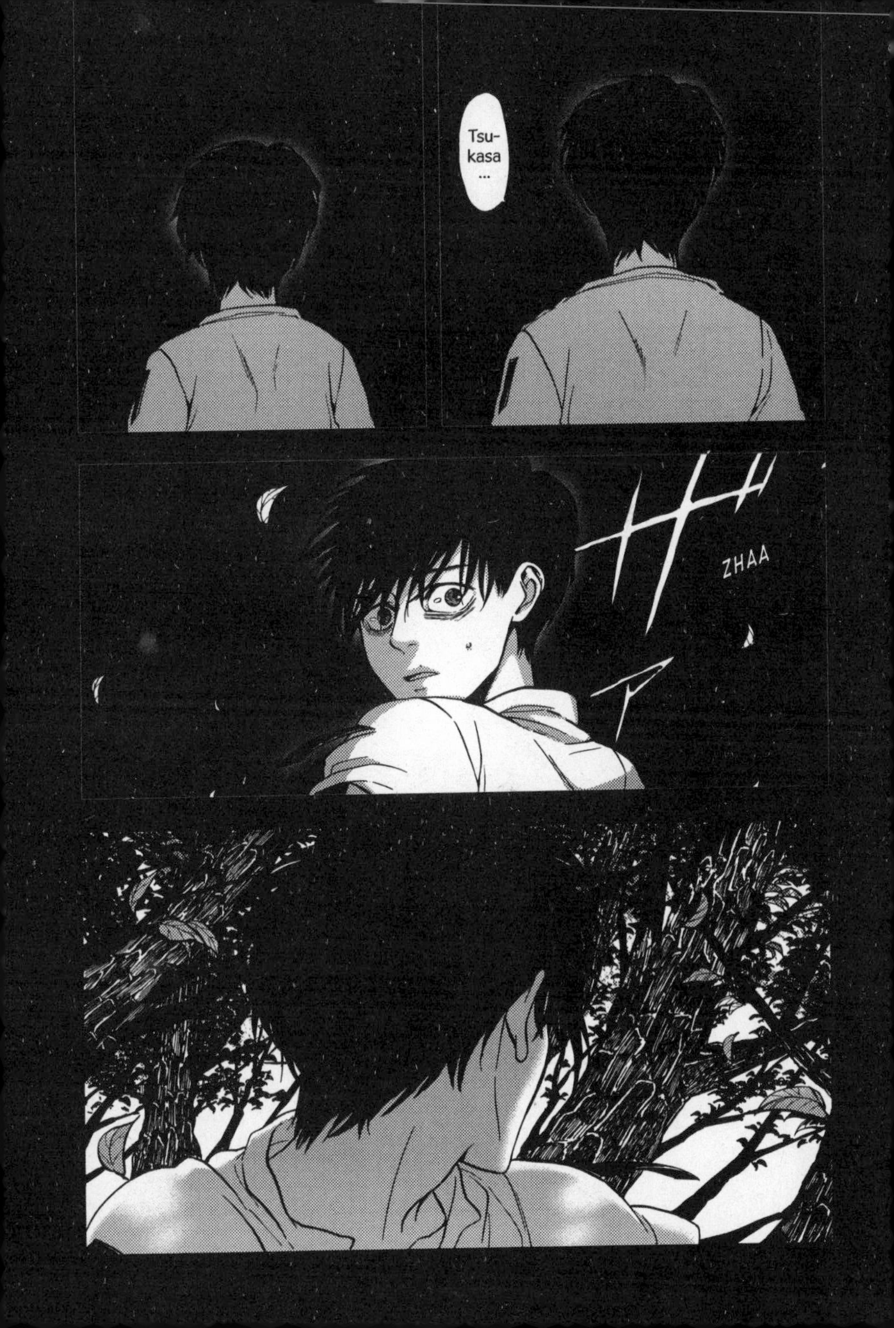
Tsu-
kasa
...
ZHAA

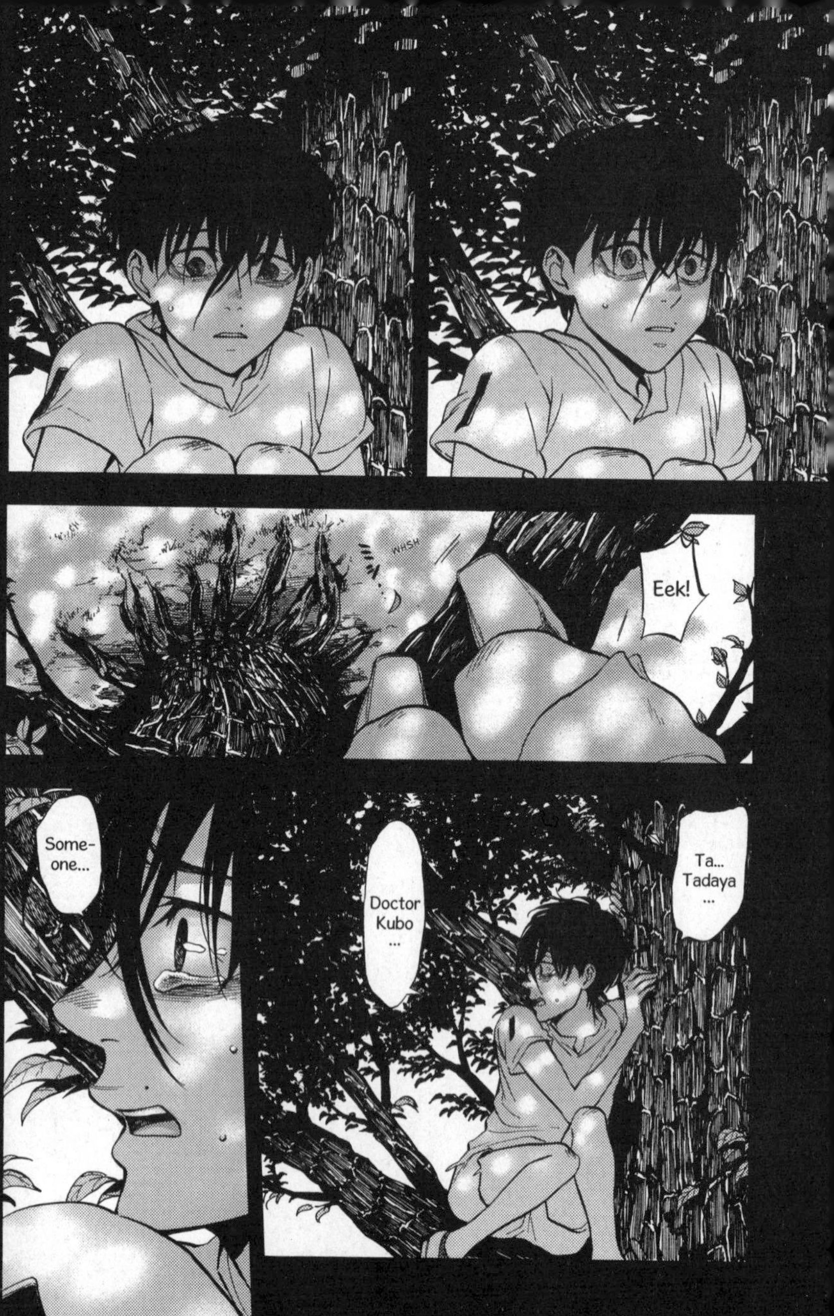
Eek!
WHSH
Ta... Tadaya ...
Doctor Kubo ...
Some- one...

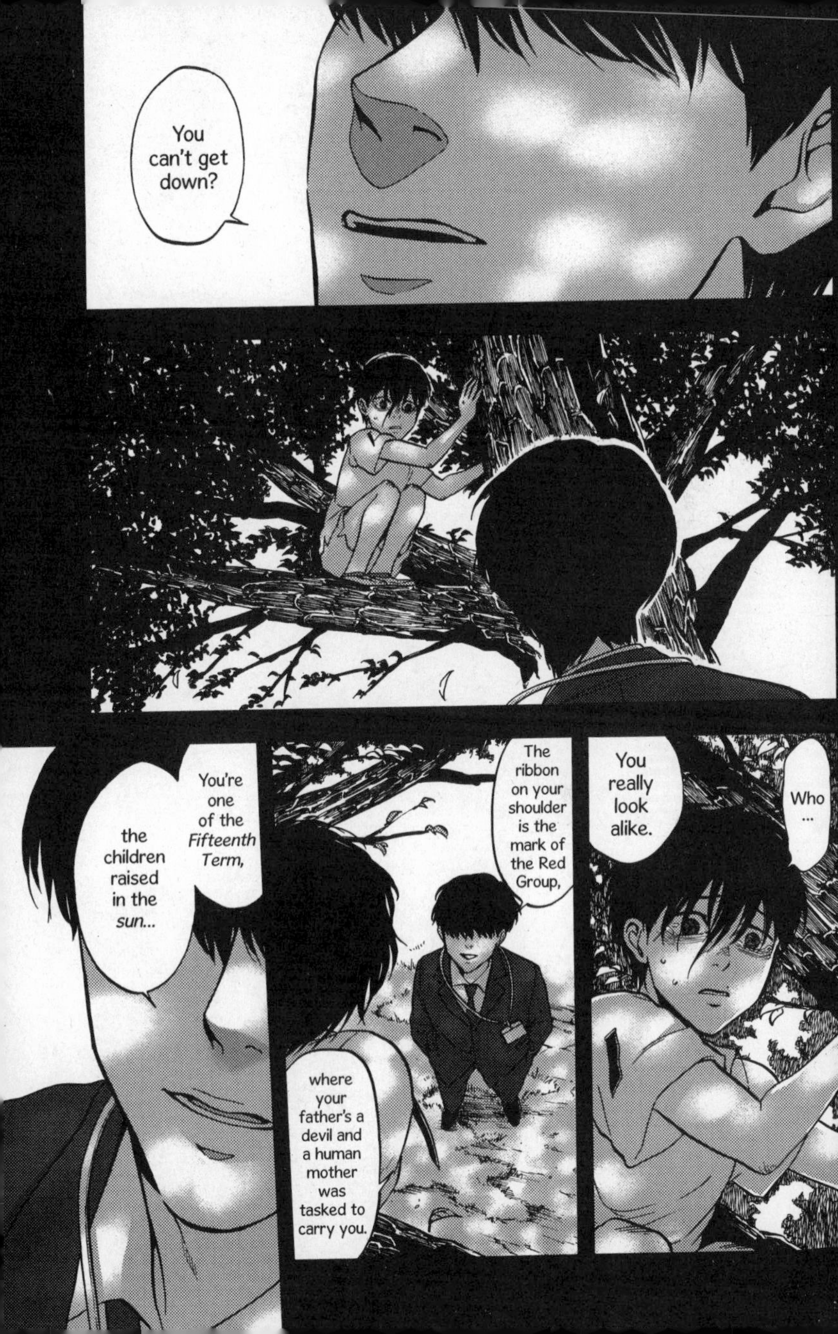
You can't get down?
Who ...
You really look alike.
The ribbon on your shoulder is the mark of the Red Group,
You're one of the *Fifteenth Term*,
the children raised in the *sun*...
where your father's a devil and a human mother was tasked to carry you.

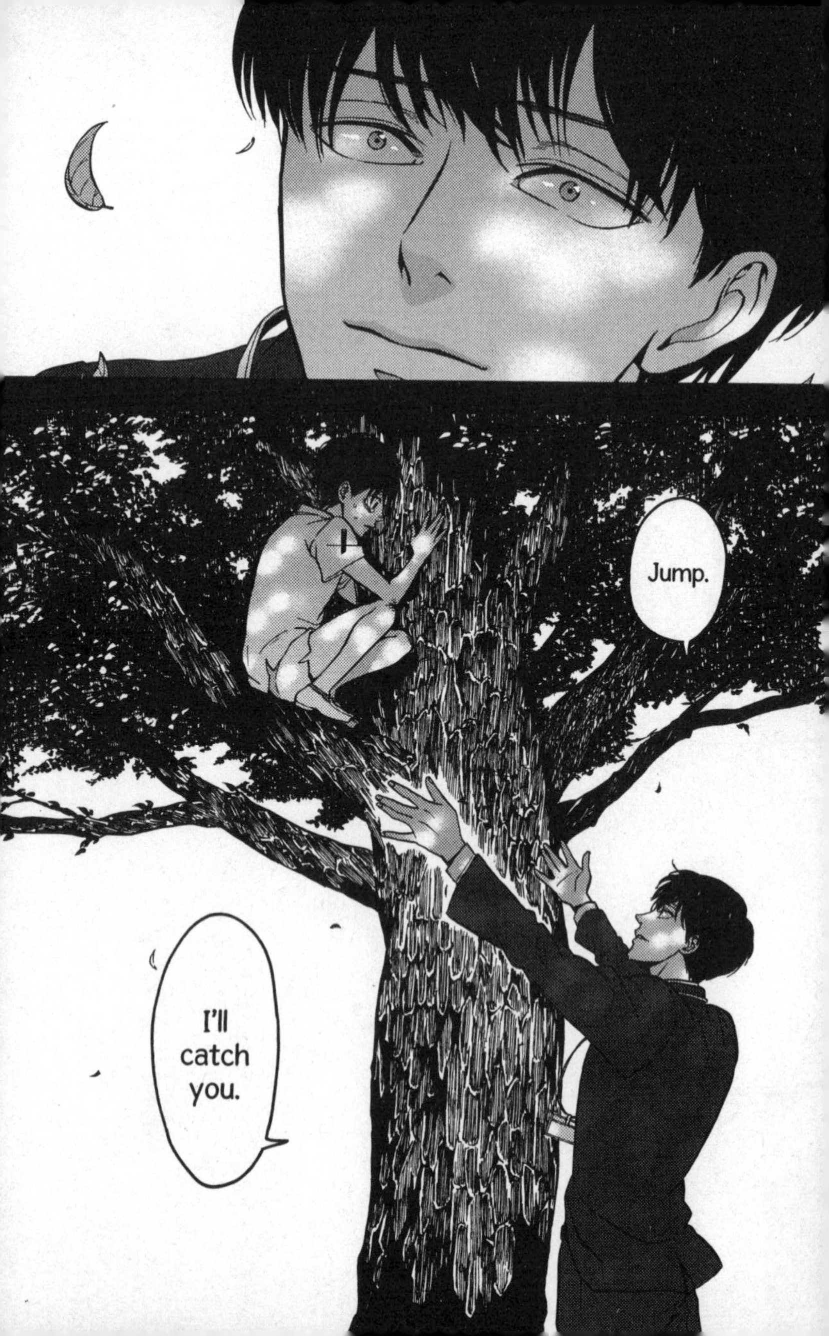
Jump.
I'll catch you.

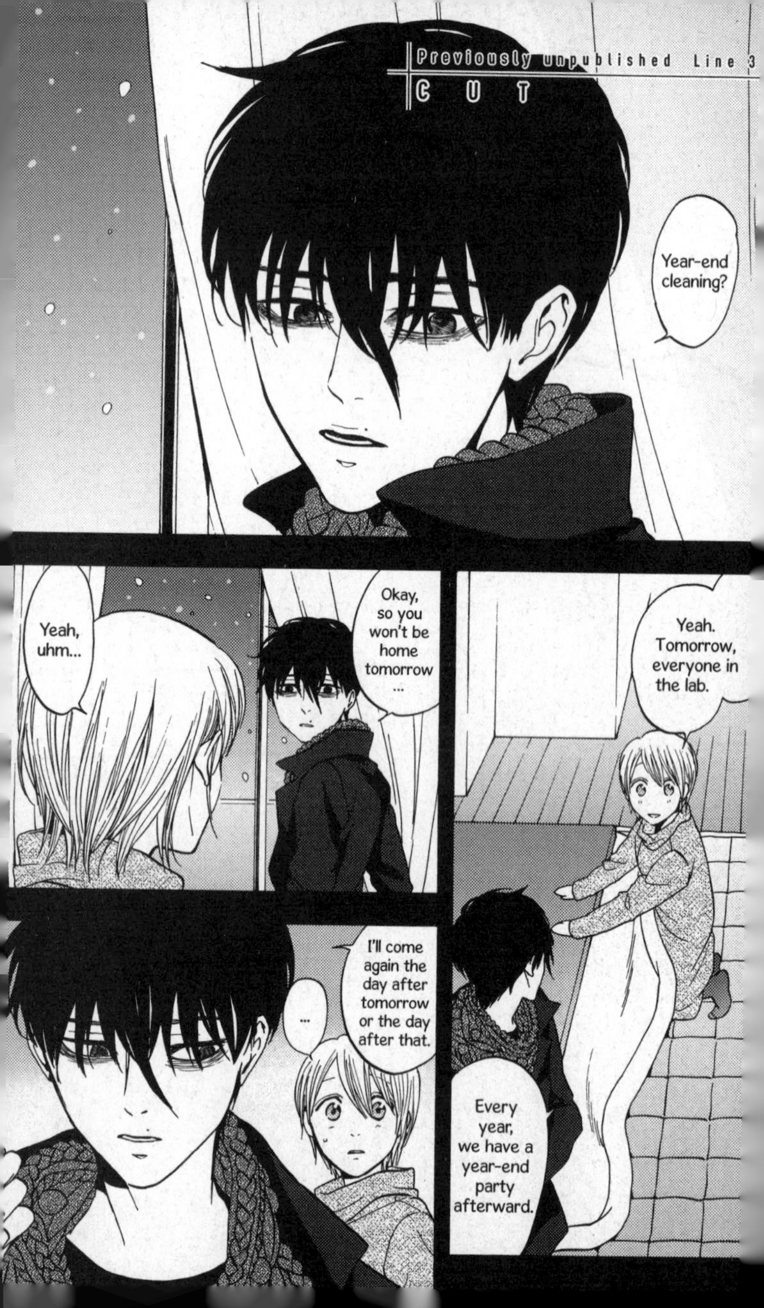
Previously Unpublished Line 3
CUT
Year-end cleaning?
Yeah. Tomorrow, everyone in the lab.
Every year, we have a year-end party afterward.
Okay, so you won't be home tomorrow ...
Yeah, uhm...
I'll come again the day after tomorrow or the day after that.
...

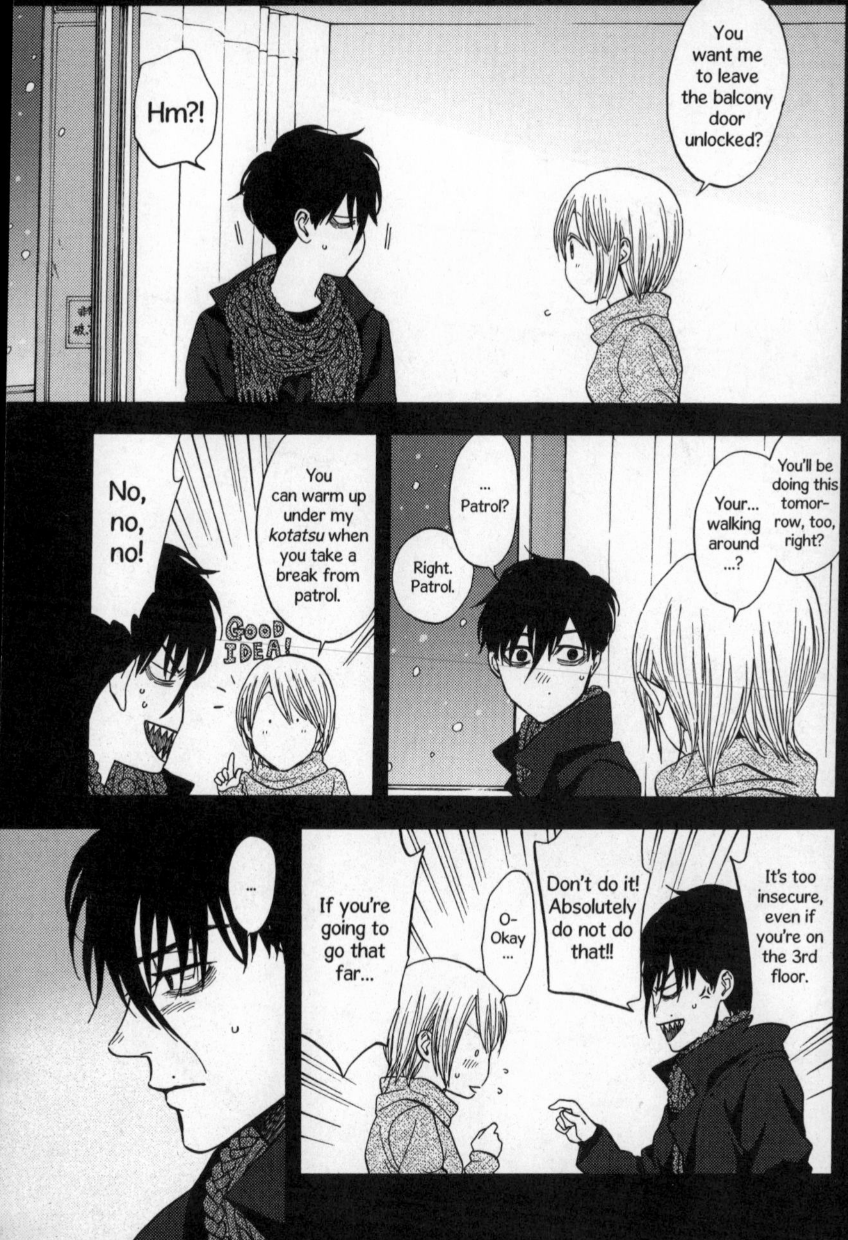
You want me to leave the balcony door unlocked?
Hm?!
You'll be doing this tomorrow, too, right?
Your... walking around ...?
... Patrol?
Right. Patrol.
You can warm up under my *kotatsu* when you take a break from patrol.
GOOD IDEA!
No, no, no!
It's too insecure, even if you're on the 3rd floor.
Don't do it! Absolutely do not do that!!
O-Okay ...
If you're going to go that far...
...

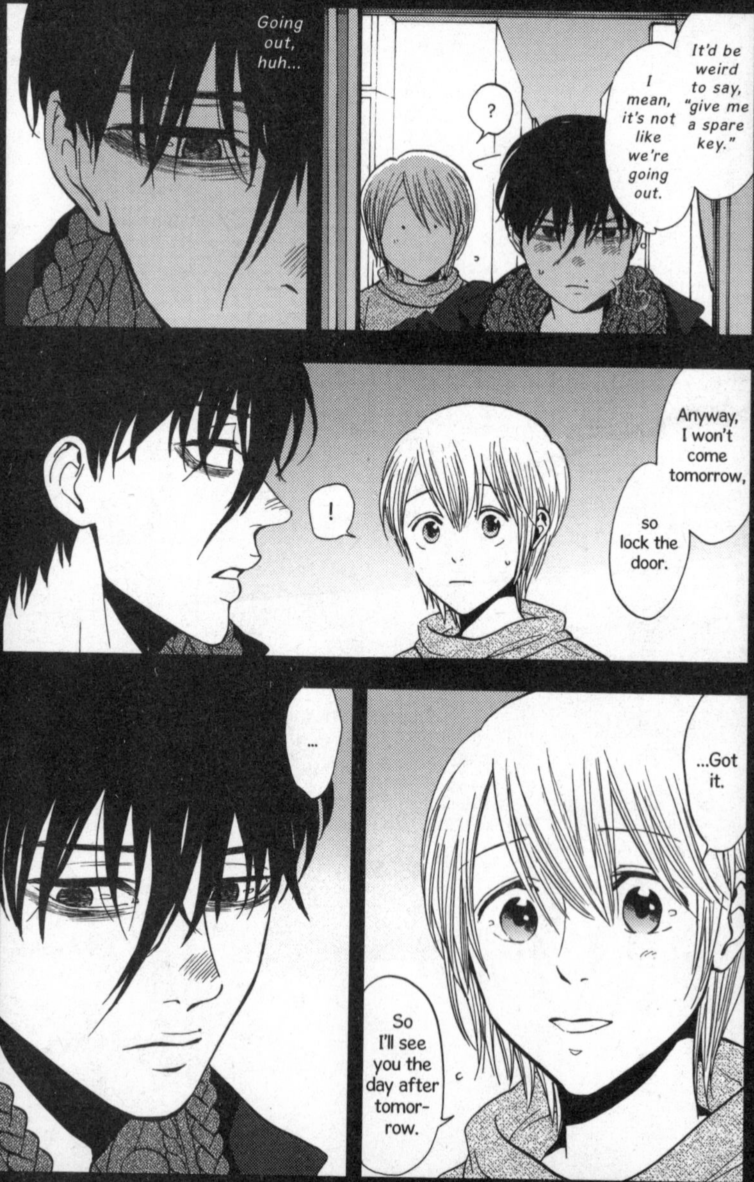
It'd be weird to say, "give me a spare key."
I mean, it's not like we're going out.
?
Going out, huh...
Anyway, I won't come tomorrow,
so lock the door.
!
...Got it.
So I'll see you the day after tomor-row.
...

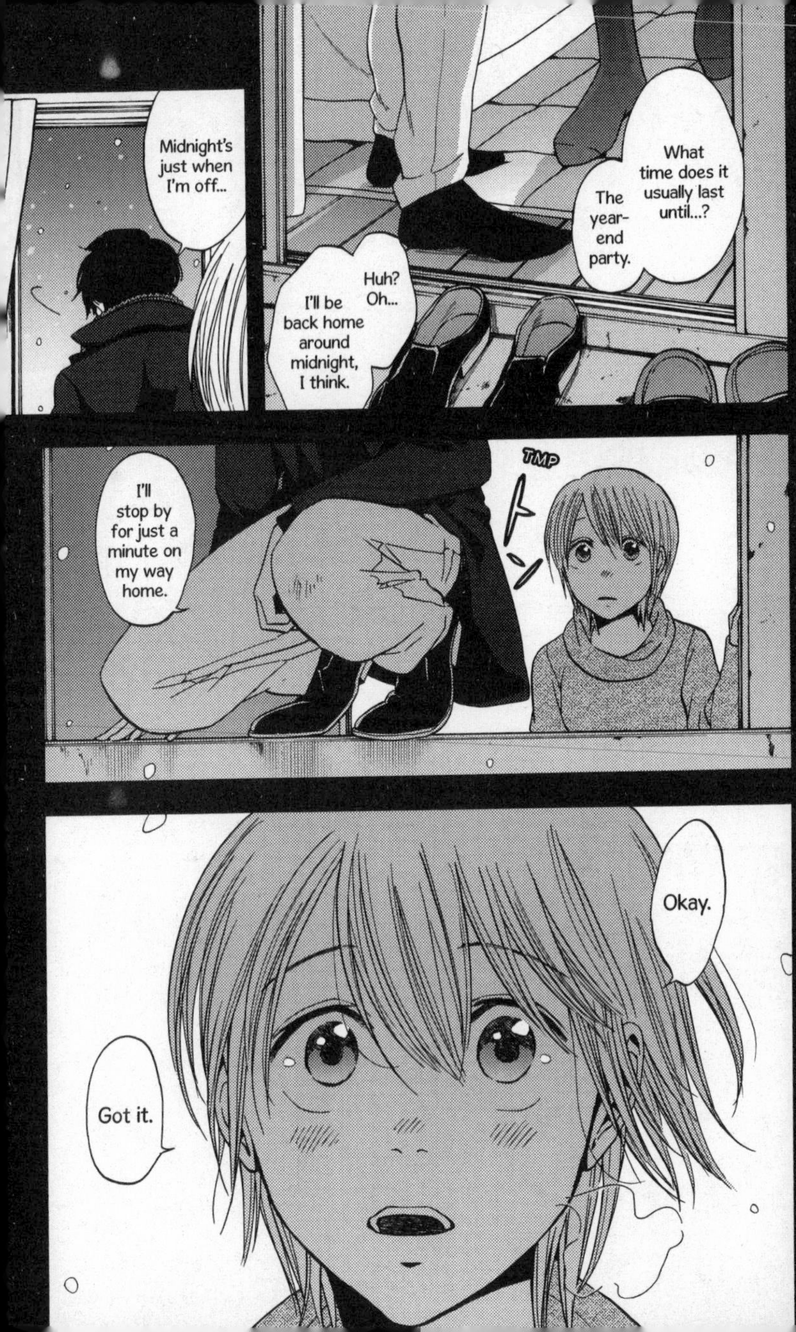
What time does it usually last until...?
The year-end party.
Huh? Oh...
I'll be back home around midnight, I think.
Midnight's just when I'm off...
TMP
I'll stop by for just a minute on my way home.
Okay.
Got it.

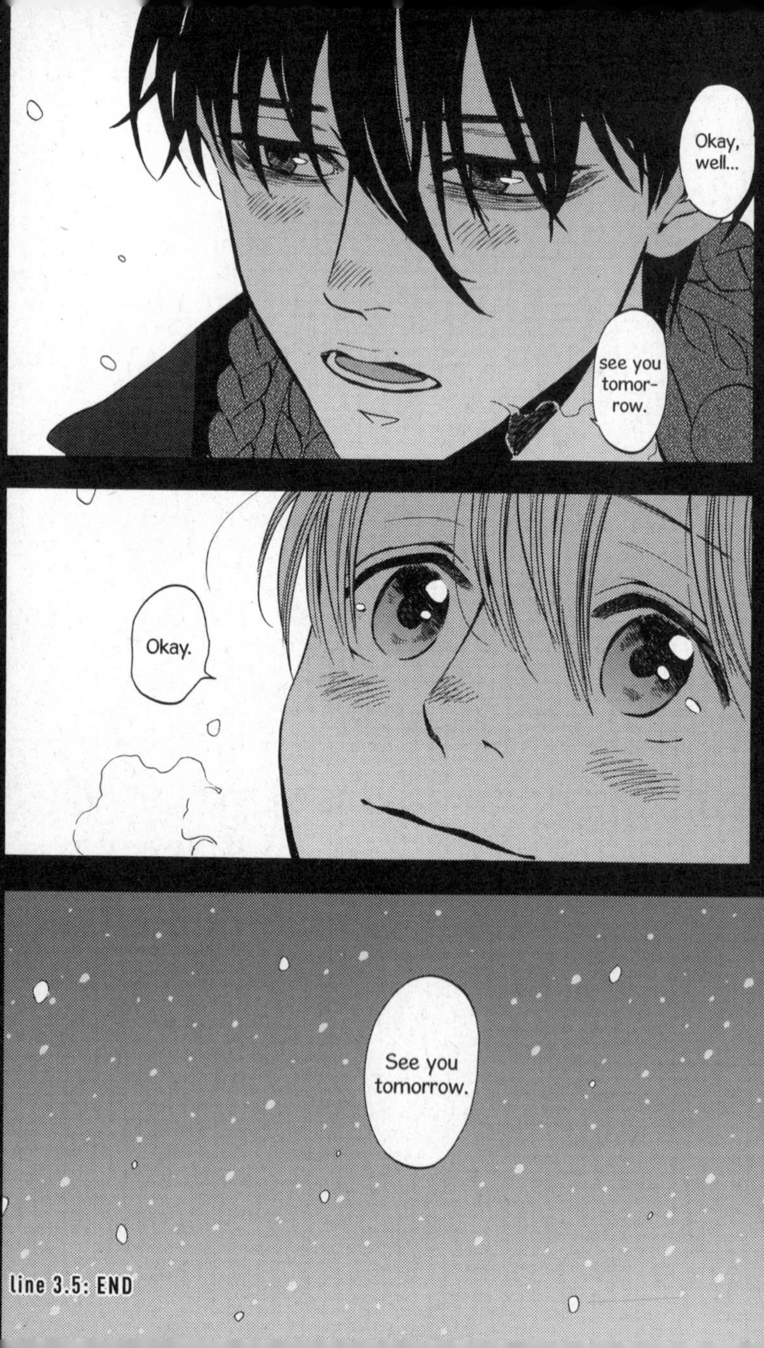
Okay, well...
see you tomor-row.
Okay.
See you tomorrow.
line 3.5: END

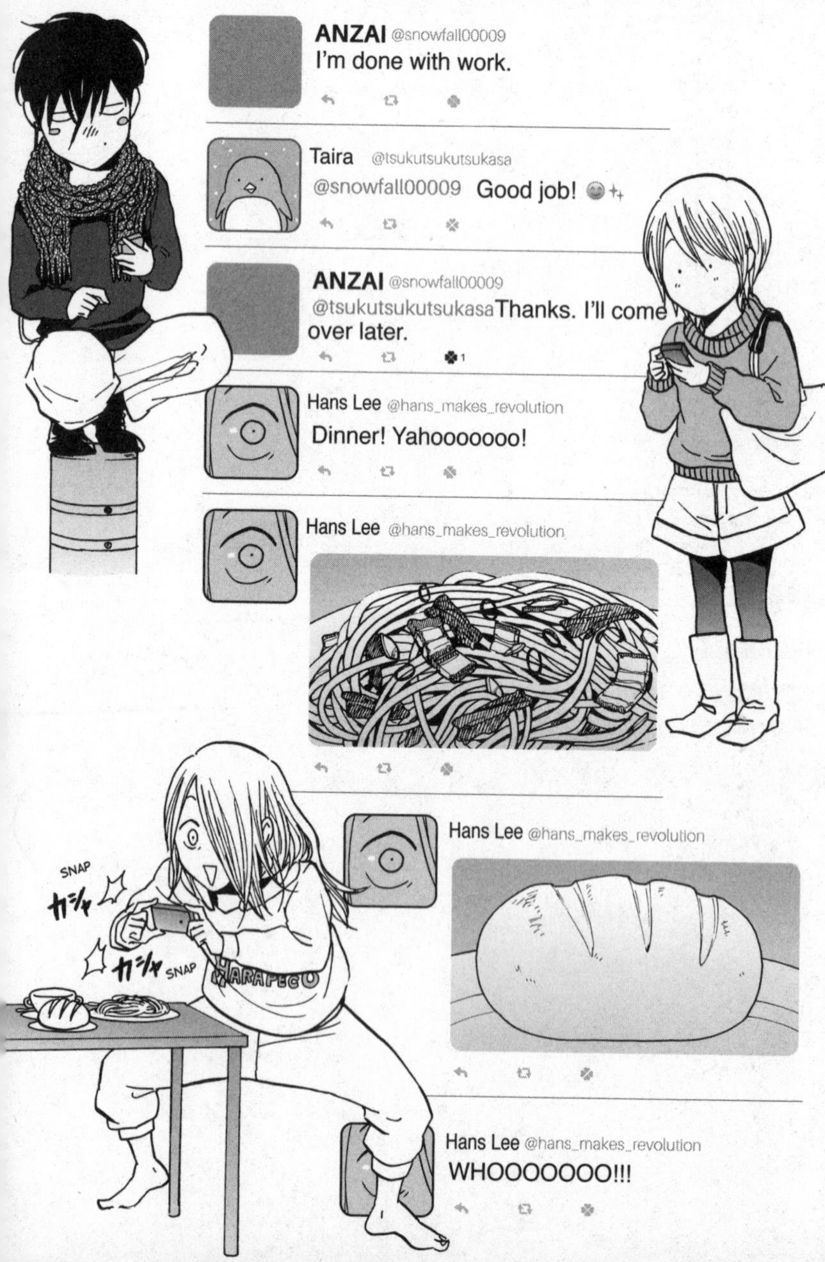
ANZAI @snowfall00009
I'm done with work.
Taira @tsukutsukutsukasa
@snowfall00009 Good job!
ANZAI @snowfall00009
@tsukutsukutsukasa Thanks. I'll come over later.
1
Hans Lee @hans_makes_revolution
Dinner! Yahooooooo!
Hans Lee @hans_makes_revolution
Hans Lee @hans_makes_revolution
SNAP
カシャ
カシャ
SNAP
HARAPECO
Hans Lee @hans_makes_revolution
WHOOOOOOO!!!

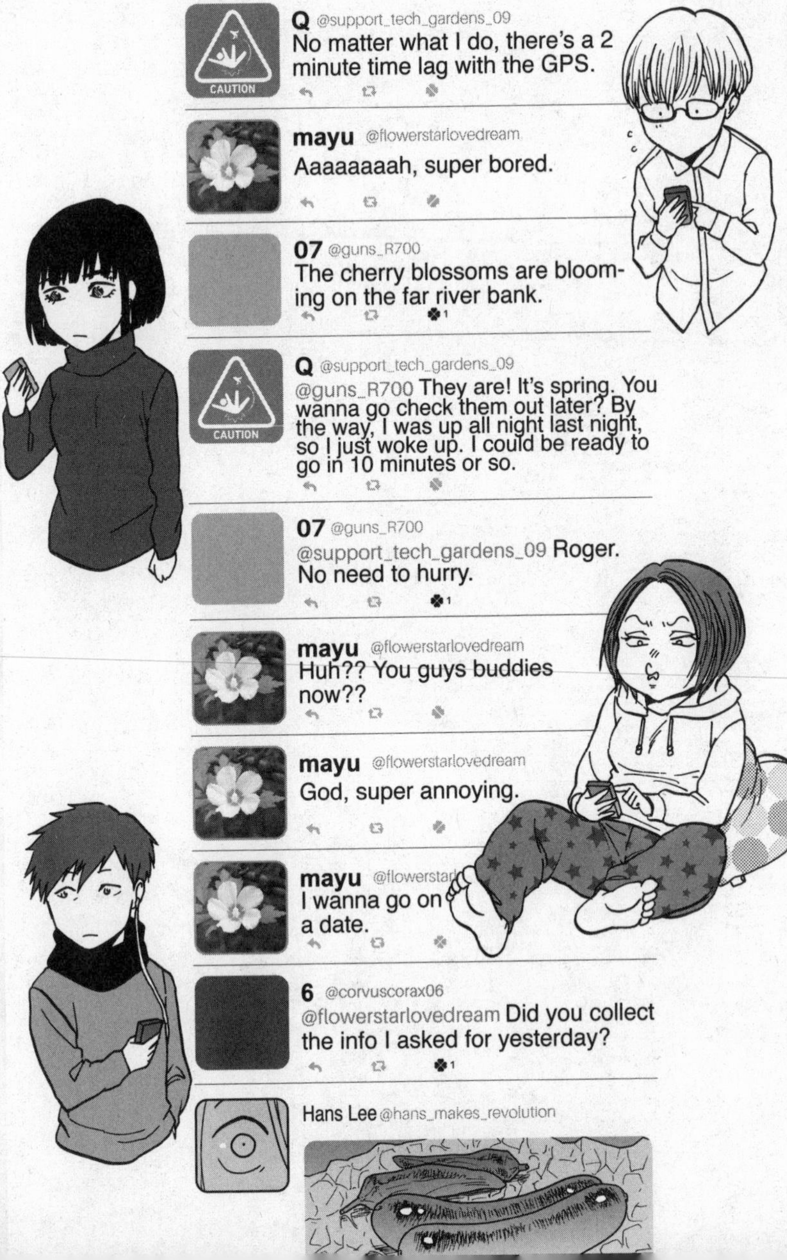
Q @support_tech_gardens_09
No matter what I do, there's a 2 minute time lag with the GPS.
CAUTION
mayu @flowerstarlovedream
Aaaaaaaah, super bored.
07 @guns_R700
The cherry blossoms are blooming on the far river bank.
1
Q @support_tech_gardens_09
@guns_R700 They are! It's spring. You wanna go check them out later? By the way, I was up all night last night, so I just woke up. I could be ready to go in 10 minutes or so.
CAUTION
07 @guns_R700
@support_tech_gardens_09 Roger. No need to hurry.
1
mayu @flowerstarlovedream
Huh?? You guys buddies now??
mayu @flowerstarlovedream
God, super annoying.
mayu @flowerstar
I wanna go on a date.
6 @corvuscorax06
@flowerstarlovedream Did you collect the info I asked for yesterday?
1
Hans Lee @hans_makes_revolution

The Basis for the Anime Series

To the Abandoned Sacred Beasts

Presented by

MAYBE

During a protracted civil war that pitted the North against the South, the outnumbered Northerners used dark magical arts to create monstrous super-soldiers—Incarnates. Now that the war has ended, those Sacred Beasts must learn how to make their way in a peaceful society, or face death at the hands of a Beast Hunter.

Nancy Schaal Bancroft, the daughter of an Incarnate soldier who met an untimely end at the hands of one such Beast Hunter, turns to hunting the hunter. But once she catches up with her quarry, she discovers hard truths about the lives of the Incarnates...

VOLUMES 1-11 AVAILABLE NOW!

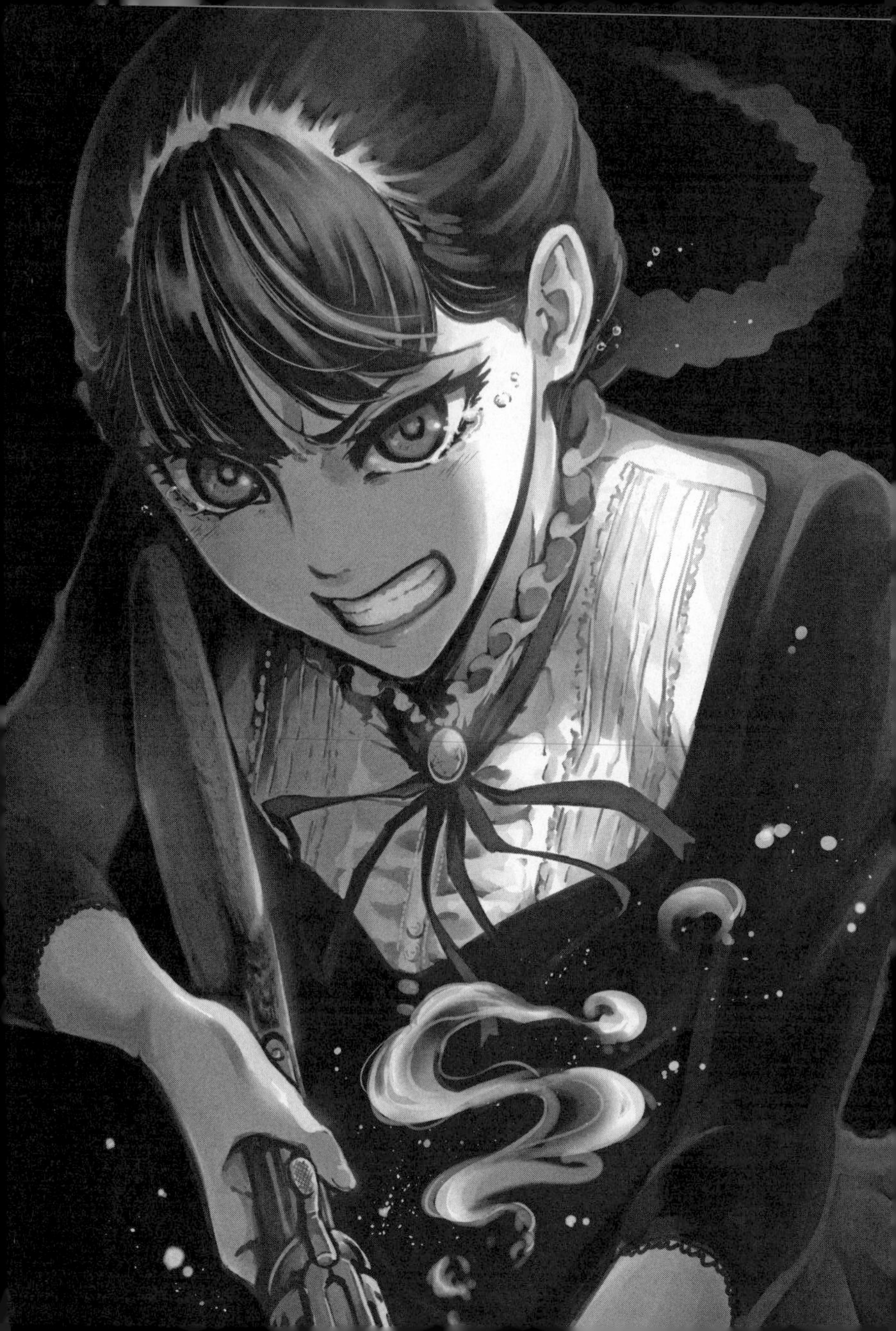

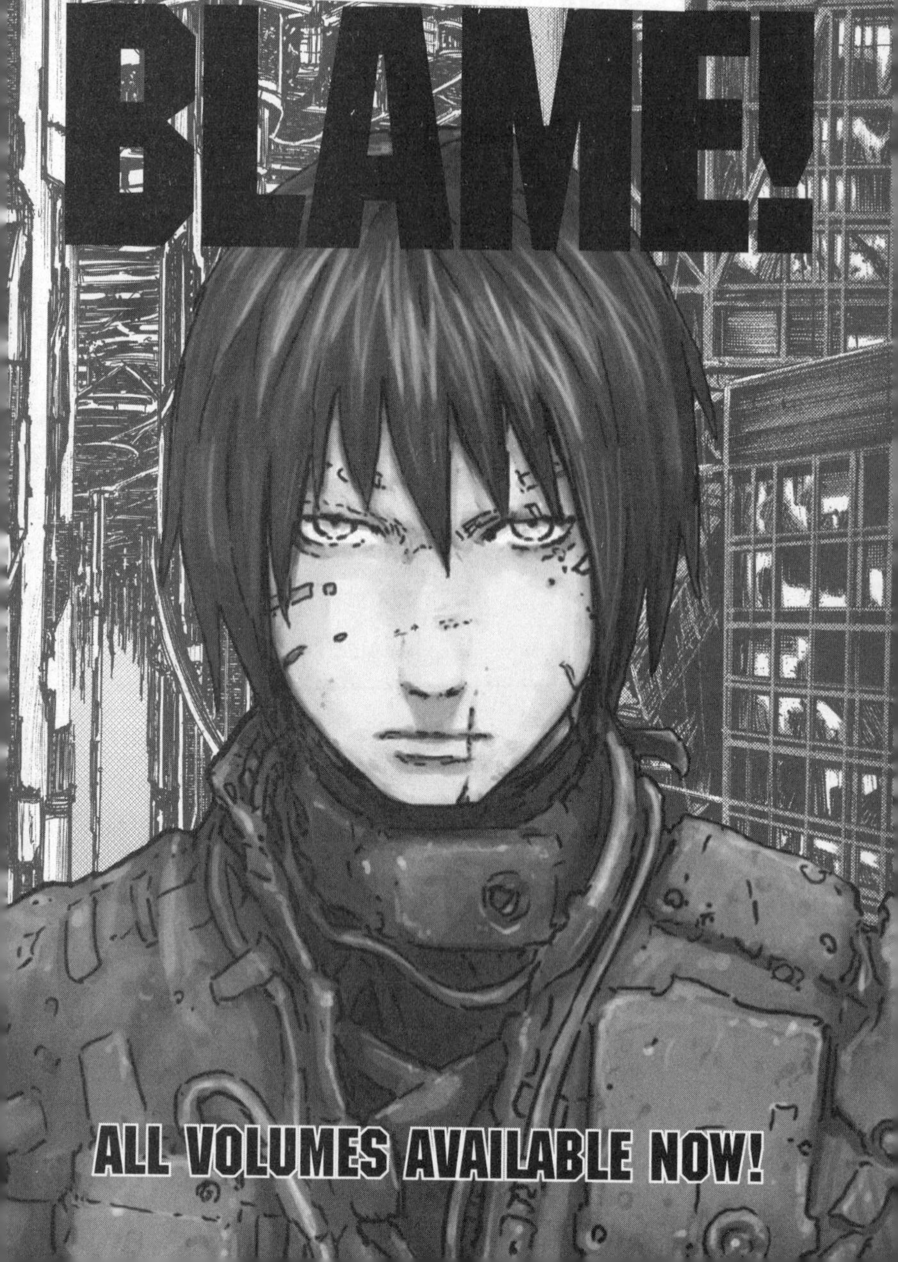
BLAME!
ALL VOLUMES AVAILABLE NOW!

IN A FUTURE VERSION OF EARTH, THERE IS A CITY GROWN SO CHAOTICALLY MASSIVE THAT ITS INHABITANTS NO LONGER RECALL WHAT "LAND" IS. WITHIN THIS MEGASTRUCTURE THE SILENT, STOIC KYRII IS ON A MISSION TO FIND THE NET TERMINAL GENE—A GENETIC MUTATION THAT ONCE ALLOWED HUMANS TO ACCESS THE CYBERNETIC NETSPHERE. ARMED WITH A POWERFUL GRAVITON BEAM EMITTER, KYRII FENDS OFF WAVES OF ATTACKS FROM FELLOW HUMANS, CYBORGS AND SILICON-BASED LIFEFORMS. ALONG THE WAY, HE ENCOUNTERS A HIGHLY-SKILLED SCIENTIST WHOSE BODY HAS DETERIORATED FROM A LENGTHY IMPRISONMENT WHO PROMISES TO HELP KYRII FIND THE NET TERMINAL GENE, ONCE SHE SETTLES A SCORE FOR HERSELF...

"WHETHER IT BE THE GREAT PACING AND LAYOUTS TO THE FRENETIC ACTION THAT OCCUPIES THE PANELS IN THESE SCENES, EVERY ONE OF THEM ALWAYS PACKS A PUNCH. THESE ARE ALL EMPHASIZED BY SOME GREAT DESIGNS ACROSS THE BOARD."

—*THE TURNAROUND BLOG*

"NIHEI'S MOODY MASTERPIECE FINALLY RELEASED IN ITS FULL DREADFUL SPLENDOR."

—*UK ANIME NETWORK*

Will you... be my friend?

NEXT VOLUME:

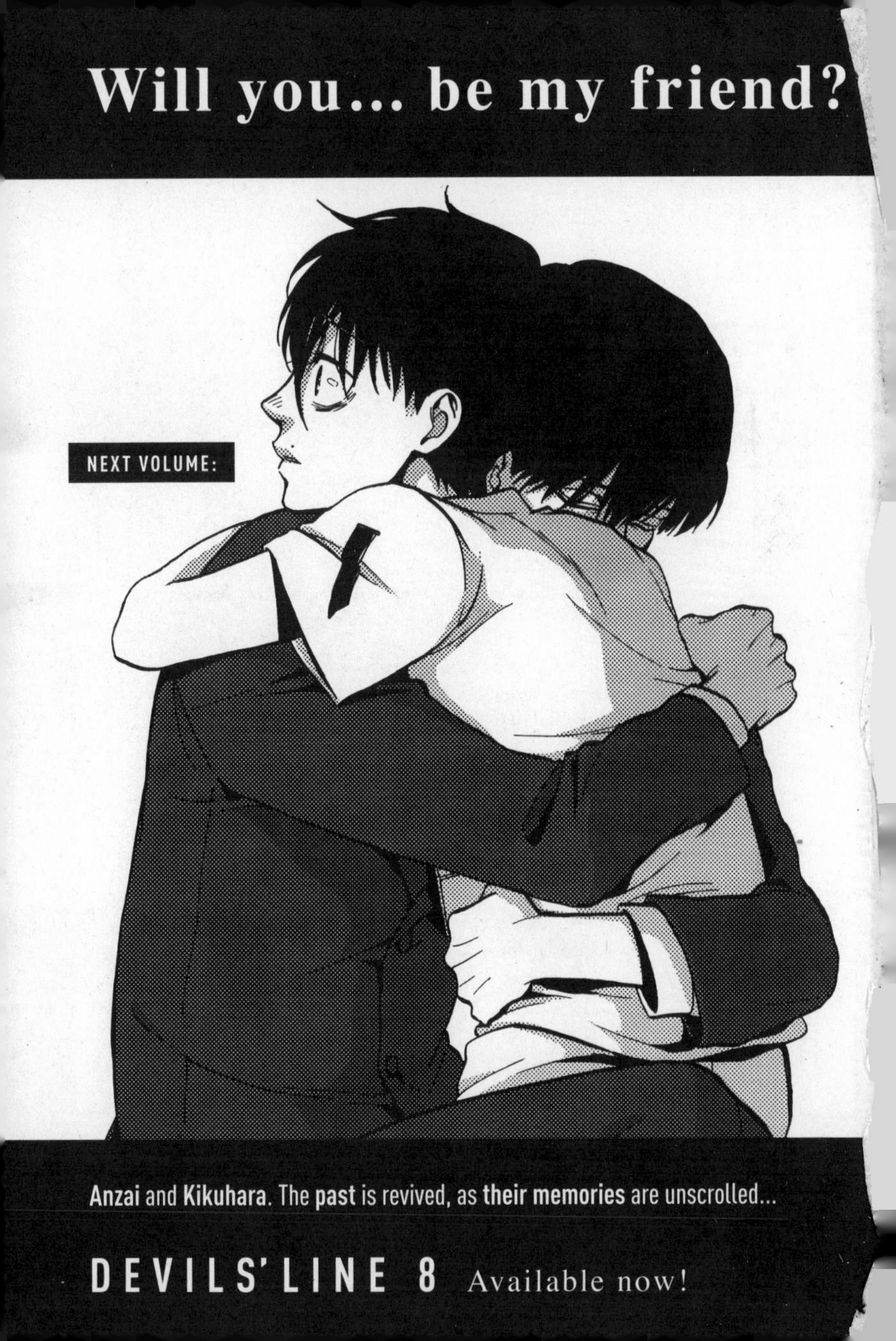

Anzai and **Kikuhara**. The **past** is revived, as **their memories** are unscrolled...

DEVILS' LINE 8 Available now!

DEVILS' LINE 7

A Vertical Comics Edition

Translation: Jocelyne Allen
Production: Risa Cho
Lorina Mapa

First published in Japan in 2016 by Kodansha, Ltd., Tokyo
Publication rights for this English edition arranged through Kodansha, Ltd., Tokyo
English language version produced by Vertical Comics, an imprint of Kodansha USA Publishing, LLC

Translation provided by Vertical Comics, 2017
Published by Kodansha USA Publishing, LLC, New York

Originally published in Japanese as *Debiruzurain 7* by Kodansha, Ltd., 2016
Debiruzurain first serialized in *Morning two*, Kodansha, Ltd., 2013-2019

This is a work of fiction.

ISBN: 978-1-945054-00-6

Manufactured in the United States of America

First Edition

Third Printing

Kodansha USA Publishing, LLC
451 Park Avenue South
7th Floor
New York, NY 10016
www.kodansha.us

Vertical books are distributed through Penguin-Random House Publisher Services.